DEEP SINGH SHAHEED

DEEP SINGH SHAHEED

DEEP SINGH SHAHEED
The Man in the Legend

HARISIMRAN SINGH

SPEAKING TIGER BOOKS LLP
125A, Ground Floor, Shahpur Jat, near Asiad Village,
New Delhi 110049

First published by Speaking Tiger Books 2022

Copyright © Harisimran Singh 2022

ISBN: 978-93-5447-236-7
eISBN: 978-93-5447-244-2

10 9 8 7 6 5 4 3 2 1

Typeset in Palatino by SÜRYA, New Delhi
Printed at Chaman Enterprises, New Delhi

All rights reserved.
No part of this publication may be reproduced, transmitted,
or stored in a retrieval system, in any form or by any means, electronic,
mechanical, photocopying, recording or otherwise,
without the prior permission of the publisher.

This book is sold subject to the condition that it shall not,
by way of trade or otherwise, be lent, resold, hired out,
or otherwise circulated, without the publisher's prior
consent, in any form of binding or cover other
than that in which it is published.

To
The True Sant-Sipahi

ਖਾਲਸਾ ਸੋਇ ਲੜੇ ਹੋਇ ਆਗੈ ॥
Khālsā sōi laṛē hōi āgai ॥
Khalsa is the one who fights in the front rank. (44)

ਖਾਲਸਾ ਸੋਇ ਨਾਮ ਰਤ ਲਾਗੈ ॥
Khālsā sō i nām rat lāgai ॥
Khalsa is the one who is infused with the divine name (47)

ਖਾਲਸਾ ਸੋਇ ਨਿਰਧਨ ਕੋ ਪਾਲੈ
Khālsā sōi nirdhan kō pālai
Khalsa is the one who looks after the poor (50)

ਖਾਲਸਾ ਸੋਇ ਦੁਸ਼ਟ ਕੋ ਗਾਲੇ ॥
Khālsā sōi dusaaṭ kō gālē ॥
Khalsa is the one who annihilates evil-doers (50)

ਖਾਲਸਾ ਸੋਇ ਜੋ ਕਰੇ ਨਿਤ ਜੰਗ ॥
Khālsā sōi jō karē nit jaṅg ॥
Khalsa is the one who fights in righteous war (53)

—Bhai Nand Lal,
Tankanamah, 106-128

And
To my dear mother who would have liked to see this in print

'Until the Lion learns to write, every story will glorify the Hunter.'
—African Proverb

'This shall remain the land of the Free so long as it is the home of the Brave.'
—Elmer Davis

'The legitimate object of war is a more perfect peace.'
—Inscription on General Sherman's statue, Washington, DC

Contents

Foreword	xi
Preface	xv

PART ONE: Life of Courage and Devotion

1. Birth and Belonging	3
2. At the Feet of the Master	17
3. Dam Dama Sahib: Guru Ki Kanshi	33

PART TWO: The Heroic Century

4. Founding a Seminary	49
5. A Cruel Yoke	67
6. The Misl Period	82
7. The Sant-Sipahi	94
8. Review	113

PART THREE: The Final Battle

9. Right to Go to War	123
10. Taking Up the Gauntlet	129
11. The Face Off	138
12. The Battle	150
13. Battle Review	170
14. Tryst with Harimandir Sahib	196

Epilogue	207
Acknowledgements	219
Appendix A: Deep Singh in Verse	222
Appendix B: Competing Claims of Birth and Belonging	264
Appendix C: Origin and Evolution of Sikhism	267
Glossary	284
Notes	296
Select Bibliography	350
Index	362

Foreword

Sikhism began in the 15th century with Baba Nanak, the first Guru. Born near Lahore as a Hindu, Nanak probably did not intend his teachings to eventually break away from his multitheistic religion when he sought to teach a reformed version of it. He emphasized simplicity, kindliness, and brotherhood, rejecting the immutable caste system of Hinduism. At the same time, he embodied some precepts of Sufism, a mystical branch of Islam. When his ideas spread, Sikhism became a religion in its own right; one that attracted more and more adherents throughout the Punjab. Gradually, Sikhs became not just believers in a religion but a race as they started marrying others of the same religious beliefs.

Inevitably, perhaps as they were newcomers in the face of prevailing belief systems, persecution and attempts at repression began and increased. Nanak's ninth successor as Guru was tortured and executed by the Moghul authorities in Delhi, to be succeeded by his nine-year old son, Govind. It was now that to survive amidst increasing persecution that Sikhism had to mutate from being just a belief system to also include militancy. Thereafter, every Sikh started taking the surname Singh and observing the Five Ks,[1] indicative of being always ready for battle.

It is primarily as soldiers that most of us think of Sikhs, the warriors of Ranjit Singh of the Kingdom of Lahore, whom the British said were their most formidable opponents in the entire subcontinent, and later a vital component of the British Indian

Army which would accept only baptized Sikhs, and insist that the Five Ks be included even in the uniform. Their gallantry and loyalty are remembered from the frontiers of India to the Western Front in the First World War, the North African deserts and Italy in the Second World War, and in the wars of Independent India since.

Although soldierly conduct is implicit in Sikh culture, there has always been a spiritual and philosophical element too. This book charts the life of Baba Deep Singh, a revered saint of Sikhism who combined the ethos of being a warrior with the original precepts of Guru Nanak. While Baba Deep Singh is revered to this day as the Soldier-Saint, this book is the first serious study to attempt to separate myth and legend from facts, and it succeeds admirably. Harisimran Singh has delved into previously unpublished sources and village records, leavened by his own understanding of military matters and his ability to compare and contrast conflicting accounts to arrive at the one that is most likely.

The book provides a fascinating account of the life and death of this extraordinary man, killed at the age of seventy-five fighting the troops of Ahmed Shah Durrani, the founder of modern Afghanistan, who had conquered most of the Punjab, much of Northern India, and was expanding into Persia. The book explains how Deep Singh became a trainer of men not only in the martial attributes of weapon handling and tactics but also how he insisted on the concept of 'just war', emphasizing the study of scriptures to be just as important as the study of war. The sheer detail of the author's research is impressive and he also writes in a style that is a pleasure to follow—indeed, anyone who has wandered about in rural India will instantly relate to his descriptive narrative style.

This is a delightful book, one of the most important additions to the history of Sikhism that will be enjoyed as well beyond the Sikh community, by anyone interested in the history of India and in the psychology of the warrior ethos. As someone who has many friends in the expatriate Sikh community and who has long admired their mixture of gallantry and honest decency, I feel honoured for having been asked to write the foreword to this splendid account of a very great man.

January 2022   Gordon Corrigan, MBE
Folkestone, Kent, UK   Military Historian and Broadcaster

Preface

Iconic Appeal

The event that I have tried to consistently attend over the past several years is the birth anniversary celebrations of Deep Singh—invariably referred to as Baba, a Persian honorific, along with the appellation Shaheed (martyr)—at his native village, Pahuwind, some forty kilometres southwest of Amritsar. This may at times coincide with India's Republic Day on 26th January or may be off by a day or two depending on when 14 Magh of the Samvat calendar falls that year. This year it fell on 27th January 2022 and the celebrations, which generally stretch over a week, began on Sunday, 23rd January.

From day one, people turned up in droves, in hundreds of thousands, to throng the expansive seven-hectare Gurdwara premises. Tractor-trollies modified for passenger carriage and night-stay, sedans, SUVs, buses, and trucks crammed every inch of the parking lots and lined the approach road while massive columns of humanity with no jostling space ponderously wound their way, inching toward the holy sanctum for obeisance.

The air resounded to exhilarating heroic verse tunefully sung with characteristic verve by dhadhis (balladeers) to the accompaniment of their traditional sarangi (string instrument played with a bow) and the percussive dhad (small hand-held two-sided drum), revisiting the ageless narrative of the 18th century hero who to many truly represents the ideal of the Khalsa sant-sipahi (warrior-saint). Exegetes, in their turn, discoursed at length, adducing from scriptures, to endorse in homilies the enormity and grandeur of a life lived with courage, virtue, and selflessness. The late evening kavi darbar (poetry recitation) celebrated and acclaimed their beau ideal and his transcendent courage, sacrifice, and resolve—qualities that matter most in crucial times.

Children and elders together frolicked in the play area with its array of Ferris wheels, merry-go-rounds, pirate ships, trampolines, toy trains, and much else before turning to a varied selection of over ten free community meals (langar) served round the clock.

I recalled with a sense of déjà vu how last year, our misgivings notwithstanding, even the powerfully united and intense farmers' agitation at the Delhi borders had failed to thin the pilgrim count. In fact, it was made special by the visit of a local Member of Parliament, announced by a sudden peal of sirens. Considerably delayed on National Highway 703B, pedestrianized for over a mile by the traffic police for the event and as a consequence, choked with pilgrims, he arrived with several functionaries of the civil administration in tow. Long a devotee, he explained in his formal address to the gathering that, prior to the elections, he had prayed at the village gurdwara for Deep Singh's blessings, and that his victory had only reaffirmed his faith. In humility, he presented a cheque of Rupees 75 lakh (7.5 million) as thanksgiving for developmental works to the village, later supplementing the amount.

Over the years, I have watched these celebrations grow in festivities, numbers, and import while the village itself has taken on the honorific, Pahuwind Sahib. Several nagar kirtans (communal hymnal singing) converge at the venue, some even on foot, from as far as Qilla Maika, over a distance of forty kilometres, and others from further afield. For some years now, the celebrations customarily culminate the following Sunday with a nagar kirtan that chants all the way, some forty-five kilometres, from Gurdwara Shaheedganj in Amritsar—where Deep Singh's mortal remains were cremated in November 1757 CE—to Pahuwind, his birth place.

Sometime in the mid-18th century, when the Khalsa sant-sipahi gave way to the conqueror, it helped the Sikhs carve out the last of the great splendiferous feudal kingdoms in modern times. Writing of its unequalled opulence in June 1845, a little before the first Anglo-Sikh war later that year, Lt Colonel Henry Steinbach states that 'although much has been abstracted from the [Sikh] royal treasury, during the constant succession of troubles, it is doubtful if any court in Europe possesses such valuable jewels as the court of Lahore.'[1]

During the Anglo-Sikh wars that followed, the Sikh martial spirit, among the preeminent legacies of the Khalsa, was widely hailed by the British when their invincible armies were repeatedly fought to a standstill. The British thereafter hastened to raise the Sikh regiment, accepting their martial prowess. They would fight with distinction in almost every theatre of war across the globe.

While Deep Singh continues to be as much the quintessential sant-sipahi as the likely unofficial patron-saint of courage and resolve for the Sikh soldier, nobody growing up in the Punjab can help but notice how profoundly ingrained he is in the Punjabi psyche.

As a cultural icon, he seems to transcend religious boundaries to resonate with Sikhs and non-Sikhs alike with totemic appeal. Car stickers of his prototypical silhouette, broadsword in hand, abound. His picture-paintings adorn homes, shops, offices, cars, buses, and trucks. He is no less represented in tattoos worn as much as a lucky charm as a symbol of a rare breed of strength, courage, and defiance. Streets, roads, housing colonies named after him, and gurdwaras in his memory, are commonplace even outside the Punjab in countries with large Punjabi diasporas.[2]

His birth and death anniversaries are commemorated with great enthusiasm and fanfare not just in his native village but across the world, and ceremonial cavalcades may stretch several miles. His memorial temple, Shaheedganj in Amritsar has an average daily pilgrim count in tens of thousands, and according to some estimates, almost eighty percent are Hindu.[3] During the special prayers, chupehra, offered each Sunday, there is little standing room for devotees who attach miraculous powers to the ceremony and may even share several illustrative incidents with moonstruck awe.[4] It is suggested that this gurdwara is next only to Harimandir Sahib (the Golden Temple in Amritsar) in footfalls and veneration.[5] It is also among the few shrines along with Harimandir Sahib which have a daily satellite telecast of the morning and evening service. Various stages of Deep Singh's last battle are marked by magnificent memorial edifices—truly a unique distinction.

While out of sheer worshipful veneration, few Sikhs adopt 'Deep' as a name, it is an unusually popular adjunct for both genders: Amandeep, Gagandeep, Pawandeep, Gurdeep, and countless others.

Deep Singh is eulogized equally by Hindu and Muslim writers and poets. Balladeers sing paeans to his scholarship and courage, and no 'kavi darbar' is complete without glowing tributes to his supreme sacrifice in rousing rhyme.

Rationale to Write

For most, this fascination for Deep Singh takes early root. For me, it was part of the cultural heritage I imbibed from my family, immediate and extended, with Deep Singh as our family guardian, incorporeal but omnipresent. My late father and my sainted aunt, Mohinder Kaur ji, were most contributive. Without this early enculturation, I would never have undertaken this study, and Deep Singh would have been to me just another absence in the overcrowded spiritual landscape of our country.

Over the years, this initial interest turned into curiosity as I sought answers to several questions. For such a profound and lasting impact, did Deep Singh actually alter the trajectory of history? Why has his narrative acquired such epic proportions and why does it continue to grip generation after generation? Often portrayed in prints with his head in one hand and a broadsword in the other, is he more myth than reality? A result of several years of academic and field research, this book seeks to faithfully answer these questions.

In my bid to discover Deep Singh the man, I have tried to eschew hagiography and to ground all research on this spiritual-cum-military leader whose life story interweaves through the turbulence of 18th century Punjab. Commenting on the period, Walker records in the 'Gazetteer of the Lahore District', how the fate of the region was tragically intertwined with that of Lahore, its provincial capital which had become 'the *point d' appui* [military base] of Sikh insurrections, and like a second Ariminum, the *itar ad bella* [route for invasion] of every invader from the West.'[6]

In overthrowing a banefully oppressive regime, the Sikhs also stemmed the upcoming tide of invasions. That they prevailed in their prolonged life-and-death struggle against stupendous odds can be attributed to their having fortuitously achieved the Clausewitzian Trinity.[7] Their unbending political objective, sovereignty, was clearly predicated; their operational instruments perfectly adapted to their context; and above all, their popular passions were powerfully articulated—chardi kala, moral ascendancy or unlimited optimism—as a social force.

Historians rightly refer to this period as the 'heroic century' because, in their insurrections against egregious tyranny, the Sikhs were enjoined by their creed 'to be supremely brave and undaunted, never to yield to an enemy under any circumstances' and in their pursuit of 'justice, to be prepared to undergo suffering, even to the point of martyrdom' (WH McLeod).[8]

'They were few in number when opposed to the legions of their enemies; they were poor and of small repute if compared with their oppressors who commanded the whole resources of Hindustan. With nothing but their faith, their brave hearts and their swords, they engaged in a death-struggle with the Mughal Empire...[while] persecutions strengthened their obstinate attachment to their faith' (Lepel Griffin).[9]

Few incidents can illustrate Sikh temerity against staggering odds better than the prequel to Deep Singh's martyrdom.

After having ravaged and plundered Delhi, Agra, Mathura, and Vrindavan during his fourth invasion, when Ahmed Shah Durrani set off from Delhi for Kabul in April 1757, his baggage train of over one hundred thousand animal-loads of loot included thousands of captive women. No sooner did he enter the Punjab than Sikh misls (warring bands),[10] Deep Singh's Shaheed misl among them, repeatedly attacked his columns, relieving him of much of his booty and rescuing many women prisoners.[11] Incensed, when he reached Lahore, Durrani had Harimandir Sahib, the gurdwara at Amritsar, demolished in May 1757 and its sacred tank defiled and filled with debris.[12]

In trying to redeem their honour, Deep Singh, then seventy-five years of age, inspired and led a motley, randomly armed band of approximately 5,000 volunteers, some with just a paihli (staff) as their primary weapon,[13] against the pernicious might of a predominantly Afghan professional army on 11th November 1757, only to find martyrdom in sacralized battle (dharmayudh or 'righteous war'), along with the bulk of his force.[14] Personally, Deep Singh rode out of the gates of history into legend that fateful day, acquiring a hallowed niche in racial memory, when he foreswore that morning before battle to keep his tryst with Sudhasar (Amritsar)—his destination—and did, although mortally wounded.

Tracing His Footsteps—Challenge and Approach

Such rare deeds of courage, sacrifice, and resolve sometimes deify and elevate ordinary mortals to sainthood, worthy only of worship. Over time, all dross tends to be winnowed out, leaving a narrative predominantly reverential in substance and tone—the primary reason why such biographies can seldom be warts-and-all accounts.

The scarcity of resource material has been another challenge. It is often said that those who create history seldom live to write it. Any researcher into this period is hamstrung by the lack of contemporary records left by the Sikhs themselves during their rise to power, possibly because they were either in hiding, or fighting a running battle with a powerful regime.

Historical fiction is a popular emerging genre to animate the page and round out even sparse received narratives, but Deep Singh's life story is too venerable and sacrosanct to readily lend itself to novelization—an area any scrupulous biographer should fear to tread.

Of the numerous contemporary Persian historiographers who wrote accounts on the Sikhs during the period, Miskin, a soldier-diarist in the employ of the Afghan-Mughal hierarchy, is significant because as part of the opposing force in Deep Singh's iconic last battle, his diary entry is the only eye-witness account and primary source for the conflict.[15] That the date of battle in his memoir should match the day of Deep Singh's martyrdom in the Panda Vahi (genealogical record) at Haridwar was for me an exciting discovery, giving a new spin to my endeavors.[16]

Researchers on Deep Singh generally accept two principal, albeit secondary, sources: Ratan Singh Bhangu's *Sri Guru Panth Prakash* (1841)[17] and Gyani Gyan Singh's *Sri Guru Panth Prakash* (1867) and *Twarikh Guru Khalsa* (1890).[18] Bhangu's work contains no single chapter on Deep Singh, only references in four sakhis (historical episodes or stories).[19] Gyani Gyan Singh's *Sri Guru Panth Parkash* (1867) written in esoteric Braj Bhasha (verse) is widely hailed as the first detailed history of the Sikhs,[20] although its author is accused at times of 'exaggerating reports in a spirit of anti-Muslim exultation.'[21] He followed this up with an equally comprehensive five-volume *Twarikh Guru Khalsa* (1890); his notes on the Shaheed misl can be found in the *Twarikh Guru Khalsa* Part 2 as well as *Raj Khalsa* Part 1. These publications together shed much light on Deep Singh's life, particularly on his last battle and include names of his companions, their places of martyrdom alongside other details of the battle, including such minutiae as casualty evacuation and last rites.

Two other studies are of particular importance on the life and times of Deep Singh. The first is a 2009 monograph by Guru Nanak Dev University, Amritsar, based on a commemorative seminar to mark Deep Singh's 250th death anniversary conducted under the auspices of two noted historians, Dr JS Grewal and Dr Indu Banga. The second is an annotated anthology in Punjabi by Professor Raijasbir Singh (2003). As a research project, it analyses all texts on Deep Singh beginning with those of Bhangu and Gyani Gyan Singh, followed by works of Gyani Thakur Singh (*Shaheed Bilas Baba Deep Singh* and *Sri Gurdware Darshan*) and a host of mostly poetic compositions down to the present time.

Much has still needed fleshing out from field research and oral traditions perpetuated by Sikh evangelists (kathavachaks) and balladeers through compositions authored very long ago, not much after the battle itself. Commemorative shrines in the erstwhile battlefield tell their own grim tale with convincing eloquence.

Interviews have been no less rewarding. In 1706 CE, Bhai Dall Singh hosted the tenth Guru for some nine months at his homestead at Talwandi Sabo, known today to the world as Dam Dama Sahib—one among the five Takhts or seats of Sikh temporal authority, a place where Deep Singh spent a major part of his life as its founder Jathedar (spiritual and administrative head). As custodians of the relics presented to Bhai Dall Singh by the tenth Guru, his descendants are an important source of information on Deep Singh and the shrine.[22]

Interaction with people from places connected with Deep Singh has been equally revealing. Residents of villages located in the area of his last battle around Gohalwar-Chabba-Chatiwind-Ramsar are a source of substantial anecdotal evidence, particularly those in-charge of cenotaphs in memory of the fallen. Usually brimming with war narratives, they can lend the battle exciting immediacy to make it all seem like yesterday.

An astounding find during my many wanderings in the area was an innominate tomb near village Chabba believed to have been built in the memory of an Afghan general who Deep Singh fought with and killed in the battle. Part of an erstwhile Muslim cemetery, it had been an object of interfaith reverence before it was razed when the area was leased out as farmland many years ago.

Bulk of the traditional material on Deep Singh is in verse, composed in the popular metre of the time, particularly as vaars (heroic ballads).[23] Some excerpts have been included in Appendix A along with a Punjabi-English translation, which is more in the nature of transcreation that seeks to retain with solicitude, the original vigor in rhythm and rhyme. Although Indian and English classical prosody are intrinsically different, relying on quantitative and qualitative metre respectively, the effect can be equally gratifying.[24]

Deep Singh's final battle has been a popular subject for poets and while some of the verse is included herein, the battle itself is the focus of an entire chapter that strives as a 'battle piece' to present, in John Keegan's sense, the real face of battle, and not just unreflective imitation.[25] Interestingly, the battle seems to obey the so-called 'Three Unities' of classical drama first observed by Aristotle. It is restricted to a single day, played out in a defined space, and the action of the belligerents is centered upon a single objective, from two opposing standpoints.

This work has tried to address several contentious issues:

- Although Pahuwind (District Tarn Taran, Punjab) is widely regarded as Deep Singh's place of birth and belonging, there are competing claims that this book has sought to examine and depose (see Appendix B).
- The Panda Vahi notes Deep Singh's name at birth as 'Deepa' and, on martyrdom, as 'Deep Singh'.[26] The first writer to cite him, Bhangu, refers to him plainly as 'Deep Singh'—a practice followed in this work.[27] The honorific prefix 'Baba' gained currency much later, at the turn of the 20th century.[28]
- Research into several intersecting narratives around the title 'Shaheed' favors an antemortem rather than a posthumous award conferred on Deep Singh for his conspicuous courage in battle. Inane or unwonted as it may seem for a living being to be awarded the title but, for this reason, he is often referred to as 'jeonda shaheed' (living martyr) even now after several centuries. Later, when the Budha Dal and the Taruna Dal were raised in 1734 by Nawab Kapur Singh on the grant of a jagir by the Mughals in a bid to pacify the Sikhs, Deep Singh's jatha was part of the former. The jatha acquired the title as a matter of course, with Deep Singh as its head just like the Shaheed misl he founded later in 1748. That the title was suffixed by all its members—rather than prefixed, as in the case of celebrated freedom fighters like Shaheed Bhagat Singh and Shaheed Udham Singh—suggests that it was more a cognomen than a title. A prefixed or pre-nominal title, 'Shaheed Deep Singh', is no less common, used in reference to him posthumously as martyr.
- Oral traditions have long hailed and sung Deep Singh's last battle as a Sikh triumph; a battle study points to a tragic and inexorable rout instead. Part Three of the book focuses wholly on the battle, including the strategy and tactics of the belligerents, and an inventory of Sikh cenotaphs in and around the erstwhile battlefield.

- Strangely, the most polemical dimension of Deep Singh's life has been his death. Opinionated perspectives on the 'severed head' lore could lie anywhere on a cline between authenticated history and phantasmal legend. Documentary and ground research on this aspect together with Deep Singh's much storied super broadsword (khanda) form part of the last chapter for readers to draw their own inferences.

According to some accounts, the Sikhs lost around four thousand in the battle. A major regret of this study has been that only a tenth of these martyrs could be identified, or at least named, despite extensive field research. The vast majority must sadly remain unknown and unsung.

In the process of collation, analysis, and synthesis, the dialectic filtering of information through the prism of logic and probability has been an essential adjunct for me, all through the study.

Foreshadowing the doctrine of military ethics by more than a century, Guru Gobind's Khalsa sant-sipahi, as an inveterate defender of all faiths and rights of others, fulfilled the principles and practice of the modern just war tradition in terms of *jus ad bellum* (right to war), *jus in bello* (right conduct in war), and *ultima ratio* (war as a last resort). Deep Singh was a mentee of Guru Gobind Singh, and to historians exploring the breadth of his personality and achievement, a rare embodiment of this Khalsa ideology, as much in life as in his martyrdom.[29] The reader would thus benefit from following the contours of Sikhism (Appendix C) in its evolution, originating in the assuaging Shaastra (scriptures or the Word), to later circumscribe Shastra (weapons) before culminating in Shahadad (martyrdom). Deep Singh inimitably epitomized the consequential binaries of bhagti-shakti (prayer-power or meditation-might) and sant-sipahi that undergird the Khalsa synthesis and praxis.

Among the foremost icons of his time, and 'one of the most revered heroes of Sikh history,'[30] Deep Singh's life is still waiting to be fully explored and chronicled. Potentially, this promises to be no mean task because, in the final analysis, any successful biography should fully address the many strands of Deep Singh's rather compendious title:

ਮਹਾਬਲੀ ਜਿਓਂਦਾ ਸ਼ਹੀਦ ਅਜਿੱਤ ਯੋਧਾ ਅਮਰ ਸ਼ਹੀਦ ਬ੍ਰਹਮ ਗਿਆਨੀ ।
Mahabali, jeonda shaheed, ajit yodha, amar shaheed, brahmgyani[31]
Pre-eminent Sacrificer, Living Martyr, Invincible Warrior, Deathless Martyr, All-knowing Spiritually-enlightened Being.

Should this work pass muster, my labour of love would have been significantly worthwhile.

February 2022   Harisimran Singh
Chandigarh

PART ONE

Life of Courage and Devotion

ONE

Birth and Belonging

A 'Deep' is Born

The view was reminiscent of an idyllic oil-on-canvas pastoral. A dim haze of mist hung in the crisp morning air, gradually lifting under the winter sun. Sequestered between sugar cane and wheat fields, a pair of translucent-white oxen ran a cane press, their heads bobbing up and down to the rhythmic jingle of their cow-bells. Bhaga, popularly known as Bhagtu (holy man) for his religious bent, had been at work since early morning, leaning over the press to feed harvested sugar cane sticks between its metallic drums that conveyed the juice through a channel into a large steaming cauldron placed over a fire.

In mid-distance, another pair of oxen trod the earth in circular motion to drive a Persian wheel, irrigating wheat fields spread as far as the eye could see, a luminous emerald but with a hint of gold that presaged the onset of Spring.

Wafted across from the mangrove yonder came the caw and shriek of crows and parrots, heard just above the cacophony of cow-bells and the grating off-key moan of the cane press and the Persian wheel.

Rather used to working alone, it took Bhagtu some time to notice the presence of a stranger. Clad in his usual saffron, his hair tied above the head in a knot, staff in one hand and a brass water pot in the other, a sadhu (itinerant holy man) was not an uncommon sight in these parts. The two soon greeted each other and, as was his wont, Bhagtu promptly offered him his yarn-spun cot to sit just when his wife, Jeoni, arrived with lunch for her husband. It was customary to offer food rather than alms to sadhus. Bhagtu and his wife waited upon him with much affection and solicitude as they served him a hearty meal.

Re-energized with wholesome food still warm from the hearth, the sadhu observed with some curiosity the absence of young helping hands.

'Do you not have any children?' he asked, his words half-muffled between munching and swallowing another morsel of unleavened flat corn bread and spinach dripping with makhan (white butter), a winter staple in the region.

No, responded Bhagtu despondently, adding how much they longed for progeny.

ਜਾਇਦਾਦ ਨੂੰ ਦੇਖ ਕੇ ਦਿਲ ਸੜਦਾ ਜਿਦੇ ਘਰ ਨਾ ਹੋਵੇ ਸੰਤਾਨ ਭਾਈ ।
ਸੇਵਾ ਪੁੱਤ ਜਹਾਨ ਤੇ ਬੜਾ ਮਿੱਠਾ ਨਾਹੀ ਏਸ ਦੇ ਹੋਰ ਸਮਾਇ ਭਾਈ ।

—Ghukewalia,
'Prasang Baba Deep Singh'[1]

jaidad nu dekh ke dil sarda jeede ghar na hovei santaan bhai.
Sewa put jahan ton bada mittha nahi ais de hor samman bhai
Their wealth to them no solace brought because they had no heir;
The world has little meaning if you have no son to care.

At this, the sadhu quaffed the tall glass of lassi (butter-milk), paused, and then briefly went into a meditative trance. Shortly, with eyes half-closed in prayer, he invoked the Lord's blessings:

ਜੋ ਜੋ ਚਿਤਵਹਿ ਸਾਧ ਜਨ ਸੋ ਲੇਤਾ ਮਾਨਿ ॥੧॥ ਰਹਾਉ ॥

—Guru Arjan Dev,
Sri Guru Granth Sahib, 817

Jo jo chitvahi sādh jan so letā mān. ||1|| *rahāo.*
Whatever God's Holy servants wish, He grants. ||1||Pause||

And then, as if to prophesy, pronounced (see ser 1 and 2 in Appendix A):

'The Lord shall soon bless thee with a son who shall excel both as a warrior and scholar, and shine like a star in the heavens. You must name him 'Deep' [Punjabi/Hindi for 'light'].'

ਸਾਡੀ ਗੱਲ ਤੂੰ ਸੁਣ ਧਿਆਨ ਲਾ ਕੇ,
ਜਨਮੇ ਪੁੱਤ ਤਾਂ ਦੀਪ ਉਸ ਨਾਮ ਰੱਖੀ ।

—Gurdeep Singh Kanwal,
Jeevan Baba Deep Singh ji[2]

Sadi gal tun sunn dhyan la ke,
Janme putt tan 'Deep' us naam rakhin.
Now, lend thine ear to what I say:
Do christen your son, 'Deep', I pray

Within a year, as if in fulfilment of the benediction, a son was born on 26th January 1682 (14 Magh, 1739 Vikram Samvat) and fondly named Deepa.[3] Some historians, however, translate the date as Thursday, 11th January 1739 (Vikram Samvat), 1683 CE.[4]

This is how folklore and oral traditions describe the uncanny circumstances of Deep Singh's birth to Bhagtu and Jeoni, a devoted, possibly, third generation Sikh couple who lived off their land in village Pahuwind, some forty kilometres southwest of Amritsar in the Punjab. Much respected in the community for their charitable disposition, they were still childless after fifteen years of marriage,[5] and longed and constantly prayed for progeny (see ser 3 in Appendix A). It is not surprising that, in time, two more sons followed (see Table 1 for family tree) because mothers conceive more readily after their first child.

Context and Conditions

Placed in its historical context, the entire episode could be completely true. Of the three great Muslim realms in the 18th century, the Ottoman, the Persian and the Moghul, the last was the most affluent, regarded as the world's richest, and in 1700-1750, accounted for twenty-three percent of the world trade. Delhi was one of the wealthiest capitals in the world.[6] Punjab was its most prosperous province after Bengal, and Lahore the pride of

Mughal India, even then regarded among the greatest cities of Asia, comparable to Istanbul.[7] It intersected with two principal trade routes: the silk route that linked Agra to Kabul through Attock to the Khyber, and then to China and Europe; and the route to Multan, Kandahar, and Persia. The other prominent city in the region was Amritsar that grew to be the biggest centre of trade in the North.[8] Pahuwind was equidistant from both, merely a half-day ride. This proximity brought economic advantage for farmers and tradesmen alike, although it was the regime that reaped maximum benefit.

Sugar cane cultivation was popular, and the Persian wheel had been diffused and generalized in the region by the 16th century.[9] Abu'l Fazal testified to the effects of well-irrigation in Punjab during the reign of Emperor Akbar: 'This province is populous, its climate healthy and its agricultural fertility rarely equaled. The irrigation is chiefly from wells.'[10] The cane-press followed in the 17th century.[11] These developments would gradually transform the area into a rich granary of food crops.[12]

Itinerant sadhus, pseudo or genuine, were fairly common in the Punjab—Persian for 'land of five rivers', among the most fertile regions of the Indian sub-continent (see Figure 1).[13] Its more prosperous segment, the Majha, seemed to attract them even more. They preferred repast to alms and often made favorable prophesies after a generous meal—or 'foresaw' misfortune, if turned away.

Panda Vahi

While historians are mostly unanimous over Deep Singh's date of birth, there is some variation over his place of birth and belonging. Ratan Singh Bhangu, the first writer to document it, records it as Chakoha (District Ludhiana). Another author, Buta Singh records it as Pero, a village near Batala, while Gyani Gyan Singh initially records it as Dakoha (District Jalandhar)—which, in fact, is where Sudh Singh, Deep Singh's close associate and

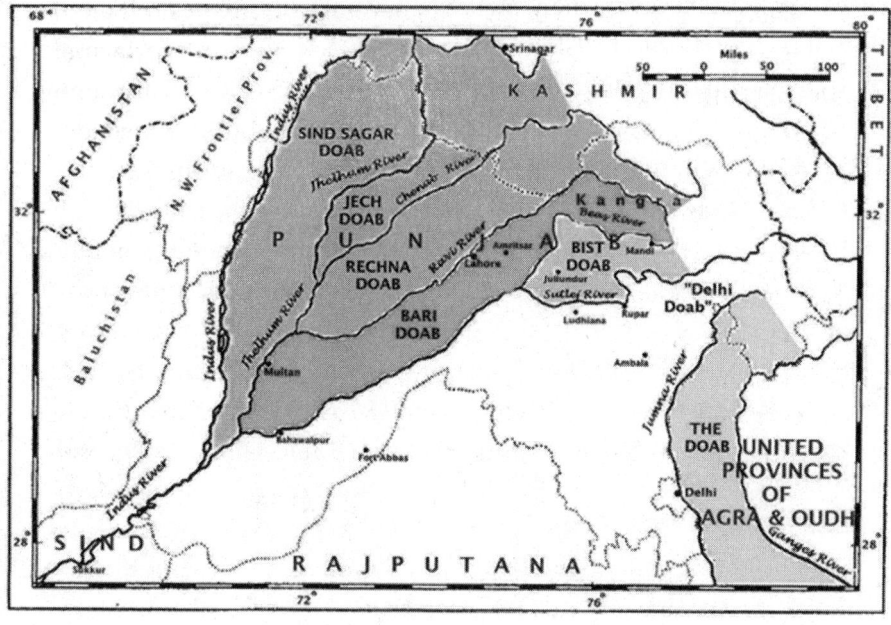

Figure 1: The Region—'Punjab Doabs'
(Source: https://en.wikipedia.org/wiki/Doaba#/media/File:Punjabdoabs1.jpg)

successor belonged.[14] In a later publication, Gyani Gyan Singh corrects it to Pahuwind, which is accepted by several subsequent writers, including Kahn Singh Nabha in his magnum opus,[15] as well as by Raijasbir Singh in his well-researched, annotated compilation.[16] Author and historian, Harjinder Singh Dilgeer goes further to record his name as Deep Singh Pahuvindia since it was customary then as now to suffix the village name.[17]

These disparities are easily resolved by referring to the Panda Vahi kept with the village Tirth Purohit (family priest), Shri Kirpa Ram Prabhakar at Haridwar, the pilgrim center,[18] which correctly records it as Pahuwind.[19] It was part of the Lahore district in Undivided India, Amritsar district after Partition, and now forms part of the newer Tarn Taran district. The much-revered Gurdwara, Janamsthan Baba Deep Singh, stands here in his memory.

There is a rival claim by village Gurm (District Ludhiana) according to which Deep Singh's mother was from Pahuwind but his father belonged to Gurm,[20] and was of the Gurm sub-caste although, strangely, there is not a single Gurm household in the village, the majority being Deol (see Appendix B).

An entry made in the genealogy register by the village Tirth Purohit in 1785 is as follows—earlier records are not available, having degraded because of the fragile parchment they were written on:

'Dasondha Singh came with the ashes of his father, mother, and brother's wife (bhabhi) in 1785 CE (1842 Samvat) and recorded the following family tree' (see Table 1 for family tree).

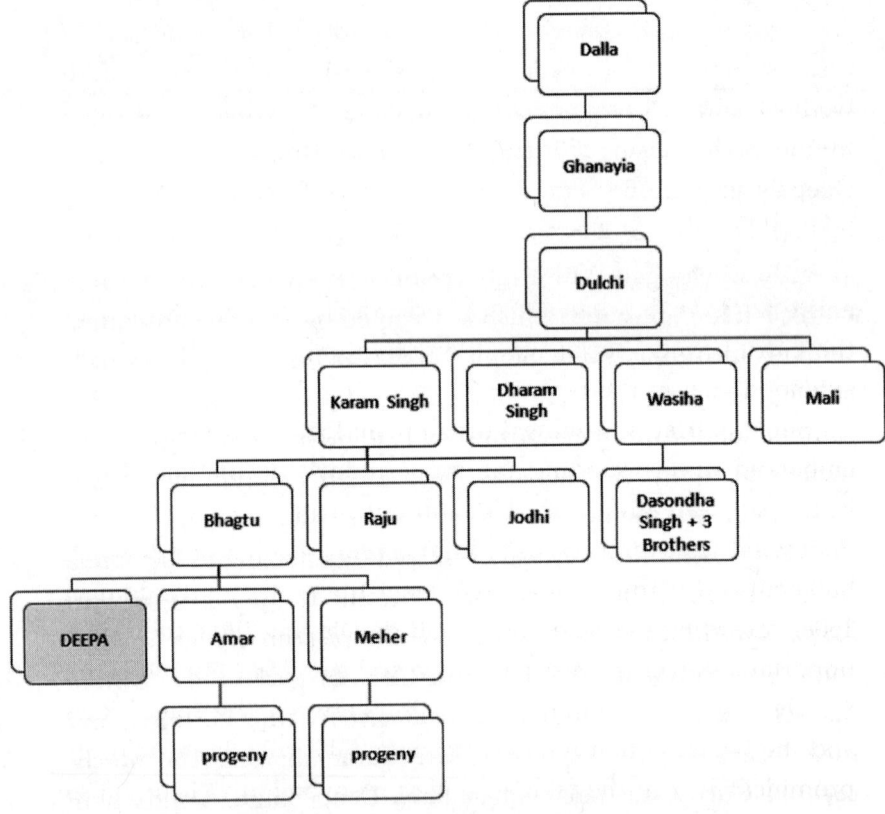

Table 1: Family Tree of Deep Singh
(Source: Panda Vahi, Haridwar, verified personally by the author)

Travel was by animal transport and since Haridwar was a long distance from Pahuwind, some 425 kilometres, it was common practice to store the ashes in urns and to make this journey once every few years to immerse the ashes in the Ganges under the aegis of the village Purohit. All such visits were recorded by the Purohit, and the family tree updated.

The genealogical record addresses several other important aspects: one, Deep Singh's family is entered as 'jat zamindar'—*jat* is the ethnicity, while *zamindar* makes them landholders; two, Deep Singh was the eldest of three brothers, and not six as recorded by the historian, Dilgeer—unlikely considering that the parents had a late start with progeny.[21] Kalsi, another historian, records the birth of a second son when Deepa was five but notes his name as 'Bhaga', which is at variance with 'Amar' in the genealogy record.[22] Three, while his brothers entered into wedlock and had progeny, Deepa led a life of celibacy dedicated to the Sikh cause.[23] Further, the suffix 'Singh' suggests that Deepa's grandfather and one great uncle were both baptized Sikhs.[24] Possibly, it was their father, Dulchi, who first embraced Sikhism during the pontificate of Guru Arjan, when almost the entire jat peasantry of the Majha had converted, influenced by the Guru's piety, social work, and standing, as well as by his extended stay in the region.[25]

Shortly after assuming guruship in 1583, Guru Arjan had embarked upon founding the modern-day city of Tarn Taran ('place of salvation') in 1585, only thirty kilometres from Pahuwind. The process took him several years during which he spent much time in the area, right up to his martyrdom in 1606, spreading the Sikh gospel and developing the city into an important Sikh centre with a temple and a sarovar (sacred lake).

The Majha, the interfluvial plains between the rivers Ravi and the Beas, is often referred to as the Sikh tract because of its prominent role in the Sikh struggle for sovereignty. It was also the main field of activities of the Gurus and later of the misls, all of which were founded by and composed mostly of men from the region. The people of Majha were called majhails. Known for their reckless courage and penchant for adventure, they were possessed of sound physique, good looks and exceptional military skills which, in time, would help them close forever the invasion routes from India's Northwest and earn the reputation of being 'the finest soldiers the world has ever known'.[26]

Early Years

Young Deepa was in every way a blessed child: a caring son, an untiring farmhand, and an energetic lad, sensitive to the tensions of his time. The animus of the Mughal emperor, Aurangzeb, towards non-Muslims was palpable in the oppressive regime and its domineering officials. All land belonged to the emperor. The governor (subedar) of a province functioned through the jagirdars, always Muslim, who were the government as far as the village was concerned, with rights to a share of the revenue. It was only with extraordinary effort that the peasant-zamindars could live in moderate comfort and yet be in constant dread of an arbitrary hike in revenue tax.[27]

Before the general adoption of the Persian wheel in the area, additional revenue was extracted for providing this technology, an inequity that created much resentment among jats. This changed when Guru Arjan, sensitive of their needs, had a well with six Persian-wheels excavated at Chheharta, and restored the ancient pool at Thatte Khera (Guru Ki Vadali) near Tarn Taran, not far from Pahuwind, endearing him to the masses.[28] On founding the modern-day city of Tarn Taran, he also built a gurdwara there in 1590 with an attached lake, then the largest sarovar in the Punjab.

Espousing the Sikh Cause

Consequently, his death from Mughal brutality in Lahore in 1606 came as a blow that only served to fester further disaffection, particularly in the Sikh tract, the Majha, always centre-stage in the struggle against Mughal excesses. According to the oral tradition, before his execution, Guru Arjan instructed his son, Hargobind (the sixth preceptor) to take up arms and resist tyranny.[29] His death seemed to stiffen this conviction among the Sikhs that personal piety must have a core moral strength. A virtuous soul must be a courageous soul. Willingness 'to suffer trial for one's conviction [thus became] a religious imperative'.[30]

Guru Arjan's death marked a turning point in an essentially pacific movement and led his son to militarize and politicize his position by raising an army and declaring Sikh sovereignty with the creation of the Akal Takht (eternal throne), as well as establishing a fort to defend Amritsar. He chose to dress like a warrior and willed fighting injustice a prime duty among his followers, thus establishing a militant tradition of resistance to persecution that remains an important motif in Sikh consciousness. His emphasis on physical courage and armed resistance were, in effect, the leavening meant to buttress moral rectitude and to defend personal honour, just as his wearing two swords symbolized his zeal to dominate both the temporal and the spiritual domains.[31]

When the attitude of Mughals further hardened with the ascension of Shah Jahan as potentate, in response, Guru Hargobind's call to arms resounded in the region, people coming forward in droves—some no doubt from Pahuwind—to join his standard and to be militarily transformed. While many found martyrdom, others would have their first taste of victory when Guru Hargobind was forced to fight three battles—Amritsar (1628), Lahira (1631), and Kartarpur (1634). Although outnumbered and out-equipped, the fact that he trounced the imperial army on all three occasions had a lasting impact on the evolution of the Sikh community.[32]

'Success against innumerable odds could not but inspire the Sikhs with self-confidence... [that] became a great national asset...

[and] considerably prepared them for the thorough transformation [...] in the hands of Guru Gobind Singh'.[33]

The people's leisure activities now took a martial turn. Equestrian sport, archery, marksmanship and gatka (traditional Sikh swordplay) came to be gradually diffused in rural Punjab by the mid-17th century.

Guru Hargobind's doughty crusade notwithstanding, in Mughal India, 'the mass of the people had no economic liberty, no indefeasible right to justice or personal freedom' (McLeod). With the ascension of Aurangzeb as potentate in 1658, the political status of a non-Muslim was degraded further to that of 'modified slavery'; their access to employment was blunted, they were liable to higher and more taxation, and many of their places of worship were ordered to be demolished. In 1670, the ancient temples of Mathura were destroyed and the city renamed Islamabad. The martyrdom of the ninth preceptor, Guru Teg Bahadur, followed in 1675 on a warrant from the Emperor when he tried to intercede in the forced proselytizing of Kashmiri Brahmins. A pious and accomplished poet, social reformer and spiritual lighthouse, the Guru's martyrdom was particularly significant in that it reflected an important principle of the Sikh faith: to stand up not only for one's own religious freedom but equally for that of others. Its impress resonates in the Sikh psyche to this day.[34] Henceforth, this empathetic and extreme benevolence would set Sikh martyrs uniquely apart from the others.

An inveterate expansionist whose reign saw the Mughal Empire reach its zenith both in territorial extent and revenue to become the world's largest economy in 1700,[35] Aurangzeb is also accused of muting and terrorizing millions who 'looked upon him as a monster, fled from his tax-gatherers, and prayed for his death [......] It was a power that had no foundation in the affection of the people'.[36]

When Guru Teg Bahadur's son, Guru Gobind, assumed guruship at the tender age of nine and made it his life's mission to fight tyranny, he found himself at loggerheads with, one, the bigotry of the Mughal court that viewed him as a threat and, two, some of the hill chiefs who looked upon him as an upstart and were jealous of his growing influence and rising social standing. The Guru deemed it expedient to move out from Chak Nanki (Kiratpur) in the Kahlur state to Paonta in Garhwal for reasons of safety.[37]

Martial Heritage

This was the world Deepa was born into, sensitive to the rampant iniquities that kindled very early in him a purposive and compelling urge for justice while the many events, narrated to him as bedtime stories by a doting mother, served to shape his socio-cultural heritage. Guru Hargobind and Guru Gobind would have been his beau ideals, and his heroes the likes of Bhai Jetha of Sidwan,[38] a village a mile from his own, and Bidhi Chand of Sur Singh, another village less than five miles away.[39]

Later, the area would spawn a generous sprinkling of heroes, many of whom were Deepa's contemporaries: Bhai Taru Singh of Poohla, Bhai Tara Singh of Vaan, Bhai Sukha Singh (Mari Kambo), Nawab Kapur Singh (Singhpura); Mai Bhago (Jhabbal), Bhagel Singh Karorsinghia (Jhabbal). Easily the most famous in recent times would be the celebrated freedom fighter, Bhagat Singh, whose place of origin is Narli, a village some ten kilometres from Pahuwind. Interestingly, a professional, chip-timed half-marathon was organized in November 2021 from Pahuwind to Narli and back to coincide with Deep Singh's martyrdom commemoration.

Education and literacy were a function of religious orientation and schools of learning were religion-based. Muslims were taught in Arabic and Persian and learned math, literature, and the Koran. The Hindus learned Sanskrit and studied astrology, pingal (poetry), palmistry, literature, and the scriptures. Gurmukhi was the medium for the Sikhs and they were taught pingal, history, math, and Sikh as well as Hindu scriptures besides law. Schools for traders were run by Mahajans where they learnt the essentials of book-keeping, accounts, etc. Persian was the official language universally taught in the region.[40]

Deepa's access to literacy was limited by his low-resource environment. It was customary to study within the village itself, where the sole resource personnel was often the village clergyman, the curriculum being mostly confined to the rudiments of the vernacular and a sprinkling of scriptural knowledge.[41] In the early 1690s, with increasing hostilities with the regime, Guru Gobind sent word throughout the Punjab for the village granthi (Sikh priest) to impart weapon training to youth and encourage physical and strength sports such as equitation, wrestling, and kabaddi.[42] Deepa had the added advantage to learn to ride from his father, an accomplished horseman.[43] He would have assimilated the religious values of his home, often accompanying his parents on pilgrimage to Harimandir Sahib, Tarn Taran Sahib, Dehra Sahib (Lahore), and Bir Baba Budha Sahib, all within easy day-return rides (see Figure 2). He grew into a tall, strapping, sensible young lad, ever willing to help the needy and when not working on the family farm, delighted and excelled in the sports of his time—hunting, equitation, gatka and kabaddi.

When Deepa was an impressionable boy of six, Guru Gobind won his first battle at Bhangani (1688). He was forced to fight many more and very soon his military exploits were legend, part of village lore, serving to further polarize both the young and the aged and, in turn, prompting them to steel themselves for the battles that lay ahead. News of armed Sikhs flocking to join his army now poured in constantly.

Deepa had just turned seventeen when came the news of the watershed moment: the founding of the Khalsa (Persian for 'the pure') on 30th March 1699 to wage war for justice against the forces of evil with the moral imperative to defend righteousness against tyranny regardless of the odds. There would be no turning back now. The spiritual and the martial were truly merged in

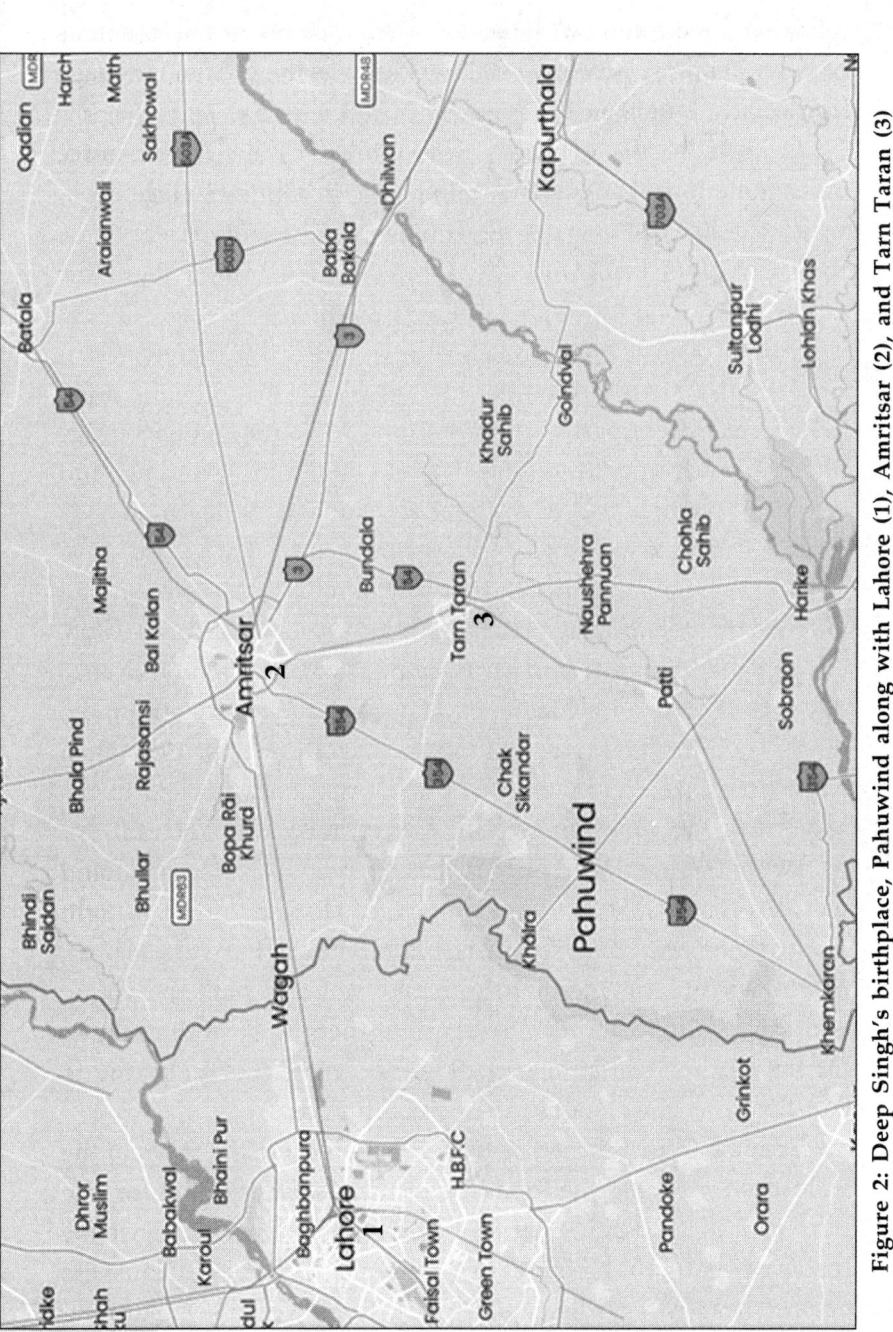

Figure 2: Deep Singh's birthplace, Pahuwind along with Lahore (1), Amritsar (2), and Tarn Taran (3)
(Source: https://mapcarta.com/33730960)

the sant-sipahi in a bid to transform a religion of self-righteous householders into warriors. The baptism ceremony involved water sweetened with sugar drop candy stirred with a steel dagger and consecrated by the recitation of scriptures.[44] The sparrow would now fight the hawk, and a solitary Sikh baptized with 'water stirred with steel' engage thousands of the enemy.[45]

TWO

At the Feet of the Master

News of the Khalsa

Spring was in the air. Ripening wheat stalks of gold danced in the breeze. It would be harvest time in a week. An ageing Bhagtu sat in the courtyard with his youngest son, Meher, a pre-teen, by his side, trying to explain to him the import and repercussions of the Khalsa baptism, now the talking point across the Punjab. Jeoni emerged from the family kitchen, carrying milk and savouries. The evening shades were beginning to fall when Deepa and Amar crossed the threshold, back from the fields. Just as well, thought Bhagtu that he now had three growing sons to help. Deepa, the eldest, had almost taken full charge at seventeen and Amar, five years younger, showed much promise as a sturdy lad with boundless reserves of youthful energy.

Before de-briefing his sons about their day's work on the farm, Bhagtu was anxious for more news about the Khalsa, recently founded by the tenth Guru on 30th March 1699. 'Anything more about the Khalsa? How many more have been baptized?' he asked.

Deepa shared village gossip to say that the event had created quite a stir in the entire land as never before, and that the number of initiates ran into several thousand.

'When is the next ceremony?' Bhagtu quizzed.

'Nobody is sure but there is talk that it might be next Vaisakhi,' said Deepa. 'We just ran into Granthiji on our way back. He says that proclamations by the Guru have been carried far and wide, beckoning all who dare to fight oppression to join the Khalsa.'

'What else did Granthiji say?' Bhagtu was curious to know more about an event that he felt was destined to have far-reaching consequences.

Deepa now reached into his pocket and pulled out a piece of paper. 'Granthiji dictated these lines that are much quoted these days because, he says, they carry the Guru's life-mission.'

Deepa slowly read out the lines in rhythmic cadence:

ਹਮ ਇਹ ਕਾਜ ਜਗਤ ਮੋ ਆਏ ॥
ਧਰਮ ਹੇਤ ਗੁਰਦੇਵਿ ਪਠਾਏ ॥
ਜਹਾ ਤਹਾ ਤੁਮ ਧਰਮ ਬਿਥਾਰੋ ॥
ਦੁਸਟ ਦੋਖਯਨਿ ਪਕਰਿ ਪਛਾਰੋ ॥੪੨॥
ਯਾਹੀ ਕਾਜ ਧਰਾ ਹਮ ਜਨਮੰ ॥
ਸਮਝ ਲੇਹੁ ਸਾਧੂ ਸਭ ਮਨਮੰ ॥
ਧਰਮ ਚਲਾਵਨ ਸੰਤ ਉਬਾਰਨ ॥
ਦੁਸਟ ਸਭਨ ਕੋ ਮੂਲ ਉਪਾਰਿਨ ॥੪੩॥

—'Chaupaee', *Dasm Granth*[1]

Hama Eih Kaaja Jagata Mo Aaee ॥
Dharma Heta Gurdevi Patthaaee ॥
Jahaa Tahaa Tuma Dharma Bithaaro ॥
Dustta Dokhyani Pakari Pachhaaro ॥42॥
Yaahee Kaaja Dharaa Hama Janaamn ॥
Samajha Lehu Saadhoo Sabha Manaamn ॥
Dharma Chalaavan Saanta Aubaaran ॥
Dustta Sabhan Ko Moola Aupaarin ॥43॥

Bhagtu listened with rapt attention, eyes half-closed as he assimilated the essence of the Guru's assertion. It was Amar who interrupted Bhagtu's train of thought, 'What does it mean, father?'

Bhagtu took time to collect his thoughts and then explained hesitantly, trying to convey the underlying meaning. 'The Guru says that he took birth only to uphold Righteousness everywhere, to destroy all evil, and to extirpate tyrants.'

It was now the turn of the youngest, Meher, 'So what will change, father? How will it affect us all?'

Bhagtu had endeavored to impart a religious upbringing to his children, and now sought to expatiate. 'It seems that with the founding of the Khalsa, Sikh ideology has been further enlarged. You're aware that with Guru Nanak, we began with the shaastra (scriptures) as a conciliatory initiative of humaneness based on shabad-guru, or the Word as a teacher that sought peace and goodwill among all.'

Well-versed in the oral narrative, Deepa now pitched in, 'Then came shastra, or weapons, under Guru Hargobind, when peaceful means alone could not prevail against brutal tyranny.'

'True,' acknowledged Bhagtu, and prompted, 'And thereafter?'

'Shahadad, or martyrdom,' continued Deepa.

'True again. The chronology of shaastra, shastra, shahadad is now complete,' explained Bhagtu. 'It seems that the clarion call made earlier by Guru Hargobind for a dharmayudh is now being intensified and formalized by Guru Gobind's call to arms. From what I gather, his message continues to reverberate strongly all through the region, and has even begun to polarize a populace long subjugated by our cruel regime.'

Like many others in the community, Bhagtu was excited by the new spin and direction that the Guru had imparted with the founding of the Khalsa but, like anybody else, he was unaware of its critical nuances. In a masterstroke of genius, as one of the greatest saviors of mankind, the Guru had, in effect, declared war in favour of human rights, civil liberties, and political freedom, anteceding the ideals of the United States Declaration of Independence and the French Revolution by almost a century.[2] Many decades before Rousseau, the Genevan philosopher, would drive the Enlightenment of Europe and argue for insurrection against oppressive rule, the Guru had thrown down the gauntlet, openly denouncing absolutism and injustice, and calling out tyrants.

Jeoni soon joined the animated discussions that followed about the likely role and impact of the Khalsa. The evening shades deepened as the sky dissolved from a bright mix of pink and crimson to inky darkness, speckled with a thousand stars radiant against a leaden orb. The topic informed every evening well into the night in every household across the Majha. Speculation was rife and mingled freely with gossip and prospect to fire Deepa and most others of his age with enthusiasm to join the crusade. Their zeal seemed to resonate with that of many in the region, including Deepa's entire family. A decision was soon made to attend the Vaisakhi celebrations the following year, in 1700 CE. Some historians suggest that they planned to attend Hola celebrations instead but this is unlikely since Guru Gobind Singh introduced these only in 1701.[3]

Travel was on horseback or by animal transport—horse or bullock cart. The journey of some 220 kilometres to Anandpur via Hoshiarpur would take a week or more, and on an appointed day in early April 1700, people gathered in thousands at Jhabal, their rendezvous, some twenty kilometres northwest of Pahuwind. From here, chanting hymns amid banter and chatter, the extended cavalcade wound its way to Anandpur, the abode of Guru Gobind, Deepa's family carrying their homemade gur (jaggery made from sugar-cane juice) as a specialty offering, customary on pilgrimage. Many, including Bhagtu would also have hauled their tithe both in kind and currency, usual among the Sikhs then.

Young, brimming with vigour and enthusiasm, Deepa chose to walk all the way along with many others.

'Deepa, it's a long way to Anandpur! You will tire! Do mount the horse and take the weight off your feet!' remonstrated Jeoni. 'For some time, at least!' she bade him.

There were horses to spare that trotted along, tethered to the back of carts but Deepa was quite inured to fatigue from the rigors of a farming life. He seemed indefatigable with his light step and buoyant mood.

'No worries, Ma! Look, there are others walking too!' he rejoined. 'I've heard it said that to walk a pilgrimage purifies and humbles us. Wouldn't that make the Lord happier?'[4]

Deepa seemed to delight in the entirely new experience: the shifting landscape, an arresting scrumble of green and auburn with red, pink and violet tasselled plants running along and away; the grass and mud tracks that dispersed and converged over expansive meadows broken by asymmetric patches of cultivation and clumps of forest; shying herds of deer, fleet of foot, that scampered away only to stop and stare, statuesque, their ears on end; the slower nilgai that brooded among tall grass and marshland; quicksilver coveys of partridge and quail starting from the brush to take wing only to settle in the near distance; the sheer glee of ferrying across two rivers, the Beas and the Sutlej; interaction among the large group of people, their halts for community meals prepared and shared from the rations they carried; the changing hues of the sky, soft, fleecy or mottled, dissolving into deeper colours before turning pale when the light sank; their bivouacs under clear and diaphanous night skies, or the snug shelter of their makeshift cart-roof against sharp April showers while thunder clapped to a show of lightning, crickets scratched the night amid the scattered disunity of frogs that thumped the darkness in deep-toned discord.

In trying to chronicle a life sketch of Deep Singh, there is little historical record available for reference. Their tumultuous and unsettled circumstances did not allow the Sikhs to pen their own early history. Yet, since in the linear, historiographical approach, the modern era begins in the early 16th century, it is acceptable to accord equal credibility to oral history, with recourse to logic where necessary.

The period of stay at Anandpur for Bhagtu and his family is estimated from two weeks to three months.[5] What is at issue here is that as a farming family, their absence would have been dictated by the crops they cultivated. Wheat and sugar cane were common in the Majha even then; of these, wheat needed relatively more irrigation.[6] Possibly, Bhagtu cultivated both; in which case, the family would need to return for the wheat harvest that normally begins mid-April, suggesting a stay of two-three weeks. In case he cultivated only sugar cane, a longer stay is possible but even this crop requires periodical tending.

Also, by some accounts, while Amar, Deepa's younger brother by five years accompanied the family to Anandpur,[7] this would have left Meher, a pre-teen, back home in the care of Bhagtu's extended family, giving further cause for their early return.

More importantly, the family had sojourned long enough for the Guru to have noticed Deepa among the multitude for his imposing stature and powerful build as much for his devotion to serve, enthusiasm to learn alongside other special traits that would distinguish him later. Now re-christened Bhai Bhag Singh, Jeevan Kaur and Bhai Deep Singh, when the family sought leave of Guru Gobind Singh, the Guru preferred Deep Singh to stay.

ਅਸਾਂ ਰਖਣਾ ਇਸਨੂੰ ਪਾਸ। ਕਈ ਕੰਮ ਇਨ ਕਰਨੇ ਰਾਸ ।
—Gyani Thakar Singh[8]

Asaan rakhna isnu pas. Kayi kamm inn karne raas.
We'll have him stay with us, for he is destined to great deeds.

Some writers suggest that Deep Singh was equally loath to leave and was the first to express this wish, initially to his father, who then spoke on his behalf to the Guru (see ser 4 in Appendix A).[9] The momentous event is recorded in popular lore:

ਦੀਪ ਸਿੰਘ ਨੂੰ ਗੁਰਾਂ ਨੇ ਪਕੜ ਬਾਹੋਂ ਨਾਲ ਪਿਆਰ ਦੇ ਪਾਸ ਬਿਠਾਇਆ ਏ ।
ਦੇ ਕੇ ਥਾਪਣਾ ਕਿਹਾ ਸ਼ਾਬਾਸ਼ ਬੇਟਾ ਭਗਤ ਸਿੰਘ ਨੂੰ ਫੇਰ ਸੁਣਾਇਆ ਏ ।
ਸਿਖਾ ਜਾਓ ਨਾ ਕਰੋ ਖਿਆਲ ਕੋਈ ਪੁੱਤਰ ਇਸ ਨੂੰ ਅਸਾਂ ਬਣਾਯਾ ਏ ।
ਇਹਦਾ ਜਸ ਸੰਸਾਰ ਵਿਚ ਬੜਾ ਹੋਸੀ ਅਸਾਂ ਇਸ ਨੂੰ ਅਮਰ ਕਰਾਇਆ ਏ ।
—Buta Singh,
'Prasang Baba Deep Singh Shaheed'[10]

Deep Singh nu guran pakad bahon naal pyar de paas bathaya ye
De ke thapna kiha shabash beta Bhagat Singh nu pher sunaya ye

Sikha jao na karo khyal koi putter is nu asan banaya ye
Ihda jas sansar vich bada hosi asan is nu amar karaya ye
The Guru held Deep Singh by the arm
And sat him down beside;
He patted him then on his back
To Bhagat Singh he said with pride:
'Go your way my fellow Sikh, no worries ever after!
Your son shall be a son to me;
His blessed future I foresee:
Much fame, acclaim shall surely be!'

Privileged Paces

For Deep Singh, this was an honour no words could pen. Howsoever much he thought and queried all those around him, he could not fathom why he had been specially chosen by the Guru to be so ordained. He could sense all along how the Guru had evinced keen interest in all he sought to do and accomplish in the short time he was there—listening to the scripture early morning, long hours of sewa (voluntary service) in the langar, his efforts to join the weapon training and equitation sessions, his curiosity to learn and assimilate the underlying spiritual message during evening katha (exegesis) but so did many others in the congregation, thought Deep Singh. Possibly, the Guru had divined latent qualities in him of which he himself was unaware.

The Guru took the new pupil under his wing and is known to have personally mentored him in the art of horsemanship, hunting, and the use of arms—a mélange that answered the training needs of the times. His education was entrusted to Bhai Mani Singh who taught him Gurmukhi, Sanskrit, Persian, and Arabic, besides guiding him through a study of Sikh scriptures and philosophy.

His day began early at amrit vela (ambrosial hour) with the recitation of scriptures followed by exegesis sessions and the study of languages along with allied subjects. The afternoon was devoted to weapon training, equitation, and mock combat. The Guru usually presided over the evening congregational service which included awareness-raising on important issues.[11]

From the outset, Deep Singh demonstrated legible and highly ornamental penmanship for which he was often sought by many of the Guru's celebrated poets such as Bhai Nand Lal and Kesho Ram to transcribe their compositions. In time, the Guru personally commended Deep Singh for this accomplishment.[12]

By some accounts, Deep Singh accompanied the Guru and his elder sons on hunting expeditions and is known to have once killed a rampant tiger, hacking off its head with one clean stroke of the sword.[13]

This feat of warding off the springing animal with the shield and then striking it in the neck with a sword was not uncommon and is attributed to many. Deep Singh would probably have been inspired by the tenth Guru himself who killed a man-eater tiger in the presence of the rajas of Nahan and Garhwal—Gurdwara Shergah marks the spot near Paonta Sahib.[14]

Though Deep Singh's length of stay at Anandpur is a matter of conjecture, it can be reasonably assumed that his scholastic and martial accomplishments would have taken him three-four years. Within this short period, he was able to master Gurmukhi alongside acquiring the rudiments of Sanskrit, Persian and Arabic. It was remarkable indeed, that a lad in his late teens could completely change course from ingenuous husbandry to a life diametrically opposite in spirit and intellect. Additionally, while training in combat and the use of arms, he could upskill and hone natural abilities of an existing skillset acquired during his growing years.

This was the period when the Khalsa were constantly under attack, singly or conjointly, by the forces of the hill rajas and the imperial army. A total of nine major and minor military engagements were fought during 1700-1705 CE. Deep Singh would have witnessed several of these, most definitely would have been blooded and begun to acquire the fighting prowess and courage that would distinguish him in later life.

It is believed that after he turned twenty-two, sometime in 1705, before the Guru's own forced evacuation from the Anandpur citadel on 5-6th December 1705, Deep Singh returned to his native village on his family's behest, taking leave of the Guru.[15] The reasons are not entirely clear though not far to see. Given the low life expectancy and poor general health in the period along with the fact that his parents had a late start to parenthood and could by now have been invalided, Deep Singh's presence back home may have become essential as the eldest in the family with two much younger siblings. It is equally likely, as some writers suggest, that his parents arranged his return to solemnize his nuptials. This, however, did not happen, not because he was shortly summoned by the Guru to Talwandi Sabo. More likely that, at a turning point in his life, he decided on celibacy to devote himself entirely to serve the Khalsa panth.[16] Any oral or written accounts that suggest his marriage and raising a family can be disregarded as aberrations by simply referring to his family tree.[17]

By another account, before the evacuation of Anandpur, the Guru deputed Bhai Mani Singh and Deep Singh to escort Mata Sundari and Sahib Devan, his wives, to Delhi, and Deep Singh visited Pahuwind on his return journey.[18] This could have been on his own volition, his parents' bidding, or both, on taking express leave of the Guru.

At the time of departure, the Guru instructed Deep Singh: 'Go in peace but I must assign to you several important tasks and responsibilities! First and foremost, spread the gospel in your area. Especially, expatiate on the essentials of our faith and encourage all to respect and adhere to Sikh praxis. Secondly, gather the youth of your region. Impart to them training in the use of arms and horsemanship. Soon enough, this should help you raise a militia. We wage an ongoing war for justice against a foe far superior in numbers and arsenal, and you could be called upon any time to supplement our forces. Thirdly, help the needy and the poor. Render all possible assistance to keep the ordinary citizen out of harm's way. Lastly, do not return until summoned. May the Lord protect you!'[19]

For a young adult who finds little mention in the annals of Anandpur, these are weighty responsibilities which endorse the high regard of the Guru for this competent and devoted young man, destined for a major role in the times to come. Although short of fighting men, it is in recognition of his strategic worth that the Guru preferred to move him out of the war zone and to entrust him with the responsibility of spreading the Sikh gospel and raising a yeomanry.

During approximately six months of his stay in Pahuwind, Deep Singh did exactly as instructed to overwhelming acclaim throughout the region, emphasizing both spiritual and military values alongside the overarching imperative to fight injustice.[20] Possibly, the band of fighting men that he trained would form the nucleus of the force that he was later formally tasked to commission.

He had made an impression deep enough on the Guru to be specially beckoned in January 1706 to Talwandi Sabo—one, to assist the Guru and Bhai Mani Singh in the finalization of the Sikh scriptures that would later be canonized as Guru Granth Sahib; two, to be picked at the very young age of twenty-three years to head the seminary at Talwandi Sabo when the Guru departed for the Deccan on 30th October 1706.

Evacuation of Anandpur

History provides no definite record of Guru Gobind Singh's evacuation of Anandpur, variously placed by writers in early 1704, early 1705, or late 1705. Even ancient Sikh sources such as Sukha Singh's Gurbilas and Attar Singh's Sakhis are at variance. In turn, this impacts the Guru's subsequent battles as well as his period of stay at Dam Dama Sahib which, accordingly, could vary from nine months to three years. Sukhdyal Singh's analyses seems the most convincing which records the evacuation on the night of 5-6th December 1705, leaving a little over nine months for the Guru's stay at Dam Dama Sahib before his departure for the Deccan on 30th October 1706.[21]

Tricked into evacuating the Anandpur citadel, the Guru was initially promised a safe passage but as soon as he left the safety of his refuge along with his entourage, the Mughals reneged on their word and attacked. As a stratagem, the Guru dispersed his force but suffered much loss of life along with several valuable manuscripts as they sought to hastily fling themselves across the swollen Sirsa river. Three separate contingents under Udey Singh, Bachitter Singh, and Jeevan Singh were detached from his force to cover their river crossing by engaging and holding off the pursuing enemy in successful rearguard actions but were killed almost to a man in their bid—Udey Singh's teg (large slashing sword) is preserved in the Akal Takth at Amritsar.

In the ensuing turmoil, the Guru was separated from his mother and two younger sons, Zorawar Singh (nine years) and Fateh Singh (six years). Betrayed by a servant, they would soon fall into Mughal hands to be martyred by immurement (being bricked alive) on 26th December 1705, after they stood firm under threats to abjure their faith. His mother, Mata Gujri, would die of grief soon after.

Accompanied by his two elder sons, Ajit Singh (eighteen years) and Jujhar Singh (fourteen years) and about fifty followers, Guru Gobind Singh hastily repaired to an orchard near Chamkaur. On learning of their arrival, the landowner welcomed the Guru and his force into his homestead. Close on their heels, the enemy was soon upon them and laid siege, thus triggering the brief but gory Battle of Chamkaur on 7th December 1705.

Capitulation was not an option for the besieged. They climbed to the top of the house and tried to defend themselves with small arms such as bows and matchlocks. As night fell, they chose to bravely sally forth in groups of five in a bid to break through the enemy cordon only to find martyrdom. Never before or since has a father personally armed his own sons and bade them to find sure-death in battle. Ajit and Jujhar thus led the last two sallies. The Guru too chose to fight and die but was dissuaded under duress of panthic edict by his colleagues. Only he and two of his followers, Daya Singh and Dharam Singh, could extricate themselves in the cover of darkness amidst a raging thunderstorm.

Popular lore recounts that, as the Guru rode out of their shelter across the surrounding plain, his horse came to an abrupt halt, lowering its head to the ground. Flashes of lightning soon revealed the blood-soaked corpse of Jujhar Singh lying among the fallen. The horse had sensed the presence of his master's son and now stood over the body, head bowed in reverence. At this, the Guru is known to have dismounted and removed his shoes out of respect for his martyred comrades-in-arms. While his companions stayed back to await an opportunity to perform the last rites for the dead, the Guru moved on. This explains why he is believed to have reached the dense Machhiwara wood alone and barefoot. Yet, the forbidding and dismal gloom of the vast forest on a bone-chilling winter night failed to subdue the muse in him. It is at this juncture that he composed the much-favored lyric 'Mitter Pyare Nu'.

He now turned to the Malwa to raise a fresh body of fighting men to continue the struggle. With brief halts, he continued through Lal Kalan-Ghulal-Rampur Katani-Alamgir-Hair-Raikot. It was at Raikot that he learnt through his host Rai Kalha of the death of his two younger sons and that of his mother. This only served to stiffen his resolve for armed resistance. At Mehde, a Muslim hakim (medicine man) tended his wounds from the recent battles.[22]

The Guru reached Dina on or about 1st January 1706 where he felt secure enough to briefly rest and recoup. The area fell in the Sirhind province but was part of the private estate of Rai Shamir of Dhaliwal. The Guru could now consolidate his followers, admitting more into the Khalsa fold mainly from the sturdy jat peasantry through baptism and training in arms. The total period of stay is unconfirmed and varies from a few days to three months-thirteen days.

According to some sources, it was here that Deep Singh along with forty warriors arrived from village Gurm to be baptized by the tenth Guru,[23] but this is at variance with mainstream writing for several reasons (see Appendix B). If indeed Deep Singh had met the Guru at Dina, he would have fought alongside him in the Battle of Muktsar but this finds no mention in oral lore either.

The Battle of Muktsar

When he learnt that the Sirhind forces were hot in pursuit once again, the Guru consulted his followers on a suitable place to engage the enemy.

'I refuse to give battle here. It could mean much collateral damage to you and your family,' said the Guru, addressing Rai Shamir, his host. 'And could also jeopardize your position with the administration as their functionary,' he continued.

As a devotee, Rai Shamir would risk his all for the Guru, 'Guru Sahib, we have the advantage of a supportive population all around, adequate arsenal, and we could reinforce our defences since there is still time.'

But the Guru was not swayed. For him the safety and well-being of his host were far more important. That's when Kapura Brar of Kot Kapura (ancestor of the Faridkot royals) suggested an alternative. He too held a private estate as an official in the Sirhind administration and was familiar with the area and terrain.

'Guru ji, I recommend that we move out about sixty kilometres west to a place called Khidrane di Dhab. It's an isolated water source in the middle of an arid wasteland. We would thus draw out the enemy and, if we can take up defences around the water source, inflict much attrition.'

The Guru readily acquiesced to the plan. By now, he had gathered a large force of loyal devotees from both Majha and Malwa, prominent from the latter were Bhai Bhalo, Bhagtu, Mul Chand, Bhunder, who arrived with their own groups of battle-ready fighting men.

The Guru had time enough to prepare entrenchments around the water source at Khidrane di Dhab but before the actual battle on 14-15th January 1706, the Sirhind force chanced upon a contingent from the Majha under Maha Singh who, along with his forty followers had earlier opted to part ways with the Guru during the Anandpur siege. Overcome with guilt and regret, they now returned to redeem themselves and, on sighting the enemy, chose to engage rather than circumvent. By some accounts, Deep Singh who was then in the Majha, influenced their return. This is highly likely given the vast responsibilities devolved on him personally by the Guru and the fact that his village, Pahuwind, was only some fifteen miles from Rataul, that of Maha Singh. He may even have considered joining them but had strict injunctions from the Guru to return only when summoned.

Outnumbered, out-equipped, and taken by surprise, they found glorious death to a man in the battlefield but each sold his life dearly, killing several of the enemy. Deeply moved by their loyalty and courage, the Guru rushed to their aid only to find a grievously wounded Maha Singh lying among his comrades. Gasping for breath, tears welling up in his eyes, with folded hands, he made an effort to rise as he begged the Guru for clemency, 'Forgive us, Guru Sahib, for forsaking you at Anandpur. Please tear the bedawa (letter abandoning the Guru) so that I may die in peace.'[24]

The Guru held Maha Singh's hand in a comforting gesture, attempting to lift him in an embrace, his head now bowed in reverence to the devotion and gallantry of these brave men who had given their all to rejoin him in battle. He then untied the bedawa from his cummerbund and tore it to shreds. At this,

Maha Singh's breathing eased, a peaceful expression spread across his countenance as he slowly dissolved into the eternal.

The Guru now had another battle on his hands but he would later return to personally oversee the cremation of his fallen comrades. The battle site was named Muktsar (pool of salvation) after the martyrdom of these brave forty muktas ('mukti' means 'salvation'), where a commemorative fair, Maghi Mela, is held in January every year.

Alerted by the battle din, the Guru's volunteer army had meanwhile completely surrounded the Sirhind troops, killing about 250 in a battle that lasted a little over four hours. By now, running out of water supplies, the Muslim commander sought Kapura's advice as their confidante and local guide for a water source. The enemy had no option but to beat a hasty retreat when informed that there was none for miles around except the one in the control of the Sikhs.[25] The Sikh stratagem had worked.

After the battle, the Guru returned to Dina where, in end-January, he wrote *Zafarnamah* (Epistle to Victory) and dispatched it to Emperor Aurangzeb through two of his trusted Sikhs, Daya Singh and Dharam Singh.[26] The Persian composition in verse, among many other things, rebuked the Emperor for reneging on an oath sworn on the Koran by his armies at Anandpur and warned him of a nemesis that inevitably awaits evil-doers. The composition is equally notable for articulating the Guru's moral justification for war in the pursuit of justice 'as a last resort' (ultima ratio):

چوں کار از ہمہ حیلتے در گزشت
حلال است بردن بہ شمشیر دست

ਚੁ ਕਾਰ ਅਜ਼ ਹਮਹ ਹੀਲਤੇ ਦਰ ਗੁਜ਼ਸ਼ਤ ॥
ਹਲਾਲ ਅਸਤ ਬੁਰਦਨ ਬ ਸ਼ਮਸ਼ੀਰ ਦਸਤ ॥੨੨॥

Chu kar az hameh heel-te dar guzasht,
Halal ast burdan b-shamshir dast (22)
In the pursuit of justice, when all stratagems are exhausted,
Only then it is righteous to unsheathe the sword. (22)

His place of stay at Dina is commemorated with a shrine called Gurdwara Lohgarh Sahib, or Zafarnamah Sahib. Thereafter, the Guru travelled South with a brief sojourn at Lakhi Jungle where now stands a commemorative Gurdwara. He is known to have composed the following lines here, possibly, recited during a kavi darbar organized in his honour:

ਲੱਖੀ ਜੰਗਲ ਖਾਲਸਾ, ਆਇ ਦੀਦਾਰ ਲਗੇ ਨੇ।
ਸੁਣਕੇ ਸਦ ਮਾਹੀ ਦਾ, ਮੇਹੀਂ ਪਾਣੀ ਮਤੇ ਨੇ।
ਕਿਸੇ ਨਾਲ ਨ ਰਲੀਆ ਕਾਈ, ਕੋਈ ਸਉਕ ਪਿਝੇ ਨੇ।
ਗਿਆ ਫ਼ਿਰਾਕ, ਮਿਲਿਆ ਮਿਤ ਮਾਹੀ, ਤਾਹਿ ਸ਼ੁਕਰ ਕੀਤੇ ਨੇ।
—Guru Gobind Singh[27]

Lakhi jungle Khalsa, aye didar lago ne
Sunke sad mahi da, mehin mato ne
Kise nal n ralia kai, koi souk piyo ne
Gia firak, milia mit mahi, tahi shuker kito ne

The devotees (Khalsa) rushed to Lakhi forest to have a glimpse of their beloved (the Guru).
As the buffalos run, leaving water and grass to hear the flute of *Ranjha*,
They all vied with one another, pulled by a magnetic force.
The separation now ended with the beloved close to their bosom.

THREE

Dam Dama Sahib: Guru Ki Kanshi[1]

Rest and Recoup

A few days later, in end-January 1706, the Guru arrived at Talwandi Sabo, near Bhatinda, a secluded, relatively secure spot that was part of Choudhary Dalla's homestead ('choudhary' was a title bestowed by Mughals on jat zamindars, or landowners). The retinue of the Guru consisted of fourteen hundred persons of whom five hundred were on horseback and the remaining on foot, some on a payroll.[2] He was received with great ceremony, his host graciously offering him his house to stay. The Guru opted for a tent as was his wont along with his followers who also stayed under canvas.[3] On their arrival much later, Mata Sundri and Sahib Kaur are known to have been put up in Bhai Dall Singh's haveli.[4]

For the first five days, Choudhary Dall served food to all until the Guru's entourage were able to set up their community kitchen. An existing high ground was developed into a makeshift stage for the Guru and it was here after a long period of tempestuous belligerency forced upon him that the Guru found peace and security to finally unbuckle his battle accouterments. Aptly, the place has since been known as Takht Sri Dam Dama Sahib (place of respite).

Historians suggest that the Guru chose this secluded spot for a number of reasons. It was already a Sikh centre previously visited by Guru Nanak in November 1515 and later by Guru Har Rai.[5] Chaudhary Dalla, the headman of the area, was a trustworthy devotee whose father, Saleem Shah, had embraced Sikhism in the time of Guru Hargobind and had even rendered military assistance during the Battle of Gurusar (1631) fought near Mehraj in the area.[6]

Later, Saleem Shah had hosted Guru Teg Bahadur during his one-month sojourn in 1674, accompanied by the young Gobind Rai, and had even initiated the digging of a sarovar. In 1693, Guru Gobind Rai revisited almost all places in Malwa earlier visited by his father, including Talwandi Sabo, making this his third visit.[7]

The Guru was equally aware of its security potential at this critical juncture. Extending from the banks of River Sutlej near Ferozepur to the wastes of Bathinda over an area of about eighty kilometres, the sequestered region was covered with dense forest known as Lakhi Jungle that, time and again, served as a retreat-cum-hideout for the Khalsa. It was also outside the jurisdiction of both the faujdar (military commander) of Sirhind and the subedar of Lahore and, instead, fell under the Subedari of Multan.[8]

On his arrival at Dam Dama Sahib, the Guru is known to have recited a quatrain that was found emblazoned at the entrance to the shrine till the mid-20th century:[9]

ਸੁਣ ਕੇ ਹਮ ਤਾਹਿ ਕੇ ਬੈਨਨ ਕੋ, ਦਮਦਮਾ ਸੁ ਮਾਲਵੇ ਵੀਚ ਸੁਧਾਰੇ ।
ਢਿਗ ਤਾਹਿ ਤਲਵੰਡੀ ਕੇ ਕਾਂਸ਼ੀ ਰਚੋਂ, ਜਹ ਬੈਲ ਪਢੇ ਹੋਏ ਬੁੱਧ ਉਦਾਰੇ ।
ਗ੍ਰੰਥ ਉਚਾਰ ਕਰੋਂ ਤਹਾਂ ਬੈਠ ਕੇ, ਬੀੜ ਸੋਊ ਜਗ ਮਾਹ ਬਿਥਾਰੇ ।
ਅਖਰ ਏਕ ਕਾ ਭੇਦ ਧਰੋ ਨਹਿ, ਮੁਮ ਦਾਸ ਗੁਰੂ ਸਮਰੱਥ ਬੀਚਾਰੇ ।

Sun ke hum tah ke bainan ko, damdama su malwe veech sudharo
Dhig tah Talwandi ke kanshi rachon, jeh bail padhe hoye budh udharo
Granth uchaar karon tahanh baith ke, bir soujag mah bitharo
Akhar ek ka bhed dharo neh, mum das guru samrath bicharo
I reached Dam Dama in Malwa, when I heard thy call
to convert Talwandi into kanshi for all;

the bovine too shall learn and mould
with Granth that we shall here unfold
across the earth to set souls free,
With true Granth it shall full agree.
To help God's servants everywhere;
Reflect on world with wisdom rare.

(NB: the true Granth herein refers to the Kartarpuri pothi)

The Adi Granth

Guru Gobind Singh felt that he had heeded an inner beckoning to arrive at Talwandi Sabo that he might elevate this arid wasteland into an oasis of learning which would overflow and spread its fragrance across the entire world. Towards this end, his first project soon after settling in was to standardize the scriptures.

The Kartarpur pothi (book from Kartarpur) compiled under the pontificate of Guru Arjan in 1604 was accepted as the authentic master scripture and had begun to be copied soon after. As the process seemed to proliferate with time, scribal decisions brought in dissimilitude, and by the end of the 17th century, there were three manuscripts claiming legitimacy: a Kartarpur version (dated 1604); a slightly longer Khara Mangat version (dated 1642); and a third Lahore version (date unknown).[10]

Guru Gobind had earlier made efforts to standardize the text at Anandpur and had commissioned Bhai Mani Singh to borrow the Kartarpur pothi from its custodian, Dhirmal's son, Bhar Mal (Dhirmal had since passed away). Dilgeer suggests in his work, that when the former presented himself before Bhar Mal on 9th August 1678, he was refused the scriptures but allowed in situ replication. Bhai Mani Singh then prepared many pothis and disseminated these among the Sikh followers far and wide.[11] However, any scriptures in the Gurus possession were, sadly, lost in the turmoil of the Guru's forced evacuation of Anandpur in December 1705. Since the Guru's request to borrow the Kartarpuri pothi now was declined in 1706, the view that has dominated

Sikh thinking since the 19th century, propagated by Gyani Gyan Singh, is that the Guru had no option but to dictate the entire text from memory at Dam Dama Sahib.

Some scholars challenge this narrative to suggest that, beginning 1682, several manuscripts were prepared at Anandpur (colophons: 1688, 1691, 1692, and three more) and that there is firm evidence of the ninth Guru's hymns having been included during his lifetime. Manuscripts inclusive of the ninth Guru's hymns have been found at Dhaka (dated 1675) and Patna (dated 1691).[12] With several manuscripts extant at the time, it is not clear whether the Guru dictated the entire granth from memory or just the ninth Guru's 115 hymns.[13]

Bhai Mani Singh was appointed the amanuensis for the task who, in turn, recommended Deep Singh as his assistant:

ਮਨੀ ਸਿੰਘ ਬੇਨਤੀ ਕਰੇ ਦੋਇ ਹੱਥ ਜੋੜ ।
ਇਸ ਕਾਰਜ ਵਿਚ ਗੁਰੂ ਜੀ ਦੀਪ ਸਿੰਘ ਦੀ ਲੋੜ ।

—Sohan Singh Ghukewalia,
'Baba Deep Singh Shaheed'[14]

Mani Singh beinti karke hatth jorh
Is karaj vich Guru ji Deep Singh de lorh
Supplicating to the Guru, Mani Singh submits
We need Deep Singh now; for this task he fits.

Deep Singh responded promptly to the message carried by Bhai Sher Singh on behalf of the Guru. On arriving at Talwandi Sabo, he was inconsolable when he learnt of the numerous tragedies that had befallen the Guru and his family and remonstrated in anguish:

'Guru ji, why did you not summon me in your time of need? Why should I live when so many of my comrades have fallen in battle?'

'Take heart, Bhai Deep Singh! A lot still needs doing to supplant the cruel regime. We are heading for worse times. There are many important responsibilities that you shall shoulder and, in time, make a special mark in history!'

Deep Singh's role in preparing the granth comprised the provisioning of writing material such as reed-pens, ink, paper, etc. In real terms, he served as understudy to Bhai Mani Singh who did the actual writing under the instructions of Guru Gobind Singh, the process finally having begun on Vaisakhi 1706 amid ceremony.[15]

Another account suggests that both Mani Singh and Deep Singh handwrote two separate copies of the recension, dictated by the tenth Guru. Mani Singh's copy accompanied the Guru to Nanded for the investiture, while Deep Singh's copy was retained at Dam Dama Sahib with instructions to prepare more copies to generalize its access among a growing and dispersed following.[16] Yet another account states that a total of four copies were prepared in the Guru's presence and conveyed to the four takths (major Sikh centers). Bhai Mani Singh was ordained as the Granthi for Harimandir Sahib, and carried one copy to that shrine.[17]

The commonly held belief suggests that only a single copy, the Dam Dami Bir, was made at the time, and that the Guru instructed Deep Singh to prepare need-based replicas later for dissemination to the four takhts.[18] This copy accompanied the Guru to Nanded, was canonized, but after the Guru's passing, returned to Dam Dama Sahib for replication by Deep Singh.

Besides launching the recension project on the day, Vaisakhi 1706 was celebrated after several years with befitting gusto. People of Malwa, mostly jats, thronged the shrine, thousands choosing to be baptized, beginning a trend that would see over a hundred thousand people baptized over nine months by the Guru himself.[19]

There was also time to reflect and engage in spiritual discussions. The Guru would dictate the scriptures during the day and render a serialized commentary in the evening mass. A select congregation of forty-eight members who attended these exegesis sessions were all accorded the title brahmgyani (enlightened individual). Deep Singh's name appears at number two in the list after that of Bhai Mani Singh and he would later perpetuate this tradition of scriptural exegesis.

The names of the Rajas of Jaipur and Jodhpur are included at serials 41 and 42, respectively, in the said list of attendees but this needs corroboration through further research.[20] According to one writer, Raja Jai Singh's visit took place when the recension and serialized exegesis were nearing completion.[21] The association of the Jaipur royals with Sikhism is, however, recorded in history and lends credence to this assertion: Raja Jai Singh Mirza was a devotee on whose behest Guru Harkishan (eighth pontificate) visited Delhi, while Raja Ram Singh had accompanied Guru Teg Bahadur to Assam.[22]

It is believed that the religious practice of the Akhand Path (uninterrupted recitation of scriptures over forty-eight hours) was also introduced here and performed for the first time to mark the completion of the project and its exegesis on Bhadon vadi teej (August 1706).[23] The opening stanza of 'Chandi di Vaar' was recited for the first time as an invocation during the ardaas (supplication) on the occasion:[24]

ੴ ਵਾਹਿਗੁਰੂ ਜੀ ਕੀ ਫਤਹਿ॥
Ek-Oankar. Waheguroo Ji Ki Fateh
God is One. All victory is of the Wondrous Guru (God).

ਸ੍ਰੀ ਭਗੌਤੀ ਜੀ ਸਹਾਇ॥
Sri Bhagouti ji Sahai
May the respected sword (God in the form of the Destroyer of evil doers) help us!

ਵਾਰ ਸ੍ਰੀ ਭਗੌਤੀ ਜੀ ਕੀ ਪਾਤਸ਼ਾਹੀ ੧੦॥
Vaar Sri Bhagouti Ji Ki Paatshaahee Dasvee
Ode of the respected sword recited by the Tenth Guru.

ਪ੍ਰਿਥਮ ਭਗੌਤੀ ਸਿਮਰਿ ਕੈ ਗੁਰ ਨਾਨਕ ਲਈਂ ਧਿਆਇ॥
Pritham Bhagouti Simar Kai, Guru Naanak Layee Dhiyae
First remember the sword (God in the form of Destroyer of evil doers); then remember and meditate upon Guru Nanak.

ਫਿਰ ਅੰਗਦ ਗੁਰ ਤੇ ਅਮਰਦਾਸੁ ਰਾਮਦਾਸੈ ਹੋਈਂ ਸਹਾਇ॥
Angad Gur Te Amar Das, Raamdaasai Hoye Sahai
Then remember and meditate upon Guru Angad, Guru Amar Das and Guru Ram Das: May they help us!

ਅਰਜਨ ਹਰਗੋਬਿੰਦ ਨੋ ਸਿਮਰੌ ਸ੍ਰੀ ਹਰਿਰਾਇ॥
Arjan Hargobind No Simrou Sri Har Rai
Remember and meditate upon Guru Arjan, Guru Hargobind and Respected Guru Har Rai.

ਸ੍ਰੀ ਹਰਿਕ੍ਰਿਸ਼ਨ ਧਿਆਇਐ ਜਿਸ ਡਿਠੇ ਸਭਿ ਦੁਖ ਜਾਇ॥
Sri HarKrishan Dhiyaa-eeai Jis Dhithe Sabh Dukh Jaye
Remember and meditate upon respected Guru Har Krishan, by whose presence all ills disappear.

ਤੇਗ ਬਹਾਦਰ ਸਿਮਰਿਐ ਘਰ ਨਉ ਨਿਧਿ ਆਵੈ ਧਾਇ॥
Teg Bahadur Simareeai Ghar Nou Nidh Avai Dhai
Remember and meditate upon Guru Tegh Bahadur; and then nine sources of wealth will hasten to your home.

ਸਭ ਥਾਂਈ ਹੋਇ ਸਹਾਇ॥
Sabh Thai Ho-e Sahaai
Oh Respected Gurus! kindly help us everywhere.

By popular belief, the first 'hukamnama' was a composition by Guru Arjan Dev.[25] This is also when the Guru declared the Dam Dama Sahib as Guru Ki Kashi, a seminary for the study of Sikhism and the spread of knowledge and learning;[26] a crucible to shape writers and poets who would throng from the West to the East;[27] a place that would vie with Guru Ki Kashi (Banaras), the revered Hindu shrine of Varanasi in the fullness of time.[28] With poets and scholars now converging at the venue, the place had already begun to reflect the glory achieved earlier at Paonta Sahib and Anandpur, acquiring a status very close to the Guru's heart.[29] Alongside, the Guru now made a concerted effort to spread the gospel, traveling extensively in the region, visiting most major villages[30] as well as dispatching preachers to different parts of the country.[31]

Hola Mohalla celebrations were revived, increasing footfall to reach numbers almost four times those witnessed at Anandpur. Gurdwaras Mahalsar (Tibi Sahib), Holgarh, and Sarovar Mahalsar bear witness to these times. Literature was produced, literary meets arranged, traditional bards and balladeers invited for congregations (Dhadi aae Mukami) to sing vaars—paeans to the martial valour of the Khalsa in the battles of Bhangani, Nadaun, Anandpur, Chamkaur, and Muktsar.

The Guru expatiated on the merits of Khande-di-Pahul (baptism by the sword) and conversely, on the evils of totems, exorcism, caste distinctions, superstitions, grave worship, and such other regressive practices. Realizing that this cultural transformation could only be accomplished through education, the Guru encouraged people to stay and study at the Ashram.

In addition to this scholarly initiative, the Guru continued to personally impart military training for proficiency in the art of war. This included daily drill and mock battles at Jandianasar. Besides a large number of volunteers always willing to risk their lives for the Panth (Khalsa community) and the Guru, his army now included a segment of paid soldiers. Some historians opine that from the military viewpoint, his position had now become stronger than ever before.[32]

Jeonda Shaheed

Ratan Singh Bhangu narrates an unusual incident in his 'Sakhi Shaheedon Singhon ki' (A Tale of Shaheed Singhs, Sakhi 79) about a test of courage that the Guru administered to his Sikhs at Dam Dama Sahib. It is not entirely clear if the shrine referred to is the one at Anandpur or Talwandi Sabo; more likely the latter considering that the incident is about panj pyaras (the five beloved ones) who in this case, are all from the Majha unlike the panj pyaras at Anandpur in 1699, who hailed from different parts of the country.

Addressing a congregation, the Guru proclaimed, 'Are there

any five Sikhs among you who would readily sacrifice their lives for the Panth!' Hurled in a tone of stern defiance, the challenge induced deathly stillness in the multitude. Finally, after the prolonged silence, five Sikhs from the Majha stepped forth, Deep Singh among them. The guru spared their lives and instead honored them with the title 'Shaheed' in recognition of their courage and predisposition for sacrifice (see ser 5 in Appendix A).

Varying rationale are advanced to explain the rare antemortem title 'Shaheed' conferred on Deep Singh prior to his martyrdom. This is one fairly credible version based as it is on information passed on to the author, Bhangu, by his illustrious paternal and maternal grandfathers, Mahtab Singh Mirankot and Sham Singh Kororia, respectively, both contemporaries of Deep Singh.[33]

This, however, contravenes the popular view of a posthumous award by Gupta and several other historians:

'As Baba Dip Singh and his followers had given up their lives [in the battle of November 1757] while performing a religious duty without causing any harm to anybody, they were all given the title of Shahids by their coreligionists.'[34]

Although readily accepted by many writers, this version fails to explain why the dera (1734) and misl (1748) headed by Deep Singh carried this title many decades before his martyrdom. Since his companions who passed muster along with him in the Guru's test of courage were also from the Majha, it is likely that some if not all had been part of the yeomanry he raised on the Guru's injunction during his brief sojourn in his village, and were subsequently included in the putative dera and misl.

Daring to Edit

Another rationale less documented but popular in the oral tradition relates to the compilation and editing of the Dasm Granth (Guru Gobind Singh's writings). When this was done is not altogether clear. Possibly, it was accomplished over many years, beginning in the presence of the Guru himself at Dam Dama Sahib.[35] Another source ascribes the compilation to Deep Singh under the guidance of Bhai Mani Singh, beginning in 1715, completed by end-1716, and later authorized by Mata Sundari, the Guru's wife.[36]

According to oral history, while Deep Singh was engaged in compiling the Dasm Granth, he chose to amend a word in the khayal 'Mitter Pyare Nu'.[37]

ਮਿਤ੍ਰ ਪਿਆਰੇ ਨੂੰ ਹਾਲੁ ਮੁਰੀਦਾ ਦਾ ਕਹਣਾ ॥
—Guru Gobind Singh, *Shabad Hazare*[38]
Mitar Piaare Nooaan Haalu Mureedaa Daa Kahanaa ॥
Convey to the dear Friend the condition of his disciples

Originally, the line read: *Haal fakiran da kehna*. Deep Singh felt that the word 'fakir'—a Muslim ascetic living on alms, by popular connotation 'bhukha-nanga' (starved and too poor to afford clothing)—was inept for Guru Gobind Singh who was a royal personage. He suggested amending it to ਮੁਰੀਦਾ 'muridaan' (disciple or follower) as more appropriate. He was immediately cautioned by Bhai Mani Singh and other Sikhs present, 'The Guru's writing is inviolable! Any amendment would amount to sacrilege!' But Deep Singh reasoned that at the time of its composition, the Guru may have found the word 'fakir' more apt for his condition as a fugitive taking refuge in the dark vastness of a jungle, pursued by a hostile army. Yet, most descriptions of the Guru portray him in regal majesty and splendor: 'very handsome [...] immaculately and richly dressed as a prince'.[39] There could be no more authentic illustration of this than the *Ganjnama* by Bhai Nand Lal, a poet par excellence, who spent several years in the company of the Guru.[40]

Since Deep Singh was unrelenting, he was further warned, 'You commit a grave error. Take heed that any amendment of the Guru's scriptures would have to be recompensed with your life!' (See ser 6 in Appendix A). Since he went ahead with the amendment, he was henceforth referred to as 'jeonda shaheed', a living martyr.

Although it is difficult to verify this narrative, such stories are seldom concocted over religious texts and scriptures held sacred, the lack of corroborative evidence notwithstanding. Deep Singh must, nonetheless, be credited for his intellect, linguistic ability and knowledge of prosody along with the moral courage to have edited one ill-fitting word for the *mot juste*. The second amendment attributed to Deep Singh, that of Khalas to Khalsa, is less significant since it merely implies the change of a grammatical category from 'khalas' (adjective) to 'khalsa' (noun).

The khayal 'Mitter Pyare Nu' was composed after the battle of Chamkaur and first recited by the Guru shortly thereafter, either before or on reaching Lakhi Jungle. Although the majoritarian view tends to challenge any such amendment, oral history cannot be completely discounted, particularly since Deep Singh was among the several compilers of the Dasm Granth. The writer Gyani Balwant Singh Kotha Guru, who is credited with in-depth research on Takth Sri Dam Dama Sahib, records a compilation that was referred to as 'Baba Deep Singh vali beerh'.[41]

Before the Guru set off for the South, he issued a Hukamnama, a royal edict (number 91) announcing his intention to depart and to invite his devotees to bid farewell. The missive included the opening lines of this khayal 'Mitter Pyare Nu' with 'muridan' and not 'fakeeran'. It must, however, be borne in mind that the edict formed part of Sakhi number 102 in *Guru ki Sakhian* completed in 1790, many decades after the event, by when any amendment would have gained full currency.[42]

Except for two compositions in Persian and one in Punjabi, the Dasm Granth was composed in Braj language using Gurmukhi between 1680 and 1705 at Paonta and Anandpur, with dharmayudh as the leitmotif. It was initially finalized at Bhabaur Sahib but recompiled several times later by Bhai Mani Singh, Deep Singh, and others.[43] The two oldest manuscripts date back to 1698 but there is none titled Dasm Granth which, in reality, was standardized much later under the Sodhak committee in 1897 from thirty-two manuscripts, and first published only in 1902.[44] A combined Adi Granth-Dasm Granth compiled and calligraphed by Bhai Mani Singh lists the Dasm Granth as Mahla 10 (writings of the tenth master), but excludes the Bhagat banis.[45]

A segment of Sikhs worldwide still accepts the Dasm Granth as the military manual, or the 'fortress' which deals with the world, while the Adi Granth is regarded as the 'temple' with a focus on the spirit. Together, the two represent miri-piri (temporal and spiritual authority).[46]

Founding Jathedar

Bhai Daya Singh and Dharam Singh returned in October 1706 with a personal invite from Emperor Auranzeb for the Guru. Before the Guru's departure, another Akhand Path was held, Sikhs turning up in large numbers from far and wide to bid farewell.[47] The ration for the communion was provided by Bhai Dall Singh on the Guru's bidding.[48]

All through the Guru's extended sojourn, Bhai Dall had endeared himself to his royal guest, showing exceptional devotion and hospitality and when the Guru decided to depart, he implored that he make Dam Dama Sahib his permanent abode. However, the Guru needed to keep his tryst with the Emperor. Yet, before leaving on 30th October 1706, accompanied by an escort of 400 chosen Sikhs, he bade Bhai Dall Singh to take special care of the nascent shrine, declaring, 'Please render all possible assistance to Deep Singh, its first Jathedar!'[49]

Sadly, Bhai Dall was destined to render no further support as enjoined by the tenth Guru. Having accompanied the Guru up to Delhi, he was tragically killed under mysterious circumstances during his return journey.[50] A cenotaph stands to his memory within the precincts of the shrine at Talwandi Sabo.

From when the Guru first set eyes on him at Anandpur and

saw a promising young lad to be trained under his supervision, the elevation of Deep Singh to Jathedar now was one among several distinctions and responsibilities bestowed upon his young shoulders. It certainly was his second watershed moment. That the Guru should completely dominate the narrative at Dam Dama Sahib, both oral and written, is understandable but that he should bequeath full charge of the fledgling institution to Deep Singh, implicitly highlights the latter's role as understudy to the Guru all through his stay in matters spiritual, temporal, and military. Deep Singh must surely have endorsed his distinctive mark of competence on all tasks assigned to him to deserve this very special honour.

His pastoral background as a novice farmer with limited access to books and learning notwithstanding, Deep Singh displayed a marked predilection to acquire knowledge in a vast array of subjects and to learn a slew of languages in a short span of a few years. Alongside, he excelled at combat skills and proved to be dauntless in war. In effect, he truly combined the rare qualities of the warrior-saint envisioned by the Guru in the Khalsa.

The Guru may also have considered Bhai Mani Singh, a mentor to Deep Singh and some thirty years his senior, for this role but he had already been appointed head Granthi at Harimandir Sahib, Amritsar in 1699, a role he was definitely more suited for. Besides, as a true scholar, Bhai Mani Singh was above most but there is no received narrative of him as a warrior whereas the seminary would require leadership in both key dimensions of sant and sipahi. Bhai Mani Singh had now also been deputed by the Guru to accompany him to the Deccan and, thereafter, to escort Mata Sahib Devan, the Guru's wife, back to Delhi.[51]

PART TWO

The Heroic Century

ਇਕ ਮੁੱਠ ਛੋਲਿਆਂ ਦੀ ਖਾਕੇ ਤੇਰੇ ਲੰਗਰਾਂ ਤੋਂ ਘੁਰ ਘੁਰ ਮੌਤ ਨੂੰ ਡਰਾਵੇ ਤੇਰਾ ਖਾਲਸਾ
ਪੰਜ ਘੁਟ ਪੀਕੇ ਤੇਰੇ ਬਾਟੇ ਉਹ ਪ੍ਰੇਮ ਵਾਲੇ, ਮਸਤੇ ਹੋਏ ਹਾਥਿਓਂ ਨੂੰ ਧਾਵੇ ਤੇਰਾ ਖਾਲਸਾ
ਤੇਰੇ ਦਰਬਾਰ ਵਿਚੋਂ ਧੂੜੀ ਲੈਕੇ ਜੋੜਿਆਂ ਦੀ, ਠੋਕਰਾਂ ਨਵਾਬੀਆਂ ਨੂੰ ਲਾਵੇ ਤੇਰਾ ਖਾਲਸਾ

—Anonymous

Transliteration

Ik mutth chholeyan di kha ke tere langaran to ghur ghur maut nu darave tera khalsa
Panj ghut pike tere bate oh prem vale, maste hoye hathion nu dhave tera khalsa
Tere darbar vichon dhuri laike joreyan di, thokran nawabian nu lave tera khalsa

Translation

Having fed on just a handful of gram from the langar,
The Khalsa is unafraid to repeatedly dare and scare Death.
Having sipped just five mouthfuls of baptismal nectar (amrit)
from the Vessel of Love, the Khalsa overpowers rogue elephants.
Having anointed the forehead with shoe-dust from the court
of the Almighty, the Khalsa battles Nawabs (Viceroys)

Transcreation

Fed on just a little gram;
We do not ask for more;
Makes us truly unafraid
Because our spirits soar.
Thereafter, we can challenge Death
To scare it full with every breath.

Baptized with thy Love benign:
Thy sips of nectar so divine,
We dare to vanquish any foe;
Rogue elephants also we lay low

The dust from thine own feet, My Lord,
We touch our foreheads with.
And then we battle troops of kings—
This surely is no myth!

FOUR

Founding a Seminary

Taking Charge

Before Deep Singh, then barely twenty-four years of age, could settle as the first Jathedar of the Dam Dami Taksal (seminary or school of learning) and serve the Khalsa Panth with full devotion in this capacity, he obeyed the Guru's injunction that bade him to return home briefly to his family:

ਭਾਈ ਦੀਪ ਸਿੰਘ ਜੀ ਨੂੰ ਹੁਕਮ ਕੀਤਾ ਘਰ ਇਕ ਵਾਰ ਜੈ ਆਉ ਫਿਰ ਨਾ ਜਾਵਣਾ, ਇਹ ਗੁਰ ਸੇਵ ਕਰਨੀ ਗੁਰਧਾਮ ਦੀ। ਗੁਰੂ ਕਿ ਕਾਂਸ਼ੀ ਕਿ ਖੁਸ਼ੀ ਹੈ ਤਾਂ ਦੀਪ ਸਿੰਘ ਆਖਿਆ ਸਤਿ ਬਚਨ ਜੀ । ਬਾਹਰੋਂ ਹਜ਼ੂਰ ਕਾ ਬਚਨ ਹੋਏ ਭਾਈ ਫਤਿਹ ਸਿੰਘ ਪ੍ਰਤੀ ਭਾਈ ਤਾਈਂ ਇਹੈ ਰਹਿਣਾ । ਭਾਈ ਦੀਪ ਸਿੰਘ ਦੇ ਅਵਣੇ ਤਕ ਕਰਨੀ ਗੁਰੂ ਕਿ ਕਾਂਸ਼ੀ ਕਿ ਸੇਵਾ ।[1]

Bhai Deep Singh ji nu hukam kita ghar ik var jai au fir na javna, iha gur sev karni gurdham di. Guru ki kanshi ki Khushi hai taan Deep Singh akhya sat bachan ji. Bahron hazur ka bachan hoa Bhai Fateh Singh prati bhai tain ihai rahna. Bhai Deep Singh de avne tak karni guru ki kanshi ki seva...

Bhai Deep Singh was asked to go home once and then return to serve Guru ki Kanshi. Bhai Deep Singh obeyed. Meanwhile, Bhai Fateh Singh was appointed to take charge in the interim period till Bhai Deep Singh returned.

An entry in the Jathedar logbook for Dam Dama Sahib records:

੧੭੬੨ (ਸੰਵਤ) ਸ੍ਰੀ ਗੁਰੂ ਗੋਬਿੰਦ ਸਿੰਘ ਜੀ ਕੇ ਦੱਖਣ ਜਾਣੇ ਕੇ ਸਮੇਂ ਇਸ ਦਰਬਾਰ ਸਾਹਿਬ ਕਿ ਸੇਵਾ ਤੇ ਸੰਗਤ ਨੂੰ ਵਿਦਿਆ ਪੜ੍ਹਾਉਣ ਵਾਸਤੇ ਭਾਈ ਦੀਪ ਸਿੰਘ ਜੀ ਨੂੰ ਛੱਡਿਆ । ਕੁਛ ਚਿਰ ਭਾਈ ਫਤਿਹ ਸਿੰਘ ਜੀ ਵੀ ਗੁਰੂ ਜੀ ਦੇ ਹੁਕਮ ਮੁਤਾਬਿਕ ਸੇਵਾ ਕਰਦੇ ਰਹੇ ।[2]

1762 (Samvat) Sri Guru Gobind Singh ji ke dakhan jaane ke samey is darbar sahib ki sewa te sangat nu vidya padhaun vaste Bhai Deep Singh ji nu chhadiya. Kuchh chir Bhai Deep Singh ji vi guru ji de hukam mutabik sewa karde rahe.

In 1762 (Samvat), at the time of departing for South India, Sri Guru Gobind Singh ji appointed Bhai Deep Singh to take charge of Dam Dama Sahib to serve the people and to educate them. According to the Guru's wish, for some time, Bhai Fateh Singh performed this function.

This explains why Bhai Fateh Singh's name appears first in the list of the custodians of Dam Dama Sahib.[3] In addition, the Guru nominated twenty-five Sikhs to be resident at the shrine. According to Bajwa and Kotha Guru, prominent among these were the eponymous Bhai Fateh Singh Malvai, Bhai Budha Singh, Bhai Desa Singh, Sudha Singh (from village Dakoha near Jalandhar), and Bhai Manohar Das (Udasi).[4] Gyani Gyan Singh suggests several more names who were also among the original initiates of the misl: Gurbaksh Singh (from village Leel near Khemkaran), Prem Singh, Dargaha Singh, Sher Singh, Hira Singh, and many more.[5] Very likely that some if not many had been part of the initial yeomanry raised by Deep Singh in 1705 at Pahuwind, on the Guru's behest.

After his return from Pahuwind, Deep Singh seldom looked homeward, devoting his life to the Khalsa to eventually become one of the supreme exemplars of its ideology—the true sant-sipahi.

As the head of this prestigious albeit nascent institution, he would need not just deep spiritual and scriptural knowledge but also the ability to discourse upon such knowledge alongside administering baptismal ceremonies. Training in combat, tactics, equitation, and skill-at-arms were to be part of his charter in order to shape the sant-sipahi. He would also provide military leadership when called upon to defend the Khalsa credo against tyranny and injustice—attributes that the Guru had discerned in him, which he would demonstrate all through his life. Within two years, he would be in a position to field an armed and trained militia of some 2000 horse.

Literary, scriptural, and martial activities initiated by Guru Gobind Singh continued at Dam Dama Sahib under Deep Singh. For the benefit of the students and the sangat (religious gathering), scriptural exegesis was part of the daily routine. In due course, the number of students increased manifold, and many of these scholars in time would excel in enunciation, exposition, and calligraphy. Multiple pothis (copies of scriptures) and gutkas (booklets with daily Sikh prayers) were prepared for devotees, while martial skills continued to be honed as an essential part of the curriculum.[6]

The novitiates rose early at amrit vela around 4 AM for an extended session of prayer and meditation. The forenoon generally focused on scriptural reading, exegesis, calligraphy; and the afternoons on weapon training and mock combat followed by evening prayers and exegesis. This curriculum was a forerunner for the three-year course now run at the Gurmat Vidyalaya at Dam Dama Sahib under the Shiromani Gurdwara Parbandhak Committee (SGPC), the apex body in-charge of Sikh affairs in the Punjab.

The Guru and the Emperor

The Guru was still in Rajputana (Bhagaur) when he received news around 17-18th March 1707 of Aurangzeb's death in February at Ahmednagar. Shortly thereafter, he received an invite from his successor, Emperor Bahadur Shah, and accordingly, returned to Delhi on 21-22nd March 1707.

When they finally met near Agra, the Guru was received with much warmth and ceremony usually reserved for royalty. On the Emperor's behest, the Guru stayed in the area and later, travelled South with him. The Emperor was on his way to fight his brother, Muhammad Azam Shah, who had challenged him for the throne. During the ensuing battle fought on 20th June 1707 at Jajau, near Dholpur, a Sikh contingent under Bhai Dharam Singh allied with the Emperor. After his victory, the Emperor moved further south to quell an insurrection by his half-brother, Muhammad Kam Baksh at Bijapur in Central India.

Historical records suggest that the Guru met the Emperor on and off during the period from March 1707 to July 1708, initially for some four months at Agra and later, while travelling South, till they finally parted ways. The Emperor moved to Hyderabad while the Guru wished to visit Sikh centers in the South,[7] beginning with Nanded which had been a Sikh centre from the times of Guru Hargobind (the sixth Guru) with a large following, some families owing allegiance since Guru Nanak's visit in the 16th century.[8]

During their extended acquaintanceship, the Guru had requested the Emperor several times to hand over Wazir Khan in the interest of justice but on the advice of his courtiers, some of whom were in league with Wazir Khan, the emperor continued to dither, leaving the Guru severely disappointed.[9]

Banda Bahadur

Based on an analysis of existing records, Sukhdyal Singh (2012) concludes that there was a Sikh sangat (regiment) comprising Sikhs and Punjabis recruited by Bahadur Shah from the Punjab into the Mughal army before he ascended the throne, and that one Lachman Dev had served as its brave and capable commander. He was a full military general, a devout Sikh also known as 'Guru da Banda' (devotee of the Guru) and was attributed miraculous powers. The Guru was in constant correspondence with this regiment, which fought with distinction at Jajua on 20th June 1707.

When the Guru was stabbed by his Pathan bodyguards at Nanded, Banda came to visit him like many others. Before the Guru passed away, he bequeathed his spiritual entity into the Adi

Granth, thus canonizing it as the Guru Granth Sahib, while he transferred his temporal energy to Banda, then about thirty-eight years. He was to be overseen by the panj pyaras—Bhai Daya Singh, Bhai Dharam Singh, Bhai Himmat Singh, Bhai Mohkam Singh, and Bhai Sahib Singh—ordained with the founding of the Khalsa during the historic devan on 30th March 1699 at Anandpur Sahib. Thereafter, Banda left the imperial army to join the guru along with his regiment.[10]

This version runs counter to the popular narrative of the Guru's meeting with Banda the bairagi (ascetic) in the latter's ashram on the banks of the Godavari. The Guru's name had also been carried far and wide for his personal courage and dogged stand against tyranny. When the two met in the last week of September 1708, Lachman Das was overwhelmed both by the Guru's charisma and the fact that he was in the presence of a national hero. Bowing in reverence, he submitted with humility:

'I am thy slave. Thou art the savior of our race!'

Their acquaintance was brief, barely two weeks,[11] during which the trained eye of the Guru perceived a man of remarkable zeal and strength of character. He baptized and re-christened him Banda Singh Bahadur (the Brave). Presenting him with some of his personal weapons, he then vested him with military command of the Khalsa and charged him with a mission to punish evil-doers, as well as to uplift the poor and downtrodden in the Punjab. He was to be accompanied by the panj pyaras along with an escort of twenty-five selected Sikhs. The Guru also dispatched hukamnamas to prominent Sikhs in the Punjab, including Deep Singh, to rally round Banda and expressed his intention to join him before the hostilities commenced.[12]

Nonetheless, it may be logical to concede not just previous combat experience to Banda but more importantly, command positions within the hierarchy of the Mughal army. Only then could he acquire the knowledge and understanding of strategy and tactics, the deployment of forces and logistics alongside a critical insight into how the Mughal army functioned in war and peace—all of which he would amply demonstrate during his bold campaigns against the Mughals shortly thereafter. Possibly, Lachman Dev did have a career in the Mughal army but later renounced it to retire into the monastery. Banda's prior acquaintance with the Guru, howsoever brief, is also likely.[13] Yet, regardless of any previous military experience, Banda's 'conversion from an inert ascetic into a commander of the forces of the Khalsa was nothing short of the Guru's miracle.'[14]

A National Hero

The Guru passed away the following month, on 7th October 1708, but only after he had ordained the Adi Granth as Guru Granth Sahib, his successor and the eternal living Guru. In the course of his armed struggle, Guru Gobind Singh lost his four sons and mother. For this reason, he is often referred to as 'sarbans dani' (one who sacrificed his family).

'Though he did not live to see his high aims accomplished, Guru Gobind Singh's labours were not lost. Though he did not actually break the shackles that bound his nation, he had set their souls free and filled their hearts with a lofty longing for freedom and national ascendancy. He had broken the charm of sanctity attached to the lord of Delhi and destroyed the awe and terror inspired by the Moslem tyranny. He had taken up sparrows and had taught them to hunt down falcons.'[15]

It does him great credit that all through his tumultuous life, when he was constantly hounded for his struggles against the religious intolerance and political iniquities of the Mughals, his conduct was unsullied by any personal animosity. He was actuated, instead, 'by patriotic feelings born of disinterested love for his people groaning for centuries under the heel of the oppressor [...] He never led any offensive expeditions [...] We always find him on the defensive, taking to the sword as the last resort. He did not occupy an inch of the enemies' lands as the result of his victories.'[16] Equally remarkable that, despite all the personal loss and treachery that he suffered at the hands of his overlords, Guru Gobind did not allow the acrimony of his bitter fight against tyranny to sully the humanistic vision set in stone by his predecessors. Pir Budhu Shah, Nabi Khan and Ghani Khan are only a few of his many Muslim followers who were among his staunchest allies, ever ready to risk their lives for him. There can be no greater proof of his unshakeable faith in humanity that transcended religious considerations than his acceptance of two Pathans as his personal bodyguards at Nanded; the very pair who would stab him while asleep, eventually leading to his death a few days later.[17] As a seer, possibly, he wished to bequeath an important message to mankind—all human beings are essentially good but may sometimes be led to evil deeds.

Deep Singh Joins Banda

Banda reached the Punjab about September 1709 and took time to consolidate his forces at the same time surveying his military objectives. The Sikhs who joined Banda in response to the Guru's edicts included Deep Singh:

ਦੀਪ ਸਿੰਘ ਤਦ ਆਪਣਾ ਜਥਾ ਲੈ ਕੇ ਬੰਦੇ ਨਾਲ ਰਲਯਾ ਆਇਕੇ ਜੀ ।
ਕੁੰਜਪੁਰੇ ਸਯੈਰੇ ਬਾਨੂੰੜ ਅੰਦਰ ਕੀਤੇ ਜੰਗ ਇਸ ਤੇਗ ਉਠਾਇਕੇ ਜੀ ।

—Ghukewalia,
'Prasang Baba Deep Singh Ji'[18]

Deep Singh tad aapna jatha laike Bande nal raliya aike ji
Kunjpure Sadhaura Banur andar kite jang teg utthai ke ji
Deep Singh then with his force to join Banda came
Fighting with his sword, Kunjpura, Sadhaura, Banur did he tame.

Disaffected by a cruel and apathetic regime, the local peasantry rose in revolt almost everywhere Banda went, greatly swelling his numbers. He first targeted Samana (near Patiala) on 26th

November 1709, the dwelling place of the executioners of Guru Teg Bahadur and Guru Gobind Singh's younger sons. He then turned on Kunjpura, Ghuram, and Thaska, all inhabited by Ranghars, notorious for rape and plunder. Damla, inhabited by the Pathans who had deserted the tenth Guru in the Battle of Bhangani (1686) came next. With surprise on his side, more military successes followed at Shahbad, Markanda and Sadhaura, his army growing on a daily basis as more non-Muslims joined his crusade against their cruel and oppressive masters.

Within a few months, by the beginning of February 1710, Banda had set up his own administrative machinery, appointed revenue collectors and police officers, with Lohgarh in the Shiwalik foothills as the capital of the first Sikh state, complete with its own mint.

Battle for Sirhind

The headquarters of the province, Sirhind, had been Banda's main military objective as he swept through its major military and administrative outposts such as Kaithal, Samana, Sadhaura, Shahabad, and Banur. He now paused to reconnoiter its military resources and spent the winter months in collecting arms, raising volunteers as well as training for battle.[19]

In response to his call for more fighting men to try and match enemy force levels, volunteers from the Majha and Doaba flocked to join him at Banur. Alerted by the movement, Wazir Khan ordered Sher Mohammed Khan, Nawab of Malerkotla, to interdict and destroy them before they crossed the Sutlej. In the sanguinary battle fought at Kiratpur near Ropar, the Sikhs were as usual no match for the trained and well-armed soldiers of the Nawab but offered stout resistance all through the day, the contest being called off at night fall. Providence brought a contingent of fresh volunteers the following day and they rejoined battle with renewed vigor. The imperial troops beat a retreat when two of their senior commanders were killed and Sher Mohammed Khan severely wounded.[20]

As some writers suggest, on account of his influence in the Majha, Deep Singh had likely raised this force of volunteers and was, possibly, in command during the battle.[21]

His bulwark gone, Wazir Khan now felt severely disadvantaged. He proclaimed jihad (holy war) and was joined by the Nawab of Malerkotla as well as other Muslim chiefs. Their trained forces totaled about twenty-five thousand and included formidable elements of artillery and about a hundred war elephants. At twenty thousand, Banda's force matched only in numbers but almost half were pillagers, lured by the prospect of loot, who would be the first to fly under enemy fire. His core fighting strength was mostly peasants 'armed with spears, hatchets, and farming implements that could be used as weapons'[22] but resolute in their cause and morale, as well as their derring-do for revenge.

Sometimes regarded as the First War of Independence, as the first decisive victory of a wholly indigenous army against their Mughal overlords, the one-day battle takes its name from the area, Chapper-Chiri (forest with many ponds), where it was fought on 22nd May 1710 (12th May according to some writers), about sixteen miles northeast of Sirhind.[23]

Initially, Banda advised caution and bade his army to stay out of the effective range of enemy cannons but when both armies advanced to contact, the Khalsa were the first to attack. They were immediately repulsed by a heavy cannonade, Wazir Khan having ordered all his batteries to open up simultaneously. The guns were well served, firing with unusual rapidity, wreaking terrible carnage among the Sikhs and engulfing the entire battlefield in a thick pall of smoke. Just when the battle seemed to be going in favor of Wazir Khan, the Khalsa rallied and, despite their heavy losses, charged the cannons to fight their way into the enemy columns. Honored with accolade and a title after the battle for fighting in the forefront, Deep Singh likely led this charge at the head of his contingent, effecting a critical turn in the battle.

Within a few hours, many of the enemy commanders had

fallen. The Khalsa now closed in on Wazir Khan, killing him and, thereafter, his army broke and ran. Achieving the near-impossible, Banda had carried the day.[24]

ਦੇਖੋ ਕਲਾ ਪ੍ਰਭ ਕੀ ਨਯਾਰੀ । ਜਿੱਤੇ ਫਕੀਰ ਸ਼ਾਹਿ ਜਾਇ ਹਾਰੀ।
ਪ੍ਰਭ ਚਾਹੇ ਮੇਰੁ ਤ੍ਰਿਣੈ ਉਠਾਇ । ਪ੍ਰਭ ਚਾਹੈ ਸਮੁੰਦ੍ਰ ਘੜਯੋ ਸੁਕਾਇ । ੧੧ ।
—Ratan Singh Bhangu, *Panth Parkash*[25]

dekhô kalâ parbh kî nayârî. jittç phakîr shâhi jâi hârî.
parbh châhç mçru tarinô uthâi. parbh châhai samundar ghardyôn sukâi .11.

It was a miracle of the Divine that a mendicant stole a victory over a powerful sovereign.
God's will can lift a mountain with a leaf of grass, or dry up a brimming ocean.

The battle ended in the complete rout and massacre of the Mughal army and the ghazis. 'Not a man of the army of Islam escaped with more than his life and the clothes he stood in,' wrote Khafi Khan.[26]

Their next target, Sirhind, was well defended with cannons mounted on the parapet of its defensive walls. The two-day siege cost the Khalsa some five hundred killed but when the defenses were breached, terrible carnage followed, and the Sikhs showed little mercy to its inhabitants. The booty that fell into Sikh hands is estimated at more than Rupees 2 crores (20 million) in money and goods.[27]

Deep Singh is known to have displayed exceptional valour at Chapper-Chiri and Sirhind, with several singular acts of bravery being ascribed to him,[28] including the slaying of Wazir Khan, Sher Mohammad Khan, and Sucha Nand—Wazir Khan's treacherous secretary:

ਇਸ ਸੂਰਮੇ ਪਕੜ ਵਜੀਦੇ ਖਾਂ ਨੂੰ ਹੈਸੀ ਮਾਰਿਆ ਸਜਾ ਭੁਗਤਾਇਕੇ ਜੀ ।
ਗਲੀ ਗਲੀ ਬਜ਼ਾਰ ਦੇ ਵਿੱਚ ਘੁਹਿਆ ਪਿਛੇ ਬੇੜੀਆਂ ਜਕੜ ਬਨਾਇਕੇ ਜੀ ।
—Ghukewalia,
'Prasang Baba Deep Singh Ji'[29]

Is soorme pakar Wajide (Wazir) Khan nu haisi mariya saza bhugtaike ji
Gali Gali Bazar de vich dhuyia picche bedia jakar banaike ji
With gallantry he killed Wazir Khan in revenge
Then dragged him through streets in chains to avenge.

Other sources, however, credit Fateh Singh for killing Wazir Khan.[30] In the absence of accurate documentation, such claims are not easily corroborated. Gupta notes that soon after his death, Wazir Khan's head was held aloft on a spear by a Sikh seated in the howdah of his elephant. He further cites the historian Yar Mohammad to state that Wazir Khan's body was dragged by oxen before being burnt.[31] While Ghukewalia attributes this act to Deep Singh, this is nowhere corroborated. By some accounts, it was Deep Singh who unfurled the Nishan Sahib atop the ramparts of the Sirhind fort after the Khalsa victory on 24th May 1710.

Panthic Investiture

Barely twenty-seven, in addition to his extraordinary courage, Deep Singh already excelled the sword, the lance, and the bow. However, in mainstream narrative, his young years and relative lack of combat experience did not allow him to be counted among the senior military commanders—Ram Singh, Maali Singh, Baaj Singh, Aali Singh, and Fateh Singh—during this battle.[32] Aulakh is among the few writers who include Deep Singh among the commanders appointed by Banda but adduces no source.[33] Nonetheless, by repeatedly distinguishing himself, fighting in the van with a readiness to risk his life,[34] he was held in awe even by the enemy and as accolade, was conferred the title 'Shaheed'—a living martyr[35]—jointly by the Panth.[36]

Kahn Singh Nabha accepts this trait of fighting in the forefront among Deep Singh's defining characteristics:

ਅਨੇਕ ਲੜਾਈਆਂ ਵਿੱਚ ਸ਼ਹੀਦ ਹੋਣ ਲਈ ਜਾਨ ਹਥੇਲੀ ਤੇ ਰੱਖਕੇ ਅੱਗੇ ਵਧਦੇ ਸਨ ।[37]
Anek larayian vich shaheed hon layi jaan hatheli te rakh ke agge vaddhe san
Would always fight in the van, carrying his head in his palm

(This is an idiomatic expression in Punjabi for 'to take great risk', 'put one's life on line', 'at the peril of one's life'.)

Having been personally mentored by the tenth Guru, it is both probable and natural for him to have acquired the courage and ability to lead in battle and to fight in the front ranks, a quality that the Guru envisioned in the true Khalsa.[38] Ostensibly, the award of the title at this juncture does call into question Bhangu's narrative (Sakhi 79) which records a similar investiture earlier by the tenth Guru himself in 1706,[39] but this subsequent award seems to be more in the nature of accolade, this time by the entire Panth in recognition of Deep Singh's role in battles fought alongside Banda Bahadur, particularly at Chapper Chiri.

After the sack of Sirhind, Deep Singh and his warriors halted briefly at village Solkhian, some thirty-five kilometres away. His visit has since been commemorated with a vibrant gurdwara located alongside the ancient Kharar-Anandpur route, now a busy highway.[40] Oral tradition suggests that Deep Singh halted here for a night where the battle-wounded were tended and those who succumbed consigned to flames. He then proceeded onward to Anandpur along with his militia where he was soon joined by Banda Bahadur. During their brief sojourn of three months, on the behest of Banda Bahadur, Deep Singh is believed to have daily expatiated on the scriptures to a large congregation that included Banda Bahadur.[41] Banda found this necessary because, although invested with military leadership of the Khalsa, his brief acquaintance with Guru Gobind Singh at Nanded precluded any assimilation of Sikh ethos, which he now sought to accomplish with Deep Singh as his spiritual guide.

After the fall of Sirhind, the highway to Anandpur was now open and it is highly probable that the Khalsa decided to reclaim and redeem their Guru's citadel, now in ruins after its sack by the Mughal armies. By popular belief, it is equally likely that the Shaheed title was conferred on Deep Singh here, in befitting ceremony, with Banda doing the honours:

'The military victories bestowed on the Panth must inevitably be ascribed to the Lord. I am, nevertheless, profoundly grateful to you all who showed boundless courage, grit, and endurance all through the prolonged campaigns.

'I am particularly beholden to Deep Singh and his formidable band of warriors. Without exception, undaunted, Deep Singh always led from the front, with redoubtable skill and gallantry. His imposing frame and daring never failed to strike terror among the enemy.

'He shines before us as a rare example of a man steeped in the Khalsa spirit of the sant-sipahi to enviably represent the true and perfect warrior!'

While Banda's tribute drew excited applause, a voice was heard from the audience that soon became a chorus:

'Hail to thee, Deep Singh! You merit the title of jeonda shaheed!'[42]

The Anandpur shrines had been left in the charge of Bhai Gurbaksh Singh Udasi by Guru Gobind Singh on his evacuation,[43] but had been pillaged by the Mughal forces thereafter. Starting 1710, both Anandgarh and Keshgarh would be gradually restored over the years, a process begun by Jalmast Singh and Sher Singh. Later, Deep Singh would appoint Gurbaksh Singh, one of his jathedars, as the custodian. A member of the Shaheed misl, Gurbaksh Singh—baptized by Bhai Mani Singh—is credited with long years of service at Anandpur, progressing the restoration work, re-establishing Sikh traditions, and developing the shrine as an important Sikh center during a difficult period in Sikh history. Much later, in 1757 and possibly 1764 as well, he would mobilize to find martyrdom in sacralized battle at Amritsar.[44]

Some doggerel by Bhangu about Deep Singh suffering toothache during this period and Banda effecting a miraculous cure seems more jest than fact (see ser 7 in Appendix A).[45]

The Fall of Banda

Mughal reprisals were not slow to follow. Banda faced his first military reversal on 16th October 1710, forcing him into hiding. He tried to reorganize his forces by sending out fresh hukamnamas for support and as a consequence, managed to recapture some lost ground in 1712. But gradually the full might of the Mughal empire was brought to bear against him, pushing him in October 1713 to seek refuge further in the remote hills near Jammu.

Finally after an eight-month siege, the Sikh garrison at Gurdas Nangal fell on 7th December 1715. Banda and 780 Sikh survivors were captured and brought to Delhi along with some 2000 Sikh heads carried aloft on spears and thousands dumped in 700 cartloads to terrorize the general populace.

Imprisoned in the Delhi fort, in a bid to convert them to Islam, the Sikhs were subjected to barbaric excruciation but none submitted, bearing their cross with rare fortitude. Starting 5th March 1716, they were executed in public in batches of 100 over a week. A Muslim scribe who was eye-witness found it 'singular [that] these people not only behaved firmly during the execution, but they would dispute and wrangle with each other for priority in execution.'[46]

Banda's death on 19th June 1716 was the last and the most brutal. He had incurred exceptional wrath of the regime and was sentenced to the most heinous death:

بہ درگاہ خواجہ ـ دین متصل مکھبرا
حضرت خلد منزل بردہ
زبان و چشمان ـ و ـ بارآمند، پوست ـ از ـ گوست بارارند
اس تخوان جدا نمایند
دل بارش را قتل نمایند

Ba Dargah Khawaja-din Mutsil Makhbara
Hazrat Khulid Manzil Bardeh.

Zubaan Va Chashmaan-O-Bar Anand, Post-az-Gosht Bar Arand.
Is-takhwaan Juda Nimayand,
Dil Barash Ra Qatal Numayand
Banda Bahadur be taken to the tomb of Khawaja Qutub-din Mutsil, the mausoleum of Hazrat 'Khulid Manzil. His tongue be cutoff and eyes gouged out. His skin be removed from flesh, bones separated out, and his little one be brutally killed.[47]

Brought to the shrine near the Qutub Minar and offered the usual choice, Islam or death, Banda refused to abjure his faith: 'His young son, Ajai Singh, about four years was then placed in his arms and he was told to take the boy's life [...] He refused [...] The executioner then hacked the child to pieces... dragged out his quivering heart and thrust it into the mouth of his father, who stood unmoved... completely resigned to God's will.'[48]

His own turn came next. Based on several eye-witness accounts, 'First of all, his right eye was removed by the point of a butcher's knife and then his left. His left foot was cut off next, and then his two hands were severed from his body, his flesh was then torn with red-hot pincers limb by limb. Banda Singh remained calm and serene amidst these tortures, completely resigned to the Will of God and [that of] the Guru.'[49] Once dead, he was disemboweled, his innards butchered out and finally, his skeleton, now white bereft of flesh, was smashed under a sledge-hammer—a death that some writers have found too barbaric to record.[50]

In Search of a Cause

Popular narrative suggests that in about 1712, his meteoric rise as a military commander seemed to turn Banda's head and he adopted the trappings of a Guru, the 11th Nanak, and also replaced the Sikh salutation with his own 'Fateh Darshan'. This may not be entirely without substance because evidence can be adduced for both the revised salutation and references to him as 'the eleventh guru' (guru yarvaan).[51] His Hukamnama of 1710 carried this salutation—'fateh darshan', instead of the traditional 'vaheguru ji ka khalsa'.[52] An eye-witness account of his martyrdom by Surman and Stephenson, Ambassadors of the East India Company to the Mughal Court, refers to him as the 'Rebel Guru'.[53] Of his own admission, before his death, he confessed to having strayed from the path ordained by the Guru:

'What power had anyone to kill me? The order of the Satguru [Guru Gobind Singh] was contravened by me, and this is the punishment for it.'[54]

These acts were viewed as grave sacrilege by the Khalsa and led a splinter group who came to be known thenceforth as Tatt (true) Khalsa to abandon support sometime in 1714, Deep Singh among them, leaving Banda with loyalists, or Bandei Khalsa.[55] Oral tradition notes the proverbial last straw during a Vaisakhi celebration at Harimandir Sahib when Banda chose to enthrone himself as the 11th Nanak, provoking general outcry that led Deep Singh and Mani Singh accompanied by several others to unceremoniously hustle him out of the premises (see ser 8 in Appendix A). Apparently, the matter was tentatively rested but the factionalism came to a head once again in 1721, this time forcing Mata Sundari, the tenth Guru's wife, to intervene in order to obviate hostilities.[56] Some writers suggest that the differences were not ideological but arose over the sharing of donations.[57] She nominated Bhai Mani Singh, then head granthi at Harimandir Sahib to resolve the stand-off, which he did with Deep Singh's assistance, employing an ingenious stratagem though sadly, not entirely without violence.

Providential resolution being sought, Bhai Mani Singh and Deep Singh wrote the names of the two sects, 'Bandeyi' and 'Tatt', separately on two slips of paper and set these afloat in the sacred tank that surrounds the sanctum sanctorum. As if by divine injunction, 'Tatt' stayed afloat while 'Bandeyi' sank. When elements of the Bandeyi Khalsa opposed this godly intervention, an armed clash ensued in which some were killed though the matter was rested, at least for the time being.[58] These are two intersecting narratives over this incident, several years apart.[59] Possibly, they reflect two separate incidents, prompted by the same factionalism—one during the life of Banda Bahadur, when the fault lines first appeared; and another after him, with Deep Singh playing a major role in both.

The complete absence of any written or oral record of a general commiseration among Sikhs or a resolution to avenge the tragic executions of Banda and his companions suggests that the Tatt-Bandeyi divide ran significantly deep even during his lifetime.

Some historians attribute Banda's eventual downfall and defeat to this rift and the resultant loss in popularity but many challenge this hypothesis.[60] Going purely by force levels, defeat of the largely untrained and ill-equipped volunteer army of the Khalsa in conventional, pitched battles against the far superior imperial forces of the world's greatest economic power of its time was inevitable when the Mughals deployed a much larger proportion of their vast military resources.

His downfall notwithstanding, Banda's confrontation with Mughal rule in North India shook the foundations of an evil empire. Although status quo ante was soon restored, he succeeded in tentatively abolishing the zamindari system and empowering the tillers as part of the agrarian uprising that he precipitated and led. As a leader, he showed remarkable tact and statesmanship in winning over many of the hill rajas to his side. Aware of the Udaipur-Amber-Jodhpur alliance to fight the Mughals, he made overtures for a Sikh-Rajput alliance—largely unsuccessful because the Rajputs preferred a wait and watch policy.[61]

Though he met an inglorious end, his politico-military achievements assured him a permanent place in history among the country's national heroes primarily because he created a will in the 'ordinary masses to resist tyranny and to live and die for a national cause'. Although the Khalsa bid for sovereignty failed, the ideal survived. Repressed under relentless persecution, this aspiration simmered like a 'smoldering fire and came out forty years later with a fuller effulgence, never to be suppressed again'.[62]

In effect, he set the stage for the rise of the Dal Khalsa which would underpin the Sikh empire in a few decades. He had, indeed, set in motion the conditions for Guru Gobind Singh's dream of political sovereignty to be realized later in the century.

Deep Singh Returns to Dam Dama Sahib

After parting ways with Banda sometime in 1714 as part of Tatt Khalsa, Deep Singh returned to Dam Dama Sahib in Talwandi Sabo and busied himself with developing the seminary both in infrastructure and as an institution of learning. This was just as well because the Khalsa had now been forced to keep a low profile, many escaping into the foothills when in the wake of Banda's capture and assassination, beginning 1716, Farrukh Siyar, the Mughal Emperor, unleashed a vicious reign of terror offering a reward of five mohurs (coins) on each Sikh head in a bid to extirpate them.[63] This forced the Sikhs to take shelter in the forests and bushy wastes of the central tracts while some also abandoned the outward articles of their faith,[64] although they continued to harass the authorities, mainly targeting government treasuries and rich landowners.[65] It was in response to such repression that in the late 1720s, having drawn lessons from their defeat in pitched battles during Banda's campaign, the Khalsa began to organize themselves into guerrilla bands to fight back at every opportunity and to keep up a running battle.[66]

FIVE

A Cruel Yoke

Fortitude to the Fore

Historians often refer to this period, starting 1716, as the second stage of the Sikh struggle for independence that would last until 1747 and would see determined Mughal attempts to stamp out their movement. The Khalsa was thrown on the defensive but remained defiant even as several prominent Sikhs were martyred.[1]

At such a time, combat and defence would have been foremost in Deep Singh's mind along with concern for his family in Pahuwind for it was the Majha, as usual, that bore the brunt of Mughal wrath. He may have found it expedient to evacuate his family out of harm's way to the remote safety of Talwandi Sabo.

Deep Singh also utilized the period 1716-1726 to provide the residents of Dam Dama Sahib with a life of stability in the Khalsa mold, blending the spiritual with the temporal, religious instruction alongside martial skill-at-arms and mock battles. Secure within the confines of thick wood, sparse shrub, and sand, Talwandi Sabo lay in largely infertile tracts of a wasteland, then untouched by any form of irrigation. As a consequence, it was thinly inhabited and for that reason less patrolled by the oppressive regime. This lent it the much-needed security for Deep Singh to gradually develop and transform Dam Dama Sahib into an oasis of learning.

Meanwhile in the Majha, Sikhs continued to be hounded

out of villages, brought in chains to Lahore and executed in hundreds. They seemed to completely disappear for a while only to mysteriously reappear some years later when the administration had wearied of the bloodletting.

A Scholastic Achievement

His relative isolation allowed Deep Singh to focus on a task that would become his greatest scholastic achievement–calligraphing four copies of the Guru Granth Sahib accomplished over a period of ten years by 1726.[2] This implies that he had access to the original, the Dam Dami Bir to copy from, which had accompanied the Guru to Nanded and had been canonized. That it was conveyed back to Dam Dama Sahib some time after the Guru's passing is a logical inference. It is also recorded that Deep Singh tallied the Dam Dami version of the scriptures with the Kartarpuri pothi over a period of six months, possibly before he made the copies.[3]

The four handwritten copies were disseminated to the four Takhts, viz. Sri Akal Takht Sahib at Amritsar, Sri Takht Patna Sahib, Sri Takht Hazur Sahib and Sri Takht Anandpur Sahib. Some historians differ and state that one copy was retained at Dam Dama Sahib and none sent to Hazur Sahib.[4] Later, Deep Singh is believed to have transcribed another copy into Arabic and conveyed it to Saudi Arabia, a claim that is difficult to verify.[5] According to another scholar, Deep Singh also transcribed the scriptures into Hindi, Marathi, Persian, and Urdu but this too is not corroborated.[6]

Sadly, the original Dam Dami Bir is believed lost to posterity. In a bid to preserve and protect it through the turbulence of the 18th century, the Khalsa would invariably carry it on the move and it is supposed to have fallen into Afghan hands during the Wada Ghallughara (Greater Holocaust) on 5th February 1762 at Kup, near Malerkotla, when about 30,000 Sikhs lost their lives in a punitive expedition under Ahmed Shah Abdali during his sixth invasion. According to Bhangu, there were two birs (copies of the holy book) at Kup, both lost in the carnage.[7] These count among the greatest losses of Khalsa heritage ever.

Some historians claim that Deep Singh also calligraphed four copies of the Dasm Granth and disseminated these to the four Takhts. Possibly, the reference here is to Sri Guru Granth Sahib although he is, nonetheless, known to have compiled and calligraphed one copy of the Dasm Granth and could well have copied more and distributed these as well.[8]

In effect, the Dasm Granth even now is the subject of debate, particularly over its authorship. Largely for this reason, it continued to exist as several disparate compositions. The letter purportedly written by Bhai Mani Singh in this regard to Mata Sundari recommending its compilation is not accepted as authentic by most scholars who believe that the book was finally compiled sometime in the 18th century.[9]

There is a popular belief that in 1740, when Sikh scholars had gathered at Dam Dama Sahib under the aegis of Deep Singh to debate the question of its compilation, Mehtab Singh and Sukha Singh arrived to pay obeisance en route to Harimandir Sahib. They had volunteered to behead Massa Rangar, the Muslim commandant of Amritsar who had converted Harimandir Sahib into a seraglio. They offered a happenstance suggestion—if they succeeded in their mission, the tenth Guru's writings should be compiled into one volume. Since they did triumph in their daring enterprise on 11th August 1740, the Dasm Granth subsequently appeared in its compiled form.[10] However, in his well-researched work on the Dasm Granth, Mann states that this incident relates not to the Dasm Granth but to the combined Adi Granth-Dasm Granth calligraphed by Bhai Mani Singh, which has survived,[11] but the year needs verification since Bhai Mani Singh was martyred much earlier in 1738.

During the period of persecution from the early 18th century, small texts of the scriptures were produced, called 'safari bir' (traveling scripture), that could be easily carried into battle.[12] Deep Singh's personal copy is an example. This was a small handwritten copy of the Dasm Granth (excluding Zafarnamah) measuring 7 x 7.25 inches of 971 pages that he usually wore in a baldric (shoulder strap) as a mark of veneration for the Tenth Master and his ideology.[13] Some writers claim that this was his own gutka which had compositions from the Guru Granth Sahib as well. He would keep another copy in a state of open reverence (parkash) during his prolonged sessions of meditation in Bhora Sahib (basement), where this copy could be seen until a few years ago but has since been removed. The two large earthen vessels (garhas) built into the wall of the Bhora have been retained—one contained black chickpeas for nourishment and the other drinking water.

It is believed that both the Guru Granth Sahib and Dasm Granth were daily installed at Dam Dama Sahib from the time of Deep Singh right up to 18th November 1966, when the management of the shrine passed to the Shiromani Gurdwara Parbandhak Committee (SGPC), who removed the latter on contentious grounds. Now, it is only the former that is found ceremonially installed or enthroned. Based on an edict by the SGPC, Dasm Granth is no longer enshrined in Gurdwaras under their charge. It may, however, still be found in Gurdwaras controlled by Nihangs for the martial fervour that it potentially reflects and invokes.

Building the Khalsa Tradition

There was ebb and flow in atrocities against the Sikhs, depending on the men at the helm of the Mughal administration. The charge that Delhi handpicked only men cruelly disposed to Sikhs as Governors (Viceroys) of Lahore is likely true. After some respite, when Sikh presence had once again become noticeable in the countryside and they were beginning to hesitatingly resume pilgrimage to important Sikh centers, Zakariya Khan was appointed Governor of Lahore province in 1726. His first step was to declare jihad against Sikhs. He ordered that their hair be cut and beards shorn, driving many into the forests and the hills once again.[14]

Zakariya Khan's long tenure of some twenty years in the Lahore province would be marked by the martyrdom of several prominent Sikhs beginning with that of Tara Singh Vaan in 1726 itself, the year of his appointment. The martyrdom of many others is directly attributed to him, including that of Haqiqat Rai (1734), Bhai Mani Singh (1738), Bhai Bota Singh and Garja Singh (1739), Bhai Taru Singh (1745), Bhai Mahtab Singh Mirankotia (1745), Bhai Shabeg Singh and son Shahbaz Singh (1745). The ruthless execution of their brethren only served to strengthen Sikh resolve for sovereignty. Deep Singh would have been personally affected by these killings since most were from his area of belonging, particularly Tara Singh Vaan and Bhai Taru Singh, both kinsmen from villages close to his own; even more by that of Bhai Mani Singh, his senior colleague, companion, and mentor.

The brutal regime, however, could not interfere much with life at Dam Dama Sahib, where some landmark contributions to the Khalsa tradition continued to be initiated:[15]

- Interpretation (arth) personally introduced by the tenth Guru and later evolved and perpetuated by Deep Singh in the form of Dam Dami taksal.
- Akhand Path of the Guru Granth Sahib personally initiated by the tenth Guru on its finalization in August 1706.
- Decision over nitnem (daily prayers): three in the morning (Japji Sahib, Jaap Sahib, Tav-Prasad Svaiya), one in the evening (Rehras), and one before retiring for the day (Kirtan Sohila).
- Decision about the four Takhts. Dam Dama Sahib was declared as the fifth Takht much later, on 18th November 1966.

- Decision to consecrate *Suraj Parkash*—a popular and monumental mainly hagiographic text about the Sikh Gurus by a Sikh poet, Santokh Singh, published in 1843 comprising legends and miracles associated with Sikh Gurus and others such as Banda Bahadur; its reading and rendering within the holy precincts of a gurdwara was thus authorized.

The Khalsa Helm

According to Gyani Gyan Singh, after Banda's martyrdom, Deep Singh was a prominent leader among the Sikhs and counted among the senior jathedars: Darbara Singh (Dewan, senior-most), Sangat Singh Khajanchi (treasurer), Hari Singh Langri (kitchen-in-charge), Bhagat Singh Modi (trader), Budha Singh Desi, Harinder Singh, Garja Singh, Sajan Singh, Ishar Singh, Gyan Singh, Sadhu Singh, Dewa Singh, Nawab Kapur Singh, Hari Singh Sukhayi, Gurbaksh Singh, Tharaj Singh, Jassa Singh, Karam Singh, Bhola Singh, Attar Singh, Siha Singh, Bachan Singh, Kehar Singh, Braj Singh, Ghanghor Singh, Amar Singh.[16]

Except for Darbara Singh (born 1644 CE), who led the Panth after Banda Bahadur till 1734 and was many years Deep Singh's senior in age, most other leaders, including Darbara Singh's successor, Kapur Singh (born 1697 CE) and Jassa Singh Ahluwalia (born 1718 CE) who, in turn, succeeded Kapur Singh, were several years younger, a fact that also served to enhance Deep Singh's respect and influence in the community.

By virtue of his exalted position as a senior spiritual-cum-military leader in the Khalsa community, Deep Singh gradually assumed a more central role in politico-military affairs, often moving out of the Malwa—Punjab region between the Sutlej and the Yamuna rivers—with his militia to participate in panthic action ranging from conferences to combat in other parts of the Punjab.

To the Aid of Ala Singh

His first major action was the assistance to Ala Singh of Patiala. In his endeavor to expand his conquest in 1731, Ala Singh found himself at loggerheads at Barnala with the combined forces of Rai Kalha of Raikot, an influential chief with a large force at his command, the Manj chiefs of cis-Satluj and Jalandhar Doab, Asad Ali Khan, the faujdar (military commander generally equivalent to Governor) of Jalandhar Doab, and Jamal Khan, Nawab of Malerkotla. Ala Singh appealed to Deep Singh for help and the latter arrived post-haste with his militia that included a contingent of Majha Sikhs to help him carry the day. He later led the thanksgiving prayer.[17] Bhangu narrates in verse how Ala Singh went barefoot in deference to thank Deep Singh and his troops, replacing all their losses and resources consumed in the battle, including horses killed.[18] According to Gupta, he also chose to be baptized by Deep Singh and to join the Khalsa brotherhood. This was the first time that Ala Singh took succor from the Majha Sikhs, establishing a union which he would harness time and again.[19]

Shaheedan Jatha

To Zakariya's consternation, no amount of harsh brutality seemed to quell Khalsa defiance for it is an 'unforgettable lesson of history that persecution stimulates the spirit that it designs to suppress.'[20] He tried reconciliation and appeasement next, extending a title, Nawab (Perso-Arab honorific, literally 'viceroy' or 'grand duke') along with a jagir (land grant and revenue) on 29th March 1733.[21]

The Sikhs initially balked at the offer only to spurn it later. They would accept no bribes or gifts from a tyrannous regime but Shabeg Singh, the Mughal representative who brought the proposition to the Akal Takht was unrelenting. He implored and coaxed his co-religionists until after extended deliberations among prominent leaders, Kapur Singh was invested with the title. Out of humility, he sought prior approval from his community by placing the royal accouterments—symbolic robes of honour (shawl, turban, jewelled plume, pair of golden bangles, necklace, row of pearls and a brocade garment)—at the feet of Panj Pyaras, Deep Singh among them, alongside Jassa Singh Ramgarhia, Karam Singh, Hari Singh Bhangi, and Buddh Singh (ancestor of Maharaja Ranjit Singh).[22] Deep Singh's high moral standing among the Panth is borne out by this rare honour.[23]

Nawab Kapur Singh's first task in 1734 was to unite the various Sikh militias into two groups—the Taruna Dal (league of the young, forty years and below) and the Budha Dal (league of the elders or veterans, above forty years).

ਦੋਹਰਾ—ਪੰਜ ਡੇਰਨ ਬਿਧ ਰਚ ਦਈ ਪੰਜ ਨਿਸ਼ਾਨ ਬਨਾਇ ।
ਪੰਜੇ ਝੰਡੇ ਤੌ ਗਡੇ ਸ੍ਰੀ ਅਕਾਲ ਬੁੰਗੇ ਤੇ ਲਿਆਇ । ੨੬ ।
ਚੌਪਾਈ—ਪ੍ਰਥਮ ਸ਼ਹੀਦਿਨ ਔ ਨਿਹੰਗਨ ਫੜਾਯੋ । ਦੀਪ ਸਿੰਘ ਕਰਮ ਸੁ ਨਾਯੋ ।
   [...] । ੨੭ ।
                              —Bhangu, *Panth Prakash*[24]

Dohra—Panj deran bidh rach dayi panj Nishan banaye
Panjo jhande tau gade sri akal bunge te leae 26
Chaupai—Pratham shaheedan au nihangan pahadayo. Deep Singh
   Karam su nayo [....] 27
Five deras with own symbols and flags
beside Akal Bunga he decreed,
First of Shaheedan and Nihangan,
Deep Singh and Karam Singh lead.

It must be noted that the title of Deep Singh's dera circumscribed both the Shaheeds and the Nihangs because originally the two were meant to be fractally synonymous. As a Khalsa, Deep Singh had been earlier awarded the title 'Shaheed' for exceptional courage and daring but he was equally a Nihang, unblemished and pure, fearless and indifferent to worldly gains and comfort. Bhangu refers even to Nawab Kapur Singh, supreme commander of the Khalsa in the mid-19th century, as 'Nihang' (Sakhi 88).[25]

The two dals collectively became known as the Dal Khalsa.[26] While the Taruna Dal was to undertake the more difficult task of defending the community, the Budha Dal was assigned the upkeep of Sikh holy places as well as the propagation of the Sikh faith.

The Budha Dal was further sub-divided into five units, each with 1300-2000 men.[27] The first batch was led by the eponymous Deep Singh (Shahidanvala Jatha), second by Karam Singh and Dharam Singh (Amritsarian da Jatha), third by Kahan Singh and Binod Singh of Goindwal (Guroo-Ansi or Sahibzadian Jatha), fourth by Dasaundha Singh of Kot Budha (Dallewalian jatha) who later founded the Nishanwala misl, and the fifth by Vir Singh Ranghreta and Jivan Singh Ranghreta (Ramdasian jatha). Each unit was assigned a unique war-drum, banner and distinctive insignia symbolic of royalty in defiance of Mughal injunctions that forbade these to non-Muslims. The Harimandir Sahib complex was assigned to them as their center. Deep Singh could now position elements of his fighting force in Amritsar but was expected to respond to all panthic requirements with promptness.

All five leaders were men of exceptional qualities but it was politically significant that this eclectic body of warriors retained their all-class character: two of the leaders were jats (Deep Singh and Dasaunda Singh); two Khatri (one Trehan and the other Bhalla, descendants, respectively, of the second and fourth Guru), while Vir Singh Rangrehta was a lowly outcaste.

Some of the other members in Deep Singh's jatha were: Natha Singh, Gurbaksh Singh, Sher Singh, Dargaha Singh, Hira Singh, and Prem Singh.[28] It is noteworthy that although fifty-two years of age, Deep Singh was nominated purely on account of his extraordinary qualities of leadership and military prowess. With this development, Deep Singh's role and responsibility were considerably enlarged beyond the Dam Dama Sahib seminary. The shrine at Anandgarh in Anandpur was already his responsibility and in the charge of his companion, Gurbaksh Singh.

The Taruna Dal was similarly sub-divided into five units headed, respectively, by: Sukha Singh Mari Kambo, Gurbaksh Singh Roranwali, Bagh Singh Hallowalia, Gurdyal Singh Dalewal, and Sham Singh Naroki. Five centers were especially created for them at Amritsar, one each at Ramsar, Bibeksar, Lacchmansar, Kaulsar, and Santokhsar.[29]

The jagir advanced by the regime was, however, confiscated in 1737 because it did not have the desired result of pacifying and subjugating the Sikhs.[30] After this brief respite, Sikhs once again came to be targeted. Dewan Lakhpat Rai, the Chief Minister of the Punjab, drove the Budha Dal out of the Bari Doab into the Malwa where they chose to ally with Ala Singh of Patiala to punish Sirhind and to help Ala Singh expand his territory. On their way back, the Budha Dal was attacked by the Dewan near Baserke with a force of 7000 and defeated. This brought the Taruna Dal into action, who now pursued the Mughal army and fought a grim action near Lahore, inflicting heavy casualties. In retaliation, the Mughal attitude hardened further. They took possession of the Amritsar temple and issued a proclamation against visiting the shrine. They also forbade the general populace from rendering any kind of assistance or shelter to Sikhs who, as a consequence, fell victim once again in thousands to a genocide.

By virtue of his location in the Malwa, Deep Singh was relatively secure, being able to exercise greater sway in the region, preaching the gospel alongside keeping combat ready a force that by 1727 had grown to approximately 2000 cavalry plus 5000 infantry. Only about 500 of this militia were garrisoned in Talwandi Sabo while the rest were under arrangement to muster on call.[31] There is little historical record that documents panthic actions of the period but it is surmised that Deep Singh and his Shaheedi jatha were in the forefront in most military actions of the Panth such as raids, defensive battles, and rescue missions.

Loss of a Mentor

As the venerable head granthi at the Amritsar temple, Bhai Mani Singh had obtained government permission to celebrate Diwali in 1737 with a ten-day fair on the condition of paying a fee of Rs 5000. When he was unable to raise the sum because the fair was thinly attended due to Mughal restrictions, he was dismembered in 1738.

The Sikhs swore revenge and when Nadir Shah invaded India the following year in 1739, routing Mughal armies, pillaging and laying waste the entire country, in the confusion that prevailed, the Sikhs built a mud-fortress at Dalewal, northwest of Amritsar on the banks of the Ravi and began exacting tribute from the whole of the upper Bari-Doab. When the ponderous, booty-laden army of Nadir Shah came within range in May 1739, it was plundered and many captive women rescued. When the monsoon further slowed the columns, the Sikhs mauled his rearguard up to the river Chenab and beyond.

Once again, Sikh actions only provoked greater severity from the administration:

- A price was put on their heads—Rs 10 for information, and Rs 50 for a Sikh, dead or alive.
- Carte blanche to plunder Sikh homes.
- Death to anyone sheltering a Sikh
- Forced conversion to Islam for anyone offering food to Sikhs.[32]

The Lesser Holocaust

A series of events that ended in great slaughter for the Sikhs began with the arrest of Bhai Taru Singh in 1745 on the charge of feeding Sikh revolutionaries. He was brought before the Governor, Zakariya Khan, in Lahore and tortured. When he bore his agony with equanimity, he was quizzed about the source of his fortitude. On declaring that he drew his strength from his unshorn hair, he was presented with the inevitable choice—apostatize or have his hair shorn. Refusing to convert, he disallowed a haircut too, instead opting to be scalped. According to Sikh sources, before he was scalped, he predicted Zakariya Khan's death from being beaten with his, Bhai Taru Singh's own shoes.

Soon after the inhuman punishment was carried out, the governor was suddenly taken ill with severe urinary retention. At once conscious of his guilt over his recent act of cruelty, he sought advice on how he might make amends with the Sikhs. He was advised an unlikely remedy—Bhai Taru Singh's shoe be hit upon his head. When this treatment was dutifully carried out by his minions, his condition seemed to miraculously improve for a while but he died twenty-one days later. Bhai Taru Singh, who had survived without his scalp all these days, passed away a day later on 1st July 1745 from blood loss and other medical complications.

Zakariya Khan's eldest son, Yahya Khan, who now succeeded as the governor, chose to attribute his father's death to the Sikhs and immediately set about his first mission of exterminating them. What fueled his rage even further was an isolated incident in January 1746 near Eminabad.

A Sikh body of some 2000 under Jassa Singh Ahluwalia and Sukha Singh Marikambo had gone to visit Gurdwara Ror Sahib in the area and hungry after a long ride, sought permission of the faujdar, Jaspat Rai, to purchase food. Instead of granting permission, the faujdar threatened to drive them off. They, however, managed to find some food and were partaking of it when Jaspat Rai personally led an assault against them. In the brief engagement that ensued, the Sikhs fought a gallant action, during which one nimble-footed Sikh, Nibahu Singh, climbed Jaspat Rai's mount, an elephant, by its tail and taking the commander completely by surprise, decapitated him. The enemy troops fled in disarray. Roiled by Mughal high-handedness, the Sikhs then plundered the city and refused to return Jaspat Rai's head for cremation until a payment was made.[33]

When news of these excesses reached Jaspat Rai's bother, Lakhpat Rai, Dewan of Lahore, he was convulsed with rage and pledged dire retaliation:

'The creed of Sikhs was started by a Khatri. As a Khatri, I shall now wipe it out from the face of the earth!' (Nanak was Khatri by ethnicity and so was Lakhpat Rai.)

To begin with, he had all Sikhs he could find in and around Lahore executed on 10th March 1746. The holy tank of the Amritsar temple was filled with debris; even the word 'gur' (jaggery) was banned because its first syllable was common with 'guru'.

In a visceral frenzy of revenge, a large army was mobilized in end-March 1746 under the personal command of the Governor, Yahya Khan, and his Dewan, Lakhpat Rai—since both now had common cause—to scour the countryside for Sikhs. Meanwhile the Sikhs, numbering about 15000, took refuge in the dense marshes of the Kahnuwan wetland. This quagmire (chhamb) or peatland was then the interfluvial floodplain of the Rivers Beas and Ravi that according to local sources, at one time stretched from Pathankot to Hargobindpur on one side and the Rivers Ravi and Beas on the other, covering an area of approximately 1000 square kilometres. Though most has now been reclaimed by agriculture, some 1000 acres remain, still overgrown with sarkanda (Saccharum bengalense) and other types of tall grass and reed as well as trees such as the Indian jujube and the babool.

Though completely inhospitable to most, the boggy marshland was familiar to the Sikhs who could use it effectively as a hideout. The Lahore army had no option but to besiege the area but suffered much attrition from harassing Sikh raids and assaults by night. Rushing out of the bushes in surprise attacks, the Sikhs would strike terror among the enemy only to disappear. Just when the wearied Lahore troops would be lulled into lowering their guard to rest their frayed nerves, the Sikhs would reappear, snaffling away their horses and rations along with much of their warlike stores and munitions.

When the cannonade proved largely ineffective, the Sikhs were finally hounded out after a month's siege with the wood being set on fire, pushing them towards the Ravi already swollen from the melting snows of the upper Himalayas in the first week of May 1746.

The main Sikh force tried to break through the cordon but not without heavy loss of life. Only about 2000 managed the river-crossing to enter the Riarki area near Gurdaspur. Their bid to escape into the hills of Basholi through Parol and Kathua was foiled by the hill Rajas whose armies were arrayed against them in deference to Mughal injunctions: 'Whosoever gives shelter to the Sikhs will meet the same fate as the Sikhs.'

Some Sikhs circumvented these hill troops, following a circuitous route to reach Kiratpur via Kullu but most had to make an opposed river crossing back across the Ravi and then try a breakout in valiant frontal attacks through the enemy in which many perished on both sides, including the son of Jaspat Rai and two sons of Yahya Khan. The Sikhs who did manage to break through had to trudge across several long miles of scorching sands along the river Beas to finally cross the Sutlej near Aliwal into the safety of Malwa.

A total of twenty-five Sikh jathas (armed bodies of men) are known to have taken part in this action, including those of Nawab Kapur Singh, Jassa Singh Ahluwalia, Charat Singh Sukerchakia, Deep Singh, and Sukha Singh Marikambo—who lost a leg from a cannon shot but tied it to his saddle and fought on. Deep Singh, then sixty-four years of age, was among the survivors. Severely wounded himself, he fought at the head of his band of warriors, many of them with critical battle injuries, and chose to extricate all of his many injured comrades back into Malwa with considerable loss of life.[34]

About 7000 Sikhs perished in this operation over two months that came to be known as the Chhota Galughara (Lesser Holocaust), while another 3000 were put to death by torture in much ignominy in Lahore.[35] Every year, commemoration ceremonies are held on 14-20th May at a shrine in Kahnuwan built on a spot where a large number of Sikhs had attained martyrdom.

A contrarian view which refutes the participation of Deep Singh and his jatha in this action must be discounted on the grounds that this was a collaborative panthic action, enjoining all to act. In a similar action some fifteen years later in 1762, the Shaheed misl fought and suffered enormous loss of life alongside their co-religionists in what came to be later known as the Wada Ghallughara (Greater Holocaust).

The Sikhs kept a low profile thereafter until the upheaval caused by Ahmed Shah Abdali's first invasion in early 1748 gave them both respite and opportunity to reappear from hiding. They plundered Abdali's baggage and also built a fortalice called Ram Rauni near Amritsar that could accommodate 500 men-at-arms.

Meanwhile, Deep Singh's legion continued to grow in these testing times, constantly infused with young volunteer recruits. There was a parallel growth in the number of fighting groups. Any daring Sikh proficient in the use of arms who could demonstrate his dexterity in battle very soon had a following. As a consequence, the number of groups thus continued to proliferate, reaching the unwieldy figure of sixty-five.

SIX

The Misl Period

Having learned an important lesson from the Kahnuwan debacle in 1746, the Sikhs felt it was time to restructure their forces and sought to effect this on Baisakhi, 29th March 1748, in a Sarbat Khalsa (general assembly of Sikhs) convened at the Akal Takht, Amritsar. In their first historic gurmatta (synod), prominent Sikh leaders who included Deep Singh resolved on more organized resistance to Mughal and Afghan oppression under the unified command of the Dal Khalsa.

Earlier, by a gurmatta on Diwali 1745, the erstwhile Taruna and Budha Dal, which had over the years grown into sixty-five jathas, were attempted with limited success to be pared down to twenty-five deras—thirty according to some writers—of 1000 each.[1] These were now reorganized into eleven misls (from Persian 'misal' meaning 'equal'), or divisions, each under its own chief with a separate banner and with Nawab Kapur Singh as supreme commander.

The misl title was derived either from the name of its progenitor, as in the case of the Shaheeds, or from his place of belonging:

- Shaheed under the eponymous Deep Singh
- Ahluwalia under Jassa Singh Ahluwalia
- Singhpuria (also called Faizulapuria) under Nawab Kapur Singh

- Karorsinghia under Karora Singh
- Nishanavali (flag-bearers) under Dasaundha Singh of Kot Budha
- Dallevalia under Gulab Singh Dallewalia
- Sukkarchakkia under Charhat Singh (grandfather of Maharaja Ranjit Singh) from Sukkarchak village
- Bhangi Misl under Hari Singh Dhillon from their addiction to bhang (cannabis)
- Kanhaiya Misl under Jai Singh
- Nakai Misl under Sardar Hira Singh
- Ramgarhia Misl under Jassa Singh Ramgarhia

Since the twelfth, Phulkian misl under Ala Singh of Patiala, was opportunist and mostly functioned independently, it was never a part of this confederacy. Ala Singh, or Ala Jat in some accounts, generally served his own Machiavellian interest and could ally with any power, although he did participate in some concerted actions of the Khalsa.

The Sikh commonwealth of eleven misls known as the 'Khalsa ji' was a kind of federal union and the leader of the Dal Khalsa was looked upon as the head of the Church and state.[2] This forging of religious and military authority was significant because it eliminated friction in the Clausewitzian sense. The misls invariably leagued together into a grand army (Dal Khalsa) to play a prominent role in the Sikh struggle of the 18th century, confederating for the common good and acting in concert against external threats. Their bi-annual meetings on Baisakhi and Diwali festivals (April and November, respectively) called Sarbat Khalsa would promulgate gurmattas on matters such as the strategy for any imminent military action, division of spoils, and other matters of common interest.[3]

Since the province of the Punjab provided a good breed of horse, Sikh soldiers were well-mounted and misl armies comprised predominantly cavalry.[4] Their overall military strength is variously estimated from around 70,000 horse to a total of approximately 2,00,000.[5]

'Each chief, in proportion of his means, furnished horses and arms of his retainers who were called bargirs; and as the first tribute exacted from a conquered district was horses, the infantry soldier was, after a successful campaign, generally transformed into a trooper.'[6]

According to Niccolò Machiavelli, the renowned Italian diplomat who has long been considered the father of modern political philosophy, a feeling of personal involvement and moral obligation to a cause provide the strongest incitement to courage and enthusiasm,[7] both of which the Khalsa demonstrated in great measure. In addition, their full-blown nationalism and the ideal of unity forged them into a disciplined and devoted brotherhood. Together, this powerful meld of qualities made them a formidable community, fused even closer under duress of extreme circumstances, eventually helping them attain sovereignty.

Elimination of Informers

This was among the first tasks that the Khalsa undertook after their restructuring—ridding themselves of a primary menace. Scattered across the length and breadth of the region were hundreds of informers. The common citizen of the region, Hindu or Muslim, lived an unsettled life, in constant dread of a pitiless regime on the one hand, and the even more brutal Afghan invaders on the other. Many opted to find favour and refuge with their overlords by providing vital intelligence on Sikh presence and movement and as a consequence, were responsible for the death of thousands of Sikh men, women, and children.

Crowned King of Afghanistan in 1747, Ahmed Shah Abdali adopted the epithet Shāh Durr-i-Durrān, 'King, Pearl of Pearls,' and changed his tribe name to 'Durrani'.[8] When he began his marauding expeditions into India in 1748, a unique opportunity presented itself to the Khalsa leadership which they seized by the forelock. The period immediately before, during, and in the wake of these expeditions was marked by panic among the populace as they ran helter-skelter trying to flee the path of Durrani's rapacious columns. In the confusion that prevailed, Deep Singh was among the Sikh leaders who organized the systematic elimination of almost all of these wily double-dealing informers.[9]

Transfer of Punjab to Afghanistan

Historians regard the years 1748-1753 as the darkest period in Punjab history with mass genocide led by the Lahore Governor, Mir Mannu, who surpassed his predecessors in the Mughal policy to extirpate the Sikhs.[10] The only extenuating influence was Kaura Mal, Dewan of the Lahore province. A Sahajdhari Sikh (believer in the Sikh faith without wearing its outward symbols), and a successful military commander, he was supportive of Sikhs and often sought their help in his military forays. In return, he would plead for leniency on their behalf and also secured permission for them to repair their Amritsar shrine in 1749.[11] In September 1750, he defeated the rebellious governor of Multan with Sikh alliance and as a reward, obtained for them jagirs at Patti, Chunian, and Jhabal, although these were forfeited a year later.[12]

Sadly for the Sikhs, Kaura Mal was killed in battle on 6th March 1752 trying to defend Lahore against Ahmed Shah Durrani during his third invasion. The Lahore army was defeated, Lahore and Multan ceded to Afghanistan, elements of the Afghan army retained in the Punjab and worse, Mir Mannu, archenemy of the Sikhs, reinstated as Governor of the Punjab, this time on behalf of Afghanistan. The Sikhs now once again became targets of Mughal-Afghan rancor.

An Unequal Contest

On one occasion in 1752, some Afghan soldiers provoked and challenged Sikhs to single combat at Kot Buddha (near Patti in the Majha). All weapons were to be allowed. The contest opened with a towering, well-built Afghan soldier with a reputation for brute strength and skill-at-arms swaggering into the makeshift arena, swinging his sword with practiced dexterity. Bhai Lakha Singh Tarkhan (carpenter by trade and brother of Bhai Sukha Singh) was nominated by the Sikhs to take up the gauntlet. The ensuing duel was an admixture of swordplay, fisticuffs, and wrestling in which the Sikh triumphed, killing his opponent. Thereupon, two Afghans leapt into the arena. Charat Singh Sukerchaka (grandfather of Maharaja Ranjit Singh) engaged them and won the unequal contest, killing them both.

Thereupon, the Afghans proved poor losers. Throwing sporting rules to the wind, four-five Afghans assaulted Charat Singh. In response, Deep Singh, then seventy years of age who was among the senior Sikh leaders watching the sanguinary contest in the front ranks leapt into the fray along with Sham Singh Karorsinghia, Jassa Singh Ahluwalia, and Hari Singh Bhangi. The Afghans seemed to be getting the worst of it in the free-for-all when it came to an abrupt halt with the sudden arrival of Nawab Kapur Singh at the head of 2000 Sikh horsemen. Outnumbered, the Afghans fled pell-mell. A commemorative gurdwara marks the site of the battle, short distance from a tomb with an adjoining mosque to the memory of one Shah Kamal, an Afghan commander who died in the contest. Gyani Gyan Singh states that several similar contests were held from time to time.[13]

Protectors of the Realm

Mir Mannu's death on 1st November 1753 brought much relief to the Sikhs along with further opportunities for territorial expansion and ownership although it is evident that misaldars (leaders of Khalsa misls) had begun to occupy territory and issue orders in their own right by 1750, even before the formal end of Mughal rule in the Punjab.

An important development in the wake of Mir Mannu's death was 'rakhi' — protective system whereby a Sikh chief would exact a fifth of the farmed income twice a year after each harvest and guarantee protection in return to Muslims and Hindus alike. Deep Singh was part of the Sarbat Khalsa on 10th April 1754 at Akal Takth (Amritsar) when a gurmatta authorized this policy,[14] which would gradually help Sikh misls become de facto owners of large fertile tracts of the Punjab. Deep Singh shared his sphere of influence with the Karorsinghias over the area south of the Sutlej though he refrained from territorial conquest—his successors, nevertheless, did.[15] Although it brought substantial long-term benefits to Sikhs in terms of power and influence, viewed in perspective, 'rakhi' was not designed to be exploitative. It was a sine qua non that grew out of the exigencies of a hazardous period in history and helped throw a blanket of security over a population living in constant dread of death and devastation.

The Swiss adventurer, Col Polier, who was a loyal supporter of the British in India, notes that around this time, the Sikhs 'began to grow formidable and assume real independence. They formed themselves into a kind of republic and in the course of a few years [especially after Adina Beg's death in 1758] possessed themselves of the full government of the province of Lahore and Multan'.[16]

By the second half of the 18th century, the northwestern parts of the Indian subcontinent comprising the fertile and productive valleys of the five rivers—Jhelum, Chenab, Ravi, Bias and Sutlej—were a conglomerate of fourteen small warring regions. Twelve of these were Sikh-controlled, one (Kasur near Lahore) was Muslim-controlled, and another in the Southeast, was held by the Irish mercenary, George Thomas (see Figure 3), who had carved his fiefdom out of the present-day districts of Hisar and Rohtak in Haryana through intrigues with the Mughals, the French, and the Marathas.[17] British records cite the year 1761 as the beginning of Sikh rule.[18] It appears that

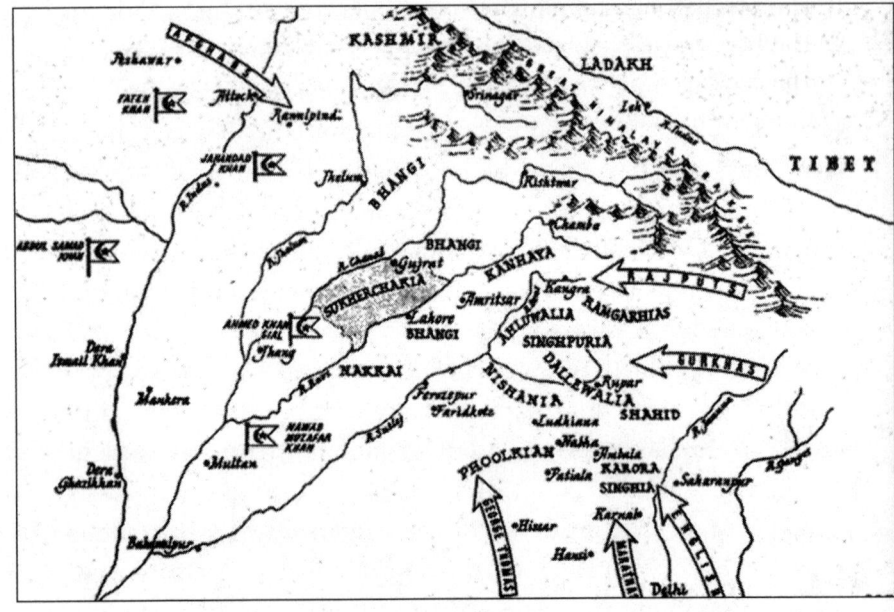

Figure 3: Area under control of the Misls in 1780
(Source: Khushwant Singh, Ranjit Singh, Penguin, Delhi, 2008)

the Sikhs had by then laid the foundations of an empire using a sort of fait-accompli strategy undergirded by the logic that while overt power-grabs create enemies and invite conflict, small bites, swallowing territories little by little, can gradually build an empire.

Syed Bulleh Shah, the famous poet of the period recorded the rising fortunes of the Sikhs in memorable verse:

ਮੁਗ਼ਲਾਂ ਜ਼ਹਰ ਪਿਆਲੇ ਪੀਤੇ ।
ਭੂਰੀਆਂ ਵਾਲੇ ਰਾਜੇ ਕੀਤੇ ।
ਸਭ ਅਸ਼ਰਫ ਫਿਰਨ ਚੁੱਪ ਕੀਤੇ ।
ਭਲਾ ਉਨ੍ਹਾਂ ਨੂੰ ਝਾਰਿਲੈ ।[19]

Mughlan zahir piale pite,
Bhurian vale Raje kite;
Sabh ashraf phirn chup kite
Bhala unhan nun jharilai.

The Mughals had drunk the cups of poison
The blanket-wearing Sikhs had become the Kings.
The noblemen do wander in silence,
Completely removed from the scene
—Kafi number 65

Miskin similarly notes of the Sikhs:

که تقسیم کردند پنجاب را
بداند هر شیخ و هر شاب را

Keh takseen kardand Punjab ra
Badand har sheikh o har shaab ra
They have divided Punjab amongst themselves and distributed the territories among the young and old.[20]

Sialkot under Sikh Sway

Adina Beg, the military governor of Jalandhar, maintained an equivocal position vis-a-vis the Sikhs. He would not hesitate to requisition their assistance to advance his own interests but could turn against them if the circumstances so demanded. Fearing for his life, he had abandoned his post during Abdali's fourth invasion beginning December 1756. In his absence, Nasir Ali held charge of the Jalandhar province, a period marked with atrocities against Sikhs and the defiling and destruction of many Sikh historic places of worship, provoking violent reactions from Sikhs.

In a bid to assert his authority with Adina Beg, the Lahore Governor summoned him into his presence but Adina Beg refused to comply, suspicious of the Afghan's intentions. When a large force was sent against him, he enlisted Sikh support and this allied force of some 25000, which included Deep Singh and Jassa Singh Ahluwalia, won a decisive victory.[21]

Thereupon, having wrought vengeance on the Mughal general who had desecrated Kartarpur, the victorious Sikh army dispersed only to learn that to regain the confidence of the Lahore government, Adina Beg had now switched loyalties and was once again beginning to target innocent Sikhs. Deep Singh had not yet reached Talwandi Sabo when he received a message from Jassa Singh Ahluwalia to return. Other misaldars were sent for to confederate a joint action in response to Adina Beg's volte-face. Meanwhile, Adina Beg had allied with the Lahore forces, soon to be joined by Amin Khan, military governor of Sialkot.

The Sikhs first invested and reduced Jalandhar—later occupied by Jassa Singh Ahluwalia—and then turned their combined might against Sialkot, defeating the Mughal forces. Some territory of Sialkot was occupied by Deep Singh which he made over to his companions, the brothers Natha Singh and Dayal Singh, appointing them administrators to run Gurdwaras Ber Sahib (Sialkot) and Baoli Sahib (Sialkot City).[22] While it is difficult to situate this incident in the mainstream Sikh history of the period, it should have happened much earlier than projected since Adina Beg died on 15th September 1758, almost a year after Deep Singh.[23] Natha Singh and Dyal Singh were baptized by Deep Singh and were prominent members of the Shaheed misl. Natha Singh was a warrior-leader of renown who participated with distinction in many significant battles of the period.[24]

In Aid of Rajputs

History records internecine conflict during the 18th century among some of the Rajput principalities now in Rajasthan. At one point, tensions were high between the houses of Bikaner and Jaisalmer. When the latter obtained the commitment of a Mughal contingent from Delhi, in a countermove, Bikaner sought military assistance from the Sikhs. In response, a combined force, twenty-thousand strong drawn from various Sikh misls, including the Shaheeds under Deep Singh, was mobilized. Sikh prowess in battle was by then legend. Somewhat dismayed by the odds, Jaisalmer pulled out of the stand-off, finding compromise more expedient.[25]

Developments at Dam Dama Sahib

On assuming charge in 1706, among the first aspects to be addressed by Deep Singh was augmenting the supply of potable water. Most drinking sources in the area provided, at best, brackish water, unfit to drink. The large well that Deep Singh commissioned provided clean drinking water. The overall development of Dam Dama Sahib was inevitably slow-paced, hamstrung by a paucity of resources. From the sojourn of the tenth Guru in 1706 until the 1740s, only tented accommodation was available. Deep Singh gradually undertook the overall infrastructural development with a sagacity that showed his long-term vision.

The sum of Rupees 1 Lakh received by the shrine in May 1739 as their share of the spoils from Nadir Shah's returning baggage train was put to good use towards construction of the main shrine (Takht Sahib), Guru Teg Bahadur's commemorative shrine (Manji Sahib), drinking water well, community kitchen, and living accommodation for scholars.[26]

Defences were improved by constructing four burjs (towers) to serve as refuge for the Khalsa as much as rallying points. The seventy-feet high observation tower for early warning, bhora for meditation and replication of texts already existed as part of Baba Dall Singh's fort but Deep Singh refurbished and repurposed these to suit his purpose. Reportedly, these were linked by a subterranean passage to the sarovar to serve as refuge in times of need.[27] The seminary was now further fortified with ten jambooraks (guns), two cannons, and a garrison of over four hundred fighting men at any time.[28]

Infrastructural development of the shrine received a major fillip with the onset of the misl period in the 1740s, when the Shaheed misl, like others, was entitled to collect up to half-share of the crop as revenue.[29] Later, the grant of a jagir by the Khalsa Panth brought annual income to the Shaheed misl for their three shrines: Rs 60,000 for Deep Singh at Dam Dama Sahib; Rs 50,000 for Baba Gurbaksh Singh at Anandgarh; Rs 25,000 for the brothers Natha Singh and Dyal Singh at Babe di Ber, Sialkot. These grants helped Deep Singh initiate and execute major developmental works at the shrine to establish it as an important Sikh centre. During the reign of Maharaja Ranjit Singh, these grants were further enhanced.[30]

Nawab Zabat Khan Rajput of Rania was a noble who held sway over a large part of the area around Dam Dama Sahib. A man of considerable authority and wealth, he was always at loggerheads with the Sikhs. After a particularly sanguinary engagement, in a bid to settle for peace, he made over twelve villages as jagir, including Dadu, Kewal, Dharampura, Singhpura, Pakka, Jogewala, Teona Pujarian, to the shrine for its langar, seven of which yielded an annual revenue of Rs 3600. In turn, Karam Singh, the then misaldar of the Shaheeds in the early 1760s, had to guarantee a truce.[31]

The entire pattern of management changed under Karam Singh who became misaldar in 1762 after Deep Singh's successor, Sudh Singh, was killed in action. With the conquest and sack of Sirhind on 14th January 1764, the misl began occupying territory around Ambala and Saharanpur, and gradually Shahzadpur became its headquarters.[32] With this came an obvious shift in focus, away from Dam Dama Sahib, and slackening of supervision and oversight in its wake. Later during the British Raj, when Talwandi Sabo and the shrine became personal fiefdoms of the Shazadpurias and the Patiala royals by an equivocal turn of events, these were further reduced to a mere resource for exploitation, soon falling into desuetude.[33]

By the 1920s, the shrine was a welter of neglect. The modest structures that did exist stood in utter disrepair beside forlorn Nishan Sahibs that continued to flutter amid complete desolation. The unpaved circumambulatory path around the sarovar had pits deep enough to hide an elephant. It was Sant Attar Singh of Mastuana who came to the rescue and set the shrine firmly on a path of modern development. Beginning 1923, the Mastuana foundation gradually transformed the premises into a complex of multiple shrines. They built magnificent edifices complete with all amenities and also fostered the flowering of educational facilities in the true image of the 'guru-ki-kanshi' envisioned by the tenth Guru.[34] The present building of the Takht Srī Damdamā Sāhib was constructed during the 1970s under the supervision of Sant Sevā Siṅgh of Srī Kesgaṛh. With a spacious high-ceilinged hall, it has a pavilion at either end.

Deep Singh's fifty-two-year stay at the shrine is commemorated even today by his picture-prints and interpretive sign-boards that are everywhere serving to remind the visitor of his seminal contribution in transforming a derelict spot in the midst of a desert into a principal educational and spiritual hub in the region.

SEVEN

The Sant-Sipahi

Savior of the Oppressed

One day, while a religious congregation was in session at Dam Dama Sahib, the shrill wailing of male and female voices rent the air, shattering the morning calm. A man and woman came staggering in, reeling from some terrible shock:

'The Lord have mercy upon us! We are ruined! We've been attacked and robbed!'

While the woman collapsed in consternation, the man sought to explain their predicament mid sobs, blood still oozing from a head wound, 'I'm Karam Chand and this is my wife. We were on a journey along with our daughter, son, and daughter-in-law, when we were suddenly set upon by Nasiruddin Bhatti's men. They mercilessly killed my son, tried to kill me too, and took away the two women!'

Some Sikhs hastened to comfort them and soon a brief investigation revealed that the incident happened some four miles away, and that the horsemen had made off in the easterly direction.

There was no time to lose. The women were in grave danger. Deep Singh ordered quick mobilization and within minutes an armed body of a hundred troopers were on their way.

Although a revenue official under the Mughal administration with jurisdiction over thirty villages, Nasiruddin was an infamous brigand who lived in the security of a fortalice in Garhi Peeran, seldom deposited the dues he collected, and terrorized the people of the area. Once in the past, Deep Singh had occasion to invest his home for a similar depravity but in the brief engagement, spared his life on the behest of Nasiruddin's wife who sought forgiveness and begged that Deep Singh adopt her as his daughter.

On reaching Nasiruddin's abode some twenty-four miles east, they cordoned it and sent word to Nasiruddin to hand over the two women captives.

Nasiruddin soon appeared on the parapet, above the ramparts, pleading his innocence:

'O Master, I swear my innocence! It is true that two Hindu ladies were brought into my homestead but they have come to no harm and have been in my custody ever since. I have already punished the two soldiers who had kidnapped them. Please come in and see for yourself! I can hand them over to you now, if you so wish?'

When Deep Singh entered the fortress along with a few of his men, Nasiruddin's wife emerged from the cloisters along with the two women:

'Dear father', began Nasiruddin's wife, who had adopted Deep Singh as her godfather. 'Here they are! We've looked upon them as our own daughters. I assure you they've come to no harm. Ask them, if you please!'

The two women were restored to their family.[1]

There are several such instances that mark Deep Singh's influence as a benefactor in the region, often going out in aid of the persecuted and distressed during this much storied period. Among several such instances of freeing captive women from Muslim overlords, mostly by force of arms, is that of Nawab Gafaru Khan.

Another lord of the realm, the Nawab enjoyed enormous extra-official power as brother-in-law to Wazir Khan, Governor of Sirhind—since Wazir Khan was killed during the battle for Sirhind in May 1710, this places the incident in 1708-1709, before Deep Singh left Talwandi to campaign alongside Banda Bahadur.

The Nawab occupied a large fort, Pakki Garhi, some seven miles from Talwandi Sabo, and was much feared as the scourge of the land, particularly for his indulgence in the royal prerogative of carrying away unmarried women. Howsoever much parents tried to solemnize their daughters' nuptials on the sly, the ceremony would invariably be disrupted by the Nawab's ubiquitous informers.

Pandit Hari Das, who was a resident of village Pukka in the area, was determined to circumvent the Nawab's salacity and conspired with his wife to wed their daughter, Laxmi Devi, their only child, in the strictest secrecy. While they were able to complete the ceremonies successfully, the doli (the last ceremony in a Hindu wedding when the groom sets off for his home along with the bride) did not escape the notice of the Nawab's men, always on the prowl. A troop of soldiers soon descended upon the festive cavalcade, wreaking havoc, and carrying away the bride.

Hari Das and his wife were beside themselves with grief. Their mournful entreaties to the soldiers went unheeded, and they dared not approach the Nawab for fear of their lives. Some village folk had heard of the new establishment under Deep Singh at Talwandi Sabo, of their respect for truth and justice and their skill-at-arms to match. With prayer on his lips, Hari Das hastened to Talwandi Sabo.

Led into Deep Singh's presence on arrival, he shared his tragedy, pleading:

'I've heard so much about how you always help the weak and the stricken. We're helpless before the Nawab. He has an evil presence but is too powerful for us. I have nowhere else to go. Please save my daughter, I beg of you!'

To help the helpless was an article of faith deeply ingrained in the Khalsa ethos, which Deep Singh had particularly imbibed from his Guru and mentor. He at once mobilized five hundred troopers and bid Hari Das to accompany them in order to verify his narrative. Hari Das was reluctant at first, aware that challenging the Nawab even indirectly could be fatal, but here was his solitary chance to rescue his daughter from worse than death.

When they reached Pakki Garhi, the Nawab's sentries informed their master of the arrival of troops. The Nawab soon appeared on the ramparts, aggressive, arrogant, and somewhat taken aback by the audacity of his visitors:

'How dare you come and threaten me thus! What do you want?'

Deep Singh's rejoinder rang out loud, clear, and firm, 'You have carried away this man's daughter. Please release her now and we shall disperse in peace.'

'What cheek!' roared the Nawab. 'Do you think you can wage war on me? Do you not know that the Governor of Sirhind is my brother-in-law? One missive to him will fetch thousands of soldiers and you will not know where to hide or run! Away with you this instant!'

Deep Singh now realized that mere words would not drive home the import of his mission. He shot off an arrow in his direction, designed to miss, but to make his intent unambiguously clear.

Incensed, the Nawab swore death and destruction: 'You know not what you do, you fool! I will destroy you and all your men!'

'Why spill more blood than is necessary, O Nawab. Let's settle this one-for-one,' bellowed Deep Singh in an even tone, his words reverberating in the stillness.

The Nawab's pathan pride was now aroused. He descended out in the open, in full armour, ready for battle. Unfortunately for him, while his years of profligacy and decadence had debilitated him, he was also in poor form as a soldier since it was his men who fought most of his battles. Unable to measure swords with his adept and spirited adversary, he was killed in the duel. Laxmi Devi was rescued and reunited with the groom, and the land thus rid of a dreadful curse.[2]

On returning from such missions where they had risked their lives for others, it was Deep Sing's wont to offer a thanksgiving followed by a prayer for humility lest their success and philanthropy should turn their head. History bears witness that this chivalrous tradition established by Deep Singh continued even after him.[3]

The Spiritual Warrior

Such instances typically portray Deep Singh as the quintessential Khalsa sant-sipahi whose praxis combined bhagti-shakti as a potent and insuperable binary to fight evil in the prevailing circumstances. In a sense, the Khalsa carried echoes of the knights of European late Middle Ages who became associated with the ideals of chivalry and a code of conduct for the perfect courtly Christian warrior. The Khalsa baptismal ceremony was not without its parallels to the 'accolade', the knighting ceremony, that usually involved a ritual bath, prayer, oath-taking, and dubbing with the sword. For the Khalsa, the baptismal nectar was consecrated with a double-edged dagger because, with Guru Gobind Singh, the sword had taken on a special, almost divine signification when it was deified as Bhagauti (sublime energy). Just as God subdues enemies, so does the Sword:[4]

ਅਸ ਕ੍ਰਿਪਾਨ ਖੰਡੋ ਖੜਗ ਤੁਪਕ ਤਬਰ ਅਰੁ ਤੀਰ ॥
ਸੈਫ ਸਰੋਹੀ ਸੈਹਥੀ ਯਹੈ ਹਮਾਰੈ ਪੀਰ ॥੩॥
—Sri Shastra Naam Mala, *Dasm Granth*

As kirpan khando kharag tupak tabar ar teer
Saif sirohi saithe yehai hamare peer |3|
The curved sword, sword, double-edged sword, broad sword, gun, battle-axe, and arrow;
The straight sword, sword, and spear are our Divine Mentors.

Akin to the melding of chivalry and religion during the Crusades in Europe when Christian armies began to devote their efforts to sacred purposes,[5] the Khalsa saw a similar transformation that increasingly witnessed a life of puritan piety combined with the use of arms chiefly for the protection of the weak and the defenseless. The Sikh daily prayer includes this supplication both to protect and to be protected.[6] A just cause was an important caveat in the Khalsa's dharmayudh, or use of physical force. Its essence truly lay in its ethical dimension. Power could be used against oppression and injustice but never to repress or exploit.

Having embarked upon a difficult asymmetric struggle, Guru Gobind realized very early in his career that to sustain it he needed to imbue his Sikhs with death defying courage on the one hand, which he achieved principally with the formation of the Khalsa—an ideal order of warrior-saints close to his heart.[7] On the other hand, he glorified death in sacralized battle as a means to salvation, reflected as the crowning sentiment of his fabled Soldier's Prayer.[8] Indeed, a military commander can do no greater service to his men than to infuse in them courage to scorn death—this may be seen to be more important than the often overrated 'killing instinct':

'Proud men—we mean, of course, pride of the genuine and true sort—know how to die; and if a man knows that, the essentials of the true soldier are in him. For though victory and success in war depend on the capacity to inflict death, if we make a psychological analysis of the martial instinct, it will be easily found that the primary constituent is the capacity to meet death proudly, and not in the capacity to inflict it.'[9]

Yet in this psychological transformation, there was one uniquely distinguishing principle of the Khalsa. Original initiates into the Khalsa fraternity such as Deep Singh bore arms and were willing to embrace death willingly as part of their ethos as defenders of religious freedom for all faiths against all forms of tyranny. It is for this reason that Sikh shaheeds became highly revered figures as unambiguous exemplars of virtue and moral justification whom Louis E. Fenech designates as 'ideal Sikh athletes of piety'.[10]

'They possessed a value system that forged them into the beau ideal of the Guru's warrior-saints. This position as saintly defenders of the Punjab and its inhabitants, irrespective of faith, endeared them to the common people. A combination of their devastating guerrilla tactics and the groundswell of support from the peasantry led to a tradition of considerable success.'[11]

George Forster, English traveler and civil servant with the East India Company, noted in 1783:

'Their success and conquests have largely originated from an activity unparalleled by other Indian nations, from their endurance of excessive fatigue, and a keen resentment of injuries. The personal endowments of the Sicques are derived from a temperance of diet, and a forbearance from many of those sensual pleasures which have enervated the Indian Mahomedans.'[12]

As a religion, Sikhism accorded the highest position to Truth. In practice too, their veneration for the truth seemed to raise their character above all other Asiatics, notes the *Asiatic Annual Register*: 'Both as a people and as individuals, they may be considered as much less addicted to the low artifice of evasion, lying or dissimulation than any other Asiatics.'[13]

Very early in their struggle, the Khalsa espoused an important tenet, drawn indubitably from the writings of the Tenth master who proscribed setting upon the defenseless:

مزن تیغ بر خون کس بے دریغ
ترا نیز خون است با چرخ تیغ

—Stanza 69, *Zafarnamah*

ਮਜ਼ਨ ਤੇਗ ਬਰ ਖੂਨਿ ਕਸ ਬੇ ਦਰੇਗ ॥ ਤੁਰਾ ਨੀਜ਼ ਖੂੰ ਚਰਖ ਰੇਜ਼ਦ ਬਤੇਗ ॥੬੯॥
Mazan teg khoon kas be dareg | Tura neej khoo charakh retaj bateg |69|
Do not strike the helpless, else the Lord will strike you.

Since their strict moral code included the scrupulous use of force, it was not uncommon for the Khalsa to inscribe excerpts from their scriptures on their weaponry as a divine remembrancer. Their abstinence from mindless slaughter even under provocation is documented no less by their foes. These unintended plaudits from Qazi Nur Mohammed who accompanied Ahmed Shah Durrani during his seventh invasion into India (1764-1765) paint the Khalsa, first-hand, in true colours of the chivalrous sant-sipahi:[14]

Besides their fighting, [there is] one more thing in which they excel all other warriors...

که نه کشند نامرد را هیچ گاه
گریزنده را هم نگیرند راه

Keh na kushand namard ra heech gah
Gurzendah ra hum nagrind rah
At no point will they kill a *namard* (powerless), nor will they chase a fugitive.

زنا هم نباشد میان سگاں
نه دزدیست بود کارِ آں بدرگاں

Zana hum na bashad miane saggan
Na duzdeest bavad kar e aan badragan
Sikhs do not maintain illicit relations with women; there are no womanizers or thieves among them. They distance themselves from evil people.

زر و زیورِ زن بتاراج نیز
نگیرند گر مهره هست و کنیز

Zaro zever-e zan bataraj neez
Nagrind gar mohra hast-o kaneez
They will not rob the jewelry of a lady—rich or poor.

نہ دُزدیست ہرگز میانِ سگاں
نہ پیداست سارق دراں بدرگاں

Na duz deest hargiz miyane saggan
Na paidast sarak daran badragan
There are no thugs, thieves, or pillagers among them.

While historians aver that the Khalsa success in battle would not have been possible without their extraordinary grit, resilience, and an endurance learnt behind the plough, they hold no less important their abstinence from general intemperance and vice as part of their strict moral code that never seemed to falter. This served to significantly deepen their acceptance and credibility because they satisfied two important principles which justify war-making according to politico-military philosophers: 'right to go to war' (jus ad bellum) and 'right conduct in war' (jus in bello). The Khalsa struggle against tyranny was defensible both in its moral compass as in its manner and conduct, belying the traditional proclivities to war and crime actuated, according to the oft-quoted Persian proverb: *zar, zan, zameen* (wealth, woman, conquest).

Strategy and Tactics

Beginning with the rapid campaigns of Banda, every minor or major military engagement of the Sikhs henceforth seemed to shape their strategy and tactics that continued to evolve till the mid-18th century. By then, their senior leaders such as Jassa Singh Ahluwalia, Jai Singh Kanhaiya, Charat Singh Sukarchakiya, Deep Singh and many others had learnt first-hand an important lesson that forms the bedrock of military strategy anywhere: it is vital to take into account the realities of geography, society, economics, and politics.[15]

As a consequence, their greatest military development of the period was the evolution of the guerrilla mode of fighting, particularly the 'running skirmish' that grew out of their asymmetric life and death struggle against the superior power of the Mughals and the rapacious Afghans. This was a lesson they had learnt rather early, during Banda's campaigns—avoid static lines of defense and pitched battles, bereft as they were of forts, garrisons, artillery, and any extraneous support.[16] They prevailed purely by mobility and adapting their fluid tactics to their limited force levels, to their rudimentary arsenal and above all, to the terrain:

ਸਝਾਨਨ ਨੇ ਯੇ ਬਾਤ ਸੁਨਾਈ ॥ ਲੜਾਈ ਕੇ ਫੱਟ ਕਹੈਂ ਸੁ ਢਾਈ ॥
ਮਿਲਨ ਭੱਜਣ ਇਹ ਸਾਰ ਦੋਇ ॥ ਲੜ ਮਰ ਮੁੱਕਣ ਆਧਾ ਸੋਇ ॥
—Bhangu, *Panth Prakash*[17]

Syannan ne yo baat sunai. Larai ke fut kahain su dhai
Milan bhajjan eh saar doi. lar mar mukkan aada soi
The battle-wise adhere to the tactics of two-and-half feet;
To strike and disengage one foot each; to die a half-foot
  indiscreet.

In their uniquely innovative 'dhai fut' strategy—literally, two-and-half feet or strikes—'Engagement' with the enemy to cause maximum damage followed by quick 'Disengagement' to minimize own casualties were paramount as the two main strikes. Pitched battles with high attrition were to be avoided and were assigned the value of half-strike. Their strategy was, in effect, a necessary expedient to conserve their limited though growing numbers. They recognized the value of initiative, with tactical surprise as their primary weapon, alongside harnessing the conditions essential for guerrilla warfare to their advantage. Having prefigured the wisdom of Liddell Hart's 'Indirect Approach',[18] they also recognized the merits of dislocating the enemy's psychological and physical balance as a vital prelude to a successful attempt at his overthrow.

Within their overall guerrilla mode of fighting, they successfully integrated a panoply of other strategic strands:[19]

- Toughened by their sustained exposure to hardship and adversity, they evolved the 'counterbalance strategy' whereby they could maintain their balance of mind amid the chaos of battle.
- Their 'death ground strategy' grew out of a constant sense of desperation that often placed them on 'death ground', with their back against the wall, accruing to them high order courage and staying power.
- Although the misls could campaign independently, when they confederated for joint action, they were placed under a unified command inevitably allowing an effective 'command and control strategy'.
- By dint of their generally irreproachable conduct in war and peace as sant-sipahis, they could retain the moral high ground, elevating their struggle to a crusade and sustaining their morale through their 'righteous strategy'.
- Their ability to retreat and avoid conflict in the face of a much stronger enemy helped them master the 'non-engagement strategy' that invariably helped them buy time and gain perspective; closely related to this was their elusive 'strategy of the void'—they gave their enemies no targets to attack, instead, constantly delivering raids and side-attacks to tire the enemy and weaken their morale.
- Their 'blitzkrieg strategy' was an important element of guerrilla warfare by which they could strike with great speed, often catching the enemy unawares.
- Combined with this, they used the 'centre of gravity strategy' when they struck at the enemy command and control centre to precipitate a strategic paralysis.
- Throughout the war-torn years, of paramount importance to the Sikhs was their 'Grand strategy': their vision that helped them look beyond individual battles at the end-objective of their crusade against an evil regime.

- Sikh commanders demonstrated remarkable skills at 'maneuver', long recognized as an important tactic to reduce attrition. Battles may be won by both slaughter and maneuver but 'the greater the general, the more he contributes to maneuver, the less he demands of slaughter.'[20]

Deep Singh and other misaldars often used a potent combination of these strategies and tactics to good effect, particularly during raids. It speaks volumes for their daring and ingenuity that in a span of fifty years, by the mid-18th century, Sikh warriors had acquired a fearsome reputation as strong-limbed guerrillas, excellent horsemen, marksmen in the Parthian mould and what gives them greatest credit, as masters of the small-scale tactical battle.

The noted scribe, Tahmas Khan Miskin, records an eye-witness account in 1754 of three Sikh horsemen driving away a full regiment of Turki soldiers under Qasim Khan between Patti and Lahore.[21]

Nonetheless, reverses in battle were not uncommon and two of the major ones are commemorated to this day as the Lesser and the Greater Holocaust (1746 and 1762, respectively). But these failed to dim the Khalsa resolve or shake their purpose. The intrepid followers of Gobind Singh consoled themselves often with unusual reasoning:

ਜੋ ਪਕੇ ਥੇ ਸੋ ਰਹੇ ਕਚੇ ਗਏ ਸੁ ਭਾਜ ॥
ਮਰੇ ਗਏ ਸਭ ਸੁਰਗ ਨੂੰ ਜੀਐ ਕਰਐ ਤਿਨ ਰਾਜ ॥[22]

Jo pakke the so rahe kache gaye su bhaaj
Mare gaye sabh surg nu jiyo karyo tin raj

The chaff has been separated from the grain.
The departed shall find peace in heaven, the living now shall reign.

ਇਕ ਨਿਹੰਗ ਬੁਕ ਤਹਿ ਕਰਐ ਉਚੇ ਬਚਨ ਸੁਨਾਇ ॥
ਤੱਤ ਖਾਲਸੇ ਮੋ ਰਹਐ ਗਏ ਸੋ ਖੇਟ ਗਵਾਇ ॥[23]

> *ik Nihang buk te kaiyo uche bachan sunai*
> *tat khalse do rahiyo gayo khot gavai.*
> A *Nihang* then lofty wisdom spoke:
> True *Khalsa* only now lives on;
> the dross could not withstand the yoke.

Their ability to repeatedly take even debilitating adversity in their stride suggests that, all along, powerfully undergirding Khalsa strategy and tactics were two principles of war now widely recognized by most armies as pre-eminent, nay, as important preconditions for military victory:

- *Selection and maintenance of aim*: a bequest from Guru Gobind Singh, the Khalsa sought and would accept nothing short of sovereignty.
- *Maintenance of morale*: their sense of chardi kahla inevitably served to bolster their morale, even in the face of severe tragedy, death, and destruction.

In the analysis and experience of Sikh history, martyrdom, in effect, was the cross the Sikhs bore for long decades before they could wrest the crown literally from the jaws of death in the shape of their ruthless overlords. Before long, the Sikhs could demonstrate their ability in maneuver warfare. In 1764, after a humiliating engagement with the Khalsa near the River Chenab, Durrani saved himself by 'putting his own horse into the river,' while his troops 'fled pell mell, like an army without defense or transport.'[24] Thereafter, the Afghans would ever hold the Sikhs in awe.[25]

Gradually, their growing numbers helped them adopt regular formations in pitched battles as in the Sikh attack on Sirhind in 1764 when they killed its Afghan administrator along with 10,000 of his cavalry, sacked the town, and began occupying territories in the plains of Sirhind, from the Sutlej to the Yamuna.[26] The following year, in the Battle of Sutlej against Durrani during his seventh invasion, they successfully forced his retreat.[27] By then, with many of the Sikh chiefs or barons gaining political ascendancy in their principalities, the Khalsa were the de facto rulers of the Punjab having declared sovereignty with self-proclaimed right to coinage in 1765 from Lahore.[28] About the same time, the voluntary basis of military service gave way to a remunerative one.[29]

There is no doubt that Ahmed Shah inflicted heavy losses upon the Sikhs but he failed to subdue them and it is an understated fact of history that the skill of the greatest military genius of his time in Asia eventually gave way before the zeal and determination of the Sikhs, animated by their religious fervor and a spirit of sacrifice.[30]

Unlikely Encomium

The Persians under Nadir Shah invaded India in 1739, and Ahmad Shah Durrani, the founder of modern Afghanistan, marched his plundering columns no less than nine times into India between 1748 and 1767. Both robber-kings had to repeatedly run the Sikh gauntlet through the Punjab. They became the greatest enemies of the Sikhs, but also their greatest admirers:

ਏਕ ਹੋਇ ਤਾਂ ਸੇ ਸੌ ਲਰੈਂ । ਮਰਨੇ ਤੇਂ ਵੈ ਮੂਲ ਨ ਡਰੈਂ ।
ਰਹੈਂ ਚਾਉ ਉਨ ਮਰਨ ਕੇ ਦੀਨ ਮਜ਼ਹਬ ਕੇ ਭਾਇ ।
ਹਮ ਮਾਰਤ ਉਨ ਥਕ ਗਏ ਉਹ ਘਟਤ ਨ ਕਿਤਹੂੰ ਦਾਇ ।

—Bhangu, *Panth Prakash*[31]

Ek hoi tam sau sau larain. Marne te vai mul na darain;
Rahai chau un maran ko din mazhab ke dhai.
Ham maarat un thak gae uh ghatat na kitahun dai.

One of them can hundred battle. Fear of Death no whit does rattle.
Always long to die for creed.
We're tired to kill; their strength won't cede.

Deep Singh was prominent among the warrior-leaders of his time who contributed to build this fearsome yet chivalrous reputation. There are numerous contemporary accounts, such as the following by Qazi Nur Mohammad, that portray the Khalsa warrior in glowing colours, often laced with invective which only affirms their authenticity:

فنِ جنگ گر خواہی آموختن
ازایشاں بیاموزائے تیغ زن

Fan-e-jang gar khaee amokhtan
Az ayshan Bhan moza-e tegh zan

If you cherish the desire to learn the art of war, come before them in the field [....] O, Swordsman! If you want to learn the modes of fighting, learn from them how to face the enemy like a hero, and then swiftly and safely disengage.

بود سنگھ القاب او دانیش
ز انصاف نبود کہ سگ خوانیش

Bavad singh alkab-e danish
Z insaf nabud keh sag khanish

Singh is their title, listen to me, o man. It is, therefore, unjust to call them dogs.

چو شیر نداالحق بہ ہنگام رزم
ز حاتم فزو نند ہنگام بزم

Chu sher nidalhaq b hangam razam
Z hatim fazu nand hangaam bazam

They are truly lions in battle, roaring with their war cries. In generosity, they surpass Hatim (companion of Mohammad known for his generosity).

چو در دست گیرند شمشیر ہند
بتازند از ہند تا ملکِ سندھ

Chu dar dast girand shamsheer-a Hind
Batazand az Hind mulk-e Sind

When they take the Indian sword in their hands, they traverse the country from Hind to Sindh. None can stand against them in battle, howsoever strong.

The Sant-Sipahi

چو در نیزه بازی در آرند دست
در آرند در فوجِ دشمن شکست

Chu dar neza bazi dar arand dast
Dar arand dar fauz-e dushman shikast
When they handle the spear, they shatter the ranks of the enemy.

سر نیزہ آسماں سے برند
اگر کوہ قاف است زہم بر درند

Sar-e neza bar asman me barand
Agar koh kaf ast z ham bar darand
When they raise the heads of their spears towards the sky, they would pierce even through the Caucasus.

در آنند زہ چوں بچاچی کماں
خدنگ عدوکش نہند اندراں

Dar arand zeh chu bchachi Kaman
Khdang adokash nihand andran
When they stretch the strings of the bow [...] the body of the enemy begins to shiver with fear.

تبر زینِ شاں گر رسد بر زرہ
ز رہ بر تنِ خصم گردد گرہ

Tabar zeen-e shan gar rasad bar zarah
Z rah bar tan-e khasam gardad garah
When their battle axes fall upon the armour of their opponents, their armour becomes their coffin.

بہ تن ہر یکے چو یک پارہ کوہ
ز پنجاہ مردش فزوں در شکوہ

B tan har yakey humcho yak para koh
Z panja mardish fazoon dar shikoh
The body of every one of them is like a piece of rock and in physical grandeur every one of them is more than fifty ghazis (Muslim warriors).

> Besides the usual arms, when they take up the musket in hand [and] come into the field of action jumping [and] roaring like lions [...] they tear asunder the chests of many and shed blood of several in the dust.[32]

'This sect abounds in giant-sized and lion-limbed youths whose stroke of the leg would certainly cause instantaneous death to a Vilayati (English) horse. Their matchlock strikes a man at a distance of nine hundred paces, and each of them covers two hundred kos (600 kilometres) on horseback.'[33]

'Five hundred of Najaf Khan's [Persian Prince who was commander-in-chief of the Mughal Army under Shah Alam II in 1772-1782 AD] horse dare not encounter fifty Sikh horsemen.'[34]

According to George Thomas, the Irish mercenary who held sway over an adjoining fiefdom and frequently came in contact with them:

'When mounted on horseback, their black flowing locks and half-naked bodies, which are formed in the stoutest and most athletic mould, the glittering of their arms, and the size and speed of their horses, render their appearance imposing and formidable, and superior to most of the cavalry in Hindostan.'[35]

Having studied the entire gamut of Sikh activities in the Punjab and the adjoining areas, Sir Jadunath Sarkar, an authority on the Mughal period, observed:

'This astonishing superiority, man for man, over all other fighting forces of India, was due to the Sikh character, training and organization.'[36] Indeed, none could hope for membership in the Khalsa 'without proficiency in equitation and arms'[37] They also displayed unusual endurance and could 'go waterless for a whole day in scorching summer.'[38]

Sikh women proved to be no less courageous. George Thomas notes: 'instances indeed have not infrequently occurred, in which they [Sikh women] have actually taken up arms to defend their habitations from the desultory attacks of the enemy, and throughout the contest behaved themselves with an intrepidity of spirit highly praiseworthy'.[39]

Jat Influx

It is militarily significant that having initially taken root in towns, when Sikhism eventually spread to the countryside in the 16th and 17th centuries, it attracted the jat people in droves, beginning in Guru Arjan's pontificate when almost the entire jat peasantry of the Majha was converted. According to the Panda Vahi, Deep Singh was jat in ethnicity and, possibly, it was his great-grandfather, Dulchi (see Table 1), who was the first to embrace Sikhism during this period. By the time of Guru Hargobind, jats were preponderant in his army.[40]

Originally pastoralists in the lower Indus river-valley of Sindh, they migrated North along the river valleys to colonize North Rajputana, the Western Gangetic Plain, and the Punjab between the eleventh and the sixteenth centuries, gaining some social ascendancy as rural grandees. Guru Gobind Singh had noted their revolutionary zeal and they formed the backbone of his Khalsa army as much as that of Banda Bahadur later.[41] Naturally assertive and virile, the attitude of non-resistance suited neither their temper nor tradition.[42] This would forge an important transformation in the Sikh movement, particularly in their response to Mughal-Afghan acts of high-handedness and tyranny.[43] Later, of the twelve misls that eventually won sovereignty for the Punjab, ten were jat-led, including the Sukerchakiyas—ancestors of Maharaja Ranjit Singh—and predominantly of a piece (the two exceptions were the Ahluwalias and Ramgarhias; Dallewalias were raised by a Khatri but the leadership soon passed to Jat-Sikhs).

After extensive research, both Maj Todd and General Cunningham, while ascribing Aryan or Indo-Scythian origin to the jats akin to the Rajputs because of their 'almost identical physique and facial character,'[44] regarded them as 'the beau ideal' of the oriental soldier—soldiers by 'instinct and tradition' who regarded 'cowardice as worse than crime.'[45]

While 'sturdy independence [...] and patient vigorous labour' were their strongest characteristics, they were also 'of all Punjab races the most impatient of tribal or communal control...and [asserted] the freedom of the individual most strongly.'[46] It was this trait of self-willed independence that especially suited the jats to spearhead and wage the unrelenting battles of the Khalsa against tyranny.

When historians refer to this period of Punjab's history as the 'heroic century', they accept the Jat-Sikhs as 'the real heroes' and the 'fighting arm' of the time.[47] Deep Singh stands out prominently among them, and if the human personality is a product of its heredity and environment, as the proverbial sant-sipahi, he was shaped as much by his ethnicity and his socio-religious heritage as the tumultuous times he was born into.

Nonetheless, the role of other castes and communities cannot be underrated in creating the propitious climate for the eventual triumph of the Khalsa:

'Just as the Khatris [along with the Brahmins] brought their sharp intellect, sense of economic and socio-political organization, love of the fine arts [...] and an idealistic view of life into the mainstream of Sikh history, the jats contributed their vigour, sense of heroism, sacrifice, and independence of character.' The unwavering loyalty and fortitude of the less-celebrated castes, including the Rangrettas, was no less contributive. It is to the eternal credit of the Gurus that they welded a spiritless aggregate of feuding tribes and caste-riven factions into a single entity, imbuing them with unrelenting courage, an egalitarian and civilized outlook, along with an overarching vision for sovereignty.[48]

EIGHT

Review

Cast in the original binary of the sant-sipahi fashioned by the tenth Guru in the founding of the Khalsa, Deep Singh stands like a colossus, clearly without peer. Historians unhesitatingly concede to him the unique distinction as the 'living embodiment of the Khalsa ideology—as much in belief and appearance, as in action and martyrdom'.[1] Indeed, the length and breadth of his spiritual worth and military leadership spanning half a century during the most crises-torn period of Sikh history has few parallels.

It was the tenth Guru who gauged the potential in a promising young lad of eighteen when he first set eyes on him in 1700 at Anandpur. A workaday husbandman from the Punjab plains, in a rare feat of learning under the tutelage of the Guru himself and Bhai Mani Singh, Deep Singh very soon excelled at both skill-at-arms and scholarly pursuits, with a penchant for language-learning.

In addition, he uniquely demonstrated very early extraordinary trustworthiness and loyalty along with the ability to lead and organize. The seer in the Guru divined considerable strategic worth in him to bade him out of the Anandpur war zone and to charge him with raising a yeomanry—which later very likely formed the nucleus of his shaheedi jatha and the misl—only to summon him later to invest him with the responsibility of the first Sikh seminary of learning at Dam Dama Sahib at the young age of twenty-four. A position of great responsibility, it called for a rare combination of qualities of the scholar, saint, leader, manager, and warrior—all of which Deep Singh would in time manifest over the next half century.

When the Guru left Dam Dama Sahib to parley with the emperor, his primary objective had been to seek justice against Wazir Khan for the wars he had forced upon the Guru and for being the principal cause of the death of his mother and sons. When the emperor was non-committal, the Guru was left with no alternative but to plan his own course. Serendipity then arranged for Banda Bahadur to cross his path. A man of exceptional qualities whom the Guru perceived as the paragon sant-sipahi, Banda would very soon demonstrate the exceptional zeal of a saint and the daring of a warrior when in the span of a few months he would wreak vengeance on all those responsible for the death of the Guru's family, conquering large parts of the Punjab amid a peasant uprising that he orchestrated and directed.

Deep Singh played a prominent role in these victories and in comparison, although twelve years his younger, was no less the perfect sant-sipahi. Indeed, if fate had not conspired to prompt the Guru southwards, and if the Guru were to make his choice some ten years later, Deep Singh could well have been picked to lead these campaigns in the Punjab.

All through his life, a large part of Deep Singh's energy and time were devoted to scholarship, preaching the gospel, scriptural replication and exegesis, pontificating on religious and spiritual matters alongside infrastructural development of the seminary. All copies of the Guru Granth Sahib extant today are replicas of the originals painstakingly calligraphed by him. In addition, Deep Singh, along with Bhai Mani Singh and Nawab Kapur Singh, was among the very few leaders extended the spiritual remit and honor of baptizing new initiates—a distinction that he conferred on several Sikh leaders of the time including Ala Singh of Patiala and Hari Singh Bhangi, progenitor of the powerful Bhangi misl.[2]

It is his military career that is even more remarkable. Deep Singh first saw action under the tenth Guru in the many battles fought at Anandpur and a few years later, led an intrepid band of men-at-arms alongside Banda Bahadur in a series of daring campaigns across the Punjab. It was his conviction and deep sense of devotion to the Khalsa ideology that saw him part ways with Banda Bahadur over the Tat-Bandeyi Khalsa controversy but not before he had demonstrated rare courage in the battlefield, always fighting in the van with a higher incidence of casualties. To have been reinvested with the title 'Shaheed', this time by the entire panth, was indeed a fitting accolade.

As the founding head of the Shaheeds, a warring band who epitomized reckless dash and daring in battle, functioning very often as force multipliers to effectively turn the tide in battles invariably fought against heavy odds, Deep Singh's contribution to Sikh military strategy and success is yet to be fully explored and acknowledged. In a sense, the Shaheeds were akin to the Knight Templars of 12-13th century Christendom who often fought as advance shock troops in key battles and were widely regarded as the most skilled fighting units of the Crusades.[3]

The span of Deep Singh's military career is equally noteworthy. Beginning in 1709 at the young age of twenty-seven alongside Banda, he was the inveterate field commander, always leading from the front, right up to his last battle in November 1757 at the age of seventy-five years. Over a span of almost fifty years, through the maelstrom of the 18th century, he rode and fought alongside all the leading warriors of the period: the veteran Darbara Singh (born 1644), the much younger Nawab Kapur Singh (born 1697) who replaced Darbara Singh as the head of the panth, as well as Charat Singh Sukerchakia (born 1721), grandfather of the great Ranjit Singh, and Jassa Singh Ahluwalia (born 1718) who succeeded Nawab Kapur Singh.

He lives on as does the memory of his martyrdom, enshrined in the daily Sikh prayer (ardas):

ਤੇਗ ਵਾਹੀ [....] ਜਿਨ੍ਹਾਂ ਸਿੰਘਾਂ ਸਿੰਘਾਇਨੀਆਂ ਨੇਧਰਮ ਹੇਠ ਸੀਸ ਦਿੱਤੇ
Teg vahi [...] jinha Singha Singhanian ne dharam heth sis ditte
Those who wielded the sword [...] the men and women who sacrificed their life for their faith'

As well as in its concluding lines:

ਖੰਡਾ ਜਾਕੇ ਹਾਥ ਮੈਂ...
Khanda jaake haath mein....
With the broadsword in hand...

As a person, he is described by Gyani Gyan Singh as almost God-like in traits:

ਸਭ ਗੁਨ ਪੂਰਨ ਰਾਵਰ ਜੈਸੇ ।
ਨਿਕਸੈਂ ਥੋਰੇ ਸਿੰਘਨ ਮੈਂ ਸੇ ।[4]
sab gunn pooran ravar jaise
niksei thorei signhan mai se
Perfect full with godlike trait.
Like him few Singhs were till date.

As a warrior, he is perceived as:

ਹੁਤੇ ਬੀਰ ਬਰ ਬਲੀ ਘਮੰਡੀ[5]
Huto bir bar bali ghamandi
Brave, strong, and proud.

This combination of qualities made him an extraordinary military leader, if somewhat irascible. His ability to provide inspirational leadership against impossible odds is, however, a largely understated facet of his personality. For instance, the response to Deep Singh's call to arms within the wider community for his last battle in 1757 was mostly restricted to the Shaheed misl which then provided the leavening for the many volunteers stirred by the prospect of martyrdom in a just cause. Overall, the event best exemplifies the core Sikh value—it is honorable to take up arms as the last recourse in the pursuit of justice, and to seek martyrdom in sacralized battle, if called for. In military terms, the battle was a defeat with very high attrition. In spiritual terms, it shall never cease to yield dividends as a dominant motif in the Sikh psyche—with Deep Singh as its effulgent icon; an enduring and rousing example to infuse fresh courage and vigour in any impersonal fight for justice and honour, anywhere, anytime.

It is often tempting to measure the greatness of a leader in the somewhat unruly and wild context of 18th century Punjab in terms of ephemeral yardsticks such as territorial conquest. As free-ranging misaldars out to occupy and subjugate large tracts of land under the stratagem of rakhi, the Sukerchakias, the Bhangis, and the Kanhaiyas were far superior. Conversely, Deep Singh as the Shaheed misaldar was bound by the selfless albeit contrarian panthic principles of 'service' and 'sacrifice' exemplified by his mentor, the tenth Guru himself. As the quintessential sant-sipahi, his mission was never territorial expansion but to fight tyranny only that goodness may prevail.

This decisively explains another less-cited facet of his character. A celibate himself, Deep Singh neither created nor bequeathed any personal estates or wealth to anyone, including to his siblings in his native village, Pahuwind.[6] This changed with the successive misaldars who demonstrated a markedly different attitude, occupying the plains south of the Sutlej, and under the hills from Ferozepur to Karnal after the sack of Sirhind in 1764.[7]

Deep Singh's unmatched contribution was his service to the Panth as the founding head of the Dam Dama seminary. His seminal efforts have made Talwandi Sabo a regional academic hub today with several universities located in the area—Guru Gobind Singh Engineering University, Yadvindra University, and Akal University. The Central University, Bhatinda, is also only a short distance away.

It is not, however, difficult to speculate the accomplishments of a man of his ability, unencumbered by the enormous responsibility of founding and running a seminary in extremely arduous times. Definitely, he could have garnered more power, pelf, and property to vie with any of the ascendant misaldars of his time. Instead, he chose in humility to follow the true path set out for him by the tenth Master.

Like no other, Deep Singh seems to fit the mold and mandate of the true Khalsa warrior-saint so faithfully reflected in rhyme:

ਖਾਲਸਾ ਸੋਇ ਲੜੇ ਹੋਇ ਆਗੈ ॥
Khālsā sōi laṛē hōi āgai ॥
Khalsa is the one who volunteers to contend in the first rank. (44)

ਖਾਲਸਾ ਸੋਇ ਨਾਮ ਰਤ ਲਾਗੈ ॥
Khālsā sō i nām rat lāgai ॥
Khalsa is the one who is infused with the divine name (47)

ਖਾਲਸਾ ਸੋਇ ਗੁਰਬਾਣੀ ਹਿਤ ਲਾਇ
Khālsā sō i gurbāṇī hit lāi
Khalsa is the one who puts his heart into Gurbani (47)

ਖਾਲਸਾ ਸੋਇ ਨਿਰਧਨ ਕੋ ਪਾਲੈ
Khālsā sōi nirdhan kō pālai
Khalsa is the one who looks after the poor (50)

ਖਾਲਸਾ ਸੋਇ ਦੁਸ਼ਟ ਕੋ ਗਾਲੇ ॥
Khālsā sōi dusaaṭ kō gālē ॥
Khalsa is the one who annihilates the evil-doers (50)

ਖਾਲਸਾ ਸੋਇ ਨਾਮ ਜਪ ਕਰੈ
Khālsā sōi nām jap karai
Khalsa is the one who remembers the divine name (51)

ਖਾਲਸਾ ਸੋਇ ਜੋ ਕਰੇ ਨਿਤ ਜੰਗ ॥
Khālsā sōi jō karē nit jaṅg ॥
Khalsa is the one who fights in righteous war. (53)

ਖਾਲਸਾ ਸੋਇ ਸ਼ਸਤਰ ਕੋ ਧਾਰੈ
Khālsā sōi saastar kō dhārai
Khalsa is the one who adorns himself with arms. (53)

ਖਾਲਸਾ ਸੋਇ ਦੁਸੰਟ ਕੋ ਮਾਰੈ ॥
Khālsā sōi dusaṇṭ kō mārai ॥
Khalsa is the one who exterminates the vicious. (54)

—Bhai Nand Lal,
Tankanamah[8]

Nowhere is the concept of the warrior-saint unpacked in such detail. As a poet laureate with a long and close association with the Guru, Nand Lal's perception of the paradigm is uniquely comprehensive and articulate. It is no surprise that as a devotee, Deep Singh strove all his life to fully achieve this vision of his Guru and mentor. His appeal for posterity rests primarily in being able to exemplify this prepossessing ideal so truly through one of the darkest periods of India's history.

As the impeccable sant-sipahi, his conduct in war and peace alongside many of his ilk, reinforced a universal military truth so crucial in battle: 'Fortitude in war has its roots in morality [...] a man of character in peace becomes a man of courage in war.' (Lord Moran)[9]

It is no coincidence that, principally, it is his last battle that immortalized him with the iconic status that seems to only gather strength with every passing year.

PART THREE

The Final Battle

> The louder din
> Of guns, and trumpets' clang, and solemn sound
> Of drums o'ercame their groans. In equal scale
> Long hung the fight, few marks of Fear were seen,
> None of retreat.

—John Philips, *Blenheim, a poem*

NINE

Right to Go to War

The Battle in History

The Panda Vahi at Haridwar records Deep Singh's death in battle in an entry made in 1785 CE (earlier records have biodegraded):

दीप सिंह अमृतसर में शहीद हुए समवत १८१४ में कार्तिक दिवाली वाले दिन ।

Deep Singh was martyred in Amritsar in Samvat 1814 on the day of Kartik Diwali.

This definitively fixes his date and place of martyrdom as Friday, 11th November 1757 at Amritsar, also the day of the Diwali festival that year (30 Kartik, 1814 Samvat).[1]

Durrani's Fourth Invasion

This date is correctly recorded in the voluminous *Dictionary of Battles and Sieges*.[2]

> '**Gohalwar, 1757, Indian Campaigns of Ahmad Shah**: Afghan ruler Ahmad Shah Durrani was returning home from the sack of Delhi in January when his force was attacked by Baba Deep Singh and he sent his son Timur Shah, Governor of Lahore, to punish the Sikhs. A few miles to the north of Amritsar at Gohalwar, the massively outnumbered Sikhs drove off the Afghans, although General Attal Khan slew Baba Deep (11th November 1757).'

Reliable historical sources log Ahmed Shah's return through the Punjab in April that year, not January,[3] and Deep Singh's was only the first of the many raids by Sikh misls on his booty-laden columns coordinated by Jassa Singh Ahluwalia, their supreme commander. The battle commenced at Gohalwar, some twelve kilometres south of Amritsar but raged right up to Amritsar, the Sikh objective for the day. It is true that the Sikhs had initial success but were later overwhelmed by the odds, when Deep Singh was killed in single combat with an enemy commander—the name varies in other sources.

It is important to understand the runup to the battle. Essentially, it formed part of a series of events set in motion by Ahmed Shah Durrani's fourth invasion. In the gubernatorial power struggle for the Lahore province, Mughlani Begum, widow of its erstwhile governor, Mir Mannu, sought Durrani's assistance. In return, she promised him the plunder of Delhi and beyond.

Reaching Delhi on 28th January 1757, Durrani's army ravaged and pillaged the city, unleashing unspeakable slaughter which, according to an eyewitness account, 'defies description'.[4] It was the turn of Mathura, Agra, and Vrindavan next. A multitude of Hindu ascetics assembled on the occasion of Holi were brutally done to death and severed heads of cows tied to them in order to abuse their faith. A large number of women were also taken away as slaves. Ahmed Shah himself took to wife Hazrat Begum, the sixteen-year-old daughter of the late emperor, Mohammed Shah, and inducted sixteen other ladies into his royal harem along with 400 attendants. He also married off his son, Taimur, to the daughter of Alamgir II.[5]

When the heat set in, heaps of corpses that now choked the river Yamuna caused pestilence and the outbreak of a cholera epidemic. This expedited Durrani's return to Delhi on 31st March and from there to Kabul soon after on 2nd April. His personal loot carried by some 28000 camels, elephants, mules, bullocks and carts, followed by 200 camel loads of property, and 80,000 horse and foot. The ruthless commandeering of animal transport left not a single horse, camel or donkey in the area. His cavalry too preferred to walk, loading their spoils on their chargers.[6]

Daring Rescue

No sooner was he clear of Delhi than his baggage train began to be plundered by bands of the Dal Khalsa, the attacks continuing all the way up to the Chenab. They cut off his rear, relieved him of much of his haul and rescued many captive women, escorting them back to their homes. Durrani's son, Taimur, was also attacked and robbed but was lucky to escape with his life.[7]

Trilok Singh describes Deep Singh's raid on an Afghan column in some detail.[8] Split into five groups of a hundred each on horseback, each trooper was armed with two swords, a lance, and assorted weapons tucked into their battledress. They posted their scouts atop trees and took positions in the undulating plains forested by kikar (babool) and tahli (North Indian rosewood) between Pipli-Thanesar and the Markanda river, awaiting the enemy.

Behind the escort that led the several miles long cavalcade were the main columns which they let pass, watching undetected from their coign of vantage a safe distance away. When the animals laden with the booty and bullock carts full of women-prisoners hove into view, at a signal from Deep Singh—Halla! (Attack!)—they charged out of their hideouts in two groups. Achieving complete surprise, one group struck at the armed escorts while the other rounded up the bullock carts. At another signal from Deep Singh—Haran! (Flee!)—they drove these off into the wilderness, rescuing some 300 women prisoners in fourteen bullock-carts, and later escorting them back to their homes.[9]

This was their typical 'dhai-phat' tactic perfected over several decades: strike the enemy by surprise, cause maximum damage, disengage as quickly, and avoid personal casualties. However, even in such brief shock action encounters, casualties were unavoidable though the enemy invariably got the worst of it. It was possible to quickly disengage because Afghan troops were forbidden pursuit to avoid dispersal and the thinning of forces, or being baited into an ambush.

Sikh reputation for such daring rescue missions was by now far-fabled and it was not uncommon for captive women to pray:

ਮੇੜੀ ਬਾਬਾ ਕੱਛ ਵਾਲਿਆ ।
ਛਈਂ । ਰੰਨ ਗਈ ਬਸਰੇ ਨੂੰ ਗਈ ।[10]
Morhi Baba kachh valiya.
Chhayin! Rann gayi Basre nu gayi!
Deliver us, O Baba in kachera (drawers)!
Listen! The woman is carried off to Basra!

(NB: women captives from India were sold in the slave markets of Basra in erstwhile Persia).

The Khalsa under the tenth Guru had shed the Indian dhoti for the kachera (drawers), a far more practical item of clothing for the lower body for a life on the move or in saddle.[11] With time, they came to be identified by this article of dress.

Elements of Deep Singh's militia dogged the cavalcade till present day Ambala after which it was the turn of other misaldars. These raids had considerably raised the Shah's dander. On reaching Lahore, he appointed his son Taimur as Viceroy of Lahore, Sirhind, Kashmir, Thatta, and Multan, with his own commander-in-chief, Jahan Khan, as his guardian along with ten thousand elite Afghan troops at his disposal.[12] He was also authorized to raise a separate army of India-born Turki, Irani, and Afghan soldiers, when necessary.[13] Durrani would have personally chastised the Sikhs for their depredations but instead instructed his commanders, he himself having to return due to the oppressive hot weather and some unrest brewing in his disjointed dominions:

ਕਬਿਤ ॥ ਗੁੱਸੇ ਵਿਚ ਅਹਿਮਦ ਸ਼ਾਹ ਨੇ ਸੱਦੇ ਜਰਨੈਲ ਸਾਰੇ,
ਕਹਿੰਦਾ ਹੁਣੈ ਗਾਜ਼ੀਆਂ ਨੂੰ ਹੱਲਾ ਕਰਵਾ ਦਿਓ ।

ਅੰਮ੍ਰਿਤਸਰ ਜਿੱਥੇ ਨਾਹ ਕੇ ਸਿੰਘ ਅਮਰ ਹੁੰਦੇ,
ਪੂਰ ਦਿਓ ਤਾਲ ਉਹਦੇ, ਵਿਚ ਮਿੱਟਟੀ ਪਾ ਦਿਓ ।
ਹਰੀ ਮੰਦਰ ਜਿਥੇ ਸਿੰਘ ਟੇਕਦੇ ਨੇ ਮੱਥਾ ਆ ਕੇ,
ਦੱਬ ਕੇ ਬਰੂਦ ਥੱਲੇ ਉਸਨੂੰ ਉਡਾ ਦਿਓ ।
ਅੜੇ ਨਹੀਂ ਸਿੰਘ ਕੋਈ ਫੇਰ ਮੇਰੇ ਅੱਗੇ ਆ ਕੇ,
ਮਾਰ ਮਾਰ ਸਾਰੇ ਹੀ ਪੰਜਾਬ ਚੋਂ ਭਜਾ ਦਿਓ ।

—Gurcharan Singh Gohalwar,
Prasang Lalkar Sahib[14]

Gusse vich Ahmed Shah ne sadde jarnail sare,
Kahenda hunein gajian nu halla kerwa deyo.
Amritsar jithe naha ke Singh amar hunde,
Poor diyo taal uhde, vich mitti pa diyo.
Hari Mandir jithe Singh tekde ne mathha a ke,
Dab ke barood thale usnu uda deyo.
Ade nahin Singh koyi pher mere agge a ke,
Mar mar sare hi Panjab chon bhaja diyo.
Ahmed Shah his Generals then did call:
Proclaimed among the people one and all.
Blow up the Singh's Harimandir in strife.
Fill their tank which gives eternal life.
How dare the Singhs incite me, he did roar—
Now kill and banish them forevermore.

Jahan Khan did exactly as enjoined by his monarch. He drove the Sikhs out into the Himalayan tracts and the deserts of Malwa. He also sent a large expeditionary force to Amritsar on 1st May 1757 that plundered the city, demolished the Sikh fort of Ram Rauni (near Ramsar) and the Sikh temple, filling its holy tank with debris.[15] The view that Gurbaksh Singh Shaheed, Deep Singh's companion, was then in-charge of the Amritsar shrine and was killed along with thirty of his men when the temple was stormed is not supported by evidence.[16] Gurbaksh Singh was then located at Anandgarh as head of that branch of the Shaheed misl, and would mobilize much later in November 1757.

This provocation, nevertheless, set the scene for Deep Singh's iconic last battle. The grave news would have taken a week or more to travel some 280 kilometres to Talwandi Sabo. The messenger, Bhag Singh Nihang, was ushered into the presence of Deep Singh who sat ensconced in routine congregation.[17] Hardly had he unburdened his tidings when there was a general outrage and a call by one and all for immediate revenge.

'Let us mobilize at once with as many men we can muster!' thundered many of his senior jathedars in one voice.

Deep Singh too was inflamed by the news and would very likely have ordered quick retaliation but after a brief discussion it was plain to all that, given their circumstances, discretion and delay were advisable. One, with the increase in hostilities, the Sikhs were now on the run, dispersed far and wide, rendering any retaliatory action in sizeable strength implausible. Two, Diwali was an important festival in November when Sikhs congregated at Amritsar in large numbers. To coincide his response with this festival seemed a better idea.

There was also a strategic factor that would confine this retributive action to Deep Singh alone. The armed reprisal he planned was alien to the guerrilla tactics of the Dal Khalsa which bade them eschew pitched or positional battles. As a consequence, no federative action could be expected from the other misls because there would be no dhai phat—no disengagement and flight. Only a steady advance to their shrine in Amritsar, against impossible odds.

Meanwhile, Deep Singh continued to discharge key panthic responsibilities. On the behest of Ala Singh of Patiala, who was under the combined threat from Mohammed Amin Khan Bhatti of Rania and the Governor of Sirhind, Deep Singh sallied forth, leading the Dal Khalsa in September 1757 as the critical countervailing force. The Sikhs brought the fierce three-day battle fought at Dharsul near Rampura to a close by delivering the coup-de-grace overnight, forcing the Afghans to flee with great loss of life. In gratitude, a beholden Ala Singh elected to be baptized by the venerable Deep Singh for a second time.[18]

TEN

Taking Up the Gauntlet

Call to Arms

ਗਗਨ ਦਮਾਮਾ ਬਾਜਿਓ ਪਰਿਓ ਨੀਸਾਨੈ ਘਾਉ ॥
ਖੇਤੁ ਜੁ ਮਾਂਡਿਓ ਸੂਰਮਾ ਅਬ ਜੂਝਨ ਕੋ ਦਾਉ ॥੧॥
ਸੂਰਾ ਸੋ ਪਹਿਚਾਨੀਐ ਜੁ ਲਰੈ ਦੀਨ ਕੇ ਹੇਤ ॥
ਪੁਰਜਾ ਪੁਰਜਾ ਕਟਿ ਮਰੈ ਕਬਹੂ ਨ ਛਾਡੈ ਖੇਤੁ ॥੨॥੨॥

—Kabir,
Sri Guru Granth Sahib, 1105

Gagan ḍamāmā bājiºo pariºo nīsānai ghāºo.
Khet jo māṅdiºo sūrmā ab jūjhan ko ḍāºo. ||1||
Sūrā so pahichānīºai jo larai ḍīn ke het.
Purjā purjā kat marai kabhū na chhāḍai khet. ||2||2||
Battle drums across the sky resound,
Aligned now weapons are, and wounds abound.
O Warrior rise, now take the field—it's time to fight!
To prove to all that Right is Might
True heroes go to war when cause is just;
Never flee, though torn to pieces in the dust.

Having decided for the moment to bide his time, Deep Singh widely disseminated his message in the region for Sikhs to celebrate Diwali at Amritsar. There were few who did not comprehend the solemnity of the motive and yet his call to arms was readily answered by many willing to take up the gauntlet at the peril of their lives to avenge so grievous an insult to their creed.

The day of Dusherra, 22nd October, that marked the onset of the Diwali season, was fixed for mobilization.[1] Perhaps, this was particularly apt because in Indian culture, the day is celebrated for the victory of good over evil. Congregational prayers were held marking the culmination of an Akhand Path to seek divine inspiration and strength. In a special ceremony, they tied the shaheedi gana on their wrists—sacred thread that symbolized resolve to fight to the finish:

ਸੁਨਿ ਸਿੰਘ ਪਾਠ-ਅਖੰਡ ਕਰਾਯੋ ।
ਹਮਨ ਕਰਯੋ ਕੰਗਨਾ ਬੰਧਵਾਯੋ ।
ਕਹਯੋ ਸਭਾ ਮੈਂ ਸਿਰ ਜੋ ਦੇ ਹੈ ।
ਸੰਗ ਹਮਾਰੇ ਸੋ ਅਬਿ ਬੈਹੋ ॥ ੧੩ ॥

—Gyani Gyan Singh, *Panth Prakash*,
Utraradh Bisram 50, Stanza 13

Sun Singh path-akhand karayo
Haman karyo kangna bandhwayo
Kahyo sabha meinsir jo dey hai
Sang hamarey so ab jahai
Akhand-patth was there performed,
Havan, and shaheedi-gana tied.
Announced he then among them all.
Only those he now did call.
who'd fight on till the bitter end,
only those he did now recommend.

They donned saffron, anointing and spraying themselves with saffron water in the tradition of Indian warriors riding out to an honorable death in battle. These lines were added to the Sikh supplicatory prayer (ardas) on the occasion:[2]

ਸ੍ਰੀ ਅੰਮ੍ਰਿਤਸਰ ਜੀ ਦੇ ਇਸ਼ਨਾਨ, ਚੋਕੀਆਂ, ਝੰਡੇ, ਬੁੰਗੇ, ਜੁਗੋ ਜੁਗ ਅਟੱਲ, ਧਰਮ ਕਾ ਜੈਕਾਰ ।
Sri Amritsar ji de ishnan; Chounkiyaa Jhande Bunge Jugo Jug Attal, Dharam Ka Jai Kaar.
Bathing in the holy waters of Sri Amritsar. O God! May thy congregations, mansions and the banners flourish forever. May Truth ever prevail.

Deep Singh addressed the assembly, lauding their mission and exhorting them to the sacralized battle that lay ahead. Most of those assembled owed allegiance to the Shaheed misl but the cause also found resonance among many others who now came forth from nearby villages such as Jage Ram Tirath, Gurusar, and Bahman.[3]

Their departure was grim because most knew they may never return. Their heads were, nevertheless, held high with a sense of honour in having chosen the path of the warrior-saint to be martyred in the fight for justice. Deep Singh sought to hand over charge of the seminary to the aged Naudh Singh, senior-most at ninety-five years, but the spirited warrior would have none of that and opted to mobilize with the rest. The charge was then handed over to Natha Singh, Deep Singh's nephew.[4]

They set off from Talwandi with a strength variously estimated from five hundred to a 2000 plus. According to Gyani Gyan Singh, of the 5000 who assembled, only 2000 were mobilized. Given the atypical circumstances, a substantial strength of the Shaheed misl needed to be retained as a necessary expedient.[5] While the misl core would provide the leavening, they counted on drawing more volunteers en route.

ਦੇਹਰਾ । ਅੰਮ੍ਰਿਤਸਰ ਵੱਲ ਕੀਤੀ ਧਾਈ, ਰਸਤੇ ਵਿਚ ਇਹ ਸਦ ਸੁਣਾਈ ।
ਜਿਨ ਜਿਨ ਹੋਣਾ ਹੋਇ ਸ਼ਹੀਦ, ਕਲਗੀਧਰ ਦੇ ਪ੍ਰੇਮ ਮੁਰੀਦ ।
ਨਾਲ ਅਸਾਡੇ ਚਲਿਆ ਆਵੇ, ਧਰਮ ਹੇਤ ਸਿਰ ਭੇਟ ਚੜਾਵੇ ।

—Lala Dhani Ram Chatrik,
Prasang Baba Deep Singh[6]

Dohra. Amritsar val kiti dhayi,, raste vich eh sad sunai
Jin jin hona hoi shaheed, kalgidhar de prem murid.
Naal asade chaliya aawe, dharam het sir bhet chadave.
He set off for Amritsar then,
en route he called to all brave men:
in true Lord's name who'd martyred be
To save their faith and set land free.

The distance of some 160 kilometres from Talwandi to Tarn Taran, their rendezvous, took them about eighteen days to traverse. Their first halt was Lakhi Jungle located within dense kandiari forests overgrown with Jand (Prosopis cineraria), Karir (Capparis decidua), Phalahi (Acacia Modesta) and other such trees that thrive in arid soil. Guru Nanak was the first of the Sikh preceptors to visit the area where he held counsel with Lakhi fakir, hence the place name. He is also credited with creating a water source near the present day Gurdwara. This perennial water supply would help develop the area into an important Sikh center-cum-hideout. Guru Hargobind and Guru Har Rai also visited the area before the tenth Guru himself, who is known to have held a kavi darbar during his brief sojourn on his way to Talwandi Sabo in January 1706.[7] The jungle has since given way to the march of intensive cultivation.

Deep Singh halted for a few days in the security of the forest, sending word to several loyalist villages around:

- Nehianwala: the largest settlement in the area close to Lakhi Jungle
- Gobindpura: a village associated with and named after the tenth Guru subsequent to his visit
- Bhuchu: long associated with Sikhism; first visited by Guru Nanak and by several other Sikh Gurus thereafter.
- Mehraj and Daraj: men from these villages had fought alongside the Sixth Guru in the Battle of Gurusar in the vicinity.[8]

Deep Singh resumed his march with an additional 500-1000 volunteers.[9] There were several halts on the way for respite as much as to rally fighting men to their cause. When they reached the ferry over the Beas at Harike Pattan, it was deemed expedient to split into smaller groups to avoid alerting the Mughal administration. For this reason, some groups made the river-crossing via as far as Khemkaran. More armed volunteers from the Majha joined at Tarn Taran Sahib where they all paid obeisance, bathed and washed their hair in the holy tank of the historic gurdwara that stands in memory of Guru Arjan Dev (fifth preceptor) who had established this settlement a century and a half before.[10]

Courage and Resolve

The army of volunteers had by now swelled to about 5000, predominantly horsed. On the morning of 11th November, the day of Diwali, Deep Singh led this force to a small thicket nearby where he briefly addressed them. In a bid to steel their resolve, he sketched a line in the ground with his broadsword and in inspirational tones, dared only those prepared for the supreme sacrifice to step across (see ser 9 in Appendix A). Popular lore suggests that not a single man turned away. A commemorative shrine, Lakeer Sahib ('Lakeer' means 'line') stands at the spot (see Figures 6 and 7).

The event carries elemental echoes of the founding of the Khalsa. Never before or after have Sikhs been so expressly tested for the principal values that the tenth Master, Deep Singh's mentor, had sought to inculcate in them by precept and example:

'Are you prepared to wage war in your fight for justice?[11] And, if called upon, are you willing to die in the cause?'[12]

Deep Singh also foreswore to live and fight till he reached Sudhasar ('sudha' means 'amrit' and 'sar' is 'lake', hence 'Amritsar') or Harimandir Sahib (Chak Guru), as some writers claim. Balladeers and commentators often compare Deep Singh favorably with Arjuna in Hindu mythology who vowed to kill Jaydaratha before sunset to avenge the death of his son, Abhimanyu. If unsuccessful, he swore to commit suicide. In contrast, Deep Singh pledged his singular resolve to live on until he reached his objective

His enduring appeal, nay, deification rests largely upon the fact that later in the day, when he would collapse from a mortal wound in the neck, he would rise again when reminded of this oath and in a feat that has no parallel, battle on till his objective. Some panegyrics ascribe these quotes to him at this juncture:

ਕਬੀਰ ਮੁਹਿ ਮਰਨੇ ਕਾ ਚਾਉ ਹੈ ਮਰਉ ਤ ਹਰਿ ਕੈ ਦੁਆਰ ॥

—*Sri Guru Granth Sahib*,
p. 1367, line 13

Kabīr muhi marne kā c̲h̲āo hai marao t̲a har kai d̲uār.
Kabir, I long to die but let this be at the Lord's Door.

ਮਰਨੇ ਮਰਨੁ ਕਹੈ ਸਭੁ ਕੋਈ ॥
ਸਹਜੇ ਮਰੈ ਅਮਰੁ ਹੋਇ ਸੋਈ ॥੨॥

—*Sri Guru Granth Sahib*,
p. 327, line 15

Marno maran kahai sab̲h̲ ko.
Sehje marai amar hoe soi. ॥2॥
Everyone says, 'I will die, I will die'.
But he alone becomes immortal,
who dies for a premeditated, noble cause. ॥2॥

Deep Singh's address fully braced his body of men, already resolute in their mission, to fight with no thought of retreat:

ਉਸ ਆਖਿਆ ਬੀਰ ਬਹਾਦਰੋ ਕਰ ਲਵੋ ਤਿਆਰਾ।
ਅੱਜ ਪੀਓ ਸ਼ਹੀਦੀ ਜਾਮ ਨੂੰ ਆ ਜਾਏ ਨਜਾਰਾ।
ਉਸ ਆਖਿਆ ਕਲਗੀ ਵਾਲਿਆ ਇਕ ਤੇਰਾ ਸਹਾਰਾ।
ਅੱਜ ਅਮ੍ਰਿਤ ਸ਼ਕਤੀ 'ਦਿਲਬਰਾ' ਵੇਖੁ ਜੱਗ ਸਾਰਾ।

—Daya Singh Dilbar,
Vaar Baba Deep Singh ji Shaheed[13]

us akhya bir bahaduro kar lavo tyara.
aj piyo shaheedi jam nu a jaye nazara.
us akhya kalgi valiya ik tera sahara.
aj amrit shakti dilbara vekhu jag sara.
Inspired all with apt advice:
'Be ready now for sacrifice!
O Lord, do lend Thy helping hand
To bless the Khalsa firebrand!'

ਮੁੜਨਾ ਖਾਲਸਾ ਜੀ ਅੱਜ ਪਿੱਛਾਂਹ ਨਹੀਂ ਜਦ ਤਕ ਰਹਿਸੀ ਸਾਡੇ ਜਾਨ ਅੰਦਰ ।
ਫਤਿਹ ਪਾਈ ਤਾਂ ਖੁਸ਼ੀਆਂ ਗੁਰੂ ਦੀਆਂ ਜੁਝ ਗਏ ਜੇ ਪਾਏ ਘਮਸਾਨ ਅੰਦਰ ।
—Kartar Singh Kalasvlia,
Jauhar Khalsa[14]

Murhna Khalsa ji aj picchan nahin jad tak rahisi sade jan ander.
Fateh payi tan khushian guru dian jujh gaye je paye ghamsan ander.
Retreat we'll not till we have breath.
Triumphant bliss, or honour in death.

It is a less known secret among veteran military commanders that a soldier is truly ready for battle only when he crosses this mental rubicon, once inspired with a do-or-die spirit.

There is an interesting parallel in an incident almost a century later, on 5th March 1836, on the other side of the globe at Alamo, Texas, when Lt Col William Travis drew a line in the ground and offered a choice to the members of his besieged garrison to leave. All but one chose to stay. They were almost killed to a man the following day when their redoubt was stormed by the Mexican army under General Santa Anna.[15]

Advance to Contact

The Shaheed jathedars and their men provided the leavening for the force that was now grouped into jathas, each led by a Jathedar—Naudh Singh, Balwant Singh, Dyal Singh, Hira Singh, Ganda Singh, Lehna Singh, Ran Singh, Gopal Singh, Bhag Singh, Sajan Singh, Bahadur Singh, under Deep Singh, then seventy-five years of age, their sainapat (commander-in-chief), in the forefront (see ser 10 in Appendix A).[16] Balladeers record their starting point as Tarn Taran:

ਤਰਨ ਤਾਰਨੋਂ ਗੁਰ ਤੇ ਦਰ ਤੋਂ, ਅਜ ਤੁਰਿਆ ਪ੍ਰਨ ਕਰ ਕੇ ।
ਅੰਮ੍ਰਿਤਸਰ ਅਜ਼ਾਦ ਕਰਾਨਾ, ਸੀਸ ਤਲੀ ਤੇ ਧਰ ਕੇ ।
—Mahinder Murti, *Teg de Dhani*[17]

Tarn Tarnon gur dey dar ton, aj turiye pran kar key
Amritsar azad karana, sees tali tey dhar key.

From the hallowed portals of Tarn Taran,
he sallied forth with vow,
to free the Amritsar temple with his head on palm somehow.

Undaunted by the odds, their sacred mission bolstered their morale. They seemed to be setting out to wed a fair bride—metaphorically, Death in their case.

ਸਬਿ ਕੇ ਮਨ ਮੈਂ ਅਤਿ ਉਤਸ਼ਾਰੈਂ ।
ਮਨੋ ਬਰਾਤ ਜੁੜੀ ਹਿਤ ਬਜਾਹੈਂ ।
ਅਸੂ ਕੁਦਾਵਤ ਜਾਵਤ ਅਧਿਕੈਂ ।
ਮਨੋ ਢੁਕਾਉ ਕਰਤ ਬਧ ਬਧ ਕੈ

—Gyani Gyan Singh, *Gur Panth Prakash II*, Utraradh Bisram 50

sab ke men mein at utsahein
mano baraat juri hit byahein
asve kudavat javat adhkein
mano dhakau karat badh badh kei ||21||

Their spirits soared up in the air
As if to wed a bride so fair;
On prancing mounts to in-laws went;
Their armor lightning flashes glent

Popular lore recounts a brief exchange between Deep Singh and his cousin, Naudh Singh, a senior Jathedar then ninety-five years of age. As a concession to his advanced years, Deep Singh suggested:

'Naudh Singh ji, keep to the flanks where the enemy is thinnest.'

In chivalrous defiance, Naudh Singh roared back his resolve, 'Nay, I shall fight where the enemy is thickest!'

Naudh Singh would lay down his life later that day much as he wished. His memorial shrine stands prominently at Chabba, his place of martyrdom on a state highway south of Amritsar, a spot of extraordinary inter-faith reverence where a langar runs 24x7.[18]

Seetal records other prominent members of this force: Sudha Singh, Ram Singh, Bir Singh, Hari Singh, Hari Basant, Hari Balwant, Mahtab Singh, Nihal Singh, Sur Singh, Bal Singh, Manna Singh, Kang Singh, Natha Singh, Nahar Singh, Tara Singh, Hari Gopal, Aghar Singh, Ram Hari, Kaur Singh, Lehna Singh, Hari Akali. Other sources cite more names: Gurdyal Singh, Dharam Singh, Santokh Singh, Harcharan Singh, Arur Singh, Didar Singh. Dev Singh. The inclusion of Sahajdhari Sikhs (without the 'Singh' suffix) in the volunteer force is notable.[19]

The Sikh army now moved out in battle formation towards their objective, Amritsar (see ser 11 in Appendix A).

ELEVEN

The Face Off

> To every man upon this earth
> Death cometh soon or late.
> And how can man die better
> Than facing fearful odds,
> For the ashes of his fathers,
> And the temples of his gods
>
> —Thomas Babington Macaulay
> *Lays of Ancient Rome*

An Eyewitness Account

Meanwhile, intelligence reports had alerted the Lahore garrison. Jahan Khan, the Afghan commander-in-chief, had declared jihad, a stratagem that seldom failed to rally Muslims for a common cause against kafirs (infidels). Documented history by Miskin, who took part in the battle, has survived as an important eyewitness account of this one-day battle:[1]

> **Jahan Khan's Operations against the Sikhs (November 1757)**
>
> 'One day, intelligence was received that a large body of Sikhs had assembled at Chak Guru [Harimandir Sahib, Amritsar] for a religious bath and were causing tumult and violence. The Viceroy's troops under Haji Atai Khan were out in the neighborhood for subduing the country, settling matters and chastising the Sikhs. The wazir wrote a letter to Sardar Haji Atai Khan informing him about the disturbances and asked him to reach the Chak by a quick march with all his troops

on a certain day promising that he also would arrive at the appointed time in order to destroy the Sikhs.

'Thereafter, the Wazir proclaimed *Ailaan Nama* ('general proclamation') throughout Lahore, asking all able-bodied men to join him in the *jihad* ('war against enemies of Islam') to fight the Sikhs. He also sent a message to Muglani Begum asking her to send as many horsemen she could spare (along with the author). She immediately gathered a force of twenty-five horsemen and dispatched them under me (the author) and one Kasim Khan. We joined the Wazir's army of 2000 horse at Lahore Cantonment and moved out to Sarai Khan, a distance of six kos by nightfall [one kos was approximately two miles, or 3.2 kilometres, making a total of nineteen kilometres, although the distance is actually approx thirty kilometres].

'Next morning, we marched to a place two kos [approx. 6.4 kilometres] on this side of the Chak Guru (village Gohalwar, five miles South of Amritsar), and were surprised to note that, despite strict instructions, Haji Attai Khan had not reached this designated rendezvous.

'As soon as the Sikhs learned of our arrival, they attacked us from all four sides. A fierce battle ensued and the opposing forces showered fire upon each other, using all available weaponry. The Sikhs seemed to have surrounded us in a tight noose that they now sought to tighten. Our force came under such pressure that many of our soldiers tried to desert but were unable to because we were completely surrounded.

'The Wazir was a brave man and fought off the enemy with great vigour. At this juncture, I was by his side along with a body of ten horse and saw the Wazir wound several of his own men with his sword who were trying to flee so that he could deter others.

'Despite being completely surrounded, we did not break our defensive formation and kept up the fight. Soon we began to run out of supplies. It was then that I showed great courage which, if I describe with my own pen, I will not be believed.

'At this point Haji Attai Khan arrived with a huge army to turn the tide of the battle. Although the Sikhs took great pride in their valour, it was now their turn to be put to the sword, or to be blown up by our cannons.

'They were defeated and took to flight towards Chak Guru but we pursued them all the way. On reaching the walled enclosure of Chak Guru, we saw five Sikh infantrymen at the gate who were all killed by our soldiers. Here, even Mir Niamtullah, a respected citizen of Lahore, was killed.

The battle over, our army set up camp near Chak Guru.'

As the only eye-witness account of the battle, it is invaluable for its authenticity. Yet, Miskin was then only a young lad of nineteen (born 1738) and as an ordinary soldier, cannot have been privy to all the intelligence reports and such other aspects as operational planning, strategic overview and the order of battle (ORBAT).[2] His record of the encounter per se would also have been physically limited by his own immediate experience. For instance, he admits of only one killed-in-action from his army whereas popular opinion puts their casualties at about a thousand. The account also warrants careful analysis and logical inferencing since of his own admission, he penned his memoirs essentially from memory over nine months in 1780, twenty-three years after the battle.[3]

Although the Sikhs had exercised sufficient caution by moving in small groups to maintain surprise, their assembling in large numbers at Tarn Taran, their rendezvous, would likely have alerted the administration, giving Jahan Khan time to plan the interception. That he proclaimed jihad and succeeded in mustering many able-bodied citizens to his cause is borne out in Miskin's memoir that records the presence (and death) of Mir Niamtullah, 'a respected citizen', in battle. Jahan Khan also chose to personally lead his troops, a clear indication that his command included many more troops in addition to the 2000 cavalry recorded by Miskin. Possibly, he mobilized whatever force he could muster in the short time available on 10th November but left instructions for more troops to join the following morning, which they did in general area Chabba:

> ਤਬੈ ਪਠਾਨ ਗੌਰ ਹੋਰ, ਆ ਗਏ ਲਾਹੌਰ ਤੇ ।
> ਅਮਾਨ ਖਾਨ ਯਾਕੂਬ ਖਾਨ, ਆਏ ਸਰਦਾਰ ਔਰ ਥੋ ॥੩੬॥
> —Gyani Gyan Singh, *Panth Prakash*, Utraradh Bisram 50[4]
>
> *Tabai pathan gaur hor, a gaye Lahore te ।*
> *Aman Khan Yakub Khan, aye Sardar aur the ।*
> More Pathans arrived from Lahore just then;
> Aman Khan, Yakub Khan, more Sardars ('commanders') with men.

Miskin also mentions the presence of artillery while the 'huge army' under Haji Attai Khan is left unquantified. On appointing his son Taimur as Governor, Durrani had positioned 10,000 elite Afghan troops under his own commander-in-chief, Jahan Khan, who very likely mobilized a large proportion of these.[5] A fairer estimate of his force would be in the range of 8,000-10,000, with a balance of cavalry (horsed and war-elephants), infantry and artillery, including approximately 3000-4000 in the task force-roving patrol under Haji Attai Khan. Gyani Gyan Singh, the first writer to record the battle in some detail in his *Twarikh* (1890) puts the strength of Jahan Khan's army at 8000.[6]

Miskin mentions an intelligence report about a 'lot of Sikhs' who had gathered at Chak Guru (Amritsar) to bathe in its holy sarovar, and that Haji Attai Khan was already out on a search and destroy mission. Firstly, that Sikhs should bathe in Chak Guru seems to contravene the historical fact of its having been filled with debris in May, earlier that year. It is, nonetheless, possible that the sarovar may have been partially cleared and restored by devotees enough to allow bathing, particularly since the shrine was once again under their charge—evidenced by the five Sikh 'infantrymen' who appeared at the gate. It was also customary for Sikhs to visit and bathe at the shrine on both Vaisakhi and Diwali, and Miskin's report refers to a period a few days prior to Diwali.

Secondly, this intelligence report alone could not justify the jihad and general mobilization ordered by Jahan Khan, neither that he personally led his army nor that he should head in the direction of Goharwal, due south of Amritsar rather than Chak Guru (Amritsar) itself. It is likely that due to his limited window on operational intelligence and planning, Miskin was not aware of another far more serious intelligence report that warned of a large Sikh army at Tarn Taran, with intent to march upon Amritsar. Only this would explain both the general mobilization of troops under personal command of Jahan Khan and their move to Goharwal, five miles south of Amritsar to intercept the Sikh army.

In contrast, the Sikhs were set upon celebrating Diwali at Chak Guru. Since they had no plans to move by stealth nor outmaneuver or outflank the enemy, in military terms, their objective translated into pitched battle. Their morale combined with the overwhelming conviction of their *jus ad bellum* (right to go to war) gave them considerable moral ascendancy, always key in battle. Add to this their desperate courage which invariably makes for a formidable army, ready to spurn fate and scorn death.

Mobilization

Watchful of surprise, Jahan Khan mobilized on 10th November 1757 from Lahore to move thirty kilometres to Sarai Amanat Khan by nightfall. After a night halt, he rode out early the following morning some seventeen kilometres to Gohalwar, deployed and prepared hasty defences, and lay in wait:

ਚਾਰ ਕੋਹ ਅੱਗੇ ਸੁਧਾ ਸਰੋਂ ਜਾ ਕੇ ਬੈਠਾ ਮੋਰਚੇ ਮੱਲ ਹੁਸ਼ਿਆਰ ਜਲਦੀ ।
—Kartar Singh Kalasvalia, *Jauhar Khalsa*[7]

Char koh agge Sudha saron ja ke baitha morche mal hoshiyar jaldi.
Four kos [eight miles] ahead of Sudharsar [Harimandir Sahib], cleverly [Jahan Khan] waited in entrenchments.

The Sikhs had their informers too. They were conveyed reports of the jihad proclaimed at Lahore, the subsequent mobilization and possibly, of the Afghan dispositions at Gohalwar that morning. Resolute in their mission dearer to them than their life, they were nevertheless undaunted, choosing to confront rather than

Figure 6: Deep Singh inspires his men before battle.
(Source: The Sikh Magazine, https://www.panthic.org/articles/2621)

Figure 7: Gurdwara Lakeer Sahib, Fateh Chak, Tarn Taran, marks the place where Deep Singh drew a line in the ground before battle and bade those prepared for the supreme sacrifice to step across.
(Photo courtesy of the author)

Figure 8: The Shaheed Bunga is located within the premises of Harimandir Sahib and enshrines the Guru Granth Sahib, the only Bunga besides the Akal Takht to do so.
(Photo courtesy of the author)

Figure 9: The Golden Temple, or Harimandir Sahib, Amritsar—literally, the abode of God.
(Source: Golden Temple Tour: http://www.sikhtours.in/golden_temple.php)

Figure 10: Tharra Sahib obelisk adjoining Manji Sahib and Guru-ka-Bagh in the periphery of the Golden Temple marks the place of cremation of 'some' of those killed in the battle; clarified butter 'jyot' (eternal flame) sits atop the pedestal.
(Photo courtesy of the author)

Figure 11: The obelisk plaque carries nine names of 'some' of those killed in battle.
(Photo courtesy of the author)

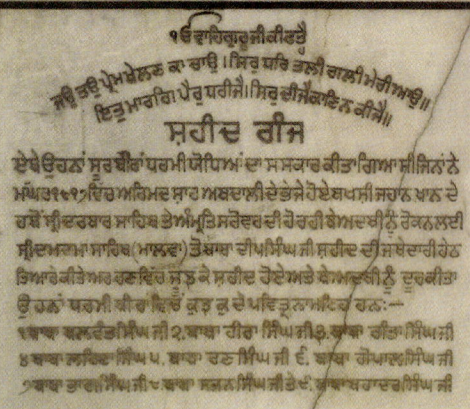

Figure 12: Deep Singh as depicted in popular colour prints.
(Source: SikhNet, https://www.sikhnet.com/news/baba-deep-singh-great-warrior-and-scholar-sikhism)

Figure 13: Gurdwara Shaheedganj, Amritsar, marks the place where Deep Singh was cremated along with some of his comrades-in-arms. The octagonal sanctum is designed as a samadh (cenotaph). It includes an original oil-on-canvas of Deep Singh by the famous Sikh artist, Sobha Singh, installed in 1976.
(Photo courtesy of the author)

Figure 14: Above: Gurudwara Lalkar Sahib, Gohalwar, marks the place where the ener was sighted and the Sikh army challenged them to battle. *(Photo courtesy of the auth*

Figure 15: Gurdwara Tahla Sahib, Chabba, marks the place where Deep Singh believed to have been decapitated in a duel with an Afghan general, and from whe he fought on, regardless, up to Amritsar. *(Photo courtesy the author)*

circumvent the enemy. In effect, neither army was surprised when they faced off at Gohalwar on the morning of 11th November.

Force Levels

- **Sikhs:** Gyani Gyan Singh estimates their strength at five thousand sowar (cavalry).[8] Other historians generally concur and describe them as a 'handful' of some 5000 peasants with assorted arms (hatchets, swords, and spears),[9] and a few guns—Deep Singh's muzzle-loading pistol is preserved in Akal Takth. According to local sources at the erstwhile battlefield, some Sikhs carried just 'swords in broken scabbards, parched gram tied in a knot as ration, and were "bhhukke dhiyae"' (starved and thirsty).[10] Ironically, some carried only a paihli (staff) as their primary weapon,[11] although this could be deadly in the hands of those trained in the Sikh martial art of Gatka (swordplay). Bhai Bota Singh and his manservant, Garja Singh, armed with just a staff each in 1739, had together felled about twenty soldiers of the one hundred sent against them before being overwhelmed. Nonetheless, the temerity of taking the field equipped with just a staff against a regular army warrants admiration.

- **Lahore Army:** Approximately 10,000 under Jahan Khan, Governor of Lahore, who proclaimed 'Jehad'; large number of war-elephants, archers, lancers; infantry, cavalry and artillery. Miskin does not specify the 'cannons', which could range from heavy to light because the Afghans had a huge array of artillery. In all probability, these were one-two pounder light artillery mobile guns such as the 'camel guns' (Shutarnal) or 'swivel guns' (Zamburak), lethal weapons of the 18th century that combined the mobility of the camel with the flexibility and heavy firepower of the swivel gun. These were key to Afghan artillery and could deliver a devastating volley when massed. However, artillery was available only in Phase 2 and 3 of the battle, and not in Phase 1 because, going by Miskin's account, Haji Attai Khan, whose force included elements of artillery, failed to report at the rendezvous on time. The artillery may also have been inducted along with the reinforcements in Phase 2.

War Aims
- **Sikhs:** evict invaders from Harimandir Sahib and bathe in the sarovar on the occasion of Diwali. As followers of Gobind and under the inspiring leadership of Deep Singh, the Sikhs had committed themselves to unsheathe the sword to fight the unjust desecration of their most sacred shrine.
- **Lahore Army:** Intercept Sikhs to thwart their aims and destroy them.

Deployment and Tactics
- **Sikhs:** Taking a leaf out of Jomini's book,[12] the Sikhs opened the battle by throwing the mass of their force upon the decisive point—the enemy command and control center. They effected a breakthrough but after the enemy rallied, they fanned out and were forced to fight pitched battles in penny packets, under respective jathedars over a frontage of some five kilometres, as evidenced from the spread of cenotaphs. The enemy, in turn, tried desperately to maneuver and mass them in order to bring down their artillery effectively but were only partially successful. Unmindful of the high attrition, the Sikhs continued to advance steadily to their objective, powered by their iron will which according to Clausewitz, the famous military theorist, can overcome all 'friction' and pulverize every obstacle.[13] This enabled many to reach their objective, fighting through the mass of the enemy and afflicting casualties to the very end.
- **Lahore Army:** defensive entrenchments at Gohalwar, seven kilometres north of Tarn Taran, with possibly a second line of defence at Chabba, four kilometres in depth, plus a roving mobile reserve, patrol or task force under Haji Attai Khan. Although unbalanced by the audacious Sikh cavalry

charge at Gohalwar, they rallied under their veteran military commander to deftly outmaneuver the Sikhs and take the offensive. Their element of artillery joined the battle later, possibly as part of reinforcements. When the Sikhs dispersed in response, the Afghans sought to mass them together in order to use their cannons but were not fully successful. Once reinforced by Haji Attai Khan, the enemy caught the Sikhs in a pincer movement, putting them to flight. To their credit, the Sikhs fled not away from the battlefield but out of range of enemy cannons and heroically towards their objective, Harimandir Sahib.

Phases of the Battle

Miskin's eyewitness jottings are a useful summary that need fleshing out with the help of Sikh accounts once their hagiographic elements are discounted. Coupled with field research, these accounts help to vividly bring alive the phases, manner, and face of this sanguinary conflict. The cluster of cenotaphs that dot the erstwhile battlefields convey with grim eloquence the areas of fierce contest and high casualties, roughly suggesting three phases in the one-day conflict (see Figures 4 and 5).

- **Phase 1 (Sikh Attack and Breakthrough):** First to attack at Goharwal, the Sikhs wrested the initiative, targeting the enemy command and control center and putting the Afghan troops to flight. The enemy commander was hard put to rally his soldiers while the Sikhs achieved a breakthrough and then broke out, making a tactical dash for their objective, Amritsar.
- **Phase 2 (The Chabba-Chatiwind Battle):** After breaking-out, the Sikhs soon reached Chabba, about four kilometres towards Amritsar almost with their full strength in tact where they now encountered stiff opposition, possibly with the arrival of reinforcements from Lahore. Intense fighting resumed. The enemy was now able to use cannon, while in response, the Sikhs dispersed over a frontage of some five kilometres, from village Mehma to Chabba, and fought under their

respective jathedars. Although suffering high attrition, they broke through and out yet again, bearing on to their objective.
- **Phase 3 (Ramsar and Beyond):** After a gap of some five kilometres, the Sikhs were caught in a pincer movement between Jahan Khan in hot pursuit, and fresh reinforcements under Haji Atai Khan, culminating in desperate close combat on the outskirts of Amritsar (Ramsar) right up to the Sikh objective, Harimandir Sahib. Sikh casualties were high but the Lahore army also suffered losses.

Terrain

In 1757, much before the extension of the Bari Doab Canal after British annexation in 1849, the cis-Ravi part of Lahore Majha was in its 'natural condition... [presenting] an almost uniformly level surface with hardly any variety of feature from end *to* end.... [with] little natural growth of any sort... [and was] sparsely populated.'[14] Sweet water wells were, however, beginning to be sunk. Generally, out of a total well area of twenty-eight acres, only between four and five acres would be sown for the kharif harvest and about twenty-two acres for the rabi because less time was available for land preparation in the summer. The kharif area would be distributed roughly among maize, cotton, sugarcane, rice, and fodder.[15]

In November at the time of the battle, only sugarcane, cotton, and fodder would have been still standing on the farmland such as there was with maize and rice already harvested. The general area would also have been dotted with the occasional kikar (Acacia arabica), ber (wild plum), and tut (mulberry). Trees that require planting such as pipal (ficus religious), bohar (ficus indica) and bakain or dhrek (Melia azadirachta) would have been fewer,[16] although oral tradition records a sheesham (North Indian Rosewood) thicket near village Chabba that served as an enemy strongpoint. Sparse low shrubbery comprising karil (Capparis aphylla), jand (Prosopis spicigera), wan (Salvadora oleordes) and mulla (Zizyphus nummularia) would have lent the landscape a somewhat green aspect amid the arid patches of brown.

The low brush by and large afforded clear fields of observation and fire. While it could hamper the swift move of massed cavalry, it posed less impediment for elephant-mounted troops. The area was devoid of any natural obstacles for use in defence but the loamy soil was conducive to digging entrenchments. Several prominent tracks allowed unhindered move of animal transport—Tarn Taran to Amritsar; Amritsar to Lahore; Lahore to Sarai Amanat Khan and Tarn Taran.

Phase 1 and 2 of the battle were fought in the vicinity of villages—Gohalwar, Chabba, Chatiwind, Varpal, Vanchari, and Mehna, stretching up to Sultanwind—each of which then were probably a cluster of one-two score houses. According to local information, Sultanwind and Chatiwind are sister villages—named after Sultan Beg and Chatti Beg, respectively—founded in the 12th century.

The population in all these villages at the time was predominantly Muslim with a sprinkling of Hindus and fewer Sikhs.[17] Sikh sympathizers, if any, along with Sahajdhari Sikhs among Hindus were unlikely to offer any overt support to the Sikh cause for fear of reprisals, especially when the Muslim population in villages was generally pro-regime, under duress if not willingly.

Phase 3 was fought on the outskirts of Amritsar in the vicinity of Ramsar, Bibeksar, and Guru-ke-bagh. Amritsar then was a city of mainly temples and a few bungas adjoining Harimandir Sahib but these had mostly been destroyed or damaged earlier in May 1757 on the directions of Durrani. However, this day being Diwali, some devotees may have risked visiting the shrine according to tradition.

Operationally, the terrain favored the imperial army. It not only lent itself to the effective use of their cavalry and artillery in addition to infantry but conversely, provided little camouflage and concealment to Sikhs for whom surprise was always key in trying to offset the odds of enemy numbers and firepower.

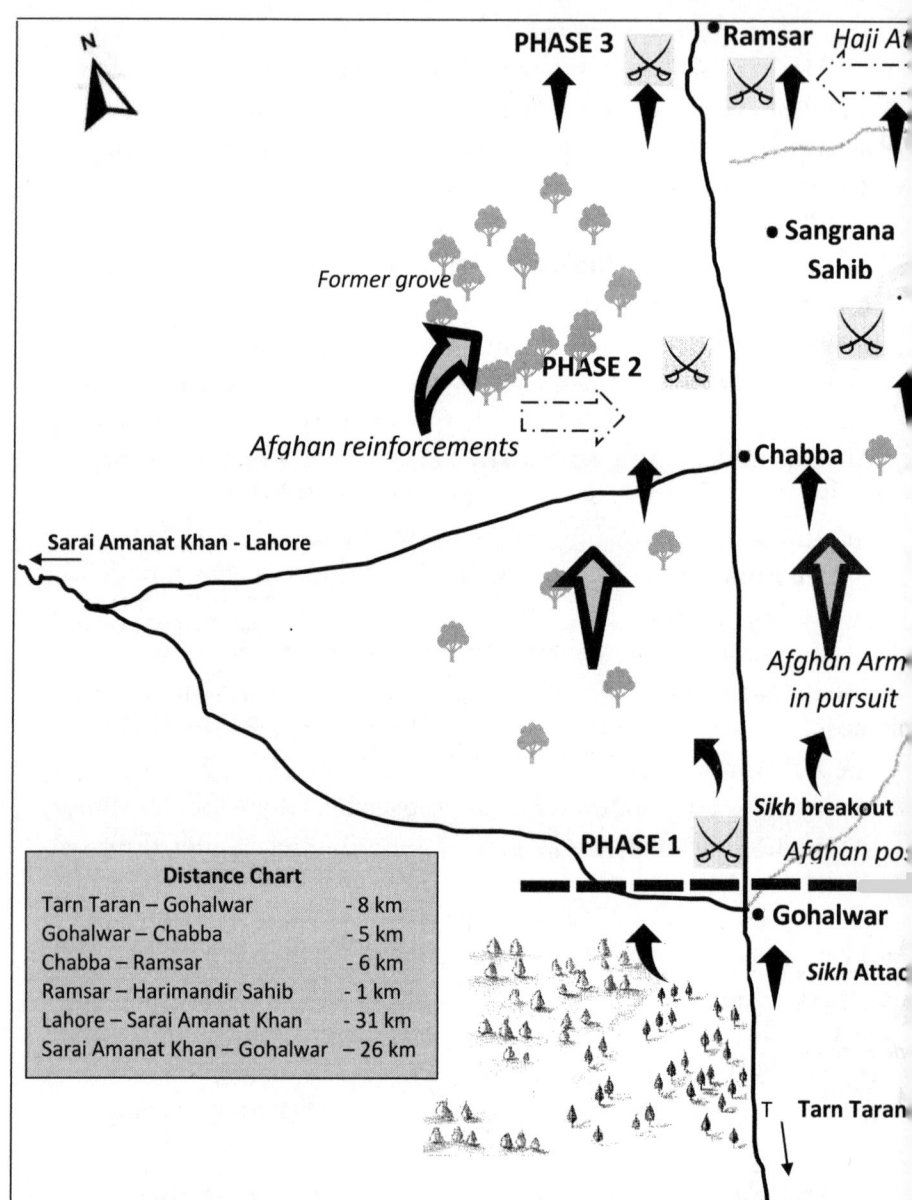

Figure 4: The Battle of Amritsar-Gohalwar, 11 November 1757

• Mehma

• Varpal

in post

Vanchari •

ded area

The Battle

Jahan Khan mobilized from Lahore on 10 November 1757 to reach Sarai Amanat Khan by nightfall. They reached Gohalwar early next morning and prepared hasty entrenchments.

Moving out from Tarn Taran on 11 November morning, when the Sikhs found their way barred at Gohalwar, they charged the enemy and effected a breakthrough.

The Afghans rallied in pursuit and fresh troops arrived at Chabba from Lahore that led to heavy fighting and high Sikh casualties. The Sikhs dispersed under cannonade, once again achieved a breakthrough, and make for their destination, Amritsar.

Haji Attai Khan arrived with his force near Ramsar. Sikhs were now caught in a pincer movement with Jahan Khan in pursuit. Heavy fighting continued right up to *Harimandir Sahib* with high Sikh casualties.

1 Km ▬▬▬

TWELVE

The Battle

> The trumpets sound, the banners fly,
> The glittering spears are ranked ready;
> The shouts o'war are heard afar,
> The battle closes thick and bloody;
> —Robert Burns, *My Bonny Mary*

For long, the battle has been a popular subject with Hindu, Muslim, and Sikh writers and poets. While Deep Singh is widely hailed and worshipped as a Sikh hero, it is his last battle that continues to be the focus of ballads sung with a verve undimmed by time. Gyani Gyan Singh was the first to chronicle the battle in any detail in his well-researched *Sri Guru Panth Prakash* Volume 2 (1867) in esoteric Braj Basha, followed by his five-volume *Twarikh Guru Khalsa* (1890), its expansion in prose. Coming twenty-three years later, it should have had the benefit of more research and yet its various parts are not entirely free of controversy in relation to the circumstances of Deep Singh's martyrdom.

Born in 1822, sixty-five years after the battle, he lived to a ripe age of ninety-nine years, and would have had the opportunity to interview the next generation of those who fought, if not some of the warriors themselves. With access to no war diaries and writing some 120 years after the battle, he is yet highly credited with seminal research, relying mainly on oral traditions and some critical field research, substantially reinforced by received narratives from his forbears Nagahia Singh, Raghu Singh, and Bakhta Singh, who had served Guru Gobind Singh, Banda Singh Bahadur, and 18th century sardars such as Nawab Kapur Singh—all contemporaries of Deep Singh. Of his own admission, he spent more than fifteen years in research, travelling extensively in quest of material. This explains why his chronicle is convincingly in sync with memorial-shrines still extant in the erstwhile battlefield.

Most subsequent writers and poets simply reimagine this narrative by Gyani Gyan Singh and their works are informed by little fresh research. Raijasbir Singh's annotated book on Deep Singh includes the compositions of seventeen writers and poets other than Ratan Singh Bhangu and Gyani Gyan Singh. The vast majority adopt Gyani Gyan Singh's narrative with minor reconceptualization, adding little to the chronicle in any historical sense.

Bearing in mind Gyani Gyan Singh's tendency to exaggerate 'in a spirit of anti-Muslim exultation,'[1] allowance must, however, be made for glamourized reporting, especially since his medium is heroic verse. With its preponderance of spondees, his poetry, nonetheless, resonates with inherent vigour and is best savoured in the original for its powerful imagery—excerpts from his verse are in Appendix A, duly referenced in this section.

Phase 1: Sikh Attack and Breakthrough

The Sikhs divvyed and organized themselves into four wings for battle. One of these was under Deep Singh, who also held overall command, while the others were in the respective command of Naudh Singh, Balwant Singh, and Dyal Singh. Having ridden some eight kilometres from Tarn Taran en route to Amritsar, when the Sikhs found their way barred by the Lahore army deployed over a wide frontage at Gohalwar, they paused briefly among clumps of trees which afforded some camouflage and concealment, where now stands a small commemorative shrine, Rann Niti (Operational Planning) Sahib.

Going by oral tradition, while the bulk of the Sikh army quietly prayed, reciting Japji Sahib, their morning prayer, the commanders—'O-Group' in military parlance—advanced within visible distance of the enemy to observe the enemy dispositions in order to weigh and finalize their tactical options. Since they had prior information of enemy artillery, they appreciated the need to avoid presenting massed targets, to fight in four wings as organized and to disperse when expedient.

It is interesting that the Lahore army maintained their defensive posture although their early warning elements would have informed them of the Sikh advance and arrival. Attack is always a more daring operation of war with potentially far higher incidence of casualties. Possibly, Jahan Khan was confident that he could bait the Sikhs into a cavalry charge and thus afflict severe attrition. That he did not use any artillery proves that he had none at this juncture. Haji Attai Khan had, for reasons unknown, failed to obey Jahan Khan's directive to join at this rendezvous. For Jahan Khan, this was an opportunity lost because a cannonade could not only have wrought havoc among the Sikhs but also prevented them from forming up for a cavalry charge.

Although informed that they would be up against enemy artillery, the Sikhs had appreciated at once that that there was none arrayed against them at Gohalwar. In the event, it would most certainly have been suicidal on their part to halt and assemble within range of enemy cannon.

Jahan Khan expected a cavalry charge from the Sikhs as was their wont but he could never have anticipated that it would be directed at his own command-and-control center. The Sikhs launched two wings with elan, Naudh Singh attacking from the right and Dyal Singh from the left. Taken by surprise, when the enemy troops were unbalanced, it was the turn of Deep Singh and Balwant Singh to charge and to try to cut down the disintegrating mass.[2]

This is how the enemy perceived this action:

'...they attacked us from all four sides. A fierce battle ensued [....] The Sikhs seemed to have surrounded us in a tight noose that they now sought to tighten. Our force came under such pressure that many of our soldiers tried to desert but were unable to because we were completely surrounded. The Wazir was a brave man and fought off the enemy with great vigour [....] I...saw the Wazir wound several of his own men with his sword who were trying to flee so that he could deter others [....] Despite being completely surrounded, we did not break our defensive formation and kept up the fight.'

—Miskin

Miskin's account suggests that the Sikhs went straight for the jugular with frontal as well as flanking attacks to overwhelm the enemy by collapsing their front and flanks. The impression the enemy had was of being attacked from 'all four sides.' As part of Jahan Khan's retinue, Miskin's impression of being thus attacked and encircled is tenable. A commemorative shrine, Lalkar Sahib ('lalkar' means 'challenge') marks the spot of this initial engagement (see photo insert, Figure 14).

Somewhat unprepared for the audacity of the Sikh offensive, the Lahore Army rallied and fought a successful defensive action under Jahan Khan, their veteran commander. Mounted on an elephant and backed by some spirited cavalry, in trying to rally his fleeing soldiers, Jahan Khan threatened, shamed, and incited them to face the Singhs but his soldiers had no heart to combat so devoted and valiant a foe, far more skilled with the sword.[3]

Miskin writes of being encircled and caught in a 'noose', which the Sikhs then began to tighten but this needs further analysis. While it may be an exaggeration to say that the Sikhs were outnumbered four-to-one,[4] they were certainly up against a numerically superior foe.[5] Miskin's diary is silent on Sikh force levels but nowhere does it mention either that the Sikhs were relatively fewer. Given the intelligence network and military resources of the Lahore Army, Jahan Khan would have mobilized enough troops to ensure an edge in both numbers and firepower. In this light, it is difficult to comprehend how a smaller army might physically encircle and get the better of a much larger one—a feat attributable to Sikh daring, military prowess, and tactical brilliance.

As hardened guerrillas, the Sikhs seemed to have employed an important principle of war—to mass their attack on the enemy command and control centre, Jahan Khan himself. Strategic paralysis or 'decapitation' by neutralizing the commander was a guerrilla tactic popular with the Sikhs, often used to good effect. Much earlier, in January 1746 at Eminabad, for example, a Sikh had climbed the enemy commander's war-elephant by its tail and killed the commander, Jaspat Rai, precipitating a rout.

This phase of the battle is best gleaned from the many reconstructions based on oral history that compare the Singh attack to lions falling upon their prey (see ser 12 in Appendix A). The ferocity of the Singhs truly demonstrated their resolve: 'We shall die only after we've killed our enemy!' They now had the upper hand and pushed the enemy back over the ground littered with the dead and dying, inducing many of the enemy soldiers to desert. Although the attack failed in its objective to kill Jahan Khan, it threw his army off-balance, scattering the fleeing soldiers (see ser 13 in Appendix A). It took Jahan Khan all his nerve and experience as a seasoned military commander to thwart a rout.

ਤੋਬਾ ਤੋਬਾ ਕਰਕੇ ਗਿਲਜੇ ਹਟਣ ਲੱਗੇ ਸਿੰਘਾਂ ਪੈਰਾਂ ਤੋਂ ਫੌਜ ਹਿਲਾ ਦਿੱਤੀ ।
ਦੋਹ ਘੜੀਆਂ ਦੇ ਵਿਚ ਘਾਣ ਲੱਥੇ ਸੂਹੀ ਧਰਤ ਨੂੰ ਚੁੰਨੀ ਪਹਿਨਾ ਦਿੱਤੀ ।
—Kartar Singh Kalaswalia,
Jauhar Khalsa[6]

Tobah tobah karke giljey hatan lage Singhan pairaan ton fauj hila dittee
Doh ghariyaan dey vich ghaan lathe suhi dharath nu chuni pahnayi ditee—
In terror did the Singhs now put the Giljas to flight
It took two gharis for them to cravenly flee the fight.

('Gilja' was the common term for an Afghan soldier. One 'ghari' is twenty-four minutes).

The Sikhs quickly disengaged, broke through, and hastened headlong for their objective (Chak Guru). According to Kartar Singh Kalaswalia, the whole action lasted two gharis (forty-eight minutes).[7]

Phase 2: The Chabba-Chatiwind Battle

> They went with songs to the battle, they were young,
> Straight of limb, true of eye, steady and aglow.
> They were staunch to the end against odds uncounted,
> They fell with their faces to the foe.
> —Laurence Binyon, *For the Fallen*

Having seized the initiative with their daring offensive, the Sikhs were able to exploit it with a breakthrough, disengaging thereafter to move swiftly towards their objective. The battle was, however, rejoined some four kilometres ahead around Chabba where the Sikhs were confronted once again by the Lahore Army. There are three possible explanations for this second encounter. One, Jahan Khan had deployed elements of his army in advance at Chabba as a second line of defence, although this finds no mention in Miskin's account. Two, recovering from the setback at Gohalwar, Jahan Khan could regroup his troops, outflank and overtake the Sikhs and in the event, reestablish contact although, according to Miskin, contact was never lost. Three, as Gyani Gyan Singh notes, reinforcements arrived from Lahore,[8] although this contravenes oral tradition which cites the arrival of fresh troops only in the last phase of battle, near Ramsar, on the outskirts of Amritsar. Miskin, however, records no reinforcements other than the timely arrival of Haji Attai Khan when their army was on the verge of defeat, yet makes no mention of the place and direction from which they came.

In fact, a combination of these possibilities is likely. Jahan Khan could reestablish contact and some reinforcements did arrive. It would not have been possible for Jahan Khan to requisition reinforcements from the battlefield because communication was by animal transport alone and the turnaround time for Lahore would make this unfeasible. It is likely that he had scrambled in haste on 10th November with instructions for more troops to report directly the following morning at the rendezvous. These now arrived, covering fifty kilometres in about three-four hours from Lahore. Besides, having thwarted a rout at Gohalwar, Jahan Khan was once again in full control and may not have felt the need to be reinforced.

In response, the Sikhs dispersed and now fought in smaller units over a wider front, possibly of five kilometres, from Chabba in the West to Mehma in the East.[9] Their extent to the East is, however, difficult to estimate since the cenotaph in Mehma stands to the memory of Didar Singh who was killed in the battle and his body retrieved for cremation in Mehma, his native village.

The battle here was far more intense, with single combat actions or duels. Soon the superior numbers and firepower of the enemy began to tell on the Sikhs. The large number of cenotaphs that dot the area around Chabba, Varpal, Sangrana Sahib, Chatiwind, Tahla Sahib tell their own grim tale.[10] Yet, the Sikhs doggedly continued their advance:

ਤਰੱਜ ਗੱਜ ਕੈ, ਗੁਰੱਜ ਤੱਜਿ ਚੁਰਨੰ ਕਰੈਂ ।
ਫਤੇ-ਕੁਮੈਤ ਪੇਲਹੀਂ, ਪਰੱਸ ਤੱਸ ਹੀ ਧਰੈਂ ।
ਟਰੰਤ ਏਕ ਪੈਰ ਨਾ, ਪਿਛਾਂਹਿ ਸਿੰਘ ਸੂਰਮੇ ।
ਬਦੰਤ ਜਾਤ ਅੱਗਰੈਂ, ਸਮੱਗਰੈਂ ਸ਼ਹੂਰ ਮੈਂ ॥ ੨੮ ॥

—Gyani Gyan Singh, *Panth Prakash II*, Utraradh Bisram 50

taraj gaj kai, guraj taj churan karein
fateh-kumait pelhi, paras tus hi dharein
tarant ek pair na, pichhant Singh surme
badhant jat agrein, samagrein shuhur mein |28|

They roared and dared, and struck with mace
Or staff and battle axe;
No single step they backward lent.
The brave Singhs forward soundly went |28|

Deep Singh was conspicuous for his initiative and gallantry, a king among men in the melee, fighting off and killing several of the enemy in the tumultuous battle that raged all around:

ਸ਼ਹੀਦ ਦੀਪ ਸਿੰਘ ਜੂ, ਮਹੀਪ ਪੰਥ ਮੈਂ ਤਹਾਂ ।
ਜਿਤੈ ਪਰੰਤ ਦੌੜ ਕੇ, ਕਰੰਤ ਚੌੜ ਹੈ ਮਹਾਂ ॥ ੩੦ ॥

—Gyani Gyan Singh, *Panth Prakash II*,
Utraradh Bisram 50

Shaheed Deep Singh ju, maheep panth main tahan.
Jitei parant daur ke, karant chaur hai mahan. |30|
Shaheed Deep Singh was the king of Panth.
Wherever he did go,
He cut a swathe right through his foe
And struck a crushing blow. |30|

If the Sikhs had been quick at the outset to identify Jahan Khan and attack his command headquarters as a strategic priority, it was now the turn of the enemy to spot Deep Singh as the Sikh commander and to target him.

ਇਕੱਲਾ ਵੇਖ ਕੇ ਬੁੱਢਾ ਜਰਨੈਲ ਲੜਦਾ,
ਘੇਰਾ ਫੌਜ ਚੁਫੇਰਿਓਂ ਪਾ ਦਿੱਤਾ ।
ਜਮਾਲ ਖਾਨ ਯੋਧਾ ਪਕੜ ਤੇਗ ਆਇਆ,
ਉਸ ਨੇ ਆਉਂਦਿਆਂ ਵਾਰ ਚਲਾ ਦਿੱਤਾ ।

—Gurdeep Singh Kanwal,
Baba Deep Singh ji Shaheed[11]

Ikala vekh ke budha jarnail larda,
Ghera fauj chuperiyon pa ditta.
Jamal Khan yodha pakar teg aya,
Us ne aundiyan vaar chala ditta.
Seeing the old General fighting alone,
The enemy did him surround.
Warrior Jamal Khan brandished sword
Attacked him hard and sound.

Riled by the reverses and somewhat emboldened by the hoariness of the man at the helm, Amir Jan Khan, a commander of 5000 men, astride a war-elephant leads the offensive at the head of his legion. When the Sikhs counterattack to blunt his assault, killing many of his soldiers, it only seems to infuriate the Pathans who now bay for Sikh blood, fighting back with even greater spirit.

Dyal Singh versus Amir Jan Khan

Sensitive to the situation and seeing his commander under attack, Dyal Singh Mahal rushes in at the head of 500 Sikhs. In the first major single combat of the battle, Dyal Singh faces off with Amir Jan Khan. Unmindful of the fact that the Khan was relatively secure mounted on an elephant, in a daring assault, Dyal Singh spurs his mount to a rampant posture and in a flash, gets the rearing horse to plant its front hoof momentarily on the elephant's forehead. Leveraged within reach, with practiced dexterity, he then lunges at the bewildered Pathan and in one clean stroke hacks off his head (see ser 14 in Appendix A). This was standard practice for a horse-rider when engaging a war-elephant with several examples from lore including that of Alexander versus Porus (Battle of Hydaspes, 326 BCE), and Maharana Partap versus Raja Man Singh (Battle of Haldighati, 1576 CE).

Wielding his sword with great skill and robustness, Dyal Singh continued his sally, killing several more of the enemy. Ayub Khan and Jahan Khan, who witnessed Dyal Singh's foray, were enraged and aroused for revenge just when reinforcements arrived from Lahore, led by several prominent Pathan commanders such as Aman Khan and Yakub Khan:

ਅਯੂਬ ਖੂਬ ਦੇਖ, ਦਿਆਲ ਸਿੰਘ ਕੀ ਬਹਾਦਰੀ ।
ਲਰੇ ਬਢਾਇ ਪਾਇ ਸੋ, ਲਗਾਇ ਜੋਰ ਨਾਦਰੀ।
ਤਬੈ ਪਠਾਨ ਗੌਰ ਹੇਰ, ਆ ਗਏ ਲਹੌਰ ਤੇ।
ਅਮਾਨ ਖਾਂ ਯਕੂਬ ਖਾਂ, ਅਏ ਸੂਦਾਰ ਔਰ ਥੇ॥੩੬॥

—Gyani Gyan Singh, *Panth Prakash II*,
Utraradh Bisram 50

Ayub khoob dekh Dyal Singh ke bahaduri.
Larei badhaei payi so, lagai jor nadari.

Tabai pathan gaur hore, aa gaye Lahore te.
Aman Khan Yakub Khan, aye Sardard aur the. |36|
Ayub was awed by Dyal Singh's gallantry
The Nadari army fought now with greater pluck and nerve
Inflamed, more Pathans from Lahore joined in verve.
Aman Khan, Yakub Khan and others came to serve |36|

Dyal Singh would later die in battle. A cenotaph-gurdwara stands, supposedly, to his memory at village Vanchari. There is, however, another commemorative shrine jointly to the memory of Dyal Singh and Arur Singh in village Varpal. Neither shrine carries any interpretative narrative of its hero and cannot be linked with certainty to the Dyal Singh mentioned-in-despatches by Gyani Gyan Singh and other writers.

Forward Ho!

The stout resistance failed to halt the advancing Sikhs who seemed to have sworn to never turn their proverbial backs; even when they fell dead, it was invariably forward, never backward:

ਡਲੰਤ ਡਾਲ ਤੇਗ ਬੇਗ, ਆਨਨੇ ਸੁ ਭਾਲ ਪੈ ।
ਜੁਝੰਤ ਸਿੰਘ ਏਕ, ਛੇਕਿ ਸ਼ੱਤਰੁ ਬਿਸਾਲ ਪੈ ।
ਸੁ ਚਾਰ ਚਾਰ ਉਂਗਲੈਂ, ਭਵੰਤ ਦੇਹ ਹੈਂ ਜਬੈ ।
ਗਿਰੰਤ ਔਨਿ ਸੰਮੁਖੈਂ, ਅਗ੍ਰਾਂਹਿ ਪੈਰ ਪਾ ਤਬੈ ॥ ੨੯ ॥

—Gyani Gyan Singh, *Panth Prakash II,*
Utraradh Bisram 50

dalant dhal teg beg, annein su bhal pai
jujant Singh ek, chhek shatru bisal pai
su char char uglein, bhavant deh hein jabei
girant aun samukhein, agahn pair pa tabei |29|
They squarely met the rapid pace of swordplay in the fight
A single Singh who fell had slain as many he would smite;
Even when his body in four pieces was so cleft;
Only forward he would fall with whatever he had left |29|.

The Face of Battle

The battle now intensified as both sides, proud of their martial traditions, stoutly dug in, neither ready to give quarter.[12] The dead and the dying, mid painful groans, lay among heaps of severed limbs, torsos, and maimed horses scattered over a distance of four-five kilometres where the earth had donned a crimson mantle from the bloodletting.[13] The face of battle is vividly captured in heroic verse that resounds with the powerful imagery of quoits flying saucer-like above the heads of the two clashing armies, the ominous thump and roll of war drums, the hiss of flying arrows, crack of bullets, trumpeting war bugles, and the clash of steel (see ser 15 in Appendix A). The contest showed no clear victors, while above the constant battle din is heard the macabre wails and whimpering of maimed men and mounts:

ਭੁਜਾਂ ਸਕੰਧ ਮੂੰਢ ਜੰਘ, ਪੈਰ ਹੱਥ ਸੱਥਲੈਂ ।
ਧਰਾ ਸਕੀਰਣੈਂ ਭਈ, ਸਰੈਣ ਮਾਸ ਗੱਟਲੈਂ ।
ਮਨੋ ਸੁ ਫਾਗ ਖੇਲਯੋ, ਝਰੇ ਮਹੀਰੁ ਕਿੰਸਕੈਂ ।
ਕਿਕਾਨ ਜੂਨ ਘਾਇਲੈਂ, ਲਿਟੈਂ ਅਧੀਰ ਚਿੰਸਕੈਂ ॥ ੩੮ ॥

—Gyani Gyan Singh, *Sri Guru Panth Prakash II*,
Utraradh Bisram 50

bhujan sakand moond jang, pair hatth santhlai
dhara sakirnai bhei, sarain maas gatlai
mano sup hag kheliyo, jharey maheer kiskain
kikaan jaan ghailain, litain adhir chiskain |38|

Fiercely fought,
Everywhere lay, limbs, shoulders, heads, feet, hands;
The earth drenched in blood
in semblance of a holi festival,
Or strewn with bright red kesu (Butea Monosprma) flowers.
Maimed horses and men
Writhed, groaned and wailed |38|.

ਦੁ ਤੀਨ ਕੋਸ ਮੈਂ ਸਰੇਸ, ਖੂਬ ਖੇਤ ਥਾਂ ਪਰਾ ।
ਮਨੋ ਉਢਾਇ ਚੁਨਰੀ, ਦਈ ਸੁਹਾਗ ਕੀ ਧਰਾ ॥ ੩੯ ॥

—Gyani Gyan Singh, *Sri Guru Panth Prakash II*,
Utraradh Bisram 50

du teen kos main sarosh, khoob khet than pera
mano udai chunri, dayi suhaag ki dhera ||39||
Over a distance of two-three kos (four-six miles)
The earth is draped
In a bridal mantle:
Vermilion

ਕਾਵਾਂ ਕੁੱਤਿਆਂ ਨੇ ਪਾਯਾ ਬਹੁਤ ਰੌਲਾ ਚੀਲਾਂ ਗਿਲਜਾਂ ਮਾਸ ਉਡਾਣ ਹਰ ਥਾਂ ।
—Kartar Singh Kalasvalia, *Jauhar Khalsa*[14]

Kavan kutian ne paya bahut raula chilan giljan maas udaan har than.
While dogs bark and jackals howl, crows, vultures, and kites keep up a steady pealing clangour as they wheel overhead waiting to prey on the stricken and the dead.

Determined Sikh Advance

Undismayed, several Sikh jathedars continued their intrepid advance along with their men in the teeth of determined resistance. Prominent among these were Deep Singh, Sudha Singh, Kehar Singh, Basant Singh, Ram Singh, Bur Singh, Hari Singh, Kaur Singh, Naudh Singh, and Dyal Singh.[15]

A Cunning Plan

Unable to stem the Sikh offensive, the Pathans now executed a cunning plan. Aware that the cow was a sacred animal for Hindus and Sikhs alike, they pushed a herd of cows in their path, expecting to stall their onslaught. In response, the Sikhs briefly converged to circumvent the bovine herd only to fan out once again like the raging waves of an ocean.[16]

Deep Singh versus Yakub Khan

Yakub Khan, Sabar Ali, and Jahan Khan tried to confront this upsurge of Sikh warriors, and this set up a duel between Deep Singh and Yakub Khan. The latter opened the contest with a shower of arrows while Deep Singh stood poised with his broadsword. They soon closed in for combat on horseback and fought for long, lunging, thrusting, and slashing at each other until their horses fell dead from cuts and wounds. Resumed on foot, the combat now became a slugfest. Shoving and pushing, they fell to the ground like two mettlesome wrestlers, each striving to get the better of the other. Fully clad in armour from head to foot, the Khan had better protection but Deep Singh proved more agile when, with a roar, he swung his thirty ser (7.7 kilograms) mace to crush the Khan's helmet and skull, killing him instantly (see ser 16 in Appendix A).[17]

Naudh Singh versus Mir Jan Khan

Mir Jan Khan saw this contest and impressed by Deep Singh's combat skills, like a true warrior, asked Deep Singh to grant him his wish for single combat—only then would he honour him as a true 'Singh'. At this, Naudh Singh, who was at hand, hotly intervened and moved his horse to face the Pathan.[18] Mid impetuous rhetoric and bellowing provocation, they opened the contest with bow and arrows until their horses were killed under them. In the ensuing combat on foot, both proved expert swordsmen, albeit too powerful in their strokes for soon their swords broke and they were left with just the grip and pommel or the blades. They now used these with rare ferocity, locked in deathly embrace, falling to the ground only to rise again with brawn, grit, and cunning until their armour was smitten through, their shields shattered and both were on the verge of exhaustion from multiple wounds. The duel came to an end when they drew their push-daggers (katars) and drove these simultaneously into each other's belly (see ser 17 in Appendix A).

Deep Singh versus Aman Khan

After another four-five Pathan commanders were similarly killed in duels, more elite troops were brought to the fore from their reserve. Among them was Aman Khan who challenged Deep Singh to personal combat. The duel unfolded in a similar pattern—

sword fight while mounted followed by hand-to-hand combat once their horses were disabled from wounds. They battled for long until their armour was in shreds and their primary weapons broken. Finally, with a common stroke of their swords, both were decapitated near Chabba. A commemorative shrine, Tahla Sahib, marks the spot of Deep Singh's fatal injury—the place takes its name from a thicket of tahlis (North Indian rosewood or shisham) that stood in the area at the time (see photo insert, Figure 15).

Seeing his head fall to the ground, his colleague, Dharam Singh (Sukha Singh Ramgarhia as per Gyani Thakur Singh),[19] reminded him of his oath of that morning to die only at Amritsar, still two-kos (six kilometres) away. With superhuman effort, Deep Singh rose, supported his head with his left hand, and continued to wield the sword with his right. He is informed by his colleagues once they reach Ramsar, where he breathes his last and is cremated (see ser 18 in Appendix A). His final duel is conceptualized differently by other writers—with Kaman Khan at Chabba (ser 19, Appendix A), with Shah Jamal at Chabba (ser 20, Appendix A), with Shah Jamal at Ramsar (ser 21, Appendix A).

In a less popular version, on reaching Ramsar, Deep Singh felt that, battle-weary, soiled and bleeding profusely, he was in no state to enter the hallowed precinct of the shrine and drawing on his extraordinary spiritual energy, flung his head from a distance of a kilometre for it to land in the parikrama. This belief is buttressed by the fact that there was a spot on the parikrama to mark the place where it fell, with no mention of the body.[20] This version is also recorded in verse by Tirlok Singh Dervesh.[21] Interpreting this legend within the realm of possibility, some analysts suggest that after Deep Singh fell to his wounds at Ramsar, his severed head was conveyed to Harimandir Sahib by solicitous comrades in an act of final obeisance.

Although up against the might of the Lahore Army, in a feat that encourages disbelief, the Sikhs continued to advance, possibly driven more by spiritual rather than physical energy to keep their tryst with Chak Guru. Miskin records their use of cannon that put the Sikhs to 'flight' but in the direction of their hallowed objective.

Phase 3: Ramsar and Beyond

Definitely the worse off, badly mauled and severely depleted from their sanguinary and bitter contest at Chabba-Chatiwind, the Sikhs managed to effect a second breakthrough at Chabba-Chatiwind to reach the outskirts of Amritsar. It is to their credit that they achieved this in the teeth of massive opposition, despite a high incidence of casualties, and with the enemy in pursuit.

Miskin notes, 'At this point, Haji Attai Khan arrived with a huge army to turn the tide of the battle. Although the Sikhs took great pride in their valour, it was now their turn to be put to the sword, or to be blown up by our cannon fire [....] we pursued them all the way.'

Miskin's is a condensed account and the point of Haji Khan's arrival is not altogether clear. That it happened when the Lahore Army was under pressure might suggest the first phase at Gohalwar, but the enemy had rallied under their commander and fought on. Possibly, they were hard pressed once again between Chabba-Chatiwind and Ramsar where the Sikhs did manage to breakthrough a second time, and that is when Haji Attai Khan joined battle.

Thereupon, Miskin records:

'They [the Sikhs] were defeated and took to flight towards Chak Guru but we pursued them all the way. On reaching the walled enclosure of Chak Guru, we saw five Sikh infantrymen at the gate who were all killed by our soldiers. Here, even Mir Niamtullah, a respected citizen of Lahore, was killed.'

Miskin's view that they used cannon against the fleeing Sikhs and also chased them are two contrasting military operations that are seldom accomplished together. It is, nevertheless, possible that after an initial cannonade that put the Sikhs to 'flight', the

Lahore Army gave chase to re-establish contact and annihilate them.

Popular Sikh accounts suggest that it is here that Haji Attai Khan joined battle, from the direction of Amritsar. With Jahan Khan in pursuit, the Sikhs were now caught in a pincer movement and this explains their high incidence of casualties in the final stage of battle. This may have restricted the use of enemy cannon but the Sikhs were now both heavily outnumbered and encircled. In a display of rare courage and tenacity of purpose, they continued to advance, many reaching their objective, the Amritsar shrine, while continuing to inflict casualties on the enemy. That Miskin records the death of a 'respected citizen of Lahore' suggests that many ordinary soldiers would have died too.

Fought around Ramsar, a kilometre short of their objective, this phase stretched all the way to the Amritsar shrine. The many cenotaphs in the area suggest that despite the crippling resistance they were up against, many succeeded in reaching their objective.

Deep Singh versus Jamal Shah, Buland Khan, Yakub Khan

In a later publication, *Twarikh Guru Khalsa* Part 3 (*Raj Khalsa, Satvin Misal Shaheedan di*), Gyan Gyan Singh records Deep Singh's final duel near Ramsar (not Chabba) with Jamal Shah, and not Aman Khan. While Deep Singh kills his adversary, he is decapitated by a stroke from his own sword to die near Ramsar, where he was cremated, a place now marked by the commemorative shrine, Shaheedganj.[22]

ਰਾਮਸਰ ਤੀਰਥ ਦੇ ਲਾਗੇ ਸ਼ਹੀਦ ਦੀਪ ਸਿੰਘ ਦੇ ਨਾਲ ਸ਼ਾਹ ਜਮਾਲ ਪੰਜ ਹਜ਼ਾਰੀ ਆ ਲੜਿਆ . ਦੋਵੇਂ ਬਹੁਤ ਲੜੇ . ਆਖਿਰ ਥੋੜੀ ਦੇਰ ਬਾਦ ਦੋਹਾਂ ਨੇ ਬਹਾਦੁਰੀ ਦੇ ਜੋਹਰ ਦਿਖਾ ਕੇ ਬਾਬਾ ਜੀ ਨੇ ਜਮਾਲ ਸ਼ਾਹ ਦਾ ਸਰ ਧੜ ਨਾਲੋਂ ਅੱਡ ਕਰ ਦਿੱਤਾ , ਤੇ ਦੀਪ ਸਿੰਘ ਜੀ ਦੀ ਤਲਵਾਰ ਨਾਲ ਉਹਨਾਂ ਦਾ ਆਪਣਾ ਸੀਸ ਵੀ ਅੱਡ ਹੋ ਗਯਾ . ਦੀਪ ਸਿੰਘ ਦਾ ਸ਼ਹੀਦ ਅਸਥਾਨ ਰਾਮਸਰ ਦੇ ਲਾਗੇ ਬਣਿਆ ਹੋਇਆ ਹੈ

—Gyani Gyan Singh, *Satvin Misal Shaheedan,*
Raj Khalsa Part 1, 36

> *Ramsar tirath de lage Shaheed Deep Singh de naal Shah Jamal panj hazari aa lariya. Dovein bahut lare. Aakhir thori der baad dohaan ne bahaduri de johaur dikha ke Baba ji ne Jamal Shah da sir dhar nalon ad kar ditta, te Deep Singh ji di talwar naal uhna da apna sees vi ad ho gaya. Deep Singh da shaheed asthan Ramsar de lage baniya hoyiya hai*

Near Ramsar Tirath, Shaheed Deep Singh dueled with Shah Jamal Panj Hazari (designated to command five thousand soldiers). They fought with great ferocity, showing rare courage, until Baba ji beheaded Shah Jamal. At this, his own head was also severed by a stroke of his own sword. Deep Singh's shaheedi asthan (memorial shrine) was raised at the spot near Ramsar.

As opposed to his initial version, Gyani Gyan Singh mentions no previous injury nor of Deep Singh battling on when decapitated in this publication that came twenty-three years later. Also, that an expert swordsman should hack off his own head in a freak strike could well be more hagiography than fact.

However, in another part of the same publication, *Twarikh Guru Khalsa*, viz, *Shamsher Khalsa* Part 2, 'Dharam Yudh', Gyani Gyan Singh omits the names of Deep Singh's adversaries altogether to state that he was decapitated in a duel at Chabba, fought on when prompted to die near Ramsar; he adduces the historians, Ghulam Sarvar and Ghanaiya Lal in support.

Other writers have described this duel in the area of Ramsar with Buland Khan and Yakub Khan (see ser 22 in Appendix A). Buland Khan is the first to strike, lunging at Deep Singh with his sword; the latter parries and, in a counter-thrust, slices off his head in one clean stroke. Seeing his comrade killed, the enemy commander now engages Deep Singh near Bibeksar but he too is killed at the hands of Deep Singh.

Balwant Singh versus Zabardast Khan and Rustam Khan

In the battle around Ramsar, Zabardast Khan (bees-hazari—designated to command twenty-thousand soldiers), a towering

Pathan, now came to the fore, his body and that of his horse completely clad in armour. He trumpeted elephant-like and hurled challenges at the Sikhs, but the elephant scares not the lion. Somewhat startled by his colossal frame, the Sikhs nevertheless, remained undaunted and soon Balwant Singh came forward to take up the gauntlet. He and his horse too were fully armour-clad. Mid-frightening roars and bluster, they maneuvered their horses this way and that, looking to strike from an advantageous position. Locked eyeball-to-eyeball, they tried to anticipate the other's next move, without the slightest flutter of their eyelids lest they should concede an edge. The armies stood aside to watch the combat between two renowned warriors comparable to the likes of the great Arjan versus Karan, or Meghnath versus Lakshman.

They open the contest with the bow and arrow, some arrows striking home to embed in the armour. Next, Balwant Singh shatters his opponent's bow with a throw of his quoit and then charges in with his twisted spear to transfix his horse in the belly. In a flash, his next quoit cleaves off the Khan's arm. Momentarily disorientated, Zabardast Khan, like a true warrior, is undismayed and thunders revenge. In quick retaliation, he drives his sword into the Singh's horse, also wounding the rider. They now close in on foot. In a flash, Balwant Singh observes that the Khan's armour is in shreds and his belly exposed. Instantly, he drives his sword into the Khan's midriff, killing him (see ser 23 in Appendix A).

Seeing his brother fall, Rustam Khan, accompanied by a group of brave Pathans, attacks Balwant Singh with great ferocity. The two duel long and hard until both are struck down by a common stroke of their swords. A memorial shrine marks Balwant Singh's place of martyrdom near Chabba. By another version, Balwant Singh gets the better of Rustam Khan, killing him, only to die later near Guru-ke-Bagh (see ser 24 in Appendix A).

Hira Singh, the Warrior

Another brave Sikh warrior, Hira Singh, fights in the van, killing several brave Pathan commanders including Sayed Sabar-Ali near Guru-ke-Bagh before he finds glorious death in the battlefield (see ser 25, Appendix A).[23]

Warriors Ram Singh and Mahat Singh

Besides Deep Singh, Gyani Gyan Singh portrays two other warriors who continued to fight even when decapitated although he makes no mention of the circumstances nor the distance thus covered. Mahat Singh Sran fights and falls near village Chatiwind. A memorial-shrine stands to his name in the village and the received narrative is still alive among the village folk who believe that Mahat Singh belonged to the village itself, and support their claim by citing his caste, Sran, which is the same in that part of the village.

Ram Singh too fights on after he is decapitated and falls near Bibeksar within Amritsar,[24] but no memorial-shrine could be traced; possibly, it was demolished as part of city development.

Several other jathedars too were martyred (see ser 26 in Appendix A, and Table 5 for their names and details of commemorative shrines).

Caring for the Dead and Wounded

Makeshift administrative arrangements had been made off the battlefield to treat the large number of Sikh wounded at a place where now stands Bachaona Sahib ('bachaona' is Punjabi for 'to save'). It was more than a dressing station because food was also provided and those who succumbed were cremated according to Sikh rites.

Going by popular lore, Sikh losses were 4000 killed and many wounded as against 1000 of the enemy killed and some wounded. Noteworthy for the scrupulous detail with which he limns the minutiae of the battle, Gyani Gyan Singh chronicles the tending of their wounded by both armies, and the last rites for those killed.

ਚੌਪਈ ॥ ਸਿੰਘ ਸ਼ਹੀਦ ਭਏ ਥੇ ਜੇਈ ।
ਕਈ ਠੌਰ ਸਸਕਾਰੇ ਤੇਈ ।
ਜ਼ਖਮੀ ਅਪਨੇ ਸਭੀ ਸੰਭਾਰੇ ।
ਤੁਰਕ ਸਿਟਾਏ ਗਢਯੋਂ ਮੜਾਰੇ ॥੯੮॥

—Gyani Gyan Singh, *Panth Prakash II*, Utararadh Bisram 50

Singh shaheed bhaye te jeyi
Kayi thor, saskare teyi
Zakhmi apne sabhi sambhare
Turk sitaye gadhyon mujhare |98|
The Singhs died scattered across the field
where they were all cremated.
Both armies nursed their wounded there;
The Turks dug pits to toss their dead,
It seemed as if they did not care |98|.

(NB: 'Turk' here refers to Afghan soldiers)

It made practical sense for the Lahore Army to bury their dead in the many cemeteries extant in the Muslim-dominated villages in the area. As a Sikh chronicler, Gyani Gyan Singh's description of the burial ceremony is predictably pejorative.

THIRTEEN

Battle Review

Sources

The first to write a history of the Sikhs in his *Panth Prakash* (1841), Bhangu did not record the battle but both Deep Singh and his Shaheedbunga find mention in his 'Sakhi Shaheed Singhon ki' (Sakhi 79). This is strong evidence since Bhangu's forbears were Deep Singh's contemporaries. Gyani Gyan Singh is credited with seminal research on the subject. In his *Sri Guru Panth Parkash* (1867), he records two duels for Deep Singh near Chabba. Deep Singh kills his first opponent, Yakub Khan, but is mortally wounded during the second duel with Aman Khan although he kills him to fight on. In his later five-volume publication, *Twarikh Guru Khalsa* (1890), Gyani Gyan Singh records another duel for Deep Singh with Shah Jamal near Ramsar during which he receives his fatal injury. Deep Singh kills his opponent, Jamal Shah, but his head too is severed by a freak stroke of his own sword.[1]

There are many variations to this narrative but the most popular tradition, in line with the commemorative shrines, favours one or more duel at Chabba and another at Ramsar. Deep Singh is decapitated at Chabba but fights on to breathe his last at Harimandir Sahib. Several ballads chronicle the sanguinary scenes around Chabba and Ramsar and a few also recount some of the other prominent duels (see Table 3). Most writers largely retain Gyani Gyan Singh's narrative, altering the names of some of the duelists.

Born in 1838, a few years after Gyani Gyan Singh, Gyani Thakar Singh had the advantage of living most of his life in Dam Dama Sahib and Amritsar, with more opportunity for field research. Yet, his narrative is completely at variance with that of Gyani Gyan Singh. It is set during Nadir Shah's invasion in 1738-40 instead of Ahmed Shah Durrani's fourth invasion in 1757. In his version, Deep Singh departs from Dam Dama Sahib along with Sukha Singh Ramgarhia and they are joined at Tarn Taran by Naudh Singh and some twenty-one Sikhs from the Majha. Most are martyred in a fierce battle fought with a large Lahore army around Chabba. Deep Singh is decapitated but when reminded of his oath by Sukha Singh, fights on, collapses from the effort at Ramsar but is once again prompted to rise until he reaches the precincts of Harimandir Sahib. Thakar Singh's version is particularly questionable because he fails to adduce any sources in support.[2]

Duels

In the campaigns of the period, during a frontal clash of two armies en masse, there was usually a melee with confused and random swordplay alongside use of the mace, spear or lance at close quarters. If they were some distance apart, other personal weapons such as the bow and arrow and the quoit could be employed. There were also duels and it was not uncommon for commanders to fight one another.

Gyani Gyan Singh names three adversaries for Deep Singh—Yakub Khan, Aman Khan, Jamal Shah. Subsequent writers added another four but without adducing any sources—Sar Buland Khan, Alla Ditta, Ali Khan Bahadur, and the Faujdar, Jahan Khan (see Table 2). This makes a total of seven of which the last, Jahan Khan, was in command of the enemy force but any account of his being killed is erroneous because he finds mention in subsequent history of the period. He returned briefly to Afghanistan the following year in April 1758,[3] but continued to play a prominent role in the Punjab and was among Durrani's several field commanders during the Third Battle of Panipat in January 1761.[4]

Similarly, Sarbuland Khan (alias Jiwan Khan) was appointed subedar of Lahore in 1760.[5] Haji Attai Khan has been excluded from this list because, as a duelist, his name figures only in a generic dictionary entry.[6]

In a battle that lasted the better part of a day, fought intensely over a distance of 11-12 kilometres, for a commander to fight seven different adversaries could be an understatement. Overall, Deep Singh may have fought many more but perhaps, dueled with just a few of the enemy commanders. Sikh records are likely based on eyewitness accounts. After all, there were survivors from the battle as also support elements off the battlefield responsible for tending the wounded and ensuring the last rites of those who succumbed. Deep Singh's battle narrative draws special strength from at least one cenotaph near Chabba believed by local knowledge to be in memory of a Muslim commander he fought with and killed.

Gurdeep Singh Kanwal names several Afghan generals who took part in the battle—Haji Attai Khan, Yakub Khan, Kasim Khan Pattiwala, Amir Jan Khan, Ayub Khan, Dina Beg, Zabardast Khan, Pir Niyamat Khan, Shah Jamal Khan, Jahan Khan.[7] Other writers name a total of six enemy duelists—Mir Jan Khan, Rustam Khan, Zabardast Khan, Kasim Khan, Sarbuland Khan, Syed Sabir Ali, and Ayub Khan (see Table 3). Of these, Miskin's account corroborates the participation of only Kasim Khan. Sikh chroniclers, particularly bards, have recorded the death of many of the enemy duelists. The death of Rustam Khan and Kasim (Qassim) Khan, however, can be ruled out because they find mention in subsequent history of the period—the former as governor of Chahar Mahal in 1760 and the latter as commander of the advance guard under Zain Khan, Governor of Sirhind, on 5th February 1762 in the Vada Ghallughara (Greater Holocaust) at Kup.[8]

It is logical to infer that, if these men did take part in the battle, the chronicled outcome of some of the duels could be more hagiographic than fact, and that the enemy may not have got the worst of it every time. It is not uncommon in heroic verse to romanticize a narrative in order to glorify one's own warriors; hyperbole and exaggeration are often the mainstay of such verse.

Places of Martyrdom and Cenotaphs

Study of the battle, both chronicle and field research, supports the popular narrative. Lasting under an hour, the first phase of the battle at Gohalwar was a cavalry charge by the Sikhs for shock action and breakthrough with little scope for any prolonged close combat. At Chabba-Chatiwind, in the second phase, the Sikhs were up against the might of the Afghan Army and had to fight every inch of their way. The large number of cenotaphs in the area speak of the high-octane conflict and loss of life. Thereafter, possibly on account of a second Sikh breakthrough, there was little opposition over the next five kilometres until Ramsar. In the final phase of the battle, they once again met stiff resistance, suffering huge casualties over the last kilometre to their objective, the Amritsar shrine.

There is a general consensus over Sikh martyrs, their circumstances, and places of martyrdom (see Table 4) although for some reason, subsequent writers have not perpetuated the legend of Mahit Singh and Ram Singh who, according to Gyani Gyan Singh, also fought on when decapitated.[9] There is even a prominent cenotaph-gurdwara in memory of Mahit Singh in village Chatiwind where he fell and according to local belief, continued to fight although beheaded in battle. No cenotaph, however, could be traced for Ram Singh near Bibeksar, though chronicled.

These are a total of nineteen names recorded for those martyred near Guru-ke-Bagh but the memorial, Thara Sahib, that stands within the premises of Manji Sahib, records only nine (see photo insert, Figures 10 and 11):[10]

ਸ਼ਹੀਦ ਗੰਜ

ਐਥੇ ਉਹਨਾਂ ਸੂਰਬੀਰਾਂ ਧਰਮੀ ਯੋਧਿਆਂ ਦਾ ਸਸਕਾਰ ਕੀਤਾ ਗਯਾ ਸੀ ਜਿਨਾਹ ਨੇ ਮੱਘਰ ੧੮੧੭ ਵਿਚ ਅਹਿਮਦ ਸ਼ਾਹ ਅਬਦਾਲੀ ਦੇ ਭੇਜੇ ਹੋਏ ਬਕਸ਼ੀ ਜਹਾਨ ਖਾਨ ਦੇ ਹੱਥੋਂ ਸ੍ਰੀ ਦਰਬਾਰ ਸਾਹਿਬ ਤੇ ਅੰਮ੍ਰਿਤ ਸਰੋਵਰ ਦੀ ਹੋ ਰਹੀ ਬੇਤਾਬੀ ਨੂੰ ਰੋਕਣ ਲਈ ਸ੍ਰੀ ਦਮ ਦਮਾਂ ਸਾਹਿਬ (ਮਾਲਵਾ) ਤੋਂ ਬਾਬਾ ਦੀਪ ਸਿੰਘ ਜੀ ਸ਼ਹੀਦ ਦੀ ਜਥੇਦਾਰੀ ਹੇਠ ਤਿਆਰੇ ਕੀਤੇ ਐਰ ਰਨ ਵਿਚ ਜੁੱਝ ਕੇ ਸ਼ਹੀਦ ਹੋਏ ਅਤੇ ਬੇਤਬੀ ਨੂੰ ਦੂਰ ਕੀਤਾ । ਉਹਨਾਂ ਧਰਮੀ ਬੀਰਾ ਚੋਂ ਕੁਝ ਕੁ ਦੇ ਪਵਿੱਤਰ ਨਾਮ ਇਹ ਹੁਣ :-

੧ ਬਾਬਾ ਬਲਵੰਤ ਸਿੰਘ ਜੀ ੨ ਬਾਬਾ ਹੀਰਾ ਸਿੰਘ ਜੀ ੩ ਬਾਬਾ ਗੰਡਾ ਸਿੰਘ ਜੀ ੪ ਬਾਬਾ ਲਹਿਣਾ ਸਿੰਘ ਜੀ ੫ ਬਾਬਾ ਰਨ ਸਿੰਘ ਜੀ ੬ ਬਾਬਾ ਗੋਪਾਲ ਸਿੰਘ ਜੀ ੭ ਬਾਬਾ ਭਾਗ ਸਿੰਘ ਜੀ ੮ ਬਾਬਾ ਸੱਜਣ ਸਿੰਘ ਜੀ ੯ ਬਾਬਾ ਬਹਾਦਰ ਸਿੰਘ ਜੀ ।

Shaheed Ganj

Aithe uhna surbiran dharmi yodhian da saskar kita gaya si jinah ne maghar 1817 vich Ahmed Shah Abdali de bheje hoye Bakshi Jahan Khan de hathon Sri Darbar Sahib te amrit sarovar di ho rahi betabi nu rokan layi Sri Dam Dama Sahib (Malwa) ton Baba Deep Singh ji Shaheed di jathedari heth tiare kite aur ran vich jugh ke shaheed hoye ate betabi nu door kita. Uhna dharmi biran shon kujh ku de paviter nam ih hun:-i

1. Baba Balwant Singh ji 2. Baba Hira Singh ji 3. Baba Ganda Singh ji 4. Baba Lehna Singh ji 5. Baba Ran Singh ji 6. Baba Gopal Singh ji 7. Baba Bhag Singh ji 8. Baba Sajjan Singh ji 9. Baba Bahadur Singh ji

Memorial to Revered Martyrs

At this spot, the brave warriors who fought for their faith were cremated who, in Maghar 1817 [should be 1814], in order to halt the desecration of Darbar Sahib and the amrit sarovar at the hands of Bakshi Jahan Khan, on the orders of Ahmed Shah Abdali, marched under the Jathedari of Baba Deep Singh ji Shaheed from Dam Dama Sahib (Malwa), put a stop to the desecration, and found glorious martyrdom in the battlefield. Here are the names of some of these holy warriors:[11]

1. Baba Balwant Singh ji 2. Baba Hira Singh ji 3. Baba Ganda Singh ji 4. Baba Lehna Singh ji 5. Baba Ran Singh ji 6. Baba Gopal Singh ji 7. Baba Bhag Singh ji 8. Baba Sajjan Singh ji 9. Baba Bahadur Singh ji

The exclusion of Deep Singh's name in this list of those cremated at this spot is significant and seems to endorse Gyani Gyan Singh's view that he fell near Ramsar, and not at Harimandir Sahib.[12] For reasons unknown, many writers exclude Balwant Singh's name although it tops the list on the memorial. Possibly, because there is another cenotaph to his memory near village Varpal that likely marks the spot of another gallant action on his part.

The general consensus over the places of martyrdom for most of the prominent Sikh warriors notwithstanding, there is a mismatch between cenotaphs documented and those found on-ground (see Figure 5). Within Amritsar, where the third and final phase of the battle was fought, no cenotaphs are to be found at Churasti Attari and Bibeksar, and only one at Pragdas Chowk against the four documented. In comparison, very few names are documented of those killed in the vicinity of Chabba-Chatiwind-Varpal but there is a profusion of cenotaphs on ground (see Table 5). There could be two possibilities. If the cenotaphs within Amritsar did exist, these have been removed, or the places of martyrdom in respect of some warriors have been mistakenly recorded within Amritsar when actually they fell in the second rather than the final phase of the battle.

This apart, there are other reasons, as curious as they are absorbing, for the diminishing cenotaphs within Amritsar on the one hand and their proliferation in the countryside on the other.

In its heyday, Amritsar was a city of baghs (gardens), havelis (manors), shaheedganjs (sepulchers or cenotaphs), and bungas. While the gardens and manors were an obvious legacy of its affluent residents, the samadhs (cenotaphs) were the scars of the many battles fought in and around Harimandir Sahib (now the Golden Temple). Both the Mughal regime and the Afghan invaders generally retaliated against Sikh acts of insurrection by destroying and desecrating their sanctum at Amritsar and also slaying the entire Sikh populace of the city.

In addition to the countless skirmishes in the area, Harimandir Sahib was thrice razed to the ground—in 1757, 1762, and 1764.[13] Every time, thousands of Sikh lives were lost, many being killed in defensive battles while others became victims of Mughal-Afghan wrath reserved for infidels.

Beginning with the Parikrama Scheme for the Golden Temple launched by the Shiromani Gurdwara Parbandhak Committee (SGPC) in 1950, most of the bungas were acquired and demolished to make way for the development and modernization of the premises. As part of this makeover, an irreparable loss was the innumerable samadhs that disappeared. Scores of samadhs that remain lack any marks of identification though locals tend to keep alive the tradition of lighting a jot (oil lamp) in the evening.[14]

In contrast, the large number of cenotaphs around Chabba-Varpal-Chatiwind, the scene of Phase 2 of the battle, tell an entirely different story. Interaction with locals suggests that some of these emerged through a rather dubious process of 'divine revelation' or 'divination' as more continue to be mysteriously added. Other cenotaphs grew out of a legacy referred to as 'jathere' (relic of ancestors)—an insubstantial mark or structure worshipped for long by the local community which gradually develops over the decades into a cenotaph-gurdwara.

While Gurdwara Bachaona Sahib in the area served as both a dressing post and cremation ground during the battle, it is equally likely that since these villages predate the battle, warriors killed in the area were cremated by the villagers where they fell. The place of cremation was then commemorated with a modest cenotaph to begin with. In the event, the location of these cenotaphs may be more reliable than the attached name—improbable that all fallen heroes could have been easily identified.[15]

Interestingly, there are several cenotaphs to Muslims in the area, mostly unnamed—Muslim religious traditions disallow nominate tombstones—but believed to be in memory of some of those killed fighting the Sikhs in this battle. According to conflicting local information, some of them were martyred fighting alongside the Sikhs rather than against them but this is nowhere corroborated. In fact, even tacit support to the Sikhs by the locals would have been improbable since these were predominantly Muslim villages at the time, averse rather than supportive of the Sikh cause or that of any subaltern community.

There was a cenotaph to the west (behind) Tahla Sahib—that marks the place of Deep Singh's fatal battle injury—in memory of a Muslim commander killed by Deep Singh in a duel. Part of village Chabba, it was located on the western edge of a rather expansive, nearly two-acre Muslim cemetery. There was even a practice among the local villagers to light a remembrance flame every evening. There is, however, no trace of it now because most cemeteries in the area have been leased out as farmland by the authorities.[16] Very likely that the cenotaph was in memory of Yakub Khan or Aman Khan, Muslim commanders Deep Singh fought with and killed in duels in the area.

With its preponderance of Muslims at the time, each village had one or more integral graveyard which still stands as such in revenue records. Gyani Gyan Singh records that Muslims killed in battle were buried in these parts. The innominate cenotaph near Tahla Sahib, supposedly of an enemy commander, had long been the object of Sikh reverence before it fell to the plough. The cenotaph is a major find and lends substantial credence to the battle narrative.

There may have been other commanders and soldiers of the Afghan Army who too fell to the Sikh sword and were buried in the area but the want of records makes any research and verification impossible.

The sole eye-witness account of the battle by Miskin

acknowledges the death of only one person—Mir Niamatullah, a prominent citizen of Lahore, and altogether omits other casualties, possibly, because of a limited view of the battle unless he deliberately chose to underreport this aspect.

Equally interesting that one of the cenotaphs in village Chabba is to the memory of a 'Moti Ram', suggesting that Sahajdhari Sikhs also fought as part of the Khalsa army. No less significant is the find of people from the area being inspired to take up cudgels in a just cause. Two cenotaphs bear testimony—Mahit Singh's in Chatiwind and Didar Singh's in Mehma. According to local sources they were natives of their respective village who joined the volunteer army at Tarn Taran. When killed in battle, their bodies were retrieved to their village for the last rites.

Put together, these records list around sixty Sikh martyrs, a figure obviously limited to the senior Sikh leadership and to those who distinguished themselves in battle since the overall Sikh casualties ran into several thousand killed or wounded.

The Khanda (Broadsword)

Deep Singh's khanda has long been the stuff of legend, often cited as weighing eighteen kilograms or ser (an obsolete Indian measure of weight). Kotha Guru who is credited with thorough research on Dam Dama Sahib records that, on hearing of the carnage at the Amritsar shrine, when Deep Singh sent edicts for Sikhs to rally for a military response:

'A Singh came forth with an offer of a khanda (broadsword) weighing eighteen ser, which Deep Singh accepted and wore in his baldric; in turn, he unstrapped and gave away his teg (large curved slashing sword) to his companions'.

This teg is now on display in the Dam Dama shrine and weighs 1.5 ser, seven tolas (approximately 1.5 kilogram).[17]

Gyani Gyan Singh, Kewal Singh Nirdosh, and Kanwal also record the weight of the khanda as eighteen ser,[18] while others cite it to be less.[19]

In the weight system prevalent at the time in the Punjab, before standardization in 1833 by the British, the katcha ser was the common measure as opposed to the pukka ser, the latter being 2.5 times the former. The conversion rate of the pukka ser in the Akbar system was 637.7 grams.[20] Accordingly, eighteen katcha ser would translate to approximately 4.6 kilograms; and twelve pukka ser as 7.7 kilograms, or approximately three kilograms in katcha ser.

A recent publication cites the weight of Deep Singh's broadsword as a mere eight katcha ser or two-three kilograms.[21] This, in fact, is the average weight of a broadsword and possibly, Deep Singh's khanda was in this range and not eighteen kilograms or ser as many tend to believe.

Deep Singh's personal weaponry preserved in Akal Takht at Harimandir Sahib and ceremonially displayed every evening after prayers includes a broadsword:[22]

- Dudhara Khanda (double-edged broadsword)
- Peshkabaj dagger stuck into the waistband for armour or chain mail piercing
- Pistol
- Medium sized Khanda
- Two kirpans
- Two small ornamental Khandas (spillikens) for the turban.
- Several quoits (chakras) of different sizes worn in the turban and also used as weapons; some are inscribed with hymns from the Sikh scriptures

Many of these weapons are inscribed with the *mool mantra* as well as excerpts from Sikh scriptures. The broadsword among this weaponry is in all probability the much storied one Deep Singh wielded in his last battle. It looks the usual size and weight alongside several others displayed—belonging to Baba Naudh Singh, Baba Gurbaksh Singh, and Akali Phula Singh. This can be gauged as much from the ease with which the functionaries handle these weapons during the display.[23]

Popular lore may depict iconic warriors as superhuman but arguably, Deep Singh adopted a personal weapon for his last battle, not overly larger nor heavier than the one he was accustomed to. As a veteran master swordsman, he knew that nimbleness is just as important as mass and momentum in swordplay.[24]

The total weight of Deep Singh's accoutrements when battle-ready, also announced during the evening weapon display at Akal Takth is put at 1.25 maund katcha or approximately sixteen kilograms.[25] His khanda and gurj (mace) together weighed above ten kilograms.[26] The quoits, peshkabaj, pistol, katar (push dagger), and chainmail made up the balance. This compares with the average iron load of twenty kilograms a Khalsa warrior carried as his accouterment.[27]

The siri sahib (sword) of Karam Singh of the Shaheed misl is also preserved in the Akal Takth. Other personal relics of Deep Singh preserved at Dam Dama Sahib—are a teg (large curved slashing sword), sarbloh jangi kara (steel bangle of wrought iron)[28] and a solid rosary of the same metal.

Outcome of the Battle

Some Sikh accounts suggest a Sikh victory, the enemy taking to their heels. Given the asymmetry in numbers and firepower, this is unlikely. When the tide of battle turned against them, Miskin's record though tragic is difficult to refute:

'Although the Sikhs took great pride in their valour, it was now their turn to be put to the sword, or to be blown up by our cannons. They were defeated and took to flight towards *Chak Guru*, but we pursued them all the way. On reaching the walled enclosure of *Chak Guru*, we saw five Sikh infantrymen at the gate who were all killed by our soldiers [....] The battle over, our army set up camp near *Chak Guru*.'[29]

Some writers erroneously record Deep Singh and Gurbaksh Singh among the five Sikhs killed at the gate.[30] Not only does this challenge the mainstream narrative but also flies in the face of the many commemorative shrines between Tarn Taran and Amritsar. Deep Singh was the head of a misl and Gurbaksh Singh a subordinate Jathedar in-charge of the Anandgarh shrine. Both could potentially field several thousand fighting men in battle. The five soldiers killed at the gate could either be advance elements of Deep Singh's own force or simply devotees visiting the shrine on the occasion of Diwali who, in a display of valour characteristic of their creed, chose the path of martyrdom when they found their shrine under attack. Miskin does mention intelligence reports of Sikhs bathing in their holy tank at Chak Guru (Amritsar).

It is, nevertheless, to the credit of the Sikhs that the Afghan Army also suffered heavily, particularly in the first phase of the battle when they broke and ran. Powered by their courage, resilience, and fighting ability, the Sikhs continued to take the fight to the enemy till the very end, many even reaching their objective against insuperable odds.

Patwant Singh is apt in his description of the battle in which the Sikhs 'fought to the last man with demonic fury,' while Deep Singh, although mortally wounded, 'hacked his way through the Afghan lines to die in the parikrama'.[31]

'A brave colonel makes a brave battalion' is a universal truth articulated by Frederick the Great.[32] There is little doubt that Deep Singh's inspiring courage and leadership helped stay and steady many on their course during the sanguinary battle which shall endure in living memory as a shining example of a handful of intrepid, randomly armed men who challenged the might of an empire only to redeem their honour, and that of their community.

As the commander of this devoted body of warriors, Deep Singh exhibited a rare meld of conspicuous courage, selflessness, tenacity of purpose, and an all-consuming mission-orientation, even after he was mortally wounded. Not far from his place of injury, the Sikhs had set up a makeshift dressing station—the commemorative Gurdwara Bachaona Sahib marks the spot—but Deep Singh chose to fight on rather than have his wounds tended. For his 'firmness of character' and the determination to bear on at all costs, he would certainly have won favour with Napoleon—perhaps, the greatest military strategist of all time—who counted these among the essential qualities of a commander-in-chief.[33]

Very early in life, Deep Singh had won the unique antemortem title 'Shaheed' as accolade for valour. His courage was even more conspicuous in his martyrdom, earning him a permanent place in history and legend:

داغِ سجود اگر تیری پیشانی پے ہو تو کیا
کوئی ایسا سجدہ کر کے زمین پے نیشان رہے

—Alama Iqbal

Daagh-e-Sajood agar teri Peshani pe ho to kya,
Koi aisa Sajda ker ke Zameen pe Nishan rahe
Your forehead bears an imprint from genuflecting at a shrine;
Leave a mark upon the earth instead, your life and deeds to shine.

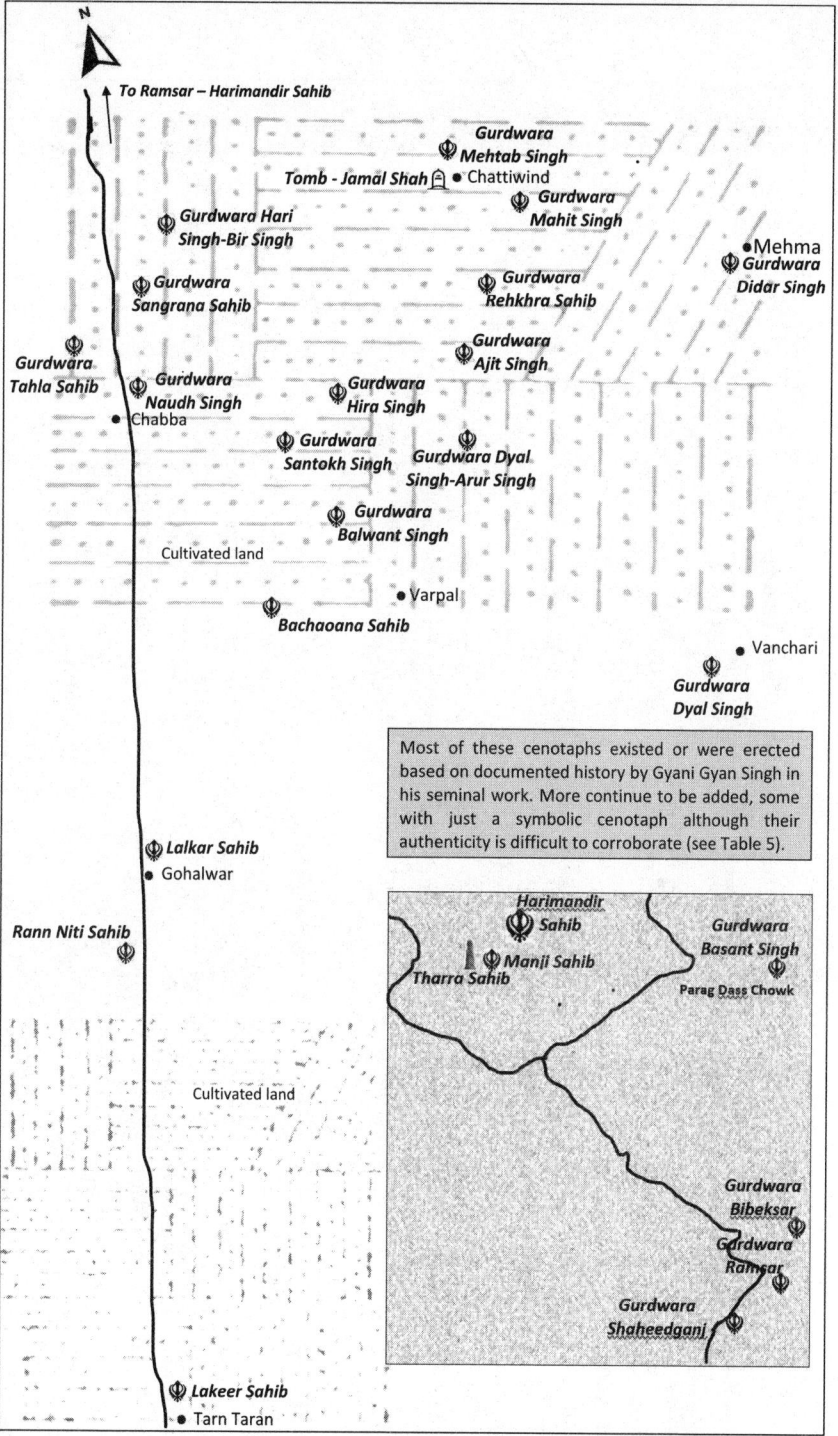

Figure 5: Prominent Battle-related Cenotaphs

Table 2: Circumstances of Deep Singh's Martyrdom

Adversary	Place	Outcome	Source
Yakub Khan and Aman Khan,	Chabba	Deep Singh is first challenged by Amir Jan Khan but Dyal Singh intervenes. Deep Singh then challenged and fought Yakub Khan, crushing his head with a mace. He was next challenged by Aman Khan. Both were beheaded, Deep Singh with his own sword.	Gyani Gyan Singh[34]
Shah Jamal	Ramsar	Reminded by a Singh of his pledge, he fought on, supporting his head with his left hand till Ramsar, where he died near the sarovar. In a later publication, Gyani Gyan Singh records a duel with Shah Jamal at Ramsar; both were beheaded—Deep Singh by a freak strike of his own sword.	
No single combat	Chabba Ramsar	Decapitated at Chabba, reminded by Sukha Singh Ramgarhia of his pledge; fought on supporting his head with his left hand. Fell a second time near Ramsar, again reminded and went up to Harimandir Sahib, where he died.	Giani Thakar Singh[35]
Shah Jamal	Ramsar	Heavy fighting near Ramsar. Shah Jamal was killed in the duel but Deep Singh also decapitated; reminded of his pledge, he fought on, his head supported by his left hand up to Harimandir Sahib, where he died.	Lala Dhani Ram Chatrik[36]

Adversary	Place	Outcome	Source
–Sar Buland Khan –Faujdar –Yakub Khan	Bibeksar	Killed his first two opponents, Sar Buland Khan and Faujdar but was wounded while fighting the third, Yakub Khan, although he killed him too. Reminded of his pledge by Dharam Singh, fought on with head supported by his left hand up to Harimandir Sahib, where he died.	Mohan Singh Ghukewalia[37]
–Yakub Khan –Shah Jamal	Chabba	First dueled with Yakub khan; both horses wounded; they dismounted and resumed combat on foot. Deep Singh bludgeoned Yakub Khan's head with a mace, killing him. Deep Singh mounted a fresh horse and was challenged by Shah Jamal, riled to see the Sikh advance. Their horses were maimed; they dismounted and resumed combat on foot; both beheaded; when reminded of his pledge, Deep Singh fought on supporting his head with his left hand. Heavy fighting at Ramsar, where he fell.	Kartar Singh Kalasvalia[38]
Jamal Shah		Both Deep Singh and Shah Jamal were killed in the encounter.	Babu Rajab Ali[39]
–Yakub Khan –Aman Khan/ Jamal Khan	Chabba	Deep Singh killed Yakub Khan; while fighting his second opponent, Aman Khan/Jamal Khan, he was decapitated but fought on and died at Ramsar.	Sohan Singh Seetal[40]

Adversary	Place	Outcome	Source
Chatur (cunning) Turk	Chabba	Deep Singh fought with great courage and was wherever the fighting was thickest. He slew many of the enemy but was decapitated by a *chatur* (cunning) Turk. Reminded of his pledge, he supported his head with his left hand and resumed fighting until he reached Harimandir Sahib where he died.	Mahinder Murti[41]
Bakshi Aman Khan	Ramsar	Heavy fighting in area Ramsar. In a duel with Bakshi Aman Khan, both decapitated. Deep Singh fought on, supporting his head with his left hand till he reached Harimandir Sahib, where he died.	Kewal Singh Nirdosh[42]
Ali Khan Bahadur and Ditta	Gohalwar–Chabba	Initially, Deep Singh attacked by 7-8 Pathan soldiers; then Ali Khan and Allah Ditta together attacked Deep Singh. Allla Ditta struck off Deep Singh's head. Pyara Singh reminded Deep Singh of his pledge; Deep Singh supported his head with his left hand and killed Alla Ditta. There was more fighting at Ramsar, where Deep Singh halted and threw his head to land in the Parkarma.	Trilok Singh Dervesh[43] Alla
Khan Jamal	Chabba	Deep Singh was challenged by Khan Jamal. In the duel both were decapitated. Reminded of his pledge, Deep Singh fought on supporting his head with his left hand until Harimandir Sahib.	Dya Singh Dilbar[44]

Adversary	Place	Outcome	Source
–General Sar Buland Khan –Faujdar (Jahan Khan)	Gohalwar–Chabba	Quite early in the battle, Deep Singh first challenged by, fought and killed the enemy general, Sar Buland Khan with one stroke. On seeing his comrade fall, the faujdar (Jahan Khan) challenged him to single combat. Both were decapitated. When reminded of his pledge, Deep Singh fought on supporting his head with his left hand till he reached Harimandir Sahib, where he died.	Buta Singh[45]
Jamal Shah	Chabba/Sangrana Sahib	Seeing the old veteran in command of the Sikh army, enemy commanders surrounded him. He was challenged by Jamal Shah. Deep Singh maimed his horse with a quoit. The combat resumed on foot. Both were decapitated but when reminded of his pledge, Deep Singh fought on supporting his head with his left hand till he reached Harimandir Sahib, where he died.	Gurdeep Singh Kanwal[46]

Table 3: Summary of Prominent Duels

Duels	Author
• In the first duel of the battle, **Amir Jan Khan** challenges **Deep Singh** but **Dyal Singh** intervenes, fights and kills Amir Jan Khan. **Deep Singh** fights and kills **Yakub Khan**; **Mir Jan Khan** applauds and would fight **Deep Singh** but **Naudh Singh** intervenes and fights **Mir Jan Khan**: both killed along with four-five other Sikhs at Chabba. **Deep Singh** fights **Aman Khan**. Aman Khan killed, and Deep Singh decapitated (near Chabba) but fights on. • **Balwant Singh** fought and killed **Zabardast Khan** with a quoit; next, he was challenged by and fought **Rustam Khan**, his brother; both were decapitated. • **Hira Singh** fought and killed **Syed Sabir Ali** near Guru-ke-bagh and many others before being martyred.	Gyani Gyan Singh[47]
• **Sher Singh Gill** fought **Mir Jan Khan**; both killed. • **Hira Singh** fought **Sabar Ali** near Guru-ka-Bagh and killed him. • **Balwant Singh** challenged and killed **Zabardast Khan** near Guru-ka-Bagh; in turn, he was challenged by his brother, **Rustam Khan**; both were killed	Kartar Singh Kalaswalia[48]
• After the Sikhs broke through from Gohalwar and were making a dash for their objective, **Amir Jan Khan** tried to intercept them on an elephant; **Dyal Singh** shot an arrow and killed him. Several Pathans now surrounded him; he was attacked by **Zabardast Khan** but **Balwant Singh** intervened and killed with a quoit. Next, **Balwant Singh** was attacked by his brother, **Rustam Khan**, both were killed.	Sohan Singh Seetal[49]

Duels	Author
• **Naudh Singh**, second-in-command of the Sikh army, fought and killed commander, **Kasim Khan Naulakhi Pattiwala**. He was killed subsequently in battle, by some accounts when seated from exhaustion and multiple wounds.	Oral tradition[50]

Table 4: Places of Martyrdom

Place	Author
• Mahit Singh was decapitated but fought on and fell at Chatiwind • Ram Singh was decapitated but fought on and fell at Bibeksar/Katra Ramgarhian • Mehtab Gill was martyred at Chatiwind • Naudh Singh was martyred at Chabba • Bir Singh and Hari Singh were martyred near Sangrana Sahib • Bir Singh, Kaur Singh, Manna Singh, Basant Singh, Sajjan Singh, Bahadur Singh, Akhar Singh, Ganda Singh, Nihal Singh, Lehna Singh, Gopal Singh, Ran Singh, Bhag Singh were martyred at Guru-ka-Bagh • Dyal Singh, Natha Singh, Mahil Singh, Nihal Singh, Bal Singh Chahil, Tara Singh, Kang Singh, Sudha Singh were martyred near Churasta Attari	Gyani Gyan Singh[51]

Place	Author
- Naudh Singh was martyred near Chabba - Hari Singh and Bir Singh were martyred near Sangrana Sahib - Dharam Singh was martyred near Bibeksar - Ram Singh was martyred near Katra Ramgarhian - Bir Singh, Basant Singh, Kaur Singh, Mana Singh (four brothers) martyred at Pragdas Chowk	Kartar Singh Kalaswalia[52]
- Naudh Singh was martyred at Chabba - Bir Singh and Hari Singh were martyred at Sangrana Sahib - Jathedar Ram Singh was martyred at Katra Ramgarhian - Several jathedars martyred at Guru-ke-Bagh: Sajjan Singh, Bahadur Singh, Akhar Singh, Hira Singh, Ganda Singh, Nihal Singh, Lehna Singh, Gopal Singh, Ran Singh, Bhag Singh, Dyal Singh, Natha Singh, Bal Singh, Tara Singh, Kang Singh - Dharam Singh was martyred near Bibeksar - Kaur Singh, Mana Singh, Basant Singh were martyred near Mangni Akhara/Parag Das Chowk	Sohan Singh Seetal[53]
- Vir (Bir) Singh, Hari Singh were martyred near Sangrana Sahib, - Aghar Singh, Ran Singh, Natha Singh, Dyal Singh, Sajjan Singh, Tara Singh, Bal Singh, Bhag Singh reached Sudhasar—cenotaph near Manji Sahib - Basant Singh, Manna Singh, etc were martyred near Pragdas Chowk - Naudh Singh near Chabba	Gurdeep Singh Kanwal[54]

Table 5: Cenotaphs: Documented versus On-Ground

Place/Village	On-ground	Documented by Gyani Gyan Singh	Remarks
Vanchari	Dyal Singh	Dyal Singh Mahal	Believed to be among the first Sikh casualties in the battle. His place of martyrdom is not documented but there is a cenotaph-gurdwara in village Vanchari supposedly to his memory. Interestingly, a few miles North, a patti (part) of village Sultanwind is of the same 'Mahal' sub-caste or gotra.
Chabba	Deep Singh, Dalip Singh, Gurbaksh Singh, Hari Singh Vir Singh Naudh Singh, Gyan Singh (separate shrine) Hari Singh-Vir Singh (near Sangrana Sahib) also called Rohri Sahib Moti Ram	Deep Singh (place of injury—Tahla Sahib), Naudh Singh (Chabba), Bir Singh–Hari Singh (near Sangrana Sahib)	According to local information, Tahla Sahib is to the memory of Deep Singh, Dalip Singh, Gurbaksh Singh, Hari Singh, and Bir Singh. There is a separate shrine for Gyan Singh, a common one for Hari Singh-Vir Singh (near Sangrana Sahib), and another for Moti Ram (in Chabba).

Place/Village	On-ground	Documented by Gyani Gyan Singh	Remarks
Chhota Varpal	Bachaona Sahib	—	This was a makeshift dressing-cum-food station as well as cremation ground for Sikh warriors in the battle. It includes a prominent samadh that enshrines the ashes as well as some weaponry of the fallen.
Varpal	Kundan Singh Raula Singh—Prem Singh Ganda Singh Bagga Singh Himmat Singh Jawaand Singh Balwant Singh Harcharan Singh Santokh Singh Dharam Singh—Tara Singh Dyal Singh—Arur Singh Baliihar Singh—Bahal Singh	—	Gyani Gyan Singh records the exploits of Balwant Singh in the battle but makes no mention of his cenotaph. His name is also included in the memorial obelisk at Tharra Sahib (Manji Sahib).

Place/Village	On-ground	Documented by Gyani Gyan Singh	Remarks
	Jawahar Singh–Narayan Singh, Jhand Singh Kartar Singh-Anokh Singh-Jagtar Singh-Shingara Singh-Kahn Singh Ajit Singh Bijla Singh (Jhand Sahib) Hira Singh— Vrisa Singh Pritam Singh— Banta Singh		
Mehma	Didar Singh	—	This is a prominent memorial Gurdwara; according to local information, Didar Singh belonged to this village and joined the army of Sikh volunteers at Tarn Taran. When he died in the battle, his body was retrieved by the village for the last rites.

Place/Village	On-ground	Documented by Gyani Gyan Singh	Remarks
Chatiwind	Mehtab Singh Sahit Singh (should be Mahit Singh) Gurlabh Singh Rakhra Sahib (langar) in memory of Resham Singh—Dharam Singh	Mehtab Singh Gill, Mahit Singh Sran	Rekhra Sahib marks the place of the langar (community kitchen) during the battle; also commemorates two cooks who were martyred—Resham Singh and Dharam Singh. The 'Boparai' clan of Chatiwind acknowledge Mehtab Singh's shrine as its jathere. It is a coincidence that a part of the village, Chatiwind, with Mahit Singh's cenotaph is of the same 'Sran' sub-caste. The locals claim that he belonged to the village and joined the crusade on the day at Tarn Taran.
Sultanwind Bibeksar/Katra (Amritsar)	Mall Singh —	Dharam Singh, Narayan Ramgarhia Singh, Ram Singh)	No cenotaph could be traced.
Prag Das Chowk/Mangni Akhara (Amritsar)	Basant Singh	Bir Singh, Basant Singh, Kaur Singh, Mana Singh (four brothers)	Mangni Ram laid the foundation of this locality, whereas Prag Das developed it.[55] The cenotaph shrine is to the memory of Basant Singh.

Place/Village	On-ground	Documented by Gyani Gyan Singh	Remarks
Churasti Atari (Amritsar)	—	Dyal Singh, Natha Singh, Mahil Singh, Nihal Singh, Bal Singh Chahil, Tara Singh, Sudha Singh, Kang Singh	No memorial or cenotaph could be found, possibly, these disappeared as part of the redevelopment.
Guru-ke-Bagh/ Manji Sahib/ Tharra Sahib (Harimandir Sahib)	Baba Balwant Singh, Baba Hira Singh, Baba Ganda Singh, Baba Lehna Singh, Baba Ran Singh, Baba Gopal Singh, Baba Bhag Singh, Baba Sajjan Singh, Baba Bahadur Singh.	Akhar Singh, Bahadur Singh, Bal Singh, Basant Singh, Bhag Singh, Bir Singh, Dyal Singh, Ganda Singh, Gopal Singh, Hira Singh, Kang Singh, Kaur Singh, Lehna Singh, Manna Singh, Natha Singh, Nihal Singh, Ran Singh, Sajjan Singh, Tara Singh.	The inscription on the memorial mentions this as the place of their cremation and that these names represent only 'some' of those martyred. Balwant Singh's name appears at the top although no writer has included it among those martyred or cremated here. Possibly, because there is a prominent shrine dedicated to his memory near village Varpal, his putative place of martyrdom and cremation. There are nineteen names documented for this spot but the memorial stands only for nine, and excludes the following eleven: Akhar Singh, Bal Singh, Basant Singh, Bir Singh, Dyal Singh, Kang Singh, Kaur Singh, Manna Singh, Natha Singh, Nihal Singh, Tara Singh.

FOURTEEN

Tryst with Harimandir Sahib

Contentious Narrative

The Deep Singh narrative is extraordinary for the circumstances of his death which tend to overshadow even his life and for that reason, never fail to generate debate and disbelief. That a handful of brave men took it upon themselves to challenge the might of a tyrannical regime is the usual saga of heroism found in many cultures across the world. But that their leader, although mortally wounded, battled on until he reached his objective in order to honor a pledge he foreswore that morning, and inspired many others to do likewise, is the stuff not of history but of legend.

Gyani Gyan Singh was the first to articulate this narrative in his *Sri Guru Panth Parkash* (1867):

ਨਰਾਜ ਛੰਦ ॥ ਹਏ ਕਿਕਾਨ ਦੋਇ ਕੈ, ਟੁਟੇ ਸੰਜੋਇ ਆਜੁਯੈਂ ।
ਭਏ ਸੁ ਹੱਥ-ਵੱਛ ਹੱਥ, ਯੋਇ ਦੋਇ ਆਜੁ ਤੇ ॥੫੫॥
ਦੋਹਰਾ ॥ ਚਲੀ ਤੇਗ ਅਤਿ ਬੇਗ ਸੈ, ਦੁਹੂੰ ਕੇਰ ਬਲ -ਵਾਰ.।
ਉਤਰ ਗਏ ਸਿਰ ਦੁਹੂੰ ਕੇ, ਪਰਸ-ਪਰੈਂ ਇਕ ਸਾਰ ॥੫੬॥
ਚੌਪਈ ॥ ਦਿਗ ਤੇ ਏਕ ਸਿੰਘ ਪਿਖ ਕਹਯੋ ।
ਪਰਣ ਤੁਮਾਰ ਦੀਪ ਸਿੰਘ ਰਹਯੋ ।
ਗੁਰਪੁਰ ਜਾਇ- ਸੀਸ ਮੈਂ ਦੈਹੋਂ ।
ਸੋ ਤੇ ਦੋਇ ਕੋਸ ਇਸ ਠੇਹੋਂ ॥੫੭॥
ਸੁਨ ਸਿੰਘ ਜੀ ਨਿਜ ਪਰਣ ਸੰਭਾਰਾ ।
ਨਿਜ ਸਿਰ ਬਾਮ-ਹਾਥ ਨਿਜ ਧਾਰਾ ।

Tryst with Harimandir Sahib

ਦਹਿਨੇ ਹਾਥ ਤੇਗ ਖਰ ਧਾਰਾ ।
ਵੱਜਨ ਜਾਂਹਿ ਥਾ ਸੇਰ ਅਠਾਰਾਂ ॥੫੮॥

—Gyani Gyan Singh, *Panth Prakash II*,
Utararadh Bisram 50, Stanza 55-58

Naraj chhand. Haye kikan doi kei, tute sanjoi ayudhein
    Bhaye su hath-vath hath, dhoi doi ayu tai (55)
Dohra. Chali teg ut beg sain, duhun ker bal-vaar.
    Utar gaye sir duhun ke, pars-perein ik saar (56)
Chaupai. Dhig tei ek Singh pikh keyo
    Paran tumar Deep Singh reheyo
    Gurpur jaye sees mein dehon
    So te doi kos is thehon (57)
    Sun Singh ji nij paran sambhara
    Nij sir bam-hath nij dhara
    Dehine hath teg khar dhara
    Vajan jan tha ser atharan

In battle both were now engaged;
their chain mail pierced but still they raged
until with swords they cut and thrust;
their heads then fell and hit the dust.
At this a fellow soldier quoth:
'Oh Deep Singh, now recall your oath.
At *Gurpur* [Amritsar] you would martyred be:
That's still four miles,[1] so God help thee!'
Now Deep Singh stirred with godly strength;
His head in left hand held at length,
And swung his sword then with his right—
Of eighteen *ser*[2] to resume the fight.

This happened in the second phase of the battle near Chabba while dueling Aman Khan, an enemy commander. By a simultaneous stroke, both are beheaded but when prompted, Deep Singh fights on (see photo insert, Figure 12). Prior to this, Deep Singh has just killed Yakub Khan, another enemy commander, bludgeoning him with his mace. In a publication that appeared twenty-three years later, after more research, Gyani Gyan Singh names Shah

Jamal as the opponent at Ramsar, not Chabba. Many historians in subsequent accounts alter the names of Deep Singh's opponents, and adopt Ramsar as the place of injury.

Commemorative Shrines

The place where Deep Singh was injured is marked with the commemorative shrine Tahla Sahib (see Figure 15) adjoining Chabba, while the Shaheed Bunga overlooks the circular spot—long since removed—where his head fell in the parikrama within Harimandir Sahib, 6.4 kilometres away (see Figure 8). Gyani Gyan Singh records the construction of this Bunga by Deep Singh in 1764 at a cost of Rs 22,000. This is inconceivable since he was martyred much earlier in 1757. It is more likely that, as Karam Singh suggests, he laid its foundations.[3] Plainly in either case, the historic structure should simply represent the Shaheed misl rather than commemorate his martyrdom. 'Bunga' simply means 'bungalow' and in this sense, it is of a piece with the sixty-nine bungas recorded by Gyani Gyan Singh along with their cost and year of construction in his *Twarikh Sri Amritsar*, all in the vicinity of Harimandir Sahib. These include the Akal Bunga (Akal Takth) constructed in 1606 by Guru Hargobind on his assuming guruship. Several misls are also represented—Kanhayia (1752), Ramgarhia (1755), Sukarchakia (1778), Nakai (1790), Ahluwalia (1804).[4]

The location of the Shaheed Bunga, however, is significant because unlike others, it serves as a cenotaph-cum-gurdwara that enshrines the Guru Granth Sahib. It is also one of only three bungas that have survived within the perimeter of Harimandir Sahib, the others being Akal Bunga and Ramgarhia Bunga. But it is the only Bunga along with the Akal Bunga (Akal Takth) that enshrines the Guru Granth Sahib, the Ramgarhia Bunga does not.

A third commemorative shrine related to Deep Singh's martyrdom is Gurdwara Shaheedganj near Ramsar, approximately a kilometre short of Harimandir Sahib (see Figure 13). Gyani

Gyan Singh maintains that it marks the place of his martyrdom while some writers refer to it as the place of his mortal injury, and others of his cremation. Having fought the good fight, this is unequivocally where his mortal remains along with those of many of his companions killed in the vicinity were cremated under the aegis of the Ramgarhias some of whom took part in the battle. In this sense, it is a samadh with an octagonal shape in the Sikh tradition but as a gurdwara, enshrines the Guru Granth Sahib. It includes an original likeness of Deep Singh by the famous Sikh artist, Sobha Singh, installed in 1976.[5]

A few yards away is the samadh of Jodh Singh Ramgarhia,[6] which attests to the region being a part of the Ramgarhia dominion. A plaque records that, thereafter, this area of some 1786 square yards served as a cremation ground for a total of twelve members of the Ramgarhia leadership until gifted to Gurdwara Shaheedganj for development and modernization.[7]

Not far, Jassa Singh Ahluwalia, had initially built a mud fortalice, Ram Rauni, in 1748 for the defence of Harimandir Sahib,[8] shortly made over to Jassa Singh Ramgarhia as its first custodian (qilladar). Destroyed initially by Mir Mannu during the Sikh struggle, it was rebuilt and fortified by the resilient Ramgarhias as the grandiose Quila Ramgarhia, giving its name to the eponymous misl besides becoming the base of Khalsa operations in 1754.[9] It was demolished yet again in May 1757 along with Harimandir Sahib on the orders of Ahmed Shah Durrani but rebuilt and further embellished until it was destroyed yet again, this time by Jahan Khan, only to be restored after 1764 when the misls came into their own. The Ramgarhia Gate has survived as an imposing remnant.[10]

Gurdwara Shaheedganj fell within Katra Ramgarhia, the largest of the Katras established in 1755.[11] The gurdwara was constructed by Jassa Singh Ramgarhia about the same time, after 1764, and gilded many decades later by Akali Phula Singh, a general in Maharaja Ranjit Singh's army and a follower of the Shaheed misl.[12]

Rationale and Ratiocination

The narrative has been part of oral traditions for over two centuries, much before it was first documented by Gyani Gyan Singh in 1867. Balladeers sing paeans to the motley group of warriors who, inspired by their daring leader, swelled from a few hundred to five thousand. They dwell passionately upon their daring in battle, recount with ardent warmth the duels with enemy commanders but save much of their fervor for the grand finale when Deep Singh, felled during single combat, rose on being reminded of his oath and supporting his severed head on one hand, continued to wield the broadsword with the other until he reached Harimandir Sahib.

For this paranormal feat, people relate to Deep Singh chiefly in two ways—some deify and worship him, while incredulous and carping dissenters deny him a place in history altogether, dismissing the narrative as myth. Ironical, indeed, that one of the most revered heroes of Sikh history should remain an enigma partly because of the reluctance on the part of many to even discuss the historicity of the battle.

A commonly articulated view among writers denies the severed head narrative to suggest that Deep Singh was only severely wounded:

'Almost every companion of the Baba [Deep Singh] lost his life. His own head had received a mortal wound. But as he had vowed not to lay down his life before visiting the precincts of the Temple, he cut through enemy forces, bleeding profusely, and fell dead only after he had arrived in the holy sanctuary.'[13]

This may seem more credible but fails to answer several questions such as the origin of the severed head narrative, the battle-related commemorative shrines, and the oral tradition.

Most academics view the narrative as apocryphal. Those who would engage with it intellectually tend to hedge as they all but debunk it to adopt a ratiocinative approach, offering ahistorical interpretations that hinge on the mythological, symbolic, or the idiomatic but their polemic begs just as many counter-arguments and questions.[14]

- A 'mythological' representation likens him, for instance, to Hanuman in Hindu mythology, often represented with Ram and Sita enshrined in his heart. But this comparison is fallacious since, unlike Hanuman, a figure from pre-history, Deep Singh lived and died in the 18th century, and various landmarks associated with his last battle exist on ground.
- A 'symbolic' representation views Deep Singh's feat in relation to Nanak's couplet:

ਜਉ ਤਉ ਪ੍ਰੇਮ ਖੇਲਣ ਕਾ ਚਾਉ ॥ ਸਿਰ ਧਰਿ ਤਲਿ ਗਲਿ ਮੇਰੀ ਆਉ ॥
ਇਤ ਮਾਰਗ ਪੈਰ ਧਰੀਜੈ ॥ ਸਿਰੁ ਦੀਜੈ ਕਾਣ ਨ ਕੀਜੈ ॥

—Guru Nanak,
Sri Guru Granth Sahib, 1412

Jau tau prem khelan ka chou. Sir dhar tali meri au.
It marag pair dharijey. Sir dijey kan na kijey
If you wish to play the Game of Divine Love, follow my path with your head in your palm; Whosoever follows my path, should be prepared to sacrifice his head without hesitation.

Here again it seems illogical to apply this scriptural couplet to Deep Singh alone and not to the scores of other famous Sikh martyrs whose sacrifice was no less significant.

- As an 'idiomatic' representation:

ਸਿਰੁ ਤਲਿ ਤੇ ਰਖ ਕੇ ਲੜਨਾ ॥
Sir dhar tali meri au.
Follow my path with your head in your palm.

is interpreted simply as to 'fight against heavy odds'.

In his magnum opus, Kahn Singh Nabha describes such daring to be characteristic of Deep Singh:

ਅਨੇਕ ਲੜਾਈਆਂ ਵਿੱਚ ਸ਼ਹੀਦ ਹੋਣ ਲਈ ਜਾਨ ਹਥੇਲੀ ਤੇ ਰੱਖਕੇ ਅੱਗੇ ਵਧਦੇ ਸਨ[15]
Anek larayian vich shaheed hon layi jaan hatheli te rakh ke agge vaddhe san
Would always fight in the van, carrying his head in his palm

In Punjabi, this idiomatic expression means 'to take great risk', 'put one's life on line', 'at the peril of one's life'.

Here too, there are several Sikh martyrs who fought equally heavy odds. For instance, Baba Naudh Singh and many others fought and fell in the same battle but are not similarly represented—except for Mahit Singh and Ram Singh recorded by Gyani Gyan Singh, although their narrative has failed to grip the popular imagination.

The circumstances of martyrdom recorded in respect of other famous Sikh martyrs over the years, besides the two Sikh Gurus, are widely accepted to be true:

- Bhai Mati Das (companion of Guru Tegh Bahadur): sawed in half on 11th November 1675.
- Bhai Sati Das (companion of Guru Tegh Bahadur): burnt alive on 11th November 1675.
- Bhai Dyala (companion of Guru Tegh Bahadur): boiled in a caulron on 11th November 1675.
- Haqikat Rai: beheaded in January 1735.
- Bhai Mani Singh: jointed or dismembered on 14th June 1738.
- Bhai Bota Singh and Bhai Garjha Singh: went down fighting with wooden staffs against a body of 100 Mughal soldiers in 1739.
- Bhai Taru Singh: scalped in 1745.
- Bhai Shabeg Singh and Bhai Shahbaz Singh (father and son): killed on the serrated wheel on 10th March 1746.

Among these Sikh martyrs, Deep Singh's martyrdom, in November 1757, is the most recent. Indeed, if the circumstances of martyrdom in respect of others are so readily accepted, it is illogical to question these for Deep Singh alone. Besides, the presence of a remembrancer, Dharam Singh or Sukha Singh, who prompts Deep Singh to bear on when wounded, although superfluous to the narrative, lends substantial authenticity.

Credited with the first comprehensive history of the Sikhs, Gyani Gyan Singh chronicles with meticulous care the life, times and roles of all major personages of any consequence in Sikh history, beginning with the Sikh Gurus right up to the kingdom of Maharaja Ranjit Singh. Yet, he attributes the extraordinary act of battling on, although decapitated, to just Deep Singh and his two comrades-in-arms, Mahit Singh and Ram Singh. This alone must infuse considerable cogency into the Deep Singh legend.

Inferences

In order to separate certitude from legend, an objective search for truth should incorporate both documented and oral history alongside field research. The only eye-witness account by Miskin notes the Afghan army pursuing the Sikhs all the way to the gates of their shrine, the diarist among them,[16] but records no instance of a warrior fighting on although beheaded. While the fog of war might prevent the recording of the full details of a battle, particularly one fought over a wide area on a full day, it might still be argued that if any soldiers did witness an unusual feat, they would surely have discussed it among themselves and possibly, shared it with others. However, a diarist eventually records only what he saw or readily believed as cannily possible. In Miskin's case, Setu Rao, the translator, has also exercised his discretion in abridging or omitting events that the diarist did not directly witness.[17] In any case, Miskin's account alone cannot be accepted as the sole arbiter to reject the received narrative of Deep Singh's martyrdom.

Medical science and reason might ever remain skeptical of this superhuman feat depicted reverentially in colour prints to this day (see Figure 12) but devotees continue to marvel and believe in its veracity. Those who welter in doubt need to answer how and why, in the first place, the 'severed head' legend arose and why it could possibly be without substance when the events occurred not so far back in time. The 18th century is subsumed under modern history characterized by meticulous detail. For instance, the record of a contemporary battle at Plassey fought the same year on 23rd June 1757 between the East India Company under Robert Clive and Siraj-ud-Daulah, with French Artillery support, includes complete details of the Order of Battle, manoeuvres, and casualties—twenty-two killed (seven Europeans and fifteen Indians), fifty wounded (fifteen Europeans and thirty Indians).

Deep Singh's battle has been chronicled and continues to be sung by troubadours and bards alike in words which, in many cases, were composed very long ago, probably not long after the battle itself, and could well be based on eye-witness accounts of survivors from the battle. This is strong evidence since much of Sikh history of the period has been similarly passed down orally.

It is also difficult to surmise the exact distance over which Deep Singh fought in the singular manner depicted—six kilometres from Tahla Sahib, or less. Alternatively, he received a second more grievous wound that may have actually or very nearly severed his head near Ramsar, a kilometre short of his objective, when Attai Khan arrived to intercept the Sikhs. This is supported by the belief that he received his fatal wound at Ramsar and not Tahla Sahib. A number of historians subscribe to this view including Ganda Singh, Teja Singh, Bhagat Singh, and Lakshman Singh.[18] Even Gyani Thakur writes that, during the battle, Deep Singh fell twice from his wounds, first near Chabba and a second time near Ramsar.[19] In the event, he could not possibly have been fatally wounded at Chabba to be able to fight another duel at Ramsar.

Conclusion

Analyses predicated on documentary and field evidence alongside oral traditions signal some aspects of the received 'severed head' narrative as non-negotiable:

- Deep Singh fought and advanced through a distance of some eleven kilometres from Goharwal to Ramsar, braving overwhelming odds all the way.

- He fought and, possibly, killed some enemy commanders in duels in area Chabba-Chatiwind. At least one Muslim cenotaph in the area, although innominate, bore testimony.
- In addition to the multiple cuts and bruises inevitable in close combat, he was twice wounded, first near Chabba, in the neck. The wound was deep enough to spawn the 'severed head' legend.
- If, indeed, he did fight his final duel near Ramsar, the wound sustained near Chabba may not have been incapacitating.
- The distance over which Deep Singh continued to fight when mortally wounded shall ever remain the subject of debate—the full six kilometres from Tahla Sahib, or the last few yards? Did he press on by dint of sheer determination until the exertions completely severed his head?

If the oldest documented account of the battle by Gyani Gyan Singh is to be believed, Deep Singh fought duels with Yakub Khan, Aman Khan, and Jamal Shah. Although wounded in the second duel, he battled on to die at Ramsar in the third duel. Gyani Gyan Singh accommodates the Shaheed Bunga coherently into his narrative. For him, it was Deep Singh himself who built it—or at least laid its foundations, as Karam Singh suggests. In any case, Gyani Gyan Singh does not relate it to Deep Singh's martyrdom, which he mistakenly postpones by ten years, to 1767 CE.

Dervesh, another writer, states that before Deep Singh died at Ramsar, he flung his severed head to land in the parikrama as if to suggest by hyperbolic tenor that it was 'conveyed' to the parikrama to rest beside the Shaheed Bunga (or its foundation stone), possibly by a mindful comrade-in-arms to fulfil their commander's wish and oath.[20] In a sense, this is in line with the popular tradition which hails Deep Singh's blistering resolve that drove him to hack his way through the enemy to die on the parikrama.

In essence, two interrelated elements constitute the mainstay of this popular narrative—one, the Shaheed Bunga and two, the circular mark below it, the putative spot where Deep Singh's head fell—there is no mention of the body. That research tends to endorse neither could be an epiphany—the bunga merely represents the Shaheed misl and not shaheedi (martyrdom), and the circular mark below it was effaced because, among other reasons, it was not backed by historical evidence.[21]

In the final analysis, it is the reader alone who must address one last question. Is this a larger than life, part-contrived-part-exaggerated portrayal of a great warrior renowned for his courage, robustness, and spiritual energy? Or was Deep Singh actually far above the ordinary and in his finest hour, outdid himself when propelled to reach beyond the frail pale of human capability?

Belief or the suspension of disbelief are a wholly personal domain and yet, in all fairness, an inclusive view undergirded by objective analyses should be the essential pre-requisite to any conclusion.

Epilogue

> How glorious fall the valiant, sword in hand,
> In front of battle for their native land.
>
> —Tyrtaeus, *Martial Elegy*

Sikh Retaliation

Sensitive to the high-risk nature of their mission and the need to conserve their core misl strength, Deep Singh had mobilized only half his fighting force at Dam Dama Sahib in October 1757. He did not ask nor expect the Anandgarh wing under Gurbaksh Singh to join in concert but when the latter heard of the fatalities, particularly that of his leader, he felt it incumbent upon himself to act. He rode out post-haste along with Dargaha Singh at the head of 2000 fighting men.[1]

Inflamed by the extent of carnage at Amritsar, they attacked and burnt several police posts. This would have happened a few days after 11th November 1757, by when the Lahore Army had struck camp and returned to base. In retaliation, a huge force from Lahore and beyond was requisitioned. Gyani Gyan Singh puts their strength at 20,000 but half that number is more probable in the short time they deployed. According to Gyani Gyan Singh, in the unequal contest on 20th November 1757 (9 Maghar 1814 Bikrami), Gurbaksh Singh, Man Singh, Basant Singh, Nihal Singh and twenty-six followers found glory in the battlefield in the best traditions of Sikh valor and sacrifice. While the memorial behind the Akal Takth commemorates the martyrdom of Gurbaksh Singh and his comrades, Basant Singh's name is included in the obelisk at Tharra Sahib; Nihal Singh's cenotaph cannot be found at Churasta Attari.[2] Some survivors are known to have taken refuge in the adjoining Basra thicket.

Not only is the differential between the large force mobilized from Anandgarh and the low battle casualties irreconcilable but mainstream history of the period records no such defensive Sikh battle either. It is more likely that Gurbaksh Singh fought two major battles in Amritsar. He survived the first along with the bulk of his force in November 1757, possibly having taken shelter in the Basra thicket and was martyred much later, in a second battle fought on 1st December 1764.

Close on the heels, in December 1757, followed another setback for the Sikhs. Sodhi Vadbhag Singh, a holy man of much substance and renown was mercilessly bludgeoned to near-death by Jahan Khan's officials sent to investigate a killing at Kartarpur near Jalandhar. Jassa Singh Ahluwalia had already called on the misaldars to avenge Deep Singh's martyrdom and this atrocity now gave them further cause to act.[3] The Sikhs rose in rebellion on all sides. A force of 20,000 horse and foot sent against them in January 1758 was trounced, its captains slain, baggage looted, and all artillery captured. Any subsequent force sent against them met the same fate. Lahore, the capital, was not spared either. For several nights, Sikh warring bands in their thousands trampled down the city under the hoofs of their horses, plundering with utter lawlessness and bringing the government to its knees from November 1757 to February 1758.[4]

There was worse to follow when, next, they leagued with Adina Beg and the Marathas to invest and reduce Sirhind on 8th March 1758, taking its governor prisoner. In the action, the Dal Khalsa comprised the Sukerchakias, Ahluwalias, Ramgarhias, Bhangis and Tara Singh Ghaiba. Animated by the victory, the armies then marched on to Lahore in April 1758. Jahan Khan and Timur Shah fled and only just managed to escape across the

Ravi. Chafing at the ignominy of defeat and relentless brutalities, the Sikhs pursued and overtook many of the fleeing Afghan soldiers only to bring them back as captives to Amritsar where they were made to cleanse the temple premises and restore its holy tank to expiate the desecration of May 1757.[5] With this action, the martyrdom of Deep Singh and his brave comrades-in-arms was fully avenged.

The Greater Holocaust

Turning the brief pause in Afghan hostilities to their advantage, the Sikhs threw up several mud forts and fortalices all over the province and in October 1760, even took Rustam Khan, governor of Chahar Mahal, prisoner along with Miskin, the soldier-diarist, now his deputy, and held both to ransom. Their hour of glory came in November 1761 when after several years of intense and sometimes desultory conflict in which they invariably showed singular courage and war-faring ability, they achieved the astonishing feat of conquering Lahore, a province that had been under foreign rule for over 750 years.[6] Lahore was now part of the Durrani empire and the Khalsa victory served to considerably dent Afghan hubris. In most of these actions, Natha Singh and Dyal Singh, both members of the Shaheed misl continued to play a prominent role, displaying the courage and zeal characteristic of their clan.[7]

Unfortunately, the Sikh triumph also invited the wrath of the Afghan Emperor. Sikh elation was soon to be eclipsed by one of their greatest tragedies when Durrani caught them unawares in a punitive expedition during his sixth invasion. The massacre on 5th February 1762 at Kup near Malerkotla has gone down in Sikh annals as the Vada Ghallughara (Greater Holocaust) in which they lost some 20,000 dead, including their hapless vahir— administrative complement comprised mostly of aged men, women, and children. What made this reversal more poignant was the loss of two historic granths, one each from Dam Dama

Sahib and Harimandir Sahib (Amritsar) that fell into enemy hands, never to be heard of again.[8] The Sikhs had been forced to carry this invaluable heritage on the move as an expedient since their places of worship were constantly under attack.

In the wake of the massacre, Harimandir Sahib was destroyed yet again on 10th April 1762.[9] However, this time, while blowing up the shrine, Ahmed Shah Durrani was hit on the nose by a flying brickbat. He would die of this wound ten years later on 16th October 1772 when it aggravated into a gangrenous ulcer.[10]

Rising Sikh Fortunes

It was not in Sikh nature to be cowed down for long. Each tragedy seemed to have just the opposite effect on a people widely diffused in the province but united by the belief in a higher destiny and the unrelenting enterprise that went with it. Malcolm observed, 'The Sikh nation, who have, throughout their early history, always appeared, like a suppressed flame, to rise into higher splendor from every attempt to crush them, had become, while they were oppressed, as formidable for their union, as for their determined courage and unconquerable spirit of resistance.'[11]

In May 1762, the Sikhs invested Sirhind yet again, exacting a tribute of Rs 50,000 from Zain Khan Sirhindi, its Mughal governor, who had earlier successfully commanded a field army under Ahmed Shah Durrani during the Third Battle of Panipat in January 1761.

By July 1762, their unbridled depredations had reduced the entire province into a state of fear and turmoil. When the Dal Khalsa assembled on 17th October 1762 to celebrate Diwali at Amritsar, Ahmed Shah Durrani attacked them but was repulsed. In turn, they counterattacked him in December as he was crossing a boat-bridge over the Ravi on his return journey to Kabul, leaving him baffled at their resilience.[12]

In March 1763, they celebrated Hola Mohalla at Anandpur

and thereafter their fortunes continued to soar. Their watershed moment came the following year on 14th January 1764. In a federal effort comprising six misls of the Budha Dal (Ahluwalias, Dallewalias, Faizullahpuria, Karorasinghias, Nishanwalias, and Shaheeds) plus the Bhangis of the Taruna Dal along with Ala Singh of Patiala, under the overall command of Jassa Singh Ahluwalia, they attacked and destroyed Sirhind, slaying its Governor, Zain Khan.[13] This was a decisive victory that added Sirhind to Khalsa dominions. It was divided among the seven misls and Ala Singh. The misaldars used this opportunity to make inroads further south beyond Saharanpur, exacting tribute and extending their control.[14]

The Shaheed misl in this action was led by Karam Singh, who had assumed leadership after his predecessor, Sudh Singh was martyred in 1762 fighting the Pathans in an action near his native village Dakoha, not far from Jalandhar.[15]

Returning with a huge booty, the first task of the Khalsa was to rebuild their Amritsar shrine. The foundation stone was laid by Sultan-e-Quam, Jassa Singh Ahluwalia, on Vaisakhi 1764 and a sum of Rupees Nine lakh (little under a million) set aside for the purpose. Their plans for reconstruction were, however, rudely interrupted by Ahmed Shah Durrani's seventh invasion when the Sikh temple once again became the target of Afghan ire.

In a defensive battle fought on 1st December 1764 behind the Akal Takht, Gurbaksh Singh was martyred along with his thirty comrades-in-arms. Although he was the custodian of Anandgarh, he had likely relocated to defend Harimandir Sahib against the invaders. HR Gupta differs on the place of battle, suggesting that it was Qilla Ramgarh—not Harimandir Sahib—a fort constructed many years earlier to garrison troops for the defence of the Sikh temple.[16]

This is at variance with Bhangu's narrative (*Panth Prakash* Volume 2, Episode 156) which records the place as Akal Takht and lauds the heroism of Nihang Gurbaksh Singh—'a strapping young warrior' (stanza 2) whose 'seat was within the Akal Takht' (stanza 12), not Anandgarh—and his opiated band of followers. A memorial behind Akal Takth commemorates the martyrdom of Gurbaksh Singh Shaheed (Nihang Singh) in 1764 CE.

An entry by Ahmed Shah's scribe, Qazi Nur Mohammad, states:

> When the Shah reached the Chak [on 1st December 1764], there was not a single *kafir* to be seen. But a few of them had remained in an enclosure [and] when they saw the renowned king and army of Islam, they came out of the enclosure. They were thirty in number. But they had not a grain of fear in them.[17]

The 'Chak' refers to Guru da Chak, the small settlement that later grew into present-day Amritsar. 'Enclosure' could mean either Fort Ramgarh or Akal Takth, though most likely the latter. This, nonetheless, explains why Gupta records the place of battle as Fort Ramgarh.

Within the Shaheed misl, the baton of leadership had already passed from Sudh Singh to Karam Singh in 1762. Now it passed from Gurbaksh Singh to Suba Singh, and from Basant Singh (Sialkot branch) to Prem Singh.[18]

The sanctum sanctorum, Amrit Sarovar, the bridge, Baba Deep Singh Shaheed Bunga, and the Darshani Deohri (entrance gate) were finally completed in 1776.[19] The parikrama and the religious places in the periphery took longer and were finished only by 1784.

Sikh Empire

In 1799, exactly 100 years after the founding of the Khalsa in 1699, Ranjit Singh rose from among his fellow-misaldars to found the Sikh empire. As the last of the feudal kingdoms of the fabled Indian subcontinent, it would dazzle with splendor and opulence seldom equaled and its treasury would include the famous Kohinoor (Persian for 'mountain of light'), the largest diamond of its time.

Among the many factors that historians cite to explain this ascension to supremacy is a power-vacuum created by the declining powers of the Afghans, the Mughals, and the Marathas. Indeed, this may well have been contributive but the principal reasons lay in the sterling leadership of the Sikhs, their indomitable courage and above all, their entrenched never-say-die spirit (chardi kala or 'ascendant energy and morale') that ever steeled them and bade them to accept nothing short of complete sovereignty.

For long, mystics and philosophers alike have championed the 'power of intention' as the magic wand for human achievement. Arguably, long-term success is often paved with good intentions. Alongside their iterative supplication for 'chardi kala', the Sikhs invariably sought the 'prosperity of all' (sarbat de bhala) in their daily prayer. Sikh praxis through the 19th century is powerful testimony to this uncanny combination of 'benevolence and morale' that eventually won them sovereignty in the face of impossible odds.

At its zenith, the Sikh empire stretched from the Sutlej in the South to the Khyber Pass in the West, and to Tibet in the North and Northeast. Maharaja Ranjit Singh would also become the first Indian in a thousand years to stem the tide of invasions from the Northwest and to carry his standards beyond the Khyber Pass into the homeland of the traditional conquerors of Hindustan. That he was able to singlehandedly found so large an empire with so little criminality is acknowledged by historians.[20] This rare feat along with the fact that his rule was exceptionally secular for its time and equally bereft of capital punishment and religious persecution is justifiably ascribed to the obdurate energy and humanity of his faith.

In an opinion poll conducted in early 2020 by BBC World Histories magazine, leading historians were asked to choose leaders who 'exercised power and had a positive impact on humanity and to explore their achievements and legacy'. Maharaja

Ranjit Singh was voted the greatest leader in history by thirty-eight per cent for establishing a 'modern empire of toleration'. Sir Winston Churchill finished a distant third, and Abraham Lincoln fourth.[21]

As if to acknowledge the inspirational and almost divine resilience and will-to-power fostered by his faith, Maharaja Ranjit Singh rebuilt Harimandir Sahib in 1809 in marble and copper and much later in 1830, decorated its sanctum with 200 kilograms of gold foil to bestow its current name, the Golden Temple (see photo insert, Figure 9).

Role of Martyrs in Nationhood

Analysts aver that while Nanak gave life new meaning, Guru Gobind Singh invested death with new purpose.[22] Indeed, the martyrdom of Gobind's younger sons would become the single most significant event in the annals of the Khalsa, a veritable inflection point to change their course of history. It imbued them with the unyielding resolve and moral impetus to repeatedly destroy Sirhind, the seat of imperial power where the two boys were immured in a wall, until it was reduced to a heap of rubble. If the foundations of the Khalsa Raj (Sikh empire) were laid on the ruins of Sirhind,[23] they were reinforced every time the Sikhs rebuilt their sanctum at Amritsar after its demolition.

Rather akin to flags and colours, places of worship are powerful rallying points, often protected with the greatest zeal and enterprise. As a corollary, their occupation usually meant the final clinching of a military victory. It was not uncommon for the victor to supplant the creed and concept of the vanquished with their own as the definitive mark of irrevocable triumphalism, and this was often the cause of much animus and controversy in the times to come. Wrangles such as the Babri Masjid-Ram Temple cause célèbre are never easily resolved.

By their courage and willingness to defend all that was sacred to them at the peril of their lives, the Sikhs could obviate such eventualities all through their conflict-torn history. The repeated resurrection from the ashes of Harimandir Sahib in Amritsar is an obvious case in point. Led by Sikh icons such as Deep Singh, martyrdom was often the price they paid. If religious institutions hold quintessential value for a community, martyrdom is an important safeguard.

Since places of worship also serve to memorialize key personages and events, particularly martyrdom, a community may go to any length to raise and preserve these as important milestones in their history. As soon as the Sikhs could wield sufficient military heft, their army marched into Delhi in March 1783 and overawed the emperor, Shah Alam II, into erecting seven memorial gurdwaras at Mughal expense, including one at the place of Guru Teg Bahadur's martyrdom (Sisgang) and another where his mortal remains were cremated (Rakabgang). The fact that mosques occupied these sites was no impediment. The emperor was dragooned into decreeing the demolition of one to erect Gurdwara Rakabganj and to allow for the construction of Gurdwara Sisganj within the compound of another by pulling down its perimeter wall. The royal firman (sanction) helped push the projects through in the face of determined opposition by Muslims, even pre-empting inter-religious disputes for the future.

After their completion in November 1783, when the Mughal emperor expressed a desire to meet the Sikh leader, Bhagel Singh, the latter initially declined and later set pre-conditions that as a Sikh, he would not bow to the emperor and would be accompanied by a contingent of troops. The meeting however, did take place, the emperor conceding the Sikh stipulations. On the day, Bhagel Singh advanced through the streets of Delhi in ceremony, seated on an elephant, followed by a Sikh escort mounted on caparisoned horses. They finally met as equals in the Red Fort but to the exuberant cheers of the traditional Sikh greeting.[24]

The same year, Jassa Singh Ramgarhia uprooted the Takhte

Taus (coronation slab)—six feet by four feet, nine inches thick—from the Red Fort by force of arms and removed it to Harimandir Sahib as a religious offering. It rests today in the Ramgarhia Bunga, in the periphery of the Sikh sanctum—a symbolic mark of royal subjugation. The slab had served as the pedestal for the Mughal throne from which Aurangzeb, the then emperor, had decreed the execution of Guru Teg Bahadur in 1675. To Jassa Singh Ramgarhia, the supra injustice was now recompensed with this imperial submission by proxy.

Throughout Sikh history, attacks on their places of worship and martyrdom seemed to trigger a cause-effect dialectic, spurring the Sikhs to revenge with renewed daring. Yet, they never took leave of their enduring code of the warrior-saint which, indeed, anticipated the modern just war tradition by more than a century. For them, the *casus belli* (occasion for war) lay in the tyrannical acts of their oppressors, which authorized their *jus ad bellum* (right to go to war) but only as a last resort (ultima ratio). During warlike acts, their conduct generally remained irreproachable—*jus in bello* (right conduct in war)—in consonance with their inbred code.

At the very least, unbeknown to them, martyrs set indelible benchmarks in courage and resolve, usually the key drivers in a struggle for independence, human rights, or political freedom, especially against a brutal regime. The onus for inspiration lies with the leadership—more by example than precept. The Sikh tradition of martyrdom was established by Guru Arjan and initially sustained by Guru Teg Bahadur and the family of the tenth Guru. Among many other leaders, Deep Singh honored and fed this glorious tradition at a critical turn in Sikh history in a manner as exceptional as it was noteworthy for him to be often regarded as the unofficial Sikh patron saint of Courage and Resolve.

In the pantheon of Sikh martyrs, for every name known and consecrated, there are thousands unnamed, unwept and unsung, who fell to the Mughal-Afghan sword in battle or perished in the implacable genocide unleashed by them, generally in response to Sikh provocation. During the 'heroic' (18th) century alone, historians estimate some 200,000 Sikh casualties, every one of which only seemed to stiffen their resolve, uplift morale, and fuel their dream for sovereignty.[25] In the words of Lepel Griffin, all along in their struggle, the blood of Sikh martyrs was, as ever, the seed of their Church.[26]

In battle, the tradition of martyrdom serves to considerably deepen the psychic reserves of hard-wired courage, setting off an ever-expanding ripple effect for posterity. Many years later, in the early part of the 19th century, Akali Phula Singh would distinguish himself both as a member of the Shaheed misl and as a trusted albeit vitriolic General under Maharaja Ranjit Singh, displaying the very same raw courage, always fighting in the van.[27]

Subsequent Sikh history is also replete with instances of Sikh warriors instinctually upholding this canon to write anew glorious chapters in courage such as the epic last man-last-round stand by twenty-one Sikhs of the 4th Battalion, the Sikh Regiment, against 10,000 Afridi tribesmen in 1897 at Saragarhi (Waziristan); the celebrated charge into roaring machine-guns during the Great War at Neuve Chapelle by the 5th Battalion, the Sikh Regiment, or the daring mission by men of the 2nd Battalion, the Sikh Regiment, at Richebourg L'Avoue in May 1915; and more recently in June 2020, the spirited unarmed combat in the icy wastes of the Galwan Valley, Ladakh, against the Peoples' Liberation Army of China.

At times, the selfsame courage may forsake its usual effulgence to take a more obdurate route such as the unbending fortitude and tenacity of Bhagat Singh, or the obsessive staying power of Udham Singh during India's freedom struggle.

The role of martyrdom in the rise of a nation though at times subliminal is always significant. No sacrifice is ever squandered nor the blood of martyrs shed in vain. In effect, it helps stay a freedom struggle on its course, ever giving strength and direction. A just cause, unsullied by personal gain, perhaps, spawns the greatest groundswell—more substantial the odds, greater the legacy. Martyrs oftentimes exercise even greater influence after death. A Caesar dead can prove more powerful than a Caesar living. Conversely, bereft of martyrdom, a movement may emasculate and slowly die.

With the evolution of the Sikh faith from its initial conciliatory pacifism to an aggressive struggle for independence, a special significance came to be attached to martyrdom with the belief that the way to sovereignty lay through one's own blood, if not that of the enemy. Over time, gurdwaras associated with martyrs assumed a significance only next to or sometimes even greater than those of the Gurus in the racial consciousness as a source of boons and fulfilment of wishes.[28] This in part explains the enduring legacy and appeal of all shrines associated with Deep Singh and his comrades-in-arms in the battle of November 1757.

Deep Singh, in particular, has emerged as the quintessential hero in a culture that deifies martyrs for their upstanding spirit, unalloyed courage, purity of purpose, and unwavering resolve—an unfailing meld that scoffs at all opposition to readily embrace martyrdom. Time has only nourished and strengthened Deep Singh's deification as a true exemplar of these primal attributes to be ever etched in living memory—worthy of not just respect but full-hearted worship.

> To live in hearts we leave behind is not to die.
> —Thomas Campbell

Acknowledgements

I profoundly acknowledge my debt to Professor Raijasbir Singh for his seminal work on Deep Singh. Credited with similar, equally authoritative studies on most Sikh icons of the period, his humility and abiding openness to further research deserve special mention. The National Seminar to mark Deep Singh's semiquincentennial year of martyrdom in 2009, held at Guru Nanak Dev University, brought together varied scholarship on his life and work. My grateful thanks to the then Vice Chancellor, Professor Roop Singh, for agreeing to hold the seminar, and to Professor Balwant Singh Dhillon and Professor Shashi Bala for organizing it with true academic rigour.

There are many who helped me with my field research. The current generation of Bhai Dall Singh's family at Talwandi Sabo were always welcoming and never seemed to run out of patience in answering my tiresome research questions. There are many others who helped me with historical and contemporary information when I toured the villages where the battle was fought—Sultanwind, Chabba, Gohalwar, Vancharii, Varpal, Mehma. In particular, Nihang Kashmir Singh of village Chabba and Vir Singh of village Chatiwind rendered crucial assistance in mapping the area. The former also shared rare inputs about the battle itself, passed down to him over several generations as a member of the Taruna Dal having spent a major part of his life as sewadar (voluntary worker) at Tahla Sahib, a commemorative shrine that marks the place of Deep Singh's mortal injury. Now in his dotage, he spends the better part of his day at a shrine in Chabba in memory of two Sikhs—Hari Singh and Bir Singh—also martyred in the same battle.

Dr Davinderpal Singh is a storehouse of information about Amritsar in general and the Golden Temple in particular and I'm much obliged to him for rare insights into the history and heritage of the area. My sincere gratitude to Dr Jogeshwar Singh of the Sikh Historical Research Board of the Golden Temple for his clear-headed and bold assertions that helped demystify several aspects of Deep Singh's martyrdom.

His young years notwithstanding, Gyani Gurlal Singh was especially proficient in unravelling for me the mystery of Gyani Gyan Singh's Braj Bhasha, the preferred literary medium of the time, with Gyani Harinder Singh of Anandpur as senior consultant.

I would be remiss if I did not express my sincere gratitude to Gordon Corrigan MBE who, like a true soldier-scholar, readily consented to write the Foreword, despite his rather full schedule as a much sought-after and highly successful military historian-presenter. For me, this is as much a privilege as a compliment.

A special thanks to Preeti Gill of Majha House who appeared just in time as the torchbearer to help find a publisher; to my colleague, Dr Iqbal Judge, for her patience in reading through the manuscript and for her invaluable suggestions, and finally to Renuka Chatterjee and Prachi Sharma who helped finalize the manuscript with a trained and discerning eye, and to Rajinder Ganju for his meticulous typesetting.

There are so many others, too numerous to name, who met me along the way and never failed to reenergize me with their enthusiasm.

Yet, I know not fully whom to thank for the allure of the journey itself nor for the occasional glimpse of the incandescence of life it has afforded.

February 2022 Harisimran Singh
Chandigarh

APPENDIX A

Deep Singh in Verse

1. A Saint Arrives

ਇਕ ਦਿਨ ਵੇਲਣਾ ਜੋਣ ਉਹ ਗਿਆ,
ਖੇਤੀ ਰੱਬ ਆਪ ਸਬੱਬ ਬਣਾਂਵਦਾ ਸੀ ।
ਰੱਬੀ ਰੂਪ ਮਹਾਤਮਾਂ ਬ੍ਰਹਮ ਗਿਆਨੀ ।
ਉਸ ਦੇ ਵੇਲਣੇ ਤੇ ਪਹੁੰਚ ਜਾਂਵਦਾ ਸੀ ।
ਭਾਈ ਭਗਤੇ ਜੀ ਬਹੁਤ ਸਤਿਕਾਰ ਕੀਤਾ,
ਖੇਸ ਬੈਠਣ ਦੇ ਲਈ ਵਿਛਾਂਵਦਾ ਸੀ ।
ਕਦੀ ਬਲਦ ਹੱਕੇ ਕਦੀ ਲਾਏ ਗੰਨੇ,
ਕਦੀ ਪੱਛੀਆਂ ਪਿੱਛੇ ਹਟਾਂਵਦਾ ਸੀ ।
ਉਸ ਨੂੰ ਵੇਖ ਇਕੱਲਿਆਂ ਕੰਮ ਕਰਦੇ,
ਰੱਬੀ ਰੂਪ ਇਉ ਮੁਖੇ ਫੁਰਮਾਂਵਦਾ ਸੀ ।
ਬਾਲ ਨਾਲ ਨਹੀ ਕੋਈ ਗੁਰਦੀਪ ਸਿੰਘਾਂ,
ਸਾਧੂ ਪ੍ਰੇਮ ਦੇ ਨਾਲ ਪੁਛਾਂਵਦਾ ਸੀ ।

—Gurdeep Singh Kanwal[1]

ik din velna jon oh gaya, kheti
rab aap sabab banavnda si.
Rabbi roop mahatma brahm gyani,
Usde velne te pahunch javnda si.
Bhai Bhagtu ji bahut satkar kita,
Khes baithan de layi vichhavnda si.
Kadi bald hakke kadi laye ganne,
Kadi panchhian pichhe hatavnda si.
Usnu vekh ikaliyan kam karde,
Rabbi roop iyon mukhon farmaunda si.

Bal nal nahi koi Gurdeep Singha,
Sadhu prem de nal puchhaunda si.
While working in his fields, one day,
The Lord devised a circumstance.
A godly figure came that way,
approached his cane press, all by chance.
Bhai Bhagtu showed him much respect;
He sat him down in comfort too,
While he did goad the oxen on,
And fed the cane, and birds did shoo.
The godly guest observed the scene,
then gently did inquire:
'Is there no son to help you on,
Alone, you'd surely tire?'[2]

2. Blessings from the Saint

ਸੰਤਾਂ ਛਕ ਪਰਸ਼ਾਦ ਅਰਦਾਸ ਕੀਤੀ,
ਭਾਈ ਭਗਤਿਆ ਭਰਨ ਭੰਡਾਰ ਤੇਰੇ ।
ਤੇਰੀ ਅਉਖ ਵੀ ਸੌਖ ਵਿਚ ਕਰਨ ਗੋਬਿੰਦ,
ਸਦਾ ਹੋਣ ਸਹਾਈ ਕਰਤਾਰ ਤੇਰੇ ।
ਗੁਰੂ ਮਿਹਰ ਹੋਵੇ ਲੱਗੇ ਭਾਗ ਤੈਨੂੰ ।
ਸਦਾ ਸੁਖ ਰਹੇ ਵਿਚ ਪਰਵਾਰ ਤੇਰੇ ।
ਪੁੱਤਰ ਹੋਏ ਐਸਾ ਜੈਸੀ ਭਾਵਨਾ ਏ,
ਜੱਸ ਹੋਣ ਭਈ ਸਦਾ ਸੰਸਾਰ ਤੇਰੇ ।
ਜਤੀ ਸਤੀ ਯੋਧਾ ਵਿਦਵਾਨ ਗਿਆਨੀ,
ਪੁੱਤਰ ਜਨਮੇ ਘਰ ਬਲੀ ਬਲਕਾਰ ਤੇਰੇ ।
ਚਮਕੂ ਸੂਰਜੇ ਵੱਧ ਜੱਗ ਤੇਜ ਉਸ ਦਾ ।
ਐਸਾ ਪੁੱਤ ਹੋਉ ਕੁਲ ਸ਼ਿੰਗਾਰ ਤੇਰੇ ।
ਗੁਰੂ ਘਰ ਵਿਚ ਵਧੇ ਸਤਿਕਾਰ ਤੇਰਾ,
ਸਦਾ ਘਰ ਵਿਚ ਰਹੇ ਬਹਾਰ ਤੇਰੇ ।

—Gurdeep Singh Kanwal[3]

Santa chhak parshada ardas kiti,
'Bhai Bhagtian bharan bhandar tere.
Teri aukh vi sukh vich karan Gobind,
Sada hon sahai kartar tere.
Guru meher hovai lagge bhag tainu,

sada sukh rahe vich parvar tere,
Puttar hovai aisa jaisi bhavna e,
Jas hovai bhai sada sansar tere.
Jati sati yodha vidvaan gyani,
Puttar janmey ghar bali balkar tere.
Chamku soorjon vadh jag tej usda,
Aisa put hovai kul shringar tere.
Guru ghar vich vadhe satkar tera,
Sada ghar vich rahe bahar tere.
As soon he'd finished lunch that day,
the holy man did pray—
'Your cup of joy shall overflow;
Convert to bliss, He'll all your woe;
The Lord shall every mercy show.
The Grace of God brings bounties All;
He'll bless your home with joy withal,
And grant you bounty of a son;
And praise of people shall be won.
Chaste warrior, saint, who'd learning love
And shine far more than sun above,
a son shall God now grant thee soon.
Adorn your home as treasured boon.
May God Almighty's love may grow
Your home in ever blossom show.'

3. Pahuwind, a Village in the Majha

ਪਹੁਵਿੰਡ ਇਸ ਮਾਝੇ ਦਾ ਨਗਰ ਉਂਘਾ,
ਇਲਾਕੇ ਲਾਹੌਰ ਵਿੱਚ ਇਹ ਸ਼ੋਭਾ ਪਾਂਵਦ ਸੀ ।
ਸੰਧੂ ਗੋਤ ਦੇ ਜੱਟ ਵਸਨੀਕ ਇਸ ਦੇ,
ਵਾਹੀਵਾਨਾਂ ਦਾ ਪਿੰਡ ਸਦਾਂਵਦਾ ਸੀ ।
ਭਾਈ ਭਗਤਾ ਜੀ ਸੰਧੂ ਬਰਾਦਰੀ ਵਿੱਚ,
ਮਾਨ, ਤਾਨ ਇੱਜਤ ਚੰਗੀ ਪਾਂਵਦਾ ਸੀ ।
ਦਸਾਂ ਨਵਾਂ ਦੀ ਕਿਰਤ ਕਮਾਈ ਕਰਦਾ,
ਦਸਵਾਂ ਹਿੱਸਾ ਗੁਰੂ ਘਰ ਪਹੁੰਚਾਂਵਦਾ ਸੀ ।
ਉਸ ਦਾ ਘਰ ਔਲਾਦ ਤੋ ਸੱਖਣਾ ਸੀ,
ਫਿਕਰ ਸਦਾ ਇਹ ਜਾਨ ਨੂੰ ਖਾਂਵਦਾ ਸੀ ।

Appendix A: Deep Singh in Verse

ਸਦਾ ਸਤਿਗੁਰਾਂ ਅੱਗੇ ਅਰਦਾਸ ਕਰਦਾ,
ਦਾਤ ਪੁੱਤਰ ਦੀ ਘਰ ਵਿੱਚ ਚਾਂਹਵਦਾ ਸੀ ।

—Gurdeep Singh Kanwal[4]

Pahuwind ik majhe da nagar uggha,
Elake Lahore vich ih sobha pavnda si.
Sandhu got de jat vasneek isde,
Vahivana da pind sadavnda si.
Bhai Bhagtu ji Sandhu baradari vich,
Man, taan izzat changi pavnde si.
Dassa novan di kirt kamai karda,
Dasvan hissa guru ghar pachavnda si.
Uss da ghar aulad ton sakhna si,
Sada satguran agge ardas karda,
Daat puttar di ghar chavnda si.

Pahuwind in the Majha region,
Far fabled in Lahore;
Inhabited by Sandhu jats,
With farming as their chore.
Bhai Bhagtu ji of Sandhu clan
Was much respected there.
He earned his bread by sweat of brow—
A tenth of which did share.
His home unblessed with children was
This vexed him to the core.
He prayed to God to grant a son
And asked for nothing more.

4. The Guru Prefers Deep Singh to Stay

ਪਾਈ ਮਿਹਰ ਦੀ ਦਿਸਟ ਗੁਰ ਮਿਹਰ ਕੀਤੀ,
ਸ੍ਰੀ ਮੁਖ ਤੋ ਇਓੁ ਫੁਰਮਾਇਆ ਏ ।
ਦੀਪ ਸਿੰਘ ਨੂੰ ਛੱਡ ਜਾਓ ਪਾਸ ਸਾਡੇ,
ਸਾਡੇ ਨਾਲ ਇਸ ਪਿਆਰ ਵਧਾਇਆ ਏ ।
ਵਿਦਿਆ ਪੜ੍ਹੂਗਾ ਰਹੂਗਾ ਪਾਸ ਸਾਡੇ,
ਇਸ ਨੇ ਵਿਦਿਆ ਵਿੱਚ ਚਿੱਤ ਲਾਇਆ ਏ ।

—Gurdeep Singh Kanwal[5]

Payi meher di drisht gur meher kiti,
Sri mukh ton iyon phurmayah e.
Deep Singh nu chhad jao paas sade,
Sade naal is pyar vadhaya ye.
Vidhya paruga, rahuga paas sade,
Is ne vidya vich chit laiya e
The Guru now looked upon with Grace
And said of Deep with kindly face:
'Deep Singh shall now stay with us—
His love for us much grows.
He'll learn so much beside us here—
His love for knowledge shows.'

5. Jeonda Shaheed

ਕਰਯੋ ਚਰਿੱਤ੍ਰ ਸਿਖਨ ਕੇ ਕਾਰਨ । ਪੱਕੇ ਕੱਚੇ ਸਿੱਖ ਦਿਖਾਰਨ ।
ਸ੍ਰੀ ਗੁਰ ਬਚਨ ਮੁਖੋਂ ਥੋ ਕਹਯੋ । ਲੈਨ ਪਰੀਖਯਾ ਤਿਮ ਹੀ ਚਹਯੋ । ੩ ।
karyô charittar sikhan kç kârna. pakkç kachchç sikkh dikhâran.
srî gur bachan mukhôn thô kahyô. lain parîkhyâ tim hî chahyô.6.

ਇਹ ਸਿੱਖਨ ਉਨ ਸੁਨੀ ਮਝੈਲਨ । ਆਏ ਸਿੱਖ ਸੁਨਤ ਚਿਤ ਚੈਲਨ ।
ਉਸ ਤੇ ਆਗੇ ਹੁਇ ਚਹੈ ਖੜਨੇ । ਸੀਸ ਕਟਾਇ ਬਹੁ ਸਿਖ ਚਹਿ ਮਰਨੋ । ੧੫ ।
ih sikkhan un sunî majhailna. âiç sikkh sunat chit chailan.
us te âge hui chahain khardnô. sîs katâi bahu sikh chahin marnô.15.

ਬਕਰਨ ਰਕਤ ਬਾਹਰ ਚਲਿ ਆਈ, ਦੇਖ ਰਕਤ ਨਠ ਗਈ ਲੁਕਾਈ ।
ਸਤਿਗੁਰ ਰਾਖੇ ਸਿੱਖ ਬਚਾਇ । ਉਨੈ ਸ਼ਹੀਦੀ ਪਦ ਦਯੋ ਲਾਇ । ੧੯ ।
bakran rakat bâhar chali âî. dçkh rakat nath gaî lukâî.
satigur râkhç sikkh bachâi. unai shahîdî pad dayô lâi.19

ਤਿਨ ਮੈ ਤੇ ਇਕ ਸਿੰਘ ਹੁਤੇ ਦੀਪ ਸਿੰਘ ਜਿਹ ਨਾਮ ।
ਦੱਛਨ ਦਿਸ ਬੁੰਗਾ ਰਚਿਓ ਸ੍ਰੀ ਅੰਮ੍ਰਿਤਸਰ ਸ਼ੁਭ ਨਾਮ । ੨੦ ।
Tin main te ik singh huto Deep Singh jih naam.
Dackhan jis bunga rachiyo Sri Amritsar shub naam.

—Ratan Singh Bhangu,
Panth Parkash, Sakhi 79[6]

Assay Sikh mettle was the aim—
sham or true: just like their name.

The Guru then spoke his mind to all,
to test them now, he all did call:
Could five Sikhs offer him their head,
To pass this test their blood would shed?
A Sikh of Majha heard this call;
And soon there stood five all in all.
The Guru then spared their lives right there;
bestowed on them 'shaheed' title rare—
One of them, Deep Singh by name.
Of Southern Amritsar Bunga fame.

6. Daring to Edit

ਰਚੀ ਰਚਨਾ ਬਾਣੀ ਦਸਮੇਸ਼ ਨੇ ਜੋ,
ਬਾਬਾ ਦੀਪ ਸਿੰਘ ਜੀ ਸਾਂਭੀ ਜਾਂਵਦੇ ਸਨ ।
ਆਦਿ ਗ੍ਰੰਥ ਜੀ ਵਾਂਗ ਗੁਰਦੀਪ ਸਿੰਘਾ,
ਇਕੱਤਰ ਕਰਕੇ ਜਿਲਦਾ ਬੰਨ੍ਹਾਵਦੇ ਸਨ ।
ਮਿੱਤਰ ਪਿਆਰੇ ਨੂੰ ਹਾਲ ਫਕੀਰਾਂ ਦਾ ਲਿਖ,
ਸਤਿਗੁਰਾਂ ਨੇ ਸ਼ਬਦ ਬਣਾਇਆ ਏ ।
ਤਾਂ ਫਕੀਰਾਂ ਦੀ ਬਾਬੇ ਮੁਰੀਦ ਲਿਖ ਕੇ,
ਲਿਖਿਆ ਗੁਰਾਂ ਦਾ ਸ਼ਬਦ ਉਲਟਾਇਆ ਏ ।
ਸਿੰਘਾਂ ਆਖਿਆ ਉਲਟਿਆ ਸ਼ਬਦ ਸਤਿਗੁਰ,
ਖਾਲਸ ਖਾਲਸਾ ਕਰ ਲਿਖਾਇਆ ਏ ।
ਬੇਟਾ ਸਤਿਗੁਰਾਂ ਸੀਸ ਦੀ ਕਰ ਅਰਪਨ,
ਏਸ ਲਿਖੇ ਦਾ ਮੁੱਲ ਚੁਕਾਇਆ ਏ ।
ਤੁਸੀਂ ਆਪਣੇ ਸੀਸ ਦੀ ਭੇਟ ਦੇਵੋ,
ਜੇਕਰ ਤੁਸਾਂ ਇਹ ਸ਼ਬਦ ਬਦਲਾਇਆ ਏ ।
ਸੁਣ ਕੇ ਹੁਕਮ ਬਾਬੇ ਜੀ ਖਾਲਸੇ ਦਾ,
ਝੱਟ ਆਪਣਾ ਸੀਸ ਝੁਕਾਇਆ ਏ ।
ਇਹ ਸੀਸ ਕੀ ਹੈ ਤਨ ਮਨ ਗੁਰੂ ਅਰਪਣ,
ਸਭ ਉਸ ਨੂੰ ਭੇਟ ਚੜ੍ਹਾਇਆ ਏ ।
ਜਦੋਂ ਚਾਹੇ ਲਉ ਸੀਸ ਗੁਰਦੀਪ ਸਿੰਘਾ,
ਕਰ ਇਹ ਬੇਨਤੀ ਸੀਸ ਨਿਵਾਇਆ ਏ ।
ਤੁਸੀਂ ਜਿੰਦਾ ਸ਼ਹੀਦ ਮੁਰੀਦ ਗੁਰ ਦੇ,
ਭਾਰੀ ਪੰਥ ਇਹ ਕਰੇ ਸਨਮਾਨ ਬਾਬਾ ।

—Gurdeep Singh Kanwal[7]

Rachi rachna bani Dasmesh ne jo,
Baba Deep Singh ji sambhi javnde san.

Adi Granth ji vaang Gurdeep Singha,
Ikattar karke jild banavnde san.
Mittar pyare nu haal fakiran da likh,
Satguran ne shabad banaya ye.
Than fakiran di babe murid likh ke,
Likhiya guran da shabad ultaya ye.
Sikhan akhya ultiya shabad satgur,
Khalas Khalsa kar likhaya ye.
Bhenta satguran sees di kar Arpan,
Eis likhe da mul chukaya ye.
Tusin apne sees di bhent devo,
Jekar tusan eh shabad badlaya ye.
Sun ke hukam babe ji khalse da,
Jhat aapna sees jhukaya ye.
Eh sees ki hai tan man Arpan,
Sab usnu bhet chadaya ye.
Jadon chaho lavo Gurdeep Singha,
Kar ye benti sees nivaya ye.
Tusin jinda Shaheed murid gur de,
Bhari panth eh kare sanman baba.

Compiling writings of Tenth Guru,
akin to Adi Granth to gather and bound,
'O, tell my Friend of this *fakir*';
Deep now changed 'fakir' to 'murid':
he thought 'murid' more apt and true.
And changed *'khalas'* into *'khalsa.'*
Sikhs chided and warned of debt to pay
Such sacrilege must he soon repay,
Would he agree, if called upon,
To sacrifice supreme?
Affirmative was then Deep's response:
He grew in their esteem.
They dubbed him 'living martyr' then—
A colossus true among all men!

7. Problem in Chewing

ਦੀਪ ਸਿੰਘ ਚੁਕੋਹੀਏ ਦਾਣੇ ਚਬੇ ਨ ਜਾਹਿ ।
ਜਿਮ ਤਿਸਕੋ ਦਾਤੈ ਦਈ, ਸੋ ਮੈ ਦੇਹੁ ਬਤਾਇ ॥
ਇਕ ਦਿਨ ਛੋਲੇ ਲਯਾਇਓ ਕੋਈ ਬੰਦੇ ਦਿਵਾਨ ॥
ਔਰ ਸਭੈ ਚਾਬਤ ਭਏ, ਇਕ ਚਬੈ ਨ ਸਿੰਘ ਜੁਵਾਨ ॥

—Ratan Singh Bhangu,
Panth Parkash[8]

Deep singh chakoyi dane chabbe na jai
Jim tisko dade dayi, so mai dey bataye
Ik din chhole leyaiyo koi bande diwan
Aur sabhei chabat bhaye, ik chabe na singh jawan

Deep Singh *Chakoyi* was unable to munch gram
Until he granted dentures was, to tell you this I am.
One day a man brought gram for all in the midst of Banda's
   diwan
All did munch away the grain, excepting the Singh *jawan*[9]

8. Factionalism

ਬੰਦਾ ਗੁਰਾਂ ਤੋ ਜਦੋ ਬੇਮੁੱਖ ਹੋਇਆ ਲੱਗਾ ਆਪ ਨੂੰ ਗੁਰੂ ਸਦਾਣ ਸਮਝੋ [....] ।
ਤਦ ਖਾਲਸੇ ਅਤੇ ਬੰਦਈਆਂ ਅੰਦਰ ਲੱਗੀ ਫੁੱਟ ਆ ਕੇ ਪੈਰ ਪਾਣ ਸਮਝੋ ।
ਤਦੇ ਮੇਲਾ ਵਸਾਖੀ ਦਾ ਆ ਗਿਆ ਅੰਮ੍ਰਿਤਸਰ ਹੋਇਆ ਕੱਠ ਆਣ ਸਮਝੋ ।
ਸੰਗਤ ਬਹੁਤ ਵਸਾਖੀ ਤੇ ਆਈ ਹੋਈ ਸੀ ਦੂਰ ਦੂਰ ਤੋ ਦਰਸਨ ਪਾਣ ਸਮਝੋ ।
ਗੱਦੀ ਲਾਈ ਤਦੇ ਬੰਦੇ ਹਰਿਮੰਦਰ ਹੈਸੀ ਜਾ ਬੈਠਾ ਨਾਲ ਸ਼ਾਨ ਸਮਝੋ ।
ਗੁਰੂ ਯਾਰਵਾਂ ਆਪ ਕਹਾਉਣ ਲੱਗਾ ਲੱਗਾ ਸੀਸ ਤੇ ਚੌਰ ਝੁਲਾਣ ਸਮਝੋ ।
ਤਦੇ ਸਿੰਘ ਜੋਸੀਲੜ ਪਕੜ ਬਾਜੂ ਪਕੜ ਬੰਦੇ ਨੂੰ ਬਾਹਰ ਬਿਠਾਣ ਸਮਝੋ ।
ਰੌਲਾ ਪੰਥ ਵਿੱਚ ਪੈ ਗਿਆ ਸੋਹਣ ਸਿੰਘਾ ਲੱਗੋ ਇਕ ਤੇ ਦੋ ਹੋ ਜਾਣ ਸਮਝੋ ।
ਮਨੀ ਸਿੰਘ ਅਤੇ ਦੀਪ ਸਿੰਘ ਦੋਹਾਂ ਵਿੱਚ ਹੋ ਕੇ ਰੌਲਾ ਮਿਟਾ ਦਿੱਤਾ ।
ਲਿਖ ਚਿੱਠੀਆਂ ਸੁਧਾਸਰ ਵਿਚ ਪਾ ਕੇ ਬੰਦਾ ਗੱਦੀਓਂ ਪਰੇ ਹਟਾ ਦਿੱਤਾ ।

—Sohan Singh Ghukewalia,
Baba Deep Singh Shaheed[10]

Banda guran ton jadon bemukh hoiya laga aap nu guru sadaan samjho
Tad khalse ate Bandiyan andar lagi phut aa ke payr pan samjho
Tadon mela vaisakhi da aa giya Amritsar katth aan samjho
Sangat bahut vaisakhi te aayihoi si door door ton darshan paan samjho
Gaddi layi tadon Bande Harmandir haisi ja baitha nal shaan samjho

Guru yarvan aap kahaun lagga lagga sees te chaur jhulan samjho
Tadon Singh joshilde pakar baju pakar Bande nu bahar bitthan samjho
Rolla panth vich pey giya Sohan Singha lagge ik te do ho jaan samjho
Mani Singh ate Deep Singh dohan vich hoke rolla mita ditta
Likh chitthiyan Sudhasar vich pa ke Banda gaddiyon pare hata ditta

Turning away from Guru's teachings, Banda declared himself the One.
With this a rift between *Khalsa* and *Bandyein* was now done.
Many gathered in Amritsar during *Vaisakhi* fair
The pilgrims came from far and wide to share the day right there.
Banda sat in Harimandir on makeshift throne and said:
'Bow before Eleventh Guru', with a whisk above his head.
Some daring *Singhs* then took his arm and showed him out of there
Mani Singh and Deep Singh then resolved this weird affair.

9. Courage and Resolve

ਬਾਬੇ ਕਰ ਅਰਦਾਸ ਲਕੀਰ ਖਿੱਚੀ,
ਉਚੀ ਵਾਹਿਗੁਰੂ ਫਤੇ ਗਜਾਇ ਬਾਬਾ ।
ਸਿੰਘੋ ਤੱਪੇ ਲਕੀਰ ਜਿਸ ਸੀਸ ਦੇਣਾ,
ਵਿਚ ਜੋਸ਼ ਦੇ ਹੁਕਮ ਸੁਣਾਇ ਬਾਬਾ ।
ਸਿੰਘ ਖੁਸ਼ੀ ਦੇ ਨਾਲ ਲਕੀਰ ਟੱਪੇ,
ਸਿੰਘ ਵਿਚ ਜੋਸ. ਦੇ ਆਇ ਬਾਬਾ ।

—Gurdeep Singh Kanwal[11]

Babe kar ardas lakir khichi,
Uchi Waheguru fateh gajai baba.
Singho tappo lakir jis sis dena,
Vich josh de hukam sunai Baba.
Singh Khushi de nal lakir tappe,
Singh vich josh de ai Baba.

Baba prayed, drew line in ground,
Then zestfully did defy:
'Step forward those who readily
Would fight and rather die!'
Rejoicing, they all crossed the line,
for courage in them all was high.

ਨਿਕਲ ਵਿਚ ਮੈਦਾਨ ਦੇ ਖੇੜ ਹੋ ਕੇ ਲੰਮੀ ਸਿੰਘ ਜੀ ਲੀਕ ਖਿਚਾਇ ਅੱਗੇ ।
ਕਹਿੰਦੇ ਧਰਮ ਤੇ ਜੇ ਸ਼ਹੀਦ ਹੋਣਾ ਪੈਰ ਉਹੋ ਹੀ ਏਸ ਤੋਂ ਪਾਏ ਅੱਗੇ ।
ਦੇਸ ਧਰਮ ਦੇ ਨਾਲ ਪਿਆਰ ਜੀਹਨੂੰ ਉਹ ਨਿਕਲ ਮੈਦਾਨ ਵਿਚ ਆਇ ਅੱਗੇ ।
ਪਿਆਰੀ ਪੰਥ ਦੀ ਆਨ ਸ਼ਾਨ ਜਿਸਨੂੰ ਸੀਸ ਤਲੀ ਉੱਤੇ ਰੱਖ ਧਾਇ ਅੱਗੇ ।

—Kartar Singh Kalaswalia,
Jauhar Khalsa[12]

Nikal vich maidaan dey khade ho ke lammi Singh ji leek khichai agge
Kahande dharam te je Shaheed hona pair uho hi ais ton paye agge
Des dharam dey naal pyar jeehnu oh nikal maidaan vich aye agge
Piyari panth di aan shaan jisnu sis tali utte rakh paye agge
Stepped Singh ji forward, front of all and then he drew a line,
He bade those cross for whom to die for country was divine:
Who value nation and their faith must surely take the field,
For honour who can give their all, to them he now appealed.

10. Advance to Contact

ਪਉੜੀ॥ ਤੁਰਿਆ ਬਾਬਾ ਦੀਪ ਸਿੰਘ ਲਾ ਚੋਟ ਨਗਾਰੇ ।
ਉਹਦੇ ਨੈਣ ਗੁੱਸੇ ਵਿੱਚ ਮਘਦੇ, ਅੱਗ ਦੇ ਅੰਗਿਆਰੇ ।
ਉਹਨੇ ਚੱਕਰ ਸਜਾਏ ਸੀਸ ਤੇ ਮਾਰਨ ਲਿਸ਼ਕਾਰੇ ।
ਉਹਨੇ ਸਾਣ ਚੜ੍ਹਾਏ ਸਾਰ ਦੇ, ਖੰਡੇ ਦੇ ਧਾਰੇ ।
ਉਹ ਕਹਿੰਦਾ ਵੱਢ-ਵੱਢ ਸੁੱਟਣੇ ਜ਼ਾਲਮ ਹਤਿਆਰੇ ।
ਮੈ ਵੈਰੀ ਤਾਈ ਦਿਖਾਵਣੇ, ਦਿਨ ਦੀਵੀ ਤਾਰੇ ।
ਹੈ ਨਿਸ਼ਚਾ ਜਿਸ ਨੂੰ ਗੁਰਾਂ ਤੇ ਕਿਉ ਜੰਗ ਵਿਚ ਹਾਰੇ ।
ਸੱਦ ਜੀਵਨ ਜੱਗ ਤੇ ਅਣਖ ਨਾਲ, ਨਿਰਦੋਸ਼ ਉਚਾਰੇ ।

—Kewal Singh Nirdosh,
Vaar Baba Deep Singh[13]

Turiya Baba Deep Singh la chot nagarey
Uhde nain gusse vich maghdey ag de angiarey
Uhne chakkar sajaye sis te maran lishkarey
Uhney shan chadhaye sar de khnade do dharey
Uh kahnda vad vad sutney jalam hatiarey
Main vairy tai dikhavney din divi tarey
Hai nischa jis nu guran te kiyo jang vich harey
Sad Jeevan jag te anakh naal nirdosh ucharey
Deep Singh now rides out in front as war drums sound their call.
His eyes emit such dash and fire while all are in his thrall.
His quoits adorn his turban bright now glinting in the sun.

His body armour glistens too; of broadsword he had one.
Resolute his mission was to fight on till they'd won.
His faith in God assured him with all success on this day.
That peace prevails on earth always and ever holds its sway.

11. Forward March

ਕੋਰੜਾ

ਸੁਣ ਕੇ ਸਿੰਘਾਂ ਦੇ ਮੁੱਖ ਆਈਆਂ ਲਾਲੀਆਂ ।
ਫੜ ਲੈ ਧਨਖ, ਤੇਗਾਂ ਨੇ ਸੰਭਾਲੀਆਂ ।
ਸੋਧ ਅਰਦਾਸਾ ਨੇ ਜੈਕਾਰੇ ਛੱਡਦੇ ।
ਕਾਹਲੇ ਪਏ ਨੇ ਸੂਰਮੇ ਹੱਥਾਂ ਨੂੰ ਵੱਢਦੇ ।
ਬਾਬਾ ਦੀਪ ਸਿੰਘ ਖੰਡਾ ਲਿਸ਼ਕਾਵਦਾ ।
ਕੂਚ ਦਾ ਹੁਕਮ ਫੌਜਾਂ ਨੂੰ ਸੁਣਾਂਵਦਾ ।
ਸੁਣਕੇ ਹੁਕਮ ਸੂਰਮੇ ਨੇ ਗੱਜਦੇ ।
ਫੌਜਾਂ ਅੱਗੇ ਲੱਗੇ ਸਰਦਾਰ ਸੱਜਦੇ ।

—Sohan Singh Seetal,
Shaheed Baba Deep Singh[14]

Korda

Sun ke Singha de mukh aiyian lalian.
Phad ke dhanak, Tegan ne sambhalian.
Sodh ardasa ne jaikare chhad de
Kahle paye ne soorme hathan nu vad de.
Baba Deep Singh khanda lashkaonda.
Kuch da hukam faujan nu sunaonda.
Sun ke hukam soormey ne gajde
Faujan agge lagge sardar sajde.

When Singhs heard orders to advance
Their faces gleamed with fire.
They brandished swords, with prayers done
And moved with restless ire.
Deep Singh leads with glinting sword—
And orders an advance.
His warriors brave, delight and cheer,
Rejoice this noble chance.
The army follows in good speed,
With sightly *Sardars* in the lead.

(NB: *Sardar* means 'commander')

12. Sikhs Attack First

ਦੋਹਰਾ ॥ ਗੋਹਲਵੜ ਕੋਲ ਸਿੰਘ ਪਹੁੰਚੇ ਆਇਕੇ ।
ਸ਼ੇਰ ਵਾਂਗ ਜ਼ਾਲਮ ਦੇ ਪਾਏ ਧਾਇਕੇ ।
ਕਾੜ ਕਾੜ ਗੋਲੀ ਤੀਰ ਛੁੱਟ ਪਏ ।
ਐਹਮੇ ਸਾਮਣੇ ਹੋ ਦੋਵੇਂ ਦਲ ਜੁੱਟ ਪਏ ।
ਦੀਪ ਸਿੰਘ ਕਹਿੰਦਾ ਸਿੰਘਾਂ ਨੂੰ ਪੁਕਾਰ ਕੇ ।
ਹੋਵਣਾ ਸ਼ਹੀਦ ਜ਼ਾਲਮਾਂ ਨੂੰ ਮਾਰ ਕੇ ।
ਤੇਗ ਉੱਤੇ ਤੇਗ ਸਾੜ ਸਾੜ ਵੱਜਦੀ ।
ਚਲੀਆਂ ਨੇ ਤੋਪਾਂ ਤੇਗ ਮਾਲਾ ਗੱਜਦੀ ।
ਤਾੜ ਤਾੜ ਤਾੜ ਹੈ ਬੰਦੂਕ ਚੱਲਦੀ ।
ਕਰੇ ਅੰਗ ਭੰਗ ਤੇ ਕਲੇਜੇ ਸੱਲਦੀ ।
ਬਾਜਾਂ ਵਾਂਗੂ ਸਿੰਘ ਪਏ ਲਲਕਾਰ ਕੇ ।
ਹੋਵਣਾ ਸ਼ਹੀਦ ਜ਼ਾਲਮਾਂ ਨੂੰ ਮਾਰ ਕੇ ।

—Sohan Singh Ghukewalia,
Baba Deep Singh Shaheed[15]

Gohalwar kol Singh pahunche aike
Sher vaang zalma dey paye dhayke
Kaar kaar goli teer chhut paye
Aihmo saamne ho dovein dal jutt peyi
Deep Singh kahnda Singha nu pukaar key
Hovena shaheed zalma nu maar ke
Teg utte teg saar saar vajdi
Chaliyan ne topaan teg mala gajdi
Taar taar taar hai bandook chaldi
Kare ang bhang te kaleje saldi
Bajaan vangu Singh paye lalkar ke
Hovena shaheed zalma nu maar ke

At Gohalwar did the Singhs attack
like lions fall on prey.
The bullets whistled thick and fast
Two armies clashed now mid the blast,
Each other did they slay.
Deep Singh loudly pledged to all
To vanquish foe, thereafter fall.
The swords did clang mid cannon boom,
The guns did crack for some their doom.

Like falcons did the Singhs now pounce;
Determined first to kill and trounce
Right there beneath the sky,
And only after die.

13. Jahan Khan Under Pressure

ਜਦ ਸਿੰਘਾਂ ਨੇ ਤੇਗ ਦੀ ਮਾਰ ਮਾਰੀ ਗਿਲਜੇ ਪੈਰ ਪਿਛਾਂ ਹਟਾਣ ਲੱਗੇ ।
ਜ਼ੋਰ ਦੇ ਕੇ ਸਿੰਘ ਸਰਦਾਰ ਯੋਧੇ ਗੁਰ ਧਾਮ ਵੱਲ ਪੈਰ ਵਧਣ ਲੱਗੇ ।
ਚੱਪੇ ਚੱਪੇ ਉੱਤੇ ਤੇਗੀ ਉਤਰੇ ਆ ਹੋਣ ਸੂਰਮੇ ਲਹੂ ਲੁਹਾਣ ਲੱਗੇ ।
ਹਾਥੀ ਉੱਤੇ ਜਹਾਨ ਖਾਨ ਸੀ ਬੈਠਾ ਖਾਨ ਹੋਰ ਭੀ ਘੋੜ ਕੁਦਾਨ ਲੱਗੇ ।
ਮੋੜ ਮੋੜ ਫੌਜ ਤਾਈਂ ਦੇਇ ਤਾਹਨੇ ਡੱਕ ਡੱਕ ਸਿੰਘਾਂ ਅੱਗੇ ਢਾਹਨ ਲੱਗੇ ।
ਤੇਗ ਝੱਲਣੀ ਸਿੰਘਾਂ ਦੀ ਹੋਈ ਔਖੀ ਦਾ ਬਚਾ ਲੜਨੀ ਮੁਸਲਮਾਨ ਲੱਗੇ ।

—Kartar Singh Kalaswalia, *Jauhar Khalsa*[16]

Jad Singhan ney teg di maar mari giljey pair pichhan hataan lagge
Zore deke Singh sardar yodhey gur dham vall pair vadhaan lagge
Chappe chappe utte teghi utre aa hone soormey lahoo luhaan lagge
Hathi utte jahan Khan si baitha Khan hore bhi ghor kudaan lagge
Morh morh fauj tain deh thane dak dak singhan agge dhan lagge
Tegh jhalni Singhan di hoi aukhi da bacha ladney musulman lagge

When Singhs with sword attacked in dash, the *Giljas* then in terror fled
The Singhs in turn did start advance to Amritsar with steady tread.
The field of battle turned so thick with blood of dying and the dead.
Jahan Khan on his elephant mount with prancing horsemen round him spread;
He bade his men with threat and taunt to face the Singhs without a dread
But they no longer could then face the swordplay of the Singhs ahead.

14. Dyal Singh Kills Amir Jan Khan

ਤਬੈ ਸ਼ਹੀਦ ਦਯਾਲ ਸਿੰਘ, ਮਾਹਲੈ ਨਿਹਾਰ ਹੈ ।
ਜੂਨ ਸਿੰਘ ਪਾਂਚ ਸੌ, ਮਿਲਾਇ ਸੰਗ ਸਾਰ ਹੈ ॥ ੩੩ ।
ਪਰਖੇ ਅਮੀਰ ਜਾਨ-ਖਾਨ ਪੈ, ਸੁ ਜਾਇ ਬੀਜ ਜਯੋ ।

Appendix A: Deep Singh in Verse

ਹਰੇ ਅਨੰਤ ਸ਼ਤਰੂ ਲਰੇ ਪਠਾਨ ਖੀਜ ਤਯੋ ।
ਹਤੇ ਅਮੀਰ ਜਾਨ ਫੀਲ ਪੈ, ਲਰੰਤ ਸੁਮਨੈ ।
ਹਰੀ-ਦਿਆਲ ਅੱਸੁ ਕੋ, ਬਧਾਇ ਸਾਮ ਬਾਂਮਨੈ ॥ ੩੪ ॥
ਧਰਾਇ ਸੁੰਭ ਫੀਲ ਮਾਥਿ, ਹਾਥ ਐਸ ਮਾਰਿਓ ।
ਉਤਾਰਿ ਮੂੰਡ ਖਾਨ ਕੋ, ਕੱਦੂ ਸਮਾਨ ਡਾਰਿਓ ॥ ੩੫ ॥

—Gyani Gyan Singh,
Sri Guru Panth Prakash II[17]

Tabai Shaheed Dyal Singh, Mahalai nihar hai.
Jawan Singh panch sau, milai sung sah hai. (33)
Pariyo Amir Jan Khan pai, su jai beej jayon.
Hare anant shatru, lare pathan kheej tayon.
Hatau Amir Jan pheel pai, larant samney.
Hari-Dyal as ko, badhai sham bamney (34)
Dharai subh pheel math, hath ais mariyo.
Udar moond Khan ko, kaddu saman dariyo. (35)

Warriors do not flee the field,
Nor give up arms, nor ever cede;
they roar and stand their ground
while Dyal Singh comes to lead
500 Singhs, for battle bound—
Attack their foe in lightning flash
to kill so many in the clash.
Inflamed Pathans bounce back in hunt
Amir Jan Khan on elephant;
He ahead of all, upfront.
Dyal Singh now advanced his mount:
Invoked gods fifty-two in count.
His horse then placed its hoof on top
Of elephant's head just as a prop,
Dyal Singh then grabbed chance to strike
And sliced Khan's head off pumpkin-like.
When many others also slain,
Ayub and Jahan Khan were roiled again.

15. Scene of Battle

ਜੰਗ ਦਾ ਨਜ਼ਾਰਾ

ਝੱਟ ਬਿਗਲ ਵੱਜ ਗਿਆ ਜੰਗ ਦਾ ਜੁੱਟੇ ਖਾ ਖਾਰਾਂ ।
ਇਕ ਦਮ ਰਣਜੀਤ ਨਗਾਰਿਆਂ ਪਾਈਆਂ ਗੁੰਜਾਰਾਂ ।

ਸਭ ਇਕ ਦੂਜੇ ਤੇ ਟੁੱਟ ਪਏ ਲੈ ਕੇ ਤਲਵਾਰਾਂ ।
ਪਏ ਤੀਰ ਚੱਲਦੇ ਨਾਗ ਜਿਉ ਮਾਰੇ ਫੁੰਕਾਰਾਂ ।

ਕਿਤੇ ਚੱਲ ਚੱਲ ਚੱਕਰ ਉਡੱਦੇ ਬੰਨ੍ਹ ਬੰਨ੍ਹ ਕਤਾਰਾਂ ।
ਕਿਤੇ ਕੜ ਕੜ ਚੱਲਣ ਗੋਲੀਆਂ ਡਾਰਾਂ ਦੀਆਂ ਡਾਰਾਂ ।

ਕਿਤੇ ਛਵੀ ਗੰਡਾਸੇ ਬਰਛੀਆਂ ਲਾਹ ਰਹੇ ਸਭਾਰਾਂ ।
ਜਿਵੇਂ ਵੱਢ ਵੱਢ ਰੱਖੀਆਂ ਖੇਤ ਵਿਚ ਕਿਰਸਾਨ ਜਵਾਰਾਂ ।

ਓਥੇ ਸੱਟਾਂ ਖਾ ਖਾ ਢਿਗਦੇ ਕਈ ਬੀਰ ਹਜ਼ਾਰਾਂ ।
ਜਿਵੇਂ ਡਿੱਗਣ ਵਿਚ ਭੂਰਲ ਦੇ ਕਈ ਮਹਿਲ ਮੁਨਾਰਾਂ ।

ਓਥੇ ਤੇਗਾਂ ਗਾਟੇ ਵੱਢਦੀਆਂ ਤੇ ਚੱਲਣ ਕਟਾਰਾਂ ।
ਜਿਵੇਂ ਵਾਢੀ ਪਾਈ ਕਣਕ ਨੂੰ ਜੱਟਾਂ ਜ਼ਿਮੀਦਾਰਾਂ ।

ਓਥੇ ਬਰਛੇ ਚੱਲਣ ਲਹੂ ਨਾਲ ਰੰਗ ਰੰਗ ਕੇ ਧਾਰਾਂ ।
ਜਿਵੇਂ ਸੁਰਖੀ ਲਾ ਕੇ ਪੈਂਦੀਆਂ ਗਿੱਧਾ ਮੁਟਿਆਰਾਂ ।

ਓਥੇ ਗੋਲੇ ਸਹਿ ਸਹਿ ਤੋਪ ਦੇ ਡਿੱਗਣ ਖਾ ਮਾਰਾਂ ।
ਜਿਵੇਂ ਮਾਰੀ ਸੱਟ ਵਦਾਣ ਦੀ ਸਿਰ ਵਿਚ ਲੁਹਾਰਾਂ ।

ਓਥੇ ਲਹੂ ਦੀਆਂ ਨਿਕਲਣ ਤਨਾਂ ਚੋ ਉਡ ਉਡ ਫੁਹਾਰਾਂ ।
ਜਿਵੂ ਟੁੱਟਣ ਕਿਸੇ ਪਹਾੜ ਚੋਂ ਚਸ਼ਮੇਂ ਦੀਆਂ ਧਾਰਾਂ ।

ਸਿਰ ਬਾਝੇ ਦਿੱਸਣ ਧੜ ਪਏ ਕੋਈ ਲਵੇ ਨਾ ਸਾਰਾਂ ।
ਜਿਉ ਮੋਢੇ ਸੁੱਟੇ ਵੱਢ ਕੇ ਤਿੱਖੇ ਹਥਿਆਰਾਂ ।

ਓਥੇ ਘੋੜੇ ਪੈਲਾਂ ਪਾਂਵਦੇ ਲਾ ਲਾ ਉਡਾਰਾਂ ।
ਜਿਵੇਂ ਮਾਲ ਰੋਡ ਤੇ ਚੱਲਦੀਆਂ ਖਹਿ ਖੀਹ ਕੇ ਕਾਰਾਂ ।

ਸਭ ਇਕ ਦੂਜੇ ਤੇ ਵੱਧ ਕੇ ਪਏ ਮਾਂਰਨ ਮਾਰਾਂ ।
ਓਥੇ ਸਿਰੀਆਂ ਦਿਸਣ ਰੁਲਦੀਆਂ ਨਲੀਏਰ ਬਜ਼ਾਰਾਂ ।

ਨਾ ਕੋਈ ਕਿਸੇ ਨੂੰ ਬਹੁੜਿਆ ਨਾ ਲਈਆਂ ਸਾਰਾਂ ।
ਉਥੇ ਕੀਤੇ ਕੌਲ ਪੁਗਾਏ ਨਾ ਮਿੰਤਰਾਂ ਤੇ ਯਾਰਾਂ ।

ਓਥੇ ਪੀਤੀ ਰੱਤ ਕਲਜੋਗਣਾਂ ਲੈ ਲੈ ਡਕਾਰਾਂ ।
ਸੀ ਜਿਹੜੀਆਂ ਕੱਲ ਸੁਹਾਗਣਾਂ ਲੁੱਟ ਰਹੀਆਂ ਬਹਾਰਾਂ ।

ਉਹਨਾਂ ਰੰਗਲੇ ਚੂੜੇ ਭੰਨ ਲਏ ਬਿਨ ਕਰੇ ਦੀਦਾਰਾਂ ।
ਕੱਲ ਸੇਜਾਂ ਮਾਨਣ ਜਿਹੜੀਆਂ ਲਾ ਹਾਰ ਸ਼ਿੰਗਾਰਾਂ ।

ਓਹ ਜੁਲਫ਼ਾਂ ਗਲ ਪਾ ਰੋਦੀਆਂ ਭੰਨ ਸੁਹਾਗ ਪਟਾਰਾਂ ।
ਜਿਹਨਾਂ ਲਾੜੇ ਤੇਰੇ ਜੰਗ ਨੂੰ ਗਾਣੇ ਬੰਨ੍ਹ ਨਾਰਾਂ ।
ਉਹ ਕੋਠੇ ਚੜ੍ਹ ਚੜ੍ਹ ਤੱਕਦੀਆਂ ਲਾ ਕੇ ਲਿਵਤਾਰਾਂ ।
ਪਰ ਸੂਰੇ ਜੁੱਟੇ ਜੰਗ ਵਿਚ ਛੱਡ ਮੋਹ ਪਿਆਰਾਂ ।
ਕਈ ਹੱਲੇ ਬੋਲੇ ਗਾਜ਼ੀਆਂ ਕਈ ਸਿੰਘ ਸਰਦਾਰਾਂ ।
ਪਰ ਕਿਸੇ ਨਾ ਛੱਡੇ ਮੋਰਚੇ ਨਾ ਮੰਨੀਆਂ ਹਾਰਾਂ ।
ਭਖ ਰਹੀਆਂ ਚਿਹਰੇ ਲਾਲੀਆਂ ਜਿਉਂ ਚੜ੍ਹੂ ਸ਼ਕਾਰਾਂ ।
'ਦਿਲਬਰ' ਢਾਡੀ ਗਾਉਣਗੇ ਮਰਦਾਂ ਦੀਆਂ ਵਾਰਾਂ ।

—Daya Singh Dilbar,
Vaar Baba Deep Singh ji Shaheed[18]

Jang da nazara
Jhat bigle vaj giya jang da jute kha kharan
Ik dum ranjit nagariyan payian gunjara

Sab ik duje te tut paye lai ke talwara
Paye teer chalde nag jiyo mare phunkaran

Kite chal chal chakkar ud de ban ban kataran
kite kar kar chalan golian daran diyan daran

kite chhavin gandanse barchiyan lah rahe satharan
jiven vad vad rakhiyan khet vich kisan javaran

uthe sattan kha kha dighde kayi bir hazaran
jiven dighan vich bhuchal de kayi mahal munaran

uthe tegan gate vad diyan te chalan kataran
jiven vaadi payi kanak nu jattan zimindaran

uthe barchhe chalan lahu nal rang rang ke dharan
jiven surkhi la ke paindiyan giddha matiyaran

uthe gole sah sah tope de dighan kha maran
jiven mari sat vadaan di sir vich loharan

uthe lahu diyan niklan tana chon ud ud phuharan
jiven phuttan kisse pahar chon chasmein diyan dharan

sir bhajon dissen dhar paye koi lave na saran
jion mochhe sutte vad ke tikkhe hathiaran

uthe ghore pailan pavnde la la udaran
jiven mal road te chaldiyan kheh kheh ke caran

sab ik duje ton vad ke paye maran maaran
uthe siriyan dissen ruldiyan nalier bazaran

na koi kisse nu bahuriyan na layian saran
uthe kite kol pujaye na mitran te yaran

uthe piti ratt kaljogna lai lai dakaran
si jehriyan kal suhagana lut rahiyan baharan

uhna rangle churre bhann lai bin kare didaran
kal sejan manan jehriyan la har shingaran

uh zulfan gal pa rondiyan bhann suhag pataran
jehna lare tore jang nu gane bann naran

oh kothe char char takdiyan la ke livtaran
par soore jutte jang vich chhad moh piyaran

kayi halle bolle gaziyan kayi Singh sardaran
par kisse na chhade morche na maniyan haran

bhak rahiyan chehre laliyan jeon chare shikaran
'Dilbar' dhadi gaonge mardan diyan varan

Scene of Battle

The bugles call now all to battle,
    war drums sound around;
Two armies have come face to face
    and sword-fights do abound.
The showers of arrows hiss and whistle,
    The quoits fly saucer-like;
The crack of bullets smash and whack
    before their billet strike.
The battle axe and spear together
    Spare no one at all;
Severed heads and limbs pile up
    wherever they do fall.
The brave lie maimed in thousands here
    As if the earth does quake
as crumble manors big and tall
    When all the earth does shake.
Akin to sheaves of millet grain
    that farmers stack afield;

The dead lie all about in heaps
   Much like a harvest yield;
The cannons boom and shells fly past,
   Above all sounds of war;
Like scores of blacksmiths, hammer and tongs—
   True image of great Thor.
High-stepping horses prance and rear
   Before they charge ahead,
Undaunted now they gallop on
   Wherever they are led.
Both armies rallied many times
   In sallies so intense,
But neither gained the upper hand
   Nor could they recompense.
The warriors fought with grit and pluck
   But victory none could score;
The bards shall to their courage sing
   Such paeans evermore.

16. Deep Singh Fights and Kills Yakub Khan near Chabba

ਦੀਪ ਸਿੰਘ ਅੜਿਆ ਜਿਸ ਤਰਫ ਆਕੇ ਖਾਂ ਯਾਕੂਬ ਅੱਗੇ ਲਲਕਾਰ ਆਯਾ ।
ਜੁੱਟੇ ਸੂਰਮੇਂ ਭਰੇ ਕਰੋਧ ਅੰਦਰ ਆਹਮੋਂ ਸਾਹਮਣੇ ਦੋਹਾਂ ਦਾ ਵਾਰ ਆਯਾ ।
ਘੋੜੇ ਦੋਹਾਂ ਦੇ ਜ਼ਖਮੀ ਹੋ ਡਿਗੈ ਖਾਂ ਯਾਕੂਬ ਉੱਠ ਲੈ ਤਲਵਾਰ ਆਯਾ ।
ਦੀਪ ਸਿੰਘ ਦੇ ਹੱਥ ਸੀ ਗੁਰਜ ਭਾਰੀ ਮਾਰੀ ਸਰ ਤੇ ਵਾਰ ਉਹ ਭਾਰ ਆਯਾ ।
ਫਿਸ ਗਿਆ ਤਰਬੂਜ ਦੇ ਵਾਂਗ ਉਥੇ ਮੀਰਜਨ ਖਾਂ ਤੇਗ ਉਲਾਰ ਆਯਾ ।

—Kartar Singh Kalaswalia, *Jauhar Khalsa*[19]

Deep Singh adiya jis taraf aake Khan Yakub agge lalkar ayaa
Jutte soormei bhare karodh andar aihmon saamney dohan da vaar ayaa
Ghorey dohaan dey zakhmi ho dighey Kjhan Yakub utth lai talwar ayaa
Deep Singh dey hath si gurj bhari mari sir tey vaar uh bhaar ayaa
Phis giya tarbooj de vaang uthhe Mirjan Khan teg ulaar aya
Yakub Khan now confronted the great Deep Singh to a fight.
In fury the two sought and fought and made a direful sight.
There horses were soon wounded, and then both did dismount;
Yakub Khan came up lunging, just as we now recount.
Deep Singh struck him then at once with full swing of his mace—
Yakub Khan couldn't dodge it and was crushed in skull and face.

The same action in the words of Gyani Gyan Singh employing with great craftsmanship the *naraj chhand,* a popular meter for heroic verse in Indian prosody. Composed predominantly in emphatic spondees with a few iambs for effect, this is powerful octameter with thumping rhythm and onomatopoeia evocative of the battle:

Line 1:   x / / / / x / / x / /   –11 syllables
Line 2:   x / / / / x / / / /   –10 syllables
Line 3:   x / x / / / x / / / /   –11 syllables
Line 4:   x / / x / / / x / x / /   –12 syllables
x = short syllable; / = long syllable

Eight feet per line, with a slight difference in the metrical arrangement; rather difficult, if not impossible, to replicate in English because of the inherent qualitative-quantitative dissimilarity of scansion.

ਤਦਾਇ ਦੀਪ ਸਿੰਘ, ਖਾਨ ਯਾਕੂਬ ਕੋ ਪ੍ਰਚਾਰ ਕੈ ।
ਕੁਵੰਡ ਖੰਡਿ ਖੈਂਚ ਕੈ, ਨਰਾਚ ਮੇਂਹ ਡਾਰ ਕੈ ।
ਉਭੈ ਸੁ ਭੱਟ ਜੁਟਗੇ ਆਘਟ ਠੱਟ ਜੰਗ ਹੈਂ ।
ਫੁਲਾਦ ਕੇ ਸੰਜੋਇ ਟੋਪ, ਥੇ ਸਜੇ ਸੁ ਅੰਗ ਹੈਂ ॥੪੫॥

—Gyani Gyan Singh,
Sri Guru Panth Prakash II[20]

Tadain Deep Singh, Khan Yakub kaun prachar kei
Kuvand khand khainch kei, narach mengh dhar kei
Ubhei su bhatt jutge aghat that jang hein
Phulad ke sanjoi tope, the saje su ang hein (45)
Deep Singh then aroused Yakub Khan to a fight;
With readied broadswords and a bow
They showered their arrows with all might
Full combat they did now engage
The Khan wore helmet-armour full.
He looked in every way a knight.

The octameter resounds with its spondees with some iambs for effect:

Line 1:   x / x / / / x / x / / x /   –13 syllables
Line 2:   x / / / x / x / x / / x /   –13 syllables

Line 3:	x / / / x / / /	–10 syllables
Line 4:	x / / / / x / / /	–10 syllables

ਮਰੇ ਕਿਕਾਨ ਦੋਇ ਕੇ, ਪੁਨਾ ਖਰੋਇ ਕੇ ਭਿਰੇ ।
ਅਖੀਰ ਹੱਥ ਵੱਥ ਹੂੈ, ਉਭੈ ਜ਼ਮੀਨ ਪੈ ਗਿਰੇ ।
ਗਰੱਜ ਸਿੰਘ, ਸਿੰਘ ਜਯੋਂ, ਗੁਰਜ ਸੇਰ ਤੀਸ ਕੈ ।
ਉਭਾਰੁ, ਭੀਮ ਪੌਨ ਪੂਤ ਕੇ ਸਮਾਨ, ਰੀਸ ਕੈ ॥ ੪੬ ॥

—Gyani Gyan Singh,
Sri Guru Panth Prakash II[21]

Mare kikan doi ke, puna kharoi ke bhire.
Akheer hatth vath hue, ubhei zameen pe girey.
Garaj Singh, Singh jion, guraj ser tees kein.
Ubhar, Bhim pon put ke saman, rees ke. (46)
Their horses killed from battle wounds;
Alighting then, they fought on ground;
Wrestling, punching, push and pound,
Fought their next round on the ground.
Lion-like now Deep Singh roared
And heaved his 30 *ser* mace.
Akin to Bhimsen-Hanuman,
With rage that showed his race.

The scansion is similar yet again:

Line 1:	x / / / x / x / / / /	–11 syllables
Line 2:	x / x / / x / x / x / /	–12 syllables
Line 3:	x / / / / x / / / x /	–11 syllables
Line 4:	x / / / / / / x /	–10 syllables

ਪ੍ਰਹਾਰ ਕੀਨ ਚੂਰਨੰ, ਸਟੋਪ ਮੂੰਡ ਖਾਨ ਕੋ।
ਮਨੇ ਤ੍ਰਬੂਜ਼, ਮੱਟ ਫੋਰਿਓ ਦਧੀ ਸੁ ਕਾਨ੍ਹ ਕੋ।
ਨਿਹਾਰਿ ਮੀਰ ਜਾਨ ਖਾਂ, ਤੁਰੰਗ ਛੇਰ ਕੈ ਅਯੋ।
ਸਮਾਨ ਮੇਘ ਗੱਜਿ, ਵਾਹ ਵਾਹ ਸਿੰਘ ਕੋ ਕਯੋ॥੪੭॥

—Gyani Gyan Singh,
Sri Guru Panth Prakash II[22]

Prahar keen chooranang, setop moond khan ko.
Mane trabooz, mat pheriyo dudhi su kan ko.
Nihar Mir Jan Khan, turang chher kai ayo.
Samaan megh gaj, wah wah Singh ko keyo.

Khan's head and helmet were now smashed
Like powder or a melon splashed;
Akin *dahi* pitchers Krishen broke.
Mir Jan Khan saw and Singh he praised;
Bellowing thunder-like, he blazed. (47)

17. Naudh Singh Fights Mir Jan Khan

ਕਹਯੋ ਕਰੈਹੁ ਦੁੰਦ-ਜੁੱਧ, ਹੌਸ ਮੋਹਿ ਪੂਰਨੰ ।
ਤੁਮਾਰ ਸਿੰਘ ਨਾਮ ਸਾਚ, ਜੇ ਲਰੈਹੁ ਤੁਰਨੰ ।
ਤਬੈ ਸਕੋਪ ਨੈਧ ਸਿੰਘ ਗਿੱਲ, ਅੱਸੁ ਛੇਰ ਕੈ ।
ਅਮੀਰ ਜਾਨ-ਖਾਨ ਸੋ, ਭਿਰਯੋ ਮਹਾਨ ਟੇਰ ਕੈ ॥ ੪੮ ॥
ਕਮਾਨ ਤਾਨ ਤਾਨ ਕੈ, ਤਕਾਇ ਬਾਨ ਝਾੜਹੀ ।
ਖਰੋ ਦਿਸਾਨ ਦੋਇ ਤੈ, ਪਠਾਨ ਸਿੰਘ ਤਾੜਹੀ ।
ਗਿਰੇ ਤੁਰੰਗ ਭੰਗ ਢੈ, ਭਿਰੇ ਕ੍ਰਿਪਾਨ ਲੈ ਪੁਨਾ ।
ਪਟੇ ਸੁ ਬਾਜ ਥੇ ਉਡੈ, ਬਲੀ ਲਰਾਕਿ ਸੋਂ ਗੁਨਾ ॥ ੪੯ ॥
ਸਰੋਹ ਲੋਹ ਮੈ ਮਢੇ, ਪਢੇ ਕ੍ਰਿਪਾਨ ਬਾਹਿਨੇ ।
ਘਨੈ ਠਨਿਆਰ ਘਾਤ ਜਖੋ, ਪੜੈ ਤ੍ਰਵਾਰ ਤਾਹਿ ਨੇ ।
ਰਹੀ ਜੁ ਮੂਠ ਮੂਠ ਮੈ, ਸੁ ਤੇਗ ਬੇਗ ਟੂਟ ਕੈ ।
ਪੁਨੇ ਘਮੰਡ ਚੰਡਿ ਮੰਡਿ, ਲੋਹ-ਦੰਡ ਛੂਟ ਕੈ ॥ ੫੦ ॥
ਗਿਰੰਤ ਔਨਿ ਪੈ ਕਬੀ, ਉਠੰਤ ਕੋਪ ਪੈ ਲਰੈ ।
ਟੂਟੀ ਸੰਜੋਇ ਢਾਲ, ਘਾਇਲੈ ਬਿਹਾਲ ਹੈ ਭਰੇ ।
ਅਤੀਵ ਦੁੱਧ-ਜੁੱਧ, ਸੁੱਧ-ਬੁੱਧਿ ਕ੍ਰੋਧ ਕੈ ਕਰਾ ।
ਅਖੀਰਿ ਬੀਰਿ ਧੀਰਿ ਵੈਗਿ, ਬੀਰ ਜੰਗ ਕੈ ਖਰਾ ॥ ੫੧ ॥
ਕਟਾਰ ਧਾਰਿ ਹੱਥ ਤੱਥ, ਹੱਤ ਵੱਥ ਹੈ ਗਏ ।
ਦਹੂੰ ਸੁ ਏਕ ਬਾਰ ਹੀ ਪਸਾਇ ਪੇਟ ਮੈ ਦਏ ।
ਭਏ ਸ਼ਹੀਦ ਸੋ ਮਹੀਦ, ਦੇਵ ਅੰਗਨਾ ਬਰੇ ।
ਬਸੇ ਬਿਕੁੰਠ ਜਾਇ, ਲਾਭ ਪਾਇ ਦੇਹ ਕੋ ਭਰੇ ॥ ੫੨ ॥
ਇਸੀ ਪ੍ਰਕਾਰ ਚਾਰ ਪਾਂਚ, ਔਰ ਹੂੰ ਸ੍ਰਦਾਰ ਜੋਂ ।
ਮਰੇ ਤੁਕਾਨ ਕੇਰ ਜੁਝਿ, ਦੁੰਦ ਜੁੱਧ ਧਾਰ ਜੋਂ ।
ਤਬੈ ਜਹਾਨ ਖਾਂ, ਯਕੂਬ ਖਾਨ ਸਾਬਰੈ ਅਲੀ ।
ਲਰੇ ਲਗਾਇ ਜੋਰ, ਹੇਰ ਸੈਨ ਐਨ ਲੈ ਭਲੀ ॥ ੫੩ ॥

—Gyani Gyan Singh,
Sri Guru Panth Prakash II[23]

kahyo karaih dud-judh, hosh moh puranang
tumar Singh naam saach, je larai turanang
tabai sakop Naudh Singh Gill, asv chher kai
Amir Jan-Khan mein, bhiryo mahant er kai |48|

kaman taan taan ke, takai baan tarhi
kharai disaan doi tei, pathan Singh tarhi
girai turang bhang hai, bhirai kirpan lai puna
patai su baaj thei ubhey, bali larak do guna |49|

saroi loh main madhe, padhey kirpan bahiney
gharain thathyar ghar jiyon, parai travar tahiney
rahi ju mooth mooth mai, su teg beg toot kai
punai ghamand chand mand, loh-dand chhoot kai |50|

girant aun pai kabi, uthant kop pai larain
tuti sanjoi dhal, ghailai bhihal hue bharein
ateev dud-judh, sudh-budh koodh kai kara
akhir bir dhir veg, dhir jang kai khara |51|

katar dhar hath that, hat vath hue gaye
duhoon sue k bar hi dhasai pet main deye
bhaye shaheed so maheed, dev angana barey
basey bikunth jai, labh pai deh kai bharey |52|

isi prakar char panch, aur hun sardar jo
marey trekan ker joojh, dud judh dhar jo
tabai Jahan Khan, Yakub Khan Sabrai Ali
larai lagai jor, hor sain ain lei bhali |53|

Mir Jan Khan now provoked Deep Singh,
And asked to grant a wish to fight.
Only then he would accept
Him as true Singh, pure and right.
Naudh Singh Gill now intervened;
In anger moved his horse between.
Mid bellowing threats, they shot their bows
Their horses killed, with swords they close. |48|
Great warriors who are so adept
at swordplay one beheld. |49|
Hammer and tongs they set upon
like blacksmiths iron meld.
Their swords then broke;
They fought with grips,
Or thrust the blades in stroke. |50|
whether on the ground they fell,

or rose, they fought with might,
their armour and their shields were rent,
both wounded, by exhaustion bent.
Warriors top rewards do gain
when battle they with brawn and brain;
patience, zeal and strength maintain. |51|
Brandished their push-daggers next,
Hand-to-hand they fought so vexed.
Swore and pushed with all their might—
drove daggers into bellies tight,
and thus they did now end the fight. |52|
In earnest as the fighting raged,
a war that hostile foes had waged,
Yakub Khan, Jahan Khan, Sabar Ali, others too.
Fought that they may Sikhs subdue |53|

18. Deep Singh Fights Aman Khan, is Mortally Wounded but Fights on to Die Near Ramsar

ਸਕੋਪ ਦੀਪ ਸਿੰਘ ਜੂ, ਯਕੂਬ ਖਾਨ ਆਦਿਕੈ ।
ਹਰੇ ਅਪਾਰ ਸੱਤਰੂ, ਲਰੇ ਜੁ ਆਇ ਬਾਦ ਕੈ ।
ਤਹਾਂ ਅਮਾਨ-ਖਾਨਹੁੰ ਸੁਦਾਰ ਪਾਉ ਰੁੱਪ ਕੈ ।
ਲਰਯੋ ਮਹਾਨ ਦੀਪ ਸਿੰਘ ਸੰਗ, ਭੂਰ ਕੁੱਪ ਕੈ ॥ ੫੪ ॥
ਹਏ ਕਿਕਾਨ ਦੋਇ ਕੈ, ਟੂਟੇ ਸੰਜੋਇ ਆਹੂਧੈ ।
ਭਏ ਸੁ ਹੱਥ-ਵੱਥ ਹੱਥ, ਧੋਇ ਦੋਇ ਆਹੂ ਤੇ ॥ ੫੫ ॥
ਦੋਹਰਾ ॥ ਚਲੀ ਤੇਗ ਅਤਿ ਬੇਗ ਸੈ, ਦੁਹੂੰ ਕੇਰ ਬਲ-ਵਾਰ ।
ਉਤਰ ਗਏ ਸਿਰ ਦੁਹੂੰ ਕੇ, ਪਰਸ-ਪਰੈ ਇਕ ਸਾਰ ॥ ੫੬ ॥
ਚੌਪਾਈ ॥ ਡਿਗਾ ਤੇ ਏਕ ਸਿੰਘ ਪਿਖਿ ਕਹਯੋ
ਪਰਣ ਤੁਮਾਰ ਦੀਪ ਸਿੰਘ ਰਹਯੋ ।
ਗੁਰਪੁਰਿ ਜਾਇ ਸੀਸ ਮੈ ਦੈਹੋ ।
ਸੋ ਤੇ ਦੋਇ ਕੋਸ ਇਸ ਠੈਹੋ ॥ ੫੭ ॥
ਸੁਨਿ ਸਿੰਘ ਜੀ ਨਿਜ ਪਰਣ ਸੰਭਾਰਾ ।
ਨਿਜ ਸਿਰ ਬਾਮ-ਹਾਥਿ ਨਿਜ ਧਾਰਾ ।
ਦਹਿਨੇ ਹਾਥਿ ਤੇਗ ਖਰ ਧਾਰਾ ।
ਵਜਨ ਜਾਂਹਿ ਤਾ ਸੇਰ ਅਠਾਰਾਂ ॥ ੫੮ ॥

—Gyani Gyan Singh,
Sri Guru Panth Prakash II[24]

Appendix A: Deep Singh in Verse

sakope Deep Singh ju, Ayub Khan adikai
hare apaar shatru, larai ju aye baad kai
tahan Aman-Khan hun sardar paun rup kai
laryo mahan Deep Singh sang, bhur kup kai |54|
haye kikan doi kai, tute sanjoi ayudhai
bhaye su hath-vath, dhoi doye ayu tai |55|
chali teg at beg mai, duhun ker bal-vaar
utar gaye sir duh ke, paras-pahein ik saar |56|
dhig tai ek singh pikh kayo
paran tumar Deep Singh rayo
gurpur jaye sees main daihon
so ted oi kos is thaihein |57|
sun singh ji nij paran sambhara
nij sir bam-hath nij dhara
dahne hath teg khar dhara
vajan jai tha ser atharan |58|

In earnest as the fighting raged,
a war that hostile foes had waged,
Yakub Khan and such others too
Whom Deep Singh killed and did subdue.
Aman Khan came and pledged to fight;
And Deep Singh angered, joined outright. |54|
The horses which they rode were killed,
Their chainmail snapped and weapons broke;
hand-to-hand they brawled and smote;
on life no longer did they dote. |55|
At once the swords flashed swift and stout;
Their heads fell down to end the bout. |56|
One Singh did prompt when Deep Singh fell.
His vow for Amritsar to tell,
Which two *kos* [six kilometres] far away did dwell. |57|
On hearing thus his comrade speak,
Now Deep Singh rose his vow to keep;
His head he lifts in his left hand
In right, eighteen *ser* Khanda grand. |58|

19. Kaman Khan Challenges Deep Singh to Single Combat

ਪਉੜੀ॥ ਇਹ ਵੇਖੇ ਖੂਨੀ ਕਾਰੇ, ਜਦੋਂ ਕਮਾਨ ਖਾਂ ।
ਉਹ ਤੋਂ ਵੇਖ ਨਾ ਗਏ ਸਹਾਰੇ, ਸਾਥੀ ਤੜਫਦੇ ।
ਉਹ ਸਾਵ੍ਹੇ ਆ ਲਲਕਾਰੇ, ਬਾਬਾ ਸਾਹਿਬ ਨੂੰ ।
ਉਹ 'ਐਲੀ ਐਲੀ' ਪੁਕਾਰੇ, ਗ਼ਾਜ਼ੀ ਦੀ ਦਾ ।
ਉਹਦੇ ਨੈਣ ਭਖਣ ਅੰਗਿਆਰੇ, ਸੁੱਟਣ ਰੱਤ ਪਏ ।
ਉਹ ਤੜਫੇ ਵਾਂਗੂੰ ਪਾਰੇ, ਭਰਿਆ ਜੋਸ਼ ਦਾ ।
ਉਹ ਚੜ੍ਹਿਆ ਲੋਚੇ ਖਾਰੇ, ਮਲਕੁਲ ਮੌਤ ਦੇ ।
ਉਹ ਰਣ ਵਿਚ ਖਲਾ ਵੰਗਾਰੇ, ਆਪਣੀ ਅਜਲ ਨੂੰ ।
ਕਹਿ, 'ਸਿੰਘਾ ! ਕਰ ਲੈ ਤਿਆਰੇ ਧੁਰ ਦਰਗਾਹ ਦੇ ।
ਮੈ ਲੱਖਾਂ ਘਾਟ ਉਤਾਰੇ ਆਪਣੀ ਤੇਗ਼ ਦੇ ।
ਤੂੰ ਐਨੇ ਕਹਿਰ ਗੁਜ਼ਾਰੇ, ਮੇਰੇ ਵਿਹੰਦਿਆਂ ।
ਮੈ ਬਦਲੇ ਲੈ ਲਾਂ ਸਾਰੇ, ਤੈਨੂੰ ਮਾਰ ਕੇ' ।

—Sohan Singh Seetal, *Shaheed Baba Deep Singh*[25]

Eh vekhe khuni kaare jadon Kaman Khan
Uh ton vekh na gaye saharey, sathi tarafde
Uh savein a lalkarey, Baba Sahib nu
Uh Ali Ali pukarey, Gazi din da
Uhde nain bhakhan angiyare, sutten rat paye
Uh tarfe vangu parey, bhariya josh da
Uh chariya loche kharey, malkul maut de
Uh rann vich khala vangarey, apni ajal nu
Keh 'Singha ! kar leh tiyari dhur dargah de
Mein lakhan ghat utarey, apni teg de
Tun aine kahar guzarey, mere vihandiya
Mein badley lai lan sarey, tainu mar ke'

Kaman Khan saw the grievous wounds inflicted on his men;
His hackles raised, he sought revenge from Deep Singh there and then.
He challenged and provoked then Baba Sahib to a fight,
Invoked his God and said a prayer that he's granted all his might.
His bloodshot eyes like embers shone and seemed to be on fire.
His frame now trembled with a rage so full of burning ire.
He stood there full of daring and so eager for the fray,
And sought his foe before him then and held them all at bay.
He boasted of his prowess and his practiced skill with sword,

Appendix A: Deep Singh in Verse

With taunts and slurs he hurled at Baba Sahib and did goad.
He pledged an oath to kill him on the ground where he now stood
And thus avenge the killing of his brethren if he could.

Deep Singh steadies himself for the fight.

ਪਾਉੜੀ।। ਇਹ ਸੁਣ ਕੇ ਬਾਬਾ ਦੀਪ ਸਿੰਘ
ਰੂਹ ਭਰਿਆ ਤੇਗ਼ ਸੁਆਰਦਾ ।
ਜਿਉਂ ਲਾਲੀ ਸੂਰਜ ਚੜ੍ਹਨ ਦੀ
ਇਉਂ ਭਖਦਾ ਰੰਗ ਸਰਦਾਰ ਦਾ ।
ਉਹਦੇ ਨੈਣੀ ਸੁਰਖ਼ੀ ਚਮਕਦੀ
ਜਿਉਂ ਟਹਿਕੇ ਫੁੱਲ ਅਨਾਰ ਦਾ ।
ਉਹਦੇ ਫਰਕਣ ਡੌਲੇ ਜੋਸ਼ ਵਿਚ
ਜਿਉਂ ਆਕੀ ਨਾਗ ਫੁੰਕਾਰਦਾ
ਉਹ ਗੱਜਿਆ ਵਾਂਗੂੰ ਸ਼ੇਰ ਦੇ
ਤੇ ਦੁਸ਼ਮਣ ਨੂੰ ਲਲਕਾਰਦਾ ।
'ਓ ਖਾਨਾਂ ! ਸੁਣ ਕੰਨ ਖੋਲ੍ਹ ਕੇ
ਤੂੰ ਉਮੱਤ ਹਜ਼ਰਤ ਸਾਹਿਬ ਦੀ
ਮੈਂ ਪੁੱਤਰ ਦਸਮ ਅਵਤਾਰ ਦਾ ।
ਅੱਜ ਤੇਗ਼ ਨਿਬੇੜੇ ਕਰੇਗੀ
ਕੌਣ ਜਿੱਤਦਾ ਹੈ ਕੌਣ ਹਾਰਦਾ?
ਮੈਂ ਤੇਰੇ ਲਹੂ ਦੀ ਧਾਰ ਵਿਚ
ਅੱਜ ਧੋਵਾਂ ਮੂੰਹ ਤਲਵਾਰ ਦਾ
ਮੈਂ ਜ਼ੁਲਮ ਮਿਟਾ ਕੇ ਦੇਸ਼ ਚੋਂ
ਫਿਰ ਸ਼ੁਕਰ ਕਰਾਂ ਕਰਤਾਰ ਦਾ ।'

—Sohan Singh Seetal, *Shaheed Baba Deep Singh*[26]

Eh sun ke Baba Deep Singh
ruh bhariya tegh swarda.
Jeon lali sooraj chadan di
Eon bhakda rang sardar da.
Ohdey nainee surkhi chamakdi
Jeon tahkei phul anaar da.
Ohdey pharkan dauley josh vich
Jeon aaki naag phukarda
Oh gajiya vangu sher dey
Tey dushman nu lalkarda.

'Oh Khana! Sun kunn khol ke
Toon putla hai hankaar da
Toon ummat Hazrat Sahib di
Main puttar dasm avatar da.
Aj tegh nibede kareygi
Kaun jiteda hai kaun harda?
Main tere lahu di dhaar vich
Aj dhovaan muh talwaar da.
Main zulm mita ke des chon
Phir shukar karan kartar da.'
When Deep Singh heard these words so said,
his sword was at the ready.
Like sunrise then his face turned red
with zeal, and yet so steady.
His eyes now glimmered with a light,
redolent and yet so bright.
He stood so tall and strapping,
his fearsome build struck awe.
He then did roar defiance
to all that he there saw.
'Oh Khan, you worship *Hazrat Sahib*;
I'm son of our Tenth Master.
Our swords shall arbitrate today,
both victory and disaster.
Your blood shall stain my sword to rid oppression from my land,
And then I shall thanksgiving give my Maker and Lord Grande!'

20. Shah Jamal Challenges Deep Singh to Single Combat Near Chabba

ਸਿੰਘ ਵਧੀਆਂ ਨੂੰ ਵੇਖ ਖਾਂ ਗੁੱਸਾ ਖੋੜਾ ਸ਼ਾਹ ਜਮਾਲ ਵਧਾ ਭਾਈ ।
ਦੀਪ ਸਿੰਘ ਜੀ ਦੇ ਅੱਗੇ ਆਣ ਡਟਆਂ ਮੂੰਹ ਆਖਦਾ ਬੋਲ ਸੁਣਾ ਭਾਈ ।
ਸਿੰਘਾਂ ਵਿਚ ਤੂੰ ਸੁਣੀਦਾ ਸੂਰਮਾ ਹੈਂ ਕੁਝ ਕਰਕੇ ਹਥ ਦਿਖਾ ਭਾਈ ।
ਦੀਪ ਸਿੰਘ ਜੀ ਗੱਜ ਕੇ ਸ਼ੇਰ ਵਾਂਗੂ ਘੋੜਾ ਫੇਰੀਆ ਵਾਂਗ ਉਠਾ ਭਾਈ ।
ਖਾਨਾ ਕਰ ਲੈ ਵਾਰ ਨਾ ਦੇਰ ਲਾ ਤੂੰ ਦੇਵਾਂ ਹੁਣੇ ਹੀ ਤੈਨੂੰ ਮੁਕਾ ਭਾਈ ।
ਦੋਵੇਂ ਸੂਰਮੇ ਜੁੱਟ ਪਏ ਰੋਹ ਮੱਥੇ ਭਾਰੀ ਹੱਥ ਭੁਲੱਥੇ ਦਿਖਾ ਭਾਈ ।

—Kartar Singh Kalaswalia, *Jauhar Khalsa*[27]

Singh vadhian nu veikh Khan gussa ghorrah Shah Jamal vadhaa bhai
Deep Singh ji dey agge aan datiya mooh aakhda bole sunaa bhai
Singhan vich tu sunida soorma hain kuj karke hath dikha bhai
Deep Singh ji gaj ke sher vangu ghorra pheriya vaang uttha bhai
Khana kar lai vaar na der la toon devaan huney hi tainu muka bhai
Dovein soormey jutt paye roh mathhey bhari hath bhulanthey dikha bhai

It galled Shah Jamal to see the Sikhs advance ahead;
He spurred his horse to Deep Singh and this to him he said:
'Your name and fame for courage and for strength are much renowned.
Let's find out now how much is true right here upon the ground!'
Deep Singh roared defiance then and inward turned his mount:
'Oh Khan! You strike the first blow now, before I make mine count.'
They lunged and thrust their swords with skill that's worthy to recount.

Deep Singh is mortally wounded in a duel with Shah Jamal at Chabba but fights on when reminded of his oath to die near Ramsar

ਵਾਰ ਦੋਹਾਂ ਵਿਚੋਂ ਕੋਈ ਖਾਵੰਦਾ ਨਾ ਘੋੜੇ ਫੇਰਦੇ ਅਖ ਮਿਲਾ ਭਾਈ ।
ਖੱਟਾ ਖੱਟ ਢਾਲਾਂ ਉੱਤੇ ਪੈਣ ਤੇਗ਼ਾਂ ਦੋਵੇਂ ਜਾਵੰਡੇ ਵਾਰ ਬਚਾ ਭਾਈ ।
ਘੋੜੇ ਦੋਹਾਂ ਦੇ ਜ਼ਖਮੀ ਹੋਈ ਡਿੱਗੇ ਪੈਦਲ ਲੜਨ ਲੱਗੇ ਗੁੱਸਾ ਖਾ ਭਾਈ ।
ਰੀਝਾਂ ਲਾਹ ਕੇ ਦੋਹਾਂ ਨੇ ਜੰਗ ਕੀਤਾ ਅੰਤ ਸਮਾਂ ਆਖ਼ਰ ਆ ਭਾਈ ।
ਕੱਠਾ ਵਾਰ ਹੋਇਆ ਦੋਹਾਂ ਯੋਧਿਆਂ ਦਾ ਦਿੱਤੇ ਦੋਹਾਂ ਦੇ ਸਰ ਉਡਾ ਭਾਈ ।
ਡਿਗ ਪਏ ਮੈਦਾਨ ਦੇ ਵਿਚ ਦੋਵੇਂ ਸੂਰਮੇ ਪੁਣੇ ਦੀ ਹੱਦ ਮੁਕਾ ਭਾਈ ।

—Kartar Singh Kalaswalia, *Jauhar Khalsa*[28]

Vaar dohaan vichon koi khavnda na ghorrey pherdey akh mila bhai.
Khata khat dhalaan uttey pain teghaan dovein javndey vaar bacha bhai.
Ghorrey dhohaan dey zakmi hoi diggey paidal ladan lagge gussa kha bhai.
Rijhan lah ke dohan ne jang keeta ant sama akhir a bhai.
Kattha vaar hoyiya dohaan yodhian da ditte dohaan dey sir udaa bhai.
Dig paye maidaan dey vich dovein sooram pune di hud muka bhai.

They thrust and blocked each other's blows; their horses nimbly stepped afield.

The swords did clang upon the shield; they parried strikes but did not yield.
Their horses were now maimed and spent, the fray resumed on ground
Until by common stroke of swords, both heads were cut and downed.

21. Deep Singh Fights Shah Jamal Near Ramsar, is Mortally Wounded but Fights on to Die in Harimandir Sahib.

ਦੋਹਰਾ॥ ਲੜਦੇ ਮਰਦੇ ਮਾਰਦੇ, ਲਹੂ ਨਦੀ ਵਹਾਇ ।
ਸ੍ਰੀ ਗੁਰਦੁਆਰੇ ਰਾਮਸਰ ਲਾਗੇ ਪਹੁੰਚੇ ਆਇ ।
ਏਥੇ ਫੌਜ ਜੁੜੀ ਸੀ ਭਾਰੀ, ਸਿੰਘਾਂ ਦੀ ਜਾਨ ਵਾਗ ਖੁਲ੍ਹਾਰੀ ।
ਤੁਰਕਾਂ, ਸਿੰਘਾਂ ਦਾ ਘਮਸਾਣ, ਬਹੁਤੇ ਲੱਥੇ ਲੋਹੂ ਘਾਣ ।
ਪੰਜ ਹਜ਼ਾਰੀ ਸ਼ਾਹ ਜਮਾਲ, ਆ ਜੁੱਟਾ ਬਾਬਾ ਜੀ ਨਾਲ ।
ਕੱਲੇ ਕੱਲੇ ਕਰਨ ਲੜਾਈ, ਲਾਂਭੇ ਸਾਰੀ ਫੌਜ ਹਟਾਈ ।
ਇਕ ਦੂਏ ਪਰ ਵਾਰ ਚਲਾਵਨ, ਆਪਣਾ ਆਪਣਾ ਦਾਉ ਬਚਾਵਨ ।
ਉਤਕ ਪੈ ਦੋਹਾਂ ਦੇ ਵਾਰ, ਦੋਹਾਂ ਦੇ ਸਿਰ ਗਏ ਉਤਾਰ ।
ਸ਼ਾਹ ਜਮਾਲ ਨੇ ਦਿੱਤੀ ਜਾਨ, ਡਿੱਗ ਪਿਆ ਹੋ ਲਹੂ ਲੁਹਾਨ ।
ਬਾਬਾ ਜੀ ਭੀ ਹੋਏ ਸ਼ਹੀਦ, ਕਲਗੀਧਰ ਦੇ ਸੱਚ ਮੁਰੀਦ ।
ਵਾਜ ਇਕ ਦੁਰੋਂਉਚੀ ਆਈ, ਬਾਬਾ ਜੀ ਕਰ ਗਏ ਚੜ੍ਹਾਈ ।
ਹਾਂ, ਹਾਂ, ਇਹ ਕਿ ਕਾਰਾ ਭਿਆਨ, ਬਚਨ ਇਨ੍ਹਾਂ ਦਾ ਐਵੇ ਗਿਆ ।
ਮਰਨਾ ਸੀ ਅੰਮ੍ਰਿਤਸਰ ਜਾ ਕੇ, ਰਹਿਮੰਦਰ ਦਾ ਦਰਸ਼ਨ ਪਾ ਕੇ ।
ਬਾਬਾ ਜੀ ਨੇ ਹੱਥ ਹਿਲਾਯਾ, ਪ੍ਰਣ ਆਪਣਾ ਨਹੀਂ ਅਸਾਂ ਭੁਲਾਯਾ ।
ਸਿਰ ਫੜਿਆ ਇਕ ਹੱਥ ਮਝਾਰ, ਦੂਜੇ ਹੱਥ ਫੜੀ ਤਲਵਾਰ ।
ਪ੍ਰੇਮੀ ਪੈਰ ਪਏ ਫਿਰ ਚੱਲ, ਸ੍ਰੀ ਹਰਿਮੰਦਰ ਪਧਾਰੇ ਵੱਲ ।
ਖੜਗ ਕਰੇ ਤੁਰਕਾਂ ਪਰ ਵਾਰ, ਪੈਰ ਤੁਰਨ ਗੁਰ ਗਲੀ ਮਝਾਰ ।
ਐਸੇ ਦਸ਼ਾ ਵਿਚ ਕਈ ਮਾਰੇ, ਆ ਪਹੁੰਚ ਆਪਣੇ ਗੁਰਦੁਆਰੇ ।
ਦੱਖਣ ਦੀ ਨੁੱਕਰ ਪਰ ਆ ਕੇ, ਹਰਿਮੰਦਰ ਦਾ ਦਰਸ਼ਨ ਪਾ ਕੇ ।
ਪ੍ਰਣ ਸਰੀਰੋ ਹੋਇ ਨਿਆਰੇ, ਜਾ ਪਹੁੰਚੇ ਗੁਰਪੁਰੀ ਮਝਾਰੇ ।

—Lala Dhani Ram Chatrik,
Prasang Baba Deep Singh[29]

Larde marde maarde, lahu nadi vahai,
Sri Gurdware Ramsar lage pahunch aye
Aithe fauj juri si bahri, Singhan di jaan vag khulari
Turkan, Singhan da ghamsan, bahute lathe lohu ghan
Panj hazari shah jamal, aa juta Baba ji naal.

Appendix A: Deep Singh in Verse

Kalle kalle karan ladai, laambe saari fauj hatai.
Ik dooje par vaar chalavan, apna apna dau bachavan
Audak pai dohan de vaar, dohan de sir gai utar
Shah Jamal ne diti jaan, dhig piya ho lahu luhan.
Baba ji bhi hoye shaheed, kalgidhar de sach mureed
Vaaj ik dooron uchhi ayi, 'Babaji kar gaye chadayi'
'Ha, ha, eh ki kara bhyan, bachan ehna da ainve giya'
'Marna si Amritsar ja ke, Harimandir da darshan pa ke'
Baba ji ne hath hilaya, pran apna nahi asi bhulaya
Sir phareya ik hath mujhar, duje hath phari talvar.
Premi pair paye phir chal, Sri Harimandir pyare val
Kharag kare Turkan par vaar, pair turan gur gali mujhar.
Aise dusha vich kayi maare, a pahunch apne gurdwara
Dakhan di nukkar par a ke, Harmandir da darshan pa ke
Pran shariton hoi nyare, ja pahunche gurpuri mujhare
They fought and killed and died beside the stream of blood that flowed.
The battle raged near Ramsar as they forward clashed and strode.
Until the foe in numbers thick assailed them so intense,
More bloodshed and fierce fighting then once more did now commence.
Commander of five thousand men, then Shah Jamal appeared.
He challenged Deep Singh to a fight; and neither seemed afeard.
They dueled single combat while their armies stood in awe.
They thrust and parried deftly so and neither did withdraw
Until by common stroke of sword they struck each other's neck,
Beheaded, then their heads fell down; it all looked quite a wreck.
Reminded of his vow then Deep Singh lifted head on palm;
with other hand, he swung his sword and moved on without qualm.
He then advanced to *Harimandir Sahib* and reached his day's abode.
The foe now scattered while the Sikhs with new grit were bestowed.
He entered from the Southern side; in deference he then bowed,
Surrendered up his soul to God, as he'd that morning vowed.

22. Deep Singh Fights Buland Khan and Yakub Khan

ਫਿਰਨਾ ਛੰਦ ॥ ਦੀਪ ਸਿੰਘ ਦੇਖ ਕੇ ਬੁਲੰਦ ਖਾਨ ਨੂੰ ।
ਪਹੁੰਚਾ ਨਜ਼ਦੀਕ ਉਹਦੇ ਹੀਲ ਜਾਨ ਨੂੰ ।
ਤਕੜਾ ਹੋ ਦੁਰਾਨੀਆਂ ਮੁਖੋਂ ਪ੍ਰਕਾਰਿਆ ।
ਬੋਲ ਕੇ ਜੈਕਾਰਾ ਸਿੰਘ ਹੱਲਾ ਮਾਰਿਆ ।
ਖਾਨ ਕੀਤਾ ਵਾਰ ਬਾਬੇ ਲਿਆ ਰੋਕ ਸੀ ।
ਫੇਰ ਵਾਰ ਆਪਣੇ ਹੈ ਦਿੱਤਾ ਠੋਕ ਸੀ ।
ਪਹਿਲੇ ਵਾਰ ਸੀਸ ਖਾਨ ਦਾ ਉਤਾਰਿਆ ।
ਬੋਲ ਕੇ ਜੈਕਾਰਾ ਸਿੰਘ ਹੱਲਾ ਮਾਰਿਆ ।
ਫੇਰ ਨੇੜੇ ਫੌਜਦਾਰ ਆਕੇ ਢੁਕਿਆ ।
ਦੇਖ ਮੌਤ ਖਾਨ ਦੀ ਨਾ ਮੂਲ ਰੁਕਿਆ [......]
ਇਕ ਦੂਜੇ ਉੱਤੇ ਵਾਰ ਹੈਣ ਕਰਦੇ ।
ਹੋਏ ਸਾਕੇ ਪਾਸ ਇਹ ਬਿਬੇਕਸਰ ਦੇ ।
ਸੂਬੇ ਨੂੰ ਵੀ ਜੋਏ ਸਿੰਘ ਕੀਤਾ ਪਾਰ ਆ ।
ਬੋਲ ਕੇ ਜੈਕਾਰਾ ਸਿੰਘ ਹੱਲਾ ਮਾਰਿਆ ।
ਫੇਰ ਆਇਆ ਸਾਮਣੇ ਯਾਕੂਬ ਖਾਨ ਹੈ ।
ਇਹ ਭੀ ਵੱਡਾ ਸੂਰਮਾ ਪਠਾਨ ਹੈ ।
ਏਸ ਨੂੰ ਭੀ ਝੱਟ ਬਾਬੇ ਨੇ ਸੰਘਾਰਿਆ ।
ਬੋਲ ਕੇ ਜੈਕਾਰਾ ਸਿੰਘ ਹੱਲਾ ਮਾਰਿਆ ।
ਸੋਹਣ ਸਿੰਘਾ ਬਾਬੇ ਨੂੰ ਵੀ ਤੇਗ ਵੱਜ ਗਈ ।
ਡਿਗ ਪਿਆ ਸੀਸ ਦੇਹੀ ਖੜੀ ਸੱਜ ਗਈ ।
ਧਰਮ ਸਿੰਘ ਕੋਲੋਂ ਬਚਨ ਉਚਾਰਿਆ ।
ਬੋਲ ਕੇ ਜੈਕਾਰਾ ਸਿੰਘ ਮਾਰਿਆ ।

—Sohan Singh Ghukewalia, *Baba Deep Singh Shaheed*[30]

Phirna Chhand. Deep Singh dekh ser Buland Khan nu
Pahuncha nazdeek uhde heel jaan nu
Takda ho Duraniya mukhon pukariya
Bol ke jaikara Singha halla mariya
Khan keeta vaar Babe liya rok si
Pher vaar aapne hai ditta thok si
Pehle vaar sees Khan da utariya
Bol ke jaikara Singha halla mariya
Pher nede faujdar ake dhukeya
Dekh maut Khan di na mool rukiya [....]
Ek duuje utte vaar hain karde
Hoye sake paas eh Bibeksar de

Sube nu vi Jodhe Singh kita paar a
Bol ke jaikara Singha halla mariya
Pher aiya saamne Yakub Khan hai
Eh bhi vada soorma pathan hei
Ais nu bhi jhat Babe ne sanghariya
Bol ke jaikara Singha halla mariya
Sohan Singha Babe nu vi teg vaj gayi
Dig piya sis dehi khadi saj gayi
Dharam Singh kolon bachan uchariya
Bol ke jaikara Singha mariya
When Deep Singh sighted Buland Khan there,
Approached him mid the battle flare.
Deep Singh called: 'Durrani, grit show!'
With zestful war cry Singhs charge foe.
Khan struck first, Deep blocked his blow;
With single stroke, dispatched him so.
The *faujdar* (commander) saw comrade die,
Then boldly Deep Singh did defy.
They now fought hard with all their might.
Deep killed him soon to end the fight.
Unfolded this near *Bibeksar*
A tale of pluck to valour stir.
Yakub Khan then crossed Deep Singh there
A brave Pathan known everywhere.
Another duel then did ensue
But Deep Singh soon Yakub Khan slew,
Though he too in the neck was slashed,
Upon the ground his head now dashed.
Dharam Singh nearby saw this all,
And prompted him his oath recall.

23. Balwant Singh Fights Zabardast Khan

ਜਬਰਦਸਤ ਖਾਂ ਬੀਸ ਹਜਾਰੀ ।
ਖਾਵਤ ਨਿਤ ਪ੍ਰਤਿ ਬਕਰੀ ਸਾਰੀ ।
ਨਿਜ ਤਨ ਅੱਸ੍ਰ ਸੰਜੋਐ ਮਢਯੋ ।
ਗਰਜ ਤਰਜ ਦਿਸ ਸਿੰਘਨ ਬਢਯੋ ॥ ੨੮ ॥

ਕੱਦ ਬਿਹੱਦ ਮਿਨਾਰ ਸਮਾਨੇ ।
ਤੀਛਨ ਅਤਿ ਤੀਛਨ ਬਲਿਵਾਨੇ ।
ਮੱਤ ਮਤੰਗ ਤੁੰਗ ਕਿ ਨ ਗਰਜੈ ।
ਕੇਹਰ ਪਿਖਿ ਲਘੁ ਭੀ ਨਹਿ ਲਰਜੈ ॥ ੭੯ ॥
ਯੱਦਪਿ ਰਹੇ ਸਿੰਘ ਪਿਖ ਤੱਜਬ ।
ਤੌ ਭੀ ਭਰੇ ਸੰਮੁਖ ਹਰਿ ਗੱਜਬ ।
ਹਰਿ-ਬਲਵੰਤ ਬਯੰਤ ਬਲਵਾਨਾ ।
ਸੰਪਟ ਆਹਨ ਆਪ ਕਿਕਾਨਾ ॥ ੮੦ ॥
ਛੇੜਿ ਤੁਰੰਗ ਉਤੈ ਭਟ ਗਰਜੇ ।
ਸੁਨਿ ਜਿਨ ਕੋ ਘਨ ਸਾਵਨ ਲਰਜੇ ।
ਆਯੁਧ ਬਿਦਜਾ ਮੈ ਜੁਗ ਪੂਰੇ ।
ਜਗਨ ਰੋਸ ਜਨੁ ਅਗਨਿ ਬਘੂਰੇ ॥ ੮੧ ॥
ਛੇਰਤ ਅੱਸੁ ਇਤ ਉਤੈ ਫਿਰੈ ਹੈ ।
ਦਾਵ ਤਕਾਵ ਘਾਵ ਕਿਝ ਚੈ ਹੈ ।
ਨੈਨ ਨੈਨ ਮੈ ਦਏ ਨ ਝਮਕੈ ।
ਸੈਨ ਸੈਨ ਮੈ ਐਨ ਸੁ ਰਮਕੈ ॥ ੮੨ ॥
ਚਮਕਤ ਨੈਨ ਰੈਨ ਜਨੁ ਤਾਰੇ ।
ਕਿਯੇ ਮਸਾਲੈ ਲੰਬੁ ਬਾਰੇ ।
ਦੁਹਿ ਦਿਸ ਕੇ ਦਲ ਖਰੇ ਨਿਹਾਰੈ ।
ਮੱਧ ਮੈਦਾਨ ਭਿਰਤ ਭਟ ਭਾਰੈ ॥ ੮੩ ॥
ਤਕਿ ਤਕਿ ਤੀਰ ਬੀਰ ਜੁਗ ਛੋਰੈ ।
ਤਨਕ ਤਨਕ ਯਸਿ ਜਿਰਹਾ ਫੋਰੈ ।
ਅਰਜਨ ਕਰਣ ਕਿ ਘਨ-ਰਵਿ ਲਛਮਨ ।
ਭਿਰਤ ਫਿਰਤ ਤਿਮ ਇਹੁ ਧਰ ਕਛਰਨ ॥ ੮੪ ॥
ਕਟਯੋ ਕੁਵੰਡ ਸਿੰਘ ਹਤਿ ਚੱਕੈ ।
ਸ਼ੀਘੁ ਫੇਰ ਸੈਥੀ ਬੱਕੈ ।
ਦਈ ਧਸਾਇ ਅੱਸੁ ਕੇ ਪੇਟੈ ।
ਧਰ ਪਰ ਗਿਰਯੋ ਅੱਸੁ ਲਗਿ ਫੇਟੈ ॥ ੮੫ ॥
ਚੱਕ੍ਰ ਐਸ ਖਰ ਫਿਰ ਸਿੰਘ ਛੋਰਾ ।
ਭੁਜਾ ਖਾਨ ਕੀ ਕਟੀ ਬਹੋਰਾ ।
ਤੌ ਭੀ ਖਾਨ ਰੋਸ ਧਰਿ ਧਾਵਾ ।
ਗਰਜਿ ਤਰਜਿ ਸਿੰਘ ਜੀ ਢਿਗ ਆਵਾ ॥ ੮੬ ॥
ਤੇਗ ਬੇਗ ਸਿੰਘ ਕੇ ਅੱਸੁ ਤਾਂਈ ।
ਮਾਰਿ ਧਰਾ ਪੈ ਦਯੋ ਗਿਰਾਈ ।
ਝਟਪਟ ਏਕ ਜ਼ਖ਼ਮ ਸਿੰਘ ਕੋ ਹੈ ।
ਲਾਯੋ ਖਾਨ, ਗੁਰੂ ਰਖਯੋ ਹੈ ॥ ੮੭ ॥

Appendix A: Deep Singh in Verse

ਜਿਰਾ ਖਾਨ ਕੀ ਕਟੀ ਪਿਖੈ ਕੈ ।
ਬੱਖੀ ਪਰ ਸਿੰਘ ਦਾਉ ਤਕੈ ਕੈ ।
ਬਲ ਧਰਿ ਰੋਸ ਹੋਸ਼ ਅਲਵੱਤਾ ।
ਕੱਤਾ ਹੱਤਾ ਕਰਿ ਗਾਖੇ ਕੱਤਾ ॥ ੮੮ ॥
ਦੂ ਧਰ ਦ੍ਰੈਵੈ ਧਰ ਖਾਨ ਗਿਰੀਓ ।
ਪੌਨ ਤੋਰ ਤਰੁ ਬਡ ਜਨੁ ਦੀਓ ।
ਦੈ ਫਲੰਗ ਸਿੰਘ ਗਰਜਖੇ ਭਾਰਾ ।
ਸਭਿ ਸਿੰਘਨ ਬੋਲਖੇ ਜੈਕਾਰਾ ॥ ੮੯ ॥

—Gyani Gyan Singh, *Sri Guru Panth Prakash II*[31]

Jabardast Khan bees hazari
khavat nit pret bakri saari
nij tan asv sanjoi madhyo
garaj taraj dis Singhan badhyo |78|

kad bihad minar samaney
bheechan at tichhan baliwaney
mat matang tung ki n garjai
kehar pikh lagh bhi nah larjai |79|

Yadap hare Sigh pikh tajab
Toi bhi bhaye sanmukh dhar gajab
Hari-Balwant bajant balwana
Sampat aahan aap kikana |80|

ter turang ubhey bhar garjai
sun jin ko ghan sawan larjai
ayudh bidhya mai jug poorey
jagan ros jan agan bhagoorey |81|

Chherat asv it utai phirai hain
Dav takav ghav kiy chaihain
Nain nain mein daye na jhamkey
Sain sain main ain su ramkey |82|

chamkat nain rain jan tarey
kidhon masaley lamboo barey
duh dis kei dal kharey niharey
madh maidan bhirat bhat bharey |83|

tak takteer bir jug chherain
tanak tanak dhas jirah phorain

arjan karan ki ghan-rav Lachman
bhirat phirat tim ih dhar kachhran |84|

Katyo kuvand Singh hat chakrai
Srigh pher saithe bakai
Dayi dhasai asv ke petai
Dhar par giryo asv lag phetey |85|

chakre ais khar phir Singh chhora
puja Khan ki kati bihora
to bhi Khan ros dhar dhava
garaj taraj Singh ji dhig ava |86|

teg beg Singh ke asv tayi
mar dhara pai day girahi
jhatpat ek zakham Singh ko hain
layo Khan, gur rakhgo hai |87|

jiha Khan ki kati pikhai kai
bakhi par Singh dau takai kai
bal dhar ros hos alvatta
kadda hadda kar gayo katta |88|

Devai dhar hua dhar Khan girio
Pon tro tar badh jan diyo
Dai phalang Singh garajyo bhara
Sab Singhan bolyo jaikara |89|

Commander of twenty thousand men,
Zabardast Khan came forward then.
A full goat he'd eat for a meal;
Armour-clad from head to heel,
His horse likewise too armour wore
The Khan advanced, and yelled and swore. |78|

Tower-like in strength and height;
A warrior brave: a frightening sight.
Mighty mammoth whom all hail
But lions never ever quail. |79|
Although startled by his sight,
The Singhs still faced him with all might.

Appendix A: Deep Singh in Verse

Balwant Singh bravely came to fore;
His horse and he, both armour wore. |80|
Moved their horses face to face
Mid frightful roars that were so loud
That shook above the thunderous cloud;
Full-skilled in war, the two do now
For combat boldly brace.
Embers of their dreadful ire
Soared and spawned a whirlwind fire. |81|
Jockeying horses, dominance seek
To strike and slash, and wounding wreak.
With locked-in eyes, without a blink
They plan their move with mindful think. |82|
Their eyes do shine like stars at night
Or, flames that leap to towering height.
Both armies pause to now behold
Two Braves who duel in combat bold. |83|
They soon let many arrows fly:
that lodge in armour by and by.
Akin to Arjan's fight with Karan
Or, Meghnath's contest with Lakshman;
Encircle like two wrestlers nigh |84|
Singh then cleaved Khan's bow with quoit;
Transfixed his horse's gut, adroit.
He'd used a spear with twisted head:
A ghastly wound that dropped it dead. |85|
With second quoit, Singh docked Khan's arm.
In powerful rage was Khan's alarm;
He thundered bravely to confront
The Singh to thus avenge affront. |86|
Khan now swiftly drove his sword
Into the horse that Singh now rode;
He also slashed a wound on Singh.
The horse fell down, the Guru saved Singh. |87|
Khan's armour now was slit and torn.
Upon his belly, none was worn.

Singh thrust his sword in gut with force;
With this Khan's life had run its course. |88|
The Khan fell down, was cleft in two,
Razed like a tree by wind that blew.
The Singh then leapt and roared and dared.
While all Singhs rousing cheers now aired. |89|

24. Balwant Singh Fights Rustam Khan

ਵਾਰ॥ ਦੋਵੇ ਜੁੱਟ ਪਏ ਧਨੀ ਤਲਵਾਰ ਦੇ
ਸਾਂਭੇ ਯੋਧਿਆਂ ਹੱਥੀ ਹਥਿਆਰ।
ਲੈਦੇ ਮੱਲ ਜਿਉ ਅਖਾੜੇ ਵਿਚ ਫੇਰੀਆਂ
ਉਧਰ ਧੋਸਿਆਂ ਨੇ ਪਾਈ ਘੁਮਕਾਰ ।
ਯੁੱਧ ਭੀਮ, ਜਰਾਸਿੰਧ ਨੇ ਆਰੰਭਿਆ
ਆਏ ਵੇਖਣ ਨੂੰ ਕ੍ਰਿਸ਼ਨ ਮੁਰਾਰ ।
ਜਾਂ ਫਿਰ ਭੀਮ, ਦੁਰਜੋਧਨ ਟੱਕਰੇ ।
ਡਾਢਾ ਗੁਰਜਾਂ ਦਾ ਹੋਏ ਖੜਕਾਰ। ।
ਤੇਗਾਂ ਢਾਲਾਂ ਉਤੇ ਇਸ ਤਰ੍ਹਾਂ ਪੈਦੀਆਂ
ਜਿਵੇ ਘਾੜ ਘੜਨ ਠਠਿਆਰ ।
ਦੋਵੇ ਵਾਰ ਬੱਚਾ ਕੇ ਮਾਰਦੇ ।
ਹੋ ਹੋ ਸੂਰਮੇ ਪੱਬਾਂ ਦੇ ਭਾਰ ।
ਜਿਵੇ ਬੱਦਲਾਂ ਚ ਭਿੜਦੀਆਂ ਬਿਜਲੀਆਂ
ਤਲਵਾਰ ਨਾਲ ਠਹਿਕੇ ਤਲਵਾਰ ।
ਢਾਲਾਂ ਵਿਚੋ ਚੰਗਿਆੜੇ ਨਿਕਲਦੇ ।
ਆਤਸਬਾਜ਼ ਜਿਉ ਚਲਾਉਂਦੇ ਅਨਾਰ ।
ਆਖ਼ਰ ਜੋਸ਼ ਵਿਚ ਐਸਾ ਆਣਕੇ ।
ਸਾਂਡਾ ਚੱਲਿਆ ਦੋਹਾਂ ਦਾ ਵਾਰ ।
ਸੀਸ ਦੋਹਾਂ ਦੇ ਧੜਾਂ ਤੋ ਲੱਥ ਗਏ
ਧੜ ਸੱਖਣੇ ਡਿੱਗੇ ਮੂੰਹ ਭਾਰ ।

—Sohan Singh Seetal,
Shaheed Baba Deep Singh[32]

Dovein jut paye dhani talvar de
Sambhey yodhiyan hathi hathiyar
Laindey mull jion akharey vich pheriyan
Udhar dhonsiyan ne payi ghamkar
Yudh Bhim, Jarasindh ne arambhiya
Aye vekhen nu Krishen murar

Appendix A: Deep Singh in Verse

Ja phir Bhim Duryodhan takre
Dhadha gurja da hoye kharkar
Tegan dhalan ute is taran paindiyan
Jivein ghar gharan thathiyar
Dovein vaar bacha ke mardey
Ho ho soormey paban te bhar
Jevein badlan ch bhirdiyan bijliyan
Talvar nal thakey talvar
Dhalan vichon changiarey nikaldey
Atam baj jion chaloundey anar
Akhar josh vich aisa ankey
Sanjha chaleya dovan da vaar
Sis dohan de dharan te latch gaye
Dhar sakhney diggey muhn bhar

Two swordsmen now came face to face,
their swordplay showed much skill.
Like wrestlers they did circle round
Mid war drums for a kill.
The crash of battleaxes rang
Above the swords on shield;
Like scores of blacksmiths all at work,
The deafening war din pealed.
With nimble feet, they dodged and swayed,
They pounced and lunged to vie;
They rushed and leapt and sprang and dove
Like lightning in the sky.
Sword clashed on sword and spear on shield,
Sparks flew now everywhere,
Until by common stroke of sword
They swung right through the air
To sever each the other's head—
lay felled on ground right there.

ਦੋਹਰਾ॥ ਜਬਰਦਸਤ ਖਾਂ ਜਬਿ ਮਰਯੋ, ਰੁਸਤਮ ਖਾਂ ਤਿਹ ਬੀਰ ।
ਅਤਿ ਕੋਪਿ ਹਮਲਾ ਕਰਯੋ, ਲੈ ਗਿਲਜਯੋ ਕੀ ਬੀਰ ॥ ੮੦ ॥
ਚੌਪਈ॥ ਰੁਸਤਮ ਖਾਂ ਸਿੰਘ ਬਲਵੰਤ ਸਹਿਲੈ ।

ਭਿਰੇ ਅਧਿਕ ਦੋਈ ਸਮ ਪਹਿਲੈ ।
ਚਲੀ ਤੇਗ ਦੁਹਿ ਕੀ ਬਲਕਾਰੀ ।
ਭਏ ਸ਼ਹੀਦ ਉਭੈ ਇਕ ਵਾਰੀ ॥ ੯੧ ॥

—Gyani Gyan Singh,
Sri Guru Panth Prakash II[33]

Zabardast Khan jab maryo, Rustam Khan tih bir
Ati kop hamla karyo, lai giljon ki bir |90|
Rustam Khan Singh Balwant Sahilain
Bhire adhik doi mas pahlain
Chali teg duin ki balkari
Bhaye shaheed ubhey ik vari |91|

Seeing Zabardast Khan upfront killed
Threw brother Rustam Khan in rage;
He forward sprang with many *Giljas*
to battle Singh, with him engage. |90|
Balwant Singh-Rustam Khan now fought
So long and hard just like they ought
Until by common strike of sword
Both died to end this episode. |91|

25. Hira Singh, the Warrior

ਸੱਯਦ ਸਾਬਰ-ਅਲੀ ਖਾਨ ਬਡ ।
ਪਾਂਚ ਹਜ਼ਾਰੀ ਜੁਝਯੋ ਤਹਿ ਖਡ ।
ਦੁੰਦ ਜੁੱਧ ਕਰਿ ਸੁੱਧ ਉਦਾਰਾ ।
ਹੀਰਾ ਸਿੰਘ ਨੈ ਤਿਸ ਕੋ ਮਾਰਾ ॥ ੭੭ ॥

—Gyani Gyan Singh,
Sri Guru Panth Prakash II[34]

Sayad Sabar-Ali Khan badh
Panch hazari jujhyo tah khad
Dud judh kar sudh udara
Hira Singh nai usko mara |77|

Sayad Sabar-Ali Khan,
Commander of five thousand men,
proficient in single combat,
Died standing at the hands of Hira Singh. |77|

Appendix A: Deep Singh in Verse

ਅਕਸਰ ਅਫਸਰ ਗਿਲਜੇ ਭਾਰੇ ।
ਹੀਰਾ ਸਿੰਘ ਬੀ ਬਹੁਤ ਪਛਾਰੇ ।
ਸੰਮੁਖ ਲਰਿ ਕਟਿ ਪੁਰਜੇ ਪੁਰਜੇ ।
ਭਯੋ ਸ਼ਹੀਦ ਮਹੀਦ ਸਫੁਰਜੇ ॥ ੯੨ ॥

—Gyani Gyan Singh,
Sri Guru Panth Prakash II[35]

Aksar afsar giljey bharey
Hira Singh bhi bahut pachharey
Sanmukh lar kat purjey purjey
Bhayo shaheed maheed saphurjey |92|
Hira Singh upfront did fight
Dispatched high-ranking *Giljas* quite
Until he too was overcome:
A glorious martyr to become. |92|

26. Deep Singh's Cremation, Cenotaph, and Other Duels

ਕੀਤਾ ਤਨ ਦਾ ਸਿੰਘਾਂ ਸਸਕਾਰ ਜਿਥੇ,
ਸ਼ਹੀਦ ਗੰਜ ਅਸਥਾਨ ਬਣਾ ਦਿੱਤਾ ।
ਸ਼ਹੀਦ ਬੁੰਗਾ ਪ੍ਰਕਰਮਾਂ ਦੇ ਵਿਚ ਬਣਿਆ,
ਜਿਥੇ ਚੌਕੜਾ ਬਾਬੇ ਨੇ ਲਾ ਦਿੱਤਾ ।
ਚਾਟੀਵਿੰਡ ਬਣੀ ਯਾਦਗਾਰ ਸੁੰਦਰ,
ਬਾਬੇ ਪੰਥ ਦਾ ਨਾਮ ਚਮਕਾ ਦਿੱਤਾ ।
ਕਬਿੱਤ-ਸੰਗ੍ਰਾਏ ਸਾਹਿਬ ਨੇੜੇ ਸੀਸ ਲੱਥਾ ਹੈਸੀ ਬਾਬੇ ਜੀ ਦਾ,
ਯਾਦਗਾਰ ਸੋਹਣੀ ਉਥੇ ਸਿੰਘਾਂ ਨੇ ਬਣਾਈ ਏ ।
ਵੀਰ ਸਿੰਘ ਹਰੀ ਸਿੰਘ ਯੋਧਿਆਂ ਨੇ ਅੰਤ ਸਮੇ,
ਚੌਕੜੀ ਸ਼ਹੀਦੀ ਪਾ ਕੇ ਐਸੇ ਥਾਂ ਤੇ ਲਾਈ ਹੈ ।
ਅਯੁੱਧ ਸਿੰਘ ਰਣ ਸਿੰਘ ਨੱਥਾ ਸਿੰਘ ਦਿਆਲ ਸਿੰਘ,
ਪਹੁੰਚੇ ਸੁਧਾ ਸਰ ਚੰਗੀ ਬੀਰਤਾ ਵਿਖਾਈ ਏ ।
ਮੰਜੀ ਸਾਹਿਬ ਲਾਗੇ ਹਨ ਇਹਨਾਂ ਦੇ ਸ਼ਹੀਦ ਗੰਜ,
ਧਰਮ ਉੱਤੇ ਸੀਸ ਵਾਰ ਖੱਟੀ ਭਲਿਆਈ ਏ ।
ਸੱਜਣ ਸਿੰਘ ਤਾਰਾ ਸਿੰਘ ਬਾਲ ਸਿੰਘ ਭਾਗ ਸਿੰਘ,
ਐਸੇ ਥਾਂ ਤੇ ਪਹੁੰਚ ਜਿੰਦ ਗੁਰੂ ਲੇਖੇ ਲਾਈ ਏ ।
ਬਸੰਤ ਸਿੰਘ ਮੰਨਾ ਸਿੰਘ ਆਦਿ ਸਿੰਘਾਂ ਸੂਰਿਆਂ ਨੇ,
ਪ੍ਰਾਗਦਾਸ ਚੌਕ ਭੇਟ ਸੀਸ ਦੀ ਚੜ੍ਹਾਈ ਏ ।
ਚੱਬੇ ਪਿੰਡ ਪਾਸ ਨੈਯ ਸਿੰਘ ਦੀ ਸਮਾਧ ਵੇਖੇ,
ਸ਼ਹੀਦ ਸਿੰਘਾਂ ਸੀਸ ਦੇ ਕੇ ਲਈ ਵਡਿਆਈ ਏ ।

ਗੁਰਦੀਪ ਸਿੰਘਾ 'ਸਿੰਘ' ਸਦਾ ਅਮਰ ਜੋ ਜਹਾਨ ਉੱਤੇ,
ਦਾਸਤਾਨ ਲਿਖ ਸੂਰਬੀਰਾਂ ਦੀ ਸੁਣਾਈ ਏ ।

—Gurdeep Singh Kanwal[36]

Kita tan da Singhan saskar jithe,
Shahidganj asthan bana ditta.
Shahid bunga parkarma de vich baniya,
jithe chonkra Babe ne la ditta.
Chativind bani yadgaar sundar,
Babe panth da naam chamka ditta.
Kabit—Sangrane Sahib nede sis latha haisi Babe ji da,
Yaadgaar sohni uthe Singhan ne banai ye.
Vir Singh, Hari Singh, yodhian ne ant samey,
Chonkri shaheedi pa ke aisey than te layi hai.
Aghar Singh, Ran Singh, Natha Singh, Dyal Singh,
Pahunche Sudhasar change veerta dikhai e.
Manji Sahib lage hun ehna de shaheed ganj,
Dharam utte sis vaar khatti bhaliai e.
Sajjan Singh, Tara Singh, Bal Singh, Bhag Singh,
Aise than te pahunch jind guru lekhe lai e.
Basant Singh, Manna Singh, aad Singhan sooriyan ne,
Pragdas Chowk bheint sis di jharai e.
Chabbe pind paas Naudh Singh di samadh vekho,
Shaheed Singhan sis de ke layi vadiai e.
Gurdeep Singha 'Singhan' sada amar jo jahan utte,
Dastan likh surbiran di sunai e.
Shaheed ganj stands exactly where
his body was cremated.
Shaheed Bunga in *Parkarma*:
where Deep Singh finally rested.
At Chattivind, a memorial stands
To ever show his name in lands.
By *Sangrana Sahib* decapitated
As such this famous deed narrated
Where Vir Singh, Hari Singh, other Brave
Did also fall to honour save.
Aghar Singh, Ran Singh, Natha Singh, Dyal Singh

Fought till *Sudhasar*, then life did fling.
Shaheedganj does near *Manji Sahib* stand
Where flutters the saffron flag so grand
Here Sajjan Singh, Tara Singh, Bal Singh, Bhag Singh
In martyrdom did honour bring.
Basant Singh, Manna Singh, other Sikhs brave
By *Pragdas Chowk* did honour crave.
The shrine at *Chabba* to Naudh Singh great
Where Singhs earned fame, embraced their fate.
Gurdeep Singh penned this valorous tale
Of Singhs whom we shall ever hail!

APPENDIX B

Competing Claims of Birth and Belonging

According to this version, after Deepa's father died fighting the Pathans of Alapur (now Lapura) in the 17th century, and since he had no brother, his widow relocated to her paternal home in Pahuwind along with Deep Singh, then only five, where he spent his childhood. He returned to Gurm as a young man in 1702 on the behest of the village panchayat (village council). By this account, his mother's maiden name was 'Virk' (sub-caste) but there is not a single 'Virk' household in Pahuwind, the majority being 'Sandhu', with a small percentage of 'Khaira'.

Although there is even a gurdwara to Deep Singh's memory in Gurm, this account has gained little traction possibly because it is out of sync with both historical records and oral traditions—one, Deep Singh's father's name in this account is Sughar Singh whereas by popular accounts his name was Bhagtu; two, the village has no genealogy record to support their claim; three, oral history tells us that, as a young adult, Deep Singh accompanied his parents to Anandpur for baptism, which contradicts any accounts of his father's early death; four, according to the genealogy register, Deep Singh's father was not the only child but the eldest of four brothers; five, according to this version, Deep Singh was born in 1688-1689,[1] which makes him barely eighteen in 1706, when appointed Jathedar at Dam Dama Sahib—highly implausible that he could attain the emotional and intellectual maturity at that age to assume so important a leadership position, nor that he would have been entrusted with such responsibility; this would also mean that he was sixty-eight years (and not seventy-five) when he

Appendix B: Competing Claims of Birth and Belonging

attained martyrdom in 1757, which contradicts both popular opinion and genealogy records.

A more serious flaw in this version is that, while departing for the South in October 1706, Guru Gobind Singh bade Deep Singh to visit his mother before he should settle into his new charge at Dam Dama Sahib. Deep Singh left and stayed five years at Gurm, spreading the gospel but mostly in meditation in a small hut, henceforth, named 'shaheedi kutiah' (hut of martyrdom).[2] But the hut stands in memory of one 'Dopehar Das' (meditated in the afternoon) who belonged to Gurm but had spent many years at Dam Dama Sahib as a follower of Deep Singh. He also suffixed 'Shaheed' to his name as a member of the misl, as did others of this sect.[3]

Further, this narrative suggests that Deep Singh returned to Dam Dama Sahib sometime in 1711. This is completely at variance with history that records his role alongside Banda Bahadur in many battles. It is equally unlikely that having been personally appointed Jathedar by the Guru to run the seminary, he would have absented himself for so long a period.

Equally irreconcilable is the assertion that Deep Singh was baptized by the tenth Guru at Dina (not Anandpur) sometime in January 1706, after the Guru had evacuated Anandpur in December 1705.[4] This leaves no scope for any prolonged scholastic or martial training for Deep Singh under the tutelage of either the Guru or Bhai Mani Singh, without which his historical claim as a warrior-leader and scholar is completely untenable.

In trying to understand the Gurm connection, some writers take the view that Deep Singh's mother (and not father) was from Gurm.[5] However, this is equally difficult to justify. Gurm village elders believe Deep Singh's mother to be of 'Virk' caste (maiden name) but there are no 'Virk' households in Gurm either. Historically, the Punjab rivers posed formidable natural obstacles, dividing the region into several geographical units (Majha, Malwa, Doaba). As a consequence, marriages tended to be restricted within these subregions and for this reason, any Pahuwind-Gurm connubial alliance is difficult to contemplate. Although oral history is silent on the sub-caste of Deep Singh's mother or her place of belonging, popular belief extant in Pahuwind suggests that

Deep Singh and Baba Naudh Singh (of Chicha near Amritsar)—who was martyred alongside him in battle—were maternal cousins, their mothers being sisters. This filial connection is fairly common knowledge in Pahuwind, but unknown in Gurm.[6]

Evidence tilts heavily in favour of Pahuwind as the place of Deep Singh's birth and belonging. In all likelihood, Deep Singh is confused with some other personage who belonged to Gurm. A sect of dopehari saints lived in Dam Dama Sahib as followers of Deep Singh at least one of whom belonged to Gurm.[7] In his authoritative study on the Malwa region, Visakha Singh records his name as 'Darera Karme', a warrior who belonged to Kila Gunghrana and was also Choudhary of forty-eight villages, including Gurm.

As a follower of Deep Singh, he divided his time between Dam Dama Sahib and Gurm where he would spread the gospel and meditate for long hours until afternoon—hence Dopehri (afternoon) saint. According to Visakha Singh, Gurm was earlier known as 'Dharam kutia' and the village gurdwara is in his memory, co-located with the 'dharam kutia,' or 'Shaheedi kutia'. He was martyred in 1817 Samvat (1760); the year Visakha Singh records Deep Singh's martyrdom, but there is no mention if both died in the same battle.[8]

This could well be the cause of the confusion and mistaken identity. Deep Singh may also have visited Gurm, possibly while traversing through the area, thereby reinforcing this narrative.

APPENDIX C

Origin and Evolution of Sikhism

Sacha Sauda (True Bargain)
The anxiety was palpable in the Bedi home. A revenue official of some standing in the local administration at Talwandi, Kalyan Chand had harboured much hope in Nanak, his only son, to perpetuate the family tradition by adopting mercantile business as his calling. To his chagrin, Nanak showed little interest in matters of the world leave alone business and spent his entire time engaging learned men in debate over spiritual topics, often demonstrating wisdom far beyond his years.

Not one to give up easily, Kalyan Chand accosted Nanak one morning, trying to curb his wayward tendencies:

'Nanak, when will you start to earn a respectable livelihood? You're almost eighteen now and it's about time you did!'

A reflective Nanak listened attentively to his father but lost in thought, made no reply. Kalyan Chand persisted and testily set him off on yet another worldly mission:

'Here, take twenty rupees! Go to the nearby town and let me see you strike a sacha sauda (good or true bargain)!'

Obedient as always, Nanak left his home for the town. He had barely walked a few miles when he chanced upon a village with the majority of its population stricken with disease and hunger. He paused, looked down at the money, and recalled his father's recent injunction for a sacha sauda. It took very little for Nanak to be convinced that there could be no truer bargain than feeding the ill and hungry. He hastened to the nearby town, bought all the food his money could buy and returned to distribute it among the destitute but beholden villagers.[1]

The tale has several versions but no biography of Nanak is complete without it. As a turning point, while it put paid to his father's dream of his son becoming a thriving businessman, it set Nanak on an altruistic path for some years before he embarked fully on the life of a mystic wanderer to become one of the greatest religious innovators of all time.

Muslim Conquest

Home to the world's oldest extant urban settlements in the form of the Indus Valley Civilization dating back to the 3rd millennium BCE, the Indian Sub-continent attracted several waves of invaders and by the 8th century CE, its Muslim conquest had begun, marked by temple demolitions, mass executions, enslavements, raids on Hindu and Buddhist kingdoms accompanied by great rapine and plunder.[2] As one Muslim dynasty attempted to supplant another, the ravages of war between 1000 AD and 1500 AD, by when the Mughal empire was established, are estimated between 60-80 million dead, the population of the region falling from 200 to 120 million.[3]

Will Durant notes:

> 'The Mohammedan Conquest of India is probably the bloodiest story in history [....] The Hindus had allowed their strength to be wasted in internal division and war; they had adopted religions like Buddhism and Jainism, which unnerved them for the tasks of life; they had failed to organize their forces for the protection of their frontiers and their capitals.'[4]

Sikhism originated during the time of the Mughal conquest in the Punjab—Persian for 'land of five rivers', among the most fertile regions of the Indian sub-continent (see Figure 1). Its founder, Guru Nanak ('guru' is Sanskrit for 'teacher' or 'preceptor') was a contemporary of Babur, founder of the Mughal dynasty. In 1521, he was at Syedpur during Babur's second invasion into the sub-continent. In a set of compositions known as Babur-Bani, Guru Nanak provides a graphic account of the Mughal conquest. Sweeping down like the whirlwind, Babur put the entire city to the sword, carrying away women and children into captivity.[5] As a poet, Nanak lamented the excoriating destruction and expressed his anguish and helplessness in a dirge, decrying the ruthless abandon with which, like a tiger preying upon a flock of sheep, Babur shed innocent blood and laid waste the entire country.[6]

In effect, the history of the Punjab during the Mughal conquest 'reads like a textbook example of brutality, exploitation, and disenfranchisement'.[7]

A Conciliatory Vision

Although born an orthodox Hindu, Nanak was a sentient being, sensitive to the tensions around him, particularly the contempt of the Muslim overlords for his Hindu co-religionists.

> As reflective lad,
> Often he was seen
> In the company of the wandering sadhus (religious ascetics)
> The roaming yogis (practitioners of yoga)
> The solitary faqirs (mendicant holy men)
> They discussed and discoursed
> The eternal truths
> The sublime verities
> Of spirit and mind
> Of this vast universe
> —HS Gill, *Baba Nanak*[8]

Oddly enough, his discussions only seemed to deepen his reservations and uncertainties:

> The more he learned
> The more he knew
> The more he was uncertain
> about the Absolute
> —HS Gill, *Baba Nanak*[9]

In his first universal and conciliatory message after his mystical encounter with the Divine, Nanak pronounced: 'There is no Hindu; there is no Musalman (Muslim),' human beings are existentially the same. This message forms the basis of the Sikh philosophy along with its egalitarian vision,[10] and Nanak cited Kabir, a mystic poet and saint who preceded him, to endorse this oneness.[11]

The oneness of God had been proclaimed by many before Nanak but not the oneness of man; this was among his more distinctive contributions.[12] If we are all one and the same, and 'One God' resides in us all, there can be no 'Other.' From this primeval 'oneness' flowed an important principle that became the cornerstone of the Sikh faith, 'sarbat the bhala' (prosperity of all). As the crowning sentiment of the daily Sikh prayer, it is evidenced in an inclusive social vision along with the Sikh belief in philanthropy: the true path lies in honest work and charity.[13] To Nanak, 'compassion' was thus an essential undertow for religion.[14] This altruistic underpinning also made him question religious dogma and as a departure from religious thought prevalent at the time, to elevate truthful living above Truth itself.[15] At a time when temples and such other places of worship were synonymous with the divine, his proclamation to dissociate spirituality and godliness from the physical and the corporeal was significantly novel and bold.[16]

Although some of his ideas drew inspiration from ancient Hindu texts such as the Upanishads, Nanak rejected multiple gods, rituals, the rigid social hierarchy of his own creed (Hinduism) and rather professed a single god, both universal and personal. Not only does He reside within each one of us but is immanent all through our being (ang-sang).

To Nanak the eternal name (nau) of God was Truth (sat) because God was ever true and all-prevailing although unknowable to ordinary mortals.[17]

Through his extensive travels and contact with people of diverse faiths, he engaged in interfaith dialogue as he sought to both learn and educate. To him, religious life meant much more than inward-looking contemplation and mendicancy. It must have a strong practical bias with ecumenical solidarity along with social, religious, and gender equality, all rooted in an ethical framework.

The institution of the langar, which was to become a defining feature of Sikh praxis, can be traced to the sacha sauda incident from Nanak's early years. Through it, Nanak stressed equality and extended it equally to congregational worship as well as social and political life thus laying the foundations for a scientific and rational vision. This would enable his successors to help ordinary people reject superstitions, the caste system, unscientific rituals, pseudo-religious ceremonies, idolatry, leading them towards a system based on the principles of faith, justice, equality and mutual respect.

At a time when gender inequality was particularly distressing in India, Nanak articulated a convincing rationale: why call woman vile when she begets kings?[18]

In contrast to the existing Hindu and Muslim worldviews, Nanak had set out to investigate for himself the reality of existence. As a consequence, his concepts of the divine Word (shabad), Name (nam), Preceptor (Guru), and divine Order (hukam) are uniquely different from the works of earlier saints (sants):

'Plainly, there is much that is profoundly original in the hymns [....] There is in them an integrated and coherent system which no other Sant has produced; there is clarity which no other Sant has matched.'[19]

As a religious innovator, Nanak propagated an exclusive vision that espoused the cause of peace at the same time extolling the virtuous warrior who fights for a righteous cause, prefiguring the sant-sipahi as well as martyrdom which would later evolve and assume a centrality in Sikh ethos and praxis.[20]

He established Kartarpur, a city where he attempted to implement his utopian vision of a just and egalitarian order among the laity, spawning a socio-political and cultural movement alongside the aesthetic flowering of the arts and music. While Martin Luther King was busy changing the course of religion in Europe, Nanak brought about a reformation of his own in the Punjab.

Several centuries later, Nanak found praise in one of India's greatest Urdu poets, Iqbal. In a composition, 'Shukar-o-Shikayat', the poet laments the prolonged subjugation of his servile fellow-countrymen:[21]

اک ولولہ تازہ دیا میں نے دلوں کو
لاہور سے تابخاکِ بخارا و سمرقند
لیکن مجھے پیدا کیا اُس دیش میں تونے
جس دیش کے بندے ہیں غلامی پے رضامند

ਇਕ ਵਲਵਲਾ-ਏ- ਤਾਜ਼ਾ ਦੀਜਾ ਮੈਨੇ ਦਿਲੋਂ ਕੋ
ਲਾਹੌਰ ਸੇ ਤਾ-ਖ਼ਾਕੇ-ਬੁਖਾਰਾ-ਓ-ਸਮਰਕੰਦ ।
ਲੈਕਿਨ ਮੁਝੇ ਪੈਦਾ ਕੀਜਾ ਉਸ ਦੇਸ਼ ਮੇ ਤੂਨੇ
ਜਿਸ ਦੇਸ਼ ਕੇ ਬੰਦੇ ਹੈ ਗੁਲਾਮੀ ਰਜ਼ਾਮੰਦ ।

Ek Walwala Taza Diya Main Ne Dilon Ko
Lahore Se Ta-Bakhak-e-Bukhara-o-Samarqand
Lekin Mujhe Paida Kiya Uss Dais Mein Tu Ne
Jis Dais Ke Bande Hain Ghulami Pe Razamand!
My songs fresh zeal to hearts of men impart,
Their charm extends to lands that lie apart.
O God, to such a land I have been sent,
Where men in abject bondage feel content.

In another, (Bang-e-Dra 143 Nanak) he sings paeans to Nanak's humanistic monotheism and egalitarian vision that rescued his country from this dark age of ignorance.[22]

پھر اُٹھی آخر سدا توہید کی پنجاب سے
ہند کو اِک مردِ کامل نے جگایا خواب سے

ਫਿਰ ਉਠੀ ਤੋਹੀਦ ਕੀ ਪੰਜਾਬ ਸੇ
ਹਿੰਦ ਕੋ ਏਕ ਮਰਦ-ਏ-ਕਾਮਿਲ ਨੇ ਜਗਾਯਾ ਖ਼ਵਾਬ ਸੇ ।

Phir Uthi Akhir Sada Touheed Ki Punjab Se
Hind Ko Ek Mard-e-Kamil Ne Jagaya Khawab Se
Again from the Punjab the call of monotheism arose
A perfect man roused India from slumber.

Instead of using highly esoteric Sanskrit—*dev bhasha* (language of the Gods)—it was to Nanak's credit that he employed Gurmukhi, literally 'from the guru's mouth', along with an idiom and analogy within reach of all. His verse incorporated vocabulary from Sanskrit, Arabic, Persian, and other South Asian languages which became characteristic of the Sikh tradition. Above all, it was the simplicity and social relevance of his message that attracted a large following among Muslims and Hindus alike—the word 'sikh' is derived from the Sanskrit 'shishya' simply meaning 'follower'.

In this sense, it is often argued that Nanak, like any other great religious leader, did not found a religion. As a gentle and mystic devotee (bhakta), he simply 'attacked religious formalism of all kinds.' It was over several generations that the creed was gradually reified and the followers religiously formalized by organizers such as Guru Arjan (the fifth preceptor) and Guru Gobind (the tenth preceptor).[23] This would include compiling the essential Sikh teachings into the Adi Granth (Punjabi for 'First Book'), which many regard as a syncretic melding of devotional Hinduism and Sufi Islam but with its own uniquely robust, reformist, and egalitarian undergirding. These scriptures would later be canonized with gurudom by the tenth preceptor in October 1708.

Guru Nanak founded a fictive lineage of successive Gurus. A khatri from a community of scribes and traders himself, all nine successive Gurus were khatri as well as townsmen. Possibly, this explains why the faith was initially confined to towns.

Formalizing the Creed

A major task that befell the second preceptor, Guru Angad, was to standardize the Brahmic Gurmukhi script. This had existed in elementary form for some time before the Sikhs appropriated it to record their writings, in the process modifying its characters and developing a complex system of usage.[24] Guru Angad also began the compilation of Sikh religious writings. This finds mention in 17th century traditions that refer to the pothi compiled at Kartarpur with Nanak's hymns ceremonially handed over to Guru Angad on ascendance.[25]

Guru Angad's second major contribution was strengthening food sharing adopted earlier by Nanak by encouraging Sikhs to tithe. It was left to the third preceptor, Guru Amar Das, to lend this innovative charity its truly egalitarian character by insisting on 'pangat'—that required all, both high and low, to partake of food seated on the ground. This classless norm was a novel initiative in a caste-ridden society and, indubitably, served to widen the appeal of the new faith. Under his leadership, the Guru Harsahai pothi was updated with the hymns of the first three preceptors to become the Govindval pothi, along with the addition of hymns of some Bhagats (saints).[26]

Babur's grandson, Akbar, supported religious freedom and, after partaking of langar under the auspices of Guru Amar Das, donated 500 bighas (a bigha is little less than half-acre) to the community for a seminary. The fourth preceptor, Guru Ramdas, purchased another 500 bighas to lay the foundations of the settlement Ramdaspur named after him, later rechristened 'Amritsar' (literally 'sacred tank') after the circumambulating water tank around Harimandir Sahib—now the Golden Temple.[27]

Guru Arjan (the fifth preceptor) was an accomplished poet and his verse reflects interfaith spirituality as an abiding principle. He also deepened rational explication with intellectual clarity on religious praxis that would be rare even today,[28] emphasizing reflection as a means to the Truth.[29]

While the Guru was much respected for his saintliness, he was widely hailed for his social work, particularly for the excavation of pools and wells operated by the Persian wheel and was popularly addressed as Sacha Padshah (the true Emperor). On his invitation, Akbar visited him in his seminary on 4th November 1598 at Govindval where, on his behest, he remitted annual revenue as relief to peasants for a failed monsoon. This served to significantly enhance the Guru's popularity among the jat peasantry who were intrinsically defiant of authority and predisposed against oppressive state structures that took away two-thirds of their production as revenue.

Mughal officials were aware of the massive influx of jats into the Sikh movement and this waiver may be viewed as part of a larger Mughal plan of providing revenue-free grants to Guru Arjan in the Majha potentially to deal with any covert resistance.[30]

The Granth

A major concern for Guru Arjan was the multiple versions of the Sikh scripture that had proliferated over the years by unknown authors. After long discussions with his confidante, Bhai Gurdas, a Sikh savant and an important poet in his own right, he realized the importance of identifying and removing interpolations in order to bequeath a single authoritative book to posterity. The painstaking compilation and organization of the Adi Granth over a period of five years became his most significant contribution to his faith.

For the purpose, he borrowed the Govindval pothi from the Bhallas of Govindval to which he added his father's and his own hymns. He dictated these to Bhai Gurdas, the amanuensis, who meticulously calligraphed and transcribed the hymns from several different languages into Gurmukhi. When complete, this would be the first text ever in Gurmukhi. It was a mammoth task arranging nearly 7000 hymns of five Sikh Gurus, fifteen Muslim and Hindu saints in precise order based on chronology and metrical structure and then setting these to thirty-one different ragas (musical measures).[31] Accomplished with exactness and intellectual discipline at a place since venerated as a shrine (Ramsar) within Amritsar, the work was 'unique among the world's religious books for its mystic ardour and catholicity of design and spirit'.[32] It comprised 974 leaves (1948 pages), was bound and then formally installed amid ceremony in the Harimandir on 4 Bhadon (16th August 1604), according the place a centrality for Sikhs ever after.[33] It came to be later known as the Kartarpuri pothi.[34] Popular tradition records another 'Bhai Banno vali pothi' created in curious circumstances: Guru Arjan charged Bhai Banno to have the original pothi bound at Lahore; Bhai Banno chose to prepare another copy with some alterations, which was later installed at his house at Khara Mangat.

The first recorded hukmnama—composition that appears when the holy book is opened at random—seemed to hail and consecrate the sacred mission.[35]

The Adi Granth is based on two fundamental assumptions: the text is revealed, hence immutable and unchangeable; it is the repository of answers to all religious and moral questions.

It is divided into three parts:

- The opening section is liturgical and includes three prayers: the Japji (Meditation) of thirty-eight stanzas and two couplets; the Rahiras (Supplication) of nine hymns (four by Nanak, three by Guru Ramdas, and two by Guru Arjan; the Sohila (Praise) of five hymns (three by Guru Nanak, one each by Guru Ramdas and Guru Arjan). These three prayers are recited at sunrise, sunset, and bedtime, respectively.
- Hymns in the main body are divided into thirty-one separate sub-sections according to musical mode (raag); each sub-section begins with hymns of four stanzas (chaupadis), followed by eight stanzas (ashtpadis), then four stanzas of six verses each (chhants), and finally longer compositions with a sequence of couplets and stanzas (vars).
- The final section consists of miscellaneous hymns not set to any musical mode and includes couplets by Guru Nanak, Guru Arjan, Guru Teg Bahadur, Kabir, Farid, and a set of panegyrics

(savaiye) by bards. The closing is with Ragmala (garland of musical modes), a hymn of twelve stanzas, grouping raags of the medieval Indian system into six families.[36]

Although the Sikh gurus composed many of their hymns in Punjabi, like other contributors of their time, they also used elements of Apabhramsha (later dialect of Sanskrit), Braj Bhasha (language of the Braj region around Mathura), Hindui (language spoken around Delhi), and a heavily Persianized Punjabi.

Martyrdom and Militarization

Akbar's successor and son, Jahangir, did not share his father's liberal outlook and, possibly, because he had come to power with the support of Muslim revivalist groups (naqshbandis), was inclined to marginalize non-Muslims: 'the glory of Islam consists in the humiliation of infidelity and the infidels. Anyone who held an infidel in esteem, caused humiliation to Islam'.[37]

He saw the Sikhs as a political threat and, within eight months of Akbar's death, had Guru Arjan Dev arrested, tortured, and put to death on 30th May 1606, allegedly for Sikh support to his son, Khusrau Mirza, in the battle for succession. There is, however, no historical evidence for any such support beyond Khusrau visiting the Guru at Tarn Taran in April 1606 to seek his blessings.[38]

> 'There was a Hindu named Arjan in Gobindwal on the banks of the Beas River. Pretending to be a spiritual guide, he had won over as devotees many simpleminded Indians and even some ignorant, stupid Muslims by broadcasting his claims to be a saint. They called him guru. Many fools from all around had recourse to him and believed in him implicitly. For three or four generations they had been peddling this same stuff. For a long time, I had been thinking that either this false trade should be eliminated or that he should be brought into the embrace of Islam. At length, when Khusraw passed by there, this inconsequential little fellow wished to pay homage to Khusraw. When Khusraw stopped at his residence, [Arjan] came out and had an interview with [Khusraw]. Giving him

some elementary spiritual precepts picked up here and there, he made a mark with saffron on his forehead, which is called cjashcja in the idiom of the Hindus and which they consider lucky. When this was reported to me, I realized how perfectly false he was and ordered him brought to me. I awarded his houses and dwellings and those of his children to Murtaza Khan, and I ordered his possessions and goods confiscated and him executed.' (The Jehangirnama)[39]

Some historians challenge the 'execution', suggesting instead that:

'He [the Guru] was imprisoned, and his death, which occurred soon after, is attributed to the rigours of his confinement; though tradition asserts that, having obtained permission from his guards to bathe in the river Ravi, which flowed by his prison, he miraculously disappeared beneath the stream.'[40]

Even if this were true, Guru Arjan would still be accepted as the first Sikh martyr because the emperor himself had ordered his execution, which would have taken place in due course. Nonetheless, his death by royal decree was a definitive indication of his socio-political importance, the growing strength of the Sikh movement, and the emergence of Ramdaspur (Amritsar) as an autonomous 'power center,' especially after the installation of the scriptures in 1604.[41] It was also the place where Guru Arjan had sought to establish the divine rule of justice and humility (halemi raj) to help people live with dignity and self-respect.[42] Unbending and steadfast before torture, Guru Arjan refused to abjure his faith, living up to his professed creed as a true man of courage.[43]

When his son, Guru Hargobind, in deference to his father's wishes, militarized the faith, he was very soon on a collision course with the regime but, in three hard fought battles forced upon him, he routed the imperial troops, the victories significantly impacting Sikh morale. Thereafter, he chose to reside in the Shivalik foothills and established a seminary at Kiratpur (Rupnagar district) in 1634. Four of his successors would likewise spend most of their lives in the area, Kiratpur and Anandpur.

In Defense of All Faiths

During his pontificate, the ninth preceptor, Guru Tegh Bahadur, travelled extensively in the Malwa region of the Punjab as well as in Bihar, Bengal, present day Bangladesh, and Assam to preach the gospel. This did not find favour with the state and he was initially arrested in 1660 though soon released on the intercession of Raja Ram Singh of Jaipur. He was re-arrested in 1670 and released again after brief confinement only to be re-arrested in 1675. This time it was for supporting Kashmiri Pandits against forced conversion to Islam under orders of the Mughal emperor, Aurangzeb, who had abandoned his predecessors' legacy of pluralism and religious tolerance. Unwavering before inducements and extreme threats to apostatize, the Guru was martyred in November 1675 in Delhi after his three companions had been tortured and killed in the most brutal manner.

In a bid to exonerate Mughals from their vile and fanatical proselytizing, revisionist Muslim accounts such as that of Latif tend to vilify the Guru, citing plunder and rapine as reasons for his arrest and execution but these do not bear logical scrutiny.[44]

When the then Governor of Kashmir, Iftikhar Khan (1671-1675) began a highly virulent movement of forced conversions, the delegation of Kashmiri Brahmins that waited upon Guru Teg Bahadur in May 1675 at Anandpur was led by one Kirpa Ram Dutt. In addition to Sikh hagiography, this event is endorsed by his descendant, the Kashmir expert, Sushil Pandit.[45] In effect, the Guru's arrest was to preempt his tour of Kashmir on the behest of this delegation.

For his singular sacrifice, the Guru is popularly known as 'Hind di chadar' (savior of India). He also lived up to the essence of one of his own beautifully cadenced hymns: 'One who frightens not; nor is himself frightened of anyone: Says Nanak, call him spiritually wise.'[46]

The Khalsa

Assuming guruship at the age of nine, Guru Gobind Singh was at once aware of how religion in the Indian context had sometimes interfered with the development of warlike virtues and he expressly strove to obviate any doctrinal enervation, instead re-energizing his followers with self-esteem with the founding of the Khalsa in March

1699.⁴⁷ He infused the creed with martial qualities alongside a strict moral code—Bhagti-Shakti (religious devotion plus righteous might). This was one of the many binaries that now began to represent the duality of the Sikh faith after Guru Hargobind initiated the Miri-Piri imperative. Military analysts concur that the founding of the Khalsa was the single most important event in the Sikh experience of history, military history in particular, in sync with Guru Nanak's vision of a righteous war conceived more than a century earlier, endorsed along the way by Guru Hargobind:

'It was reserved for Nanak to perceive the true principles of reform, and to lay those broad foundations which [enabled] his successor Gobind to fire the minds of his countrymen with a new nationality, and to give practical effect to the doctrine that the lowest is equal with the highest, in race as in creed, in political rights as in religious hopes.'⁴⁸

The casteless nature of the faith was reinforced in the original baptismal ceremony more by accident than design. The voluntary panj pyare (the 'beloved five')—the first five to be baptized—represented a cross-section of high and low castes from different parts of India.

The Khalsa were enjoined to wear five outward distinguishing symbols:

- Kesh (uncut hair): symbol both of holiness and strength.
- Kara (steel bracelet): reminder for righteous action.
- Kanga (wooden comb): to keep uncut hair neat and tidy; symbol of clean mind and body.
- Kachha (special underwear or breeches): symbol of chastity; also suitable when riding a horse.
- Kirpan (dagger): symbol of justice as well as temporal and spiritual power.

In addition, five weapons were now made obligatory (panj hathiar)—sword, war quoits (chakram), arrow, noose, and a gun.⁴⁹

Commenting on Guru Gobind Singh's writings later compiled as the Dasm Granth, John Malcolm states that 'Courage is throughout... placed above every other virtue; and Govind, like Muhammed, makes martyrdom for the faith which he taught, the shortest and most certain road to honour in this world, and eternal happiness in the future.'⁵⁰

Equally contributive to his success was his leadership style, far ahead of his time. His image as the first among equals belies his self-effacing modesty. He feted the supremacy of the Khalsa, the commune over their leader; the battalions over their commander:

ਜੁਧ ਜਿਤੇ ਇਨਹੀ ਕੇ ਪ੍ਰਸਾਦਿ....॥

Judhh Jithae Einehee Kae Prasadh.... ||

It is by the Grace of the Khalsa that we have been victorious in battle.

ਇਨਹੀ ਕੀ ਕ੍ਰਿਪਾ ਸਭ ਸੱਤ੍ਰ ਮਰੇ ॥

Einehee Kee Kripa Sabh Sathr Marae ||

It is through their Grace that we could prevail over our enemies.

ਇਨਹੀ ਕੀ ਕ੍ਰਿਪਾ ਕੇ ਸਜੇ ਹਮ ਹੈਂ ਨਹੀ ਮੋ ਸੋ ਗਰੀਬ ਕਰੋਰ ਪਰੇ ॥ ੨ ॥

Einehee Kee Kripa Kae Sajae Ham Hain Neheen Mo So Gareeb Karor Parae || 2 ||

It is by their Grace that I have been elevated to this lofty status, else I would be one among millions of poor ordinary mortals.

—Guru Gobind Singh,
Dasm Granth, p. 284

Sant-Sipahi

Clearly, in Sikh theology, shaastra and shastar ('divine word' and 'weapon'), miri and piri (the 'spiritual' and the 'temporal'), sant and sipahi ('saint' and 'soldier') represent no dichotomy but instead, a thesis, anti-thesis and synthesis that underpin the 'warrior-saint', ever bound to rightful living, righteous action and when called upon, to righteous war in order to supplant any oppressive and hegemonic political structures with an egalitarian order—*Khalsa Raj (Rule of the Pure)*.

The word-order of the compound sant-sipahi (saint-soldier) is relevant: the first duty of the Sikh is to be saintly and wise; next, he must practice arms to fight injustice and to defend the weak.

This essential spiritual underpinning stood firm even in times of bitter conflict. Outnumbered and ill-equipped, the Khalsa never lost their humanity. Members of the faith such as Bhai Ghanaiya would even tend wounded enemy soldiers. When Afghan invaders would take away thousands of Hindu and Muslim girls as slaves, warring bands of Sikhs would liberate them at great peril, escorting them back to their homes.

A Bequest to the Nation

By his uncanny ability to perceive and seize what was vital in his time, Guru Gobind Singh relumed his people with Promethean fire.[51] Banerjee counts him 'among the greatest of Indians of all ages' and credits him with a rare vision in that he left subsequent leadership to the collective wisdom of a community that threw up its own leaders during the Sikh war of Independence; a leadership so highly evolved that it eventually 'blunted the edge of Abdali's aggressive power which even the Marathas failed to resist, and turned his great triumph at Panipat a barren victory'.[52]

Later, the Nobel laureate, Rabindranath Tagore, would adopt Guru Gobind Singh as a nationalist icon to inspire the youth of his time, goading them to take up arms in India's freedom struggle:[53]

> To jump on the bosom of tyranny
> And to slay it with my sharp sword (Stanza 6)
>
> In my heart I am lighting a lamp,
> Which no storm can blow out.
> It will give light to the whole of humanity[54] (Stanza 24)

Besides his own prodigious poetry, an important bequest of Guru Gobind was finalizing the Sikh scriptures by incorporating hymns of his father, Guru Teg Bahadur, as well as standardizing it as the Granth Sahib from among several variations in 1706 at Talwandi Sabo, a place since venerated as Dam Dama Sahib.[55] This recension was later ordained in October 1708 as the canon with the prefix 'Guru'—the final, sovereign, and eternal living guru—by Guru Gobind Singh himself a few days before his demise on 7th October 1708.

Before departing for South India, he also established a seminary at Dama Dama Sahib, appointing Deep Singh as its first Jathedar. A discerning choice, Deep Singh would later be recognized as the 'living embodiment' of the Khalsa ideology, 'as much in belief and appearance, as in action and martyrdom.'[56]

Blessed and baptized by the Guru and backed by all prominent Sikhs of the time such as Deep Singh, Banda Singh Bahadur would be the first Sikh ever to comprehensively challenge Mughal hegemony in what some historians designate as India's first war of independence when his wholly indigenous ragtag army defeated their imperious overlords. His success, however, was short-lived partly because he lost the support of a large segment of the Sikh population, Deep Singh among them, when he chose to arrogate to himself powers and status beyond his brief and altered some key traditions of the Khalsa. Nevertheless, on the foundations laid by him, the Sikhs would later establish one of the great feudal kingdoms of the period under Ranjit Singh after having borne the cross for over a century.

A Modern Legacy

When Guru Nanak, the founder of the religion, attained enlightenment in 1505 AD at the age of twenty-seven, all those around him were incredulous of his spiritual edification except his own sister, Nanaki, who became his first disciple. Today, there are over 27 million Sikhs worldwide. While the vast majority live in the Indian state of the Punjab, about twenty percent have migrated to form prosperous communities in every continent with the largest emigrant populations settled in Canada and the United Kingdom.[57] The monotheistic and spiritual appeal of the religion has also caught the imagination of communities and cultures worldwide and large numbers continue to adopt the Sikh way of life, including its external symbols.

Several principal Sikh legacies have gained momentum. Sikhs continue to distinguish themselves as soldiers, many reaching top echelons of the armed forces in India and abroad. The concept of miri-piri (temporal and spiritual authority) is still highly regarded and seems to equip them with the political acumen to assume positions of leadership and key appointments in legislative bodies around the world, including those of the leading democracies such as the USA, UK, and Canada.

Nanak's original message that sought sarbat-da-bhala (well-being of all) has been for Sikhs the lodestar through the ages. As far back as 1783, when a dreadful famine struck the whole of North India,

Sikh langars continued to welcome all and sundry. According to the Gazetteer of Montgomery district, in a feat of rare munificence, a Sikh chief went to the extent of selling off all his property to be able to feed grain to the starving general populace.[58]

The institution of the langar has now diversified into larger, ubiquitous charity initiatives for humanitarian aid worldwide—for war-displaced Syrian refugees in Turkey and Lebanon, Rohingya refugees in Bangladesh, to the millions affected by the crippling COVID-19 pandemic across the globe, or in other trouble spots ravaged by conflict and natural calamities.

At the age of thirty years, Guru Nanak sought leave of his parents—who would have rather had him care for them in their dotage—to spread his gospel, saying: 'There is a call from Heaven. I must go whither He directs me.'

Over the next twenty-four years, Nanak undertook five long missionary journeys mostly on foot in different directions, visiting the principal holy centers of his time as far as Sri Lanka, Bangladesh, Tibet, Nepal, Bhutan, Southwest China, Afghanistan, Iran, Iraq, and Saudi Arabia. Today, the sapling that Guru Nanak planted and nurtured more than five hundred years ago with love and humility has taken root across the world when Sikhism ranks among the world's many prominent religions. His hymnal compositions can be heard dawn, dusk, and night in homes and places of worship across the globe.

Among the greatest religious innovators and social reformers of all time, Guru Nanak lives on in a benign bequest that continues to shine a beacon of compassion and rationality all around us:

> 'With the emergence of Guru Nanak, the mist cleared and light shone all around.
> Akin to sunrise that dispels the stars and darkness.'[59]

Glossary

Adi Granth: Sikh scriptures compiled by Guru Arjan in 1604 and later updated in 1706 and canonized in October 1708 by Guru Gobind Singh; now Guru Granth Sahib.

Amrit Sanchar, Amrit Sanskar, Khande-di-Pahul: baptism of the sword; rite of initiation into the Khalsa brotherhood introduced by Guru Gobind Singh when he founded the Khalsa in March 1699.

Amrit vela: ambrosial hour, usually around 4 AM considered ideal for meditation in Sikh belief and practice.

Amrit: elixir; sweet water used in Sikh baptism ceremonies prepared by stirring sugar drop candies in an iron bowl with a double-edged sword to the recitation of five banis (hymns from the Sikh scriptures) by five members of the Khalsa.

Amritdhari: baptized Sikh who has undergone Amrit Sanchar.

Ang-sang: 'inside every part of the body', Sikh religious concept that God is immanent all through living beings.

Ardas: prayer, supplication; supplicatory prayer.

Baint: in Arabic and Persian poetry a poem of two lines though the number of syllables per line can vary.

Bairagi: ascetic

Baisakhi, Vaisakhi: annual celebration on 13th April; Guru Gobind Singh founded the Khalsa order on this day in 1699.

Bandei Khalsa: a breakaway faction led by Banda Bahadur; opposed to the Tat Khalsa who remained true to the teachings of the tenth Guru.

Bani: abbreviation of 'Gurbani' applied to any of the writings in Guru Granth Sahib.

Bargirs: soldiers, part of a misl, who were provided a horse and equipment by the misaldar (leader); very often they acquired their own as war trophies in their first successful military campaign.

Bhagat Bani: writings in the Guru Granth Sahib not written by the Gurus but by Bhagats (other saints).

Bhagauti: sublime energy; Guru Gobind Singh elevated the sword to this divine pedestal.

Bigha: little less than half-acre of land.

Brahmgyani: enlightened individual; select congregation of forty-eight members who attended the exegesis sessions by Guru Gobind Singh at Dam Dama Sahib (1706).

Braj Bhasha: dialect of Hindi also known as Brij or Brijbhoomi after a region in India on both sides of the Yamuna River with its center at Mathura-Vrindavan in Uttar Pradesh; it included Hodal in Haryana and Bharatpur in Rajasthan. It is a Western Hindi language predominant in the literary tradition of North India along with Awadhi.

Buddha Dal: 'army of veterans' (above forty years) formed by Nawab Kapur Singh along with the Taruna Dal (army of the young, below forty years) in 1734 to look after Sikh holy places, preach, and initiate new converts to the Khalsa order.

Bunga: derived from the Persian 'bungah' meaning hospice or dwelling place. In the Sikh tradition, it specifically refers to the dwelling places and mansions which grew around Harimandir Sahib (Amritsar) or other centres of Sikh pilgrimage; primarily built by conquering misl sardars and chiefs, or Sikh schoolmen and sectaries to house the warriors responsible for the defence of Harimandar Sahib. The Akal Bunga (now the Akal Takth) was the first to be constructed, opposite Harimandir Sahib by Guru Hargobind in 1606. There were scores of bungas in the vicinity of the temple. The Shaheed Bunga is located within the perimeter of Harimandir Sahib and represents the Shaheed misl; also serves as a cenotaph-cum-gurdwara to mark the place of Deep Singh Shaheed's martyrdom in November 1757.

Chakre: quoit; worn in the Nihang style turban (dastar bunga or 'towering fortress') and used as a weapon of war when hurled like a discus.

Chal: rhyme

Chali Mukte (Forty Immortals): forty Sikhs martyred in the Battle of Muktsar (Khidrane di Dhab) in January 1706 and personally blessed by Guru Gobind Singh for salvation (mukti).

Chardi Kala: 'chardi' means 'rising', 'kala' is Sanskrit for 'energy'; literally 'rising' or 'ascendant energy'; an important expression in Sikhism for a 'positive, buoyant and optimistic' mindset; always in 'high spirits', 'ever progressive', 'always cheerful'; sustained and steady high morale even in adversity; incorrigible optimism. As an attribute, it is central to the Sikh faith, and part of the concluding line of the daily Sikh prayer in tandem with the benevolence for 'sarbat da bhala' (prosperity of all).

Chaupai: quatrain; poetry stanza of four lines.

Chhand bandi: prosody; although intrinsically different, Indian and English classical prosody are not mutually exclusive. English poetry relies on qualitative meter—stressed (accented) syllables coming at regular intervals, interspersed with unstressed ones. Punjabi poetry uses quantitative meter, instead, based on syllabic weight or length—Laghu (short vowel) and Guru (long vowel). The effect can be similar.

Chhand: verse or writing arranged in lines which have rhythm (meter) and rhyme. Sometimes written in quatrains (four-line stanzas) in the poetic traditions of North India and Pakistan. The contents of Jaap Sahib are divided into various chhands bearing the name of the type of meter as per the prevalent system of Indian prosody.

Chupehra: (paher is an ancient Indian unit of time roughly equal to three hours). Chupehra would be four pahers (twelve hours)—time spent in meditating at gurdwaras, generally for the grant of personal wishes, includes choral recitation of scriptures. Generally—Japji Sahib (five times), Chopai (once), Sukhmani Sahib (once).

Dal Khalsa: the Khalsa army set up on Baisakhi 1748 and divided into eleven misls; the twelfth misl (Phulkian) was independent.

Dan, daan: charity; an essential article of Sikh faith that requires tithing (giving away a tenth of income to the needy or less advantaged).

Dasm Granth: the book of writings of Guru Gobind Singh believed to have been compiled after his death.

Dastar: pugree (turban); inseparable part of Sikh dress for men according to the Sikh 'Code of Conduct'; turban in the Nihang style.

Dastar-bunga: literally 'towering fortress', the tall turban in the Nihang style.

Daswand, dasvand (tithe): ten percent of earnings donated to the needy or less advantaged as part of Sikh practice.

Deg-Teg: 'deg' is a large cooking cauldron and 'teg' a large slashing sword; together they symbolize the dual responsibility of the Sikh Panth to provide food and protection for the needy and oppressed.

Dera: type of socio-religious organization in Northern India akin to a 'monastery'; extended residential sites of religious leaders often glossed as sect. Originally, the five Sikh deras or fighting groups of the Taruna Dal founded in 1734 by Nawab Kapur Singh of 1300-2000 men each, with a separate drum and banner. The first was commanded by Deep Singh known as Shahidanvala Jatha. The second was commanded by Bhai Karam Singh and Dharam Singh of Amritsar known as Amritsarian da Jatha. The third was led by Baba Binod Singh and his son Baba Kahn Singh called Sahibzadian da Jatha or Guru-Ansi Jatha. The fourth was commanded by Bhai Dasaundha Singh of Kot Buddha, and the fifth by Bhai Bir Singh Ranghreta. They were located separately in the five holy Sarovars (sacred pools) in Lacchmansar (1586), Santokhsar (1587-88), Ramsar (1602-03), Kaulsar (1627), and Bibeksar (1628).

Dewan (Diwan): a high-ranking government officer; chief minister of a province.

Dhadi: one who sings the praises of God usually heroic ballads in a particularly rousing style and tradition to the accompaniment of traditional instruments; introduced by Guru Hargobind.

Dhai Phat: literally, two-and-half feet, or two-and-half strikes. An important Sikh guerrilla tactic that grew out of their asymmetric struggle. First strike—unbalance the enemy with surprise to cause maximum damage; Second Strike—disengage with minimum personal casualties; Half-strike—engage in pitched battle (and be killed). It implied giving full importance to Attack and Disengagement, and half importance to being wounded or killed.

Dhall: shield

Dharma: religion, teaching, or lifestyle as in Sikh Dharma.

Dharmayudh: war in the defence of righteousness, sacralized battle.

Dhonsa: large war drum

Dhoti, chaadra: rectangular piece of unstitched cloth usually around 4.5

metres long, worn as a traditional men's garment over the lower body all through the Indian subcontinent.

Diwali: Hindu festival of lights also celebrated by Sikhs; marks 'Bandi Chor Divas' to commemorate Guru Hargobind's release from Mughal incarceration when he insisted on freeing another fifty-two Hindu kings imprisoned in the Gwalior Fort.

Doaba: area falling between the rivers Sutlej and Beas in the Punjab.

Doha, Dohra: self-contained rhyming couplet, or two rhyming lines.

Dumala: loose end of a turban deliberately left to hang as a style statement; the high, Nihang-style turban.

Emir (Arabic Amīr): 'commander,' or 'prince', in the Muslim Middle East, a military commander, governor of a province, or a high-ranking military official.

Fakir: a pious person; often a mendicant.

Fateh Darshan: greeting introduced by Banda Bahadur through a Hukamnama in 1710 to replace 'Waheguru ji ka Khalsa, Waheguru ji ki Fateh'; led to a schism and two splinter groups: Bandei Khalsa (loyal to Banda Bahadur) and Tat Khalsa (loyal to the teachings of the Sikh gurus).

Fateh: victory

Faujdar: military commander of a province.

Ghallughara: holocaust

Ghari: ancient system of measuring time, at the rate of twenty-four minutes.

Giani: a person with spiritual knowledge.

Gilja: commonly used to refer to Afghan soldiers in 18th century Punjab.

Granthi: one who performs the reading of Guru Granth Sahib.

Gresthi: Sikh ideal of being married, having a family and earning ones living by honest, socially useful means, serving one's fellow human beings and worshipping God.

Gurbani: the writings of the Gurus.

Gurdwara, gurudwara: literally 'God's door' or 'God's place'; Sikh place of worship.

Gurj: mace

Gurmat: general term for Sikhism including the teachings of the Gurus as well as the Rahit Maryada (code of conduct).

Gurmatta: synod; resolution passed in a council presided over by the Guru or the advice of the Guru.
Gurmukh: God-oriented instead of being self-centered; opposite of manmukh (controlled by one's own mind and will).
Gurmukhi: the written form of Punjabi used in Sikh scriptures developed and propagated by Guru Nanak and Guru Angad.
Gursikh: someone deeply and sincerely devoted to the service of the Guru and the Sikh way of life.
Gutka: book containing daily Sikh prayers.
Haleemi Raj: divine rule of justice and humility, a Sikh ideal.
Harimandir Sahib (Sudhasar): 'abode of God' or 'Darbār Sahib' (exalted court). Gurdwara in the city of Amritsar, the preeminent spiritual site of Sikhism built in the middle of a man-made pool, completed by Guru Ram Das in 1577; today, the Golden Temple.
Hola Mohalla: annual spring gathering of Sikhs at Anandpur Sahib for sporting contests, hymnal singing, and poetry recitation initiated by Guru Gobind Singh in 1701.
Hukam: the ordained will of God.
Hukamnama, Hukamnamah: royal edict generally given by Sikh gurus.
Jagir: an assignment of land revenue in lieu of salary for service to the state or government.
Jagirdar: a holder or recipient of a jagir
Jambura: small light cannon carried in a camel-pack
Janamsakhi: A hagiographic account of the life of Guru Nanak or other Gurus; generally, in the form of parables.
Janjail: long heavy musket with a range of 600 yards.
Jatha: a band or group; generally, an armed body of men.
Jathedar: the appointed head of a Sikh body of men; also, its spiritual and administrative head.
Jhoke: dialogue in Punjabi verse.
Jira, sanjoi: chain mail or armour.
Kaband: headless body
Kacchera: a specially designed undergarment akin to boxer shorts in appearance with a tie-knot (drawstring); it replaced the 'dhoti'. It is one of five Sikh articles of faith called the Five Ks (ਪੰਜ ਕ੍ਕਾਰ), or outer symbols ordained by Guru Gobind Singh on Baisakhi, 1699 during the amrit sanchar ceremony; it symbolizes chastity. The

other symbols are kanga (comb), kara (steel bracelet), kes (uncut hair), kirpan (sword or dagger).

Kanga: comb; one of five physical symbols that a baptized Sikh must wear; symbol of hygiene and discipline.

Kar Seva: voluntary work for religious purposes especially the building of gurdwaras; desilting the holy tank at Harimandir Sahib every fifty years.

Kara: steel bracelet, one of the five physical symbols that a baptized Sikh must wear; symbol of restraint and remembrance of God.

Karah Parsad: sacramental or communion food distributed in gurdwaras or elsewhere as part (generally at the end) of a religious ceremony in the presence of Guru Granth Sahib; somewhat akin to Christian communion or sacrament; prepared with equal quantities of wheat flour, sugar, and ghee (clarified butter).

Katar: a push dagger

Katha: a religious lecture, exegesis, homily, or expatiation of Sikhism.

Kathavachak: sectary or schoolman who interprets and expatiates on religious texts.

Kaur: middle or last name of a Sikh female; mandatory last name for a Khalsa Sikh female.

Kes: uncut hair, one of the five physical symbols that a baptized Sikh must have; symbol of spirituality.

Keshdhari: a Sikh who does not cut their hair; may or may not be amritdhari (baptized).

Khande-di-Pahul, Amrit Sanchar, Amrit Sanskar: baptism by the sword; the rite of initiation into the Khalsa brotherhood with amrit; see Amrit Sanchar.

Khilat: robe of honour

Kirpan: dagger or sword, one of five physical symbols that a baptized Sikh must wear; symbol of the duty to fight injustice and defend the weak.

Kirtan: musical rendering of gurbani.

Korda: poem generally of thirteen syllables per line.

Kos: ancient Indian unit of measurement; one kos was equal to two miles, or 3.2 kilometres.

Langar: free community kitchen found in all Sikh Gurdwaras; may be organized anywhere; cornerstone of the Sikh religion; symbol of

Glossary

charity and equality instituted by Guru Nanak.

Maderdesh: Punjab

Maghi: Sikh festival on 14th January to commemorate the martyrdom of the forty mukte (forty immortals) in the Battle of Muktsar (Khidrane-di-Dhab).

Majha: The Punjab rivers sub-divide the region into somewhat distinctive geo-cultural units. This is the interfluvial tract north of the Beas, between the rivers Beas and Ravi, also referred to by historians as the 'Sikh tract' being central to the Sikh struggle for sovereignty in the 17-19th centuries. The Rechna Doab, between the Chenab and the Ravi, is also considered to be part of Majha.

Makhan: home-made butter, generally white, popular in rural parts of North India.

Mala: rosary; made of wood, plastic, steel or iron.

Malwa: area southeast of the Sutlej where the erstwhile cis-Sutlej states flourished.

Marsiya: elegy

Maya: the delusion of being wrapped in the material world.

Miri-piri: the 'spiritual' and the 'temporal; one of the many binaries that define the duality of the Sikh faith; has parallels in shaastra and shastar (divine word' and 'weapon'); sant and sipahi ('saint' and 'soldier'); concept of spiritual and worldly upliftment initiated by Guru Hargobind symbolized by his wearing two swords.

Misl, misal: Persian for 'similitude' or 'equal;' created by a gurmatta (synod) by the Sarbat Khalsa (general assembly of Sikhs) on Vaisakhi 1748 at Akal Takht (Amritsar) when various Sikh groups were organized into twelve misals for better coordination, command and control; came to represent sovereign states of the Sikh Confederacy, commonwealth or 'aristocratic republic' that foreran the Sikh empire. The Shaheed misl was headed by Deep Singh.

Nagara: kettledrum found in some gurdwaras; introduced by Guru Hargobind for announcements.

Narsingha, Ransingha: a type of primitive trumpet used in parts of India and Nepal; made of two metal curves joined together to form an 'S' shape; used in battles and also in some prominent Gurdwaras early morning during the enthronement of Guru Granth Sahib.

Nihang: order of Sikhs who follow the soldier lifestyle from the times of Guru Gobind Singh; they dress in traditional blue robes, bear arms, and spurn creature comforts.

Nishan Sahib: Khalsa flag found in all gurdwaras; a symbol of sovereignty.

Nitnem: daily Sikh prayers comprising Japji (Guru Nanak), Jap Sahib and Ten Swayyas (Guru Gobind Singh) in the morning; Rahiras (nine hymns by Guru Nanak, Guru Amar Das and Guru Arjun) at sunset; and Kirtan Sohila (five hymns by the same three Gurus at bedtime).

Padas: Sanskrit term for 'foot' (cognate of English metrical foot); metrical form of hymns in Guru Granth Sahib; varies in length from one to four line verses.

Paher: ancient Indian unit of time, roughly three hours.

Panda Vahi: village genealogy record of families maintained at Haridwar by the Tirth Purohit (family priests located beside holy rivers or holy tanks). After cremation of the mortal remains in the Punjab, it was customary for the ashes to be brought to Haridwar for immersion in the Ganges under the auspices of the Tirth Purohit who would then update the family record of births, deaths, marriages, and visits. This tradition changed over the centuries. Most Sikhs now prefer to immerse the ashes in the Sutlej at Patal Puri, a gurdwara in Rupnagar district where the sixth preceptor (Guru Hargobind) was cremated and the ashes of the seventh and eighth preceptors immersed.

Panj Hathiar (five weapons): on founding the Khalsa in 1699, Guru Gobind Singh also made it obligatory to carry five weapons—sword, war quoits (chakram), arrow, noose, and a gun.

Panj Kakke (Five Ks): five physical symbols worn by baptized Sikhs; kachha or kacchera (briefs), kanga (comb), kara (steel bracelet), kes (unshorn hair), and kirpan (ceremonial sword or dagger); These respectively symbolize 'chastity', 'hygiene and discipline', 'restraint and remembrance of God', 'spirituality', and 'duty to fight injustice and defend the weak'.

Panj Piaras: literally the five beloved ones; the first five Sikhs initiated into the Khalsa order by Guru Gobind Singh on Vaisalhi 1699 when he founded the Khalsa.

Panth: the entire Sikh community.

Parkarma, Parikrama: the walkway around the sarovar (pool) found in many gurdwaras.

Patth: reading of the Guru Granth Sahib.

Pauri: poetic meter or stanza common in Guru Granth Sahib.

Peshkabz: literally 'fore-grip', type of pointed Indo-Persian knife designed to penetrate chain mail or other types of armor.

Phirna Chhand: poetic measure that is varied within a larger piece to provide contrast and relief.

Phulantha: sleight-of-hand especially in a swordfight.

Phultha, patebazi, gatkabazi: swordplay

Phunha: derived from the Sanskrit punha meaning 'again'; poetic metre in which a particular term or phrase occurs repeatedly in each chhand or verse of a poem.

Pingal: poetry

Pothi: manuscript forms of Sikh scriptures that predate the canonized version.

Rag, raag, raga: literally 'coloring, tingeing, dyeing'; a tuneful measure of five to seven notes based on the system of Hindustani sangeet; melodic framework for improvisation; each rāga is an array of melodic structures with musical motifs considered in the Indian tradition to have the ability to 'colour the mind' and affect emotions.

Ragi: a musician who sings the hymns of Guru Granth Sahib in the tradition of ragas.

Rahit Maryada: Sikh Code of Conduct conceived by the Shiromani Gurdwara Parbandhak Committee (SGPC).

Rakhi: protection; protective system introduced by the Khalsa in mid-18th century Punjab whereby a Khalsa leader would exact a fifth of the farmed income twice a year after harvest for guaranteed protection to Muslims and Hindus alike.

Ransingha: see Narsingha.

Rehkela: small wheeled cannon that can be manhandled.

Sahibzadas: four sons of Guru Gobind Singh martyred in Dec 1705—Ajit Singh, Jujhar Singh, Zorawar Singh, Fateh Singh.

Sainapat: military commander-in-chief.

Saithi brek: twisted spear

Sakhi: a story, usually of Gurus.

Samadh: place of cremation of warriors or other important personages marked with a dome-like octagonal structure and held in reverence; for warriors, may include token weaponry, blood-soaked earth, and ashes (the skeletal remnants from cremation are dispersed in the Ganges), stored in earthen or brass urns under the floor. The roof often portrays sixteen petals, reflecting 'Solah kalan sampooran' (important sixteen qualities). Somewhat akin to mausoleum or sepulcher.

Sangat: congregation of Sikhs.

Sant: saint

Sant-sipahi: 'saint' and 'soldier;' has parallels in shaastra and shastar ('divine word' and 'weapon'); miri and piri (the 'spiritual' and the 'temporal').

Sarbans dani: 'one who sacrificed his entire family'; attributed to Guru Gobind Singh who lost both parents and four sons in the struggle for justice against tyranny.

Sarbat da bhala: 'well-being of all humanity'; an essential attitudinal trope in Sikhism; the concluding line of the daily Sikh ardas (prayer) alongside the supplication for 'chardi kala' (ascendant morale and energy). Flows out of their belief in the 'oneness of mankind', which precludes the 'other' in Sikh theology.

Sarbat Khalsa: representative meeting of all Sikhs to consider important matters related to the panth.

Sarovar: sacred tank found in most gurdwaras.

Sat Sri Akal: Sikh greeting; means 'God is Truth and Immortal'.

Savvayya: poem in praise of God or a patron; often of four lines though the meter can vary.

Ser: an ancient now archaic unit of weight. At the time of Akbar, the katcha ser was the common standard of measure as opposed to the pukka ser, which was 2.5 times the former. The conversion rate of the pukka ser was at the rate of 637.7 grams. Later, this was revised to .933 kilograms; one tola at the rate of 11.67 grams; one pukka ser = 80 tolas = .933 kilograms; one maund (forty ser) = 37.32 kilograms.

Shaastra: 'divine word'; often contrasted with shastar (weapons of war); other contrasting parallels: miri and piri (the 'spiritual' and the 'temporal'); sant and sipahi ('saint' and 'soldier').

Shabad: religious hymns contained in Sikh scriptures.

Shabdan: syllable

Shaheed: martyr; also, a misl of that name founded by Deep Singh in the 18th century.

Shaheedbunga: the Bunga built in 1764 within the perimeter of Harimandir Sahib to represent the Shaheed misl or mark the place of Deep Singh's martyrdom; serves as cenotaph-cum-gurdwara with an independent Nishan Sahib.

Shastra: weapons of war. See Kahn Singh Nabha for an illustrated definition of Sikh weapons of the 17-19th century (Mahankosh, 331-334).

Shlok, slok: unit of verse, often short like a doha or rhyming couplet; common in the Guru Granth Sahib.

Shiromani Gurdwara Parbandhak Committee (SGPC): Committee which oversees the administration of many Gurdwaras in Punjab, Haryana and Himachal Pradesh; also responsible for publication and education related to Sikhism.

Sikhi: Sikh teachings.

Singh: Lion; common last or middle name of male Sikhs.

Siri Sahib: sword

Subedar: provincial governor

Sukhmani Sahib: literally 'psalm of peace'; major composition by Guru Arjun in Guru Granth Sahib.

Tahli: the Indian Rosewood, native to the Indian subcontinent.

Takht: total five seats of Sikh authority—Akal Takth (Amritsar), Patna Sahib (Patna), Hazur Sahib (Nander), Keshgarh Sahib (Anandpur), Dam Dama Sahib (Talwandi Sabo).

Taruna Dal: league of the young (forty years and below) created in 1734 by Nawab Kapur Singh along with the Budha Dal (league of the elders or veterans above forty years). The former were responsible for the protection of religious shrines and the community, the latter for the recruitment of young initiates, their training and instruction. The two collectively became known as the Dal Khalsa.

Teer: short spear, spike or arrow.

Teg: large slashing sword

Vaar: heroic ode or ballad that generally narrates the story of Punjabi folk heroes.

Zafarnama: 'Epistle of Victory'; a letter written by Guru Gobind Singh to the Mughal emperor, Aurangzeb in 1706 CE.

Notes

Foreword

1 'Panj Kakke' are the five physical symbols worn by baptized Sikhs: kachha or kacchera (briefs or drawers), kanga (wooden hair-comb), kara (steel bracelet), kes (unshorn hair), and kirpan (ceremonial sword or dagger); These respectively symbolize 'chastity', 'hygiene and discipline', 'restraint and remembrance of God', 'spirituality', and 'duty to fight injustice and defend the weak'.

Preface

1 Henry Steinbach, *The Punjab—being a brief account of the Country of the Sikhs* (London: Smith, Elder and Co, 1845), 16-17.
2 Sukhdyal Singh, "Baba Deep Singh ji Shaheed: Jeevan, Sama ate Prapetian" in compendium of papers presented at *Baba Deep Singh: Jeevan te Yogdaan* National Seminar (Amritsar: Guru Nanak Dev University, 2009), 58: Sukhdyal Singh feels that Deep Singh is embedded in the Sikh psyche and emotions (jajbat), far beyond his historic relevance.
3 This information was shared by Davinderpal Singh who has authored a book on the city.
4 Paher is an Indian unit of time. One paher is roughly three hours. Chupehra would be four pahers or twelve hours but is generally less. It commences mid-noon in this shrine and involves the choral recitation of scriptures: five times Japji Sahib; once Chopai and once Sukhmani Sahib.
5 Ajit Singh Aulakh, *Illustrated Stories of Baba Deep Singh ji Shaheed, Baba Banda Singh ji Bahadur, Bhai Mani Singh ji Shaheed* (Amritsar: Chattar Singh Jeevan Singh, 2010), 34.

6   GC Walker, *Gazetteer of the Lahore District 1893-1894* (Lahore: Panjab Government, 1894), 23, 33.
7   Michael Howard: "The Dimensions of Strategy" in *War*, ed. Lawrence Freedman (New York: Oxford University Press, 1994), 199.
8   Cited in JS Grewal, *WH McLeod and Sikh Studies*, Journal of Punjab Studies, 17 (2010): 1-2, 132; the view of the 'heroic century' was initially popularized by such writers as Gopal Singh, Teja Singh, Ganda Singh and even JD Cunningham in reference to the Sikh struggle against their regimes in the 18th century.
9   Lepel Griffin, *Ranjit Singh* (Oxford: Clarendon Press, 1892), 70-71.
10 Misl or misal: Persian for 'similitude' or 'equal'; created by a gurmatta (synod) by the Sarbat Khalsa (general assembly of Sikhs) on Vaisakhi 1748 at Akal Takht (Amritsar) when various Sikh groups were organized into twelve misls for better coordination, command and control; came to represent sovereign states of the Sikh Confederacy, commonwealth or 'aristocratic republic' that foreran the Sikh empire. The Shaheed misl was headed by Deep Singh.
11 Tony Jacques, *Dictionary of Battles and* Sieges (Westport: Greenwood, 2007), 400; Trilok Singh, *Amar Shaheed Baba Deep Singh* (Amritsar: Chattar Singh Jeevan Singh, 2015), 65-70; Mehnga Singh Kalsi, *Sirlath Shaheed Baba Deep Singh* (Chandigarh: Unistar Books, 2015), 84-85.
12 Khushwant Singh, *The History of the Sikhs* Vol. I (Delhi: Oxford University Press, 1999), 138.
13 Gyani Gyan Singh, "Baba Deep Singh Shaheed ji di katha: Utraradh Bisram 50", *Panth Prakash II*, stanza 28.
14 Khushwant Singh, *History*, I: 139-140; HR Gupta, *History of the Sikhs* Vol. II (New Delhi: Munshiram Manohar Lal, 2007), 130-135; Tony Jacques, *Dictionary*, 400.
15 Tahmas Khan Miskin, *Tahmas Nama*, Abridged and translated by P. Setu Madhav Rao (Bombay: Popular Prakashan, 1967).
16 *Ibid.*, p. 61, Miskin notes only the month, November 1757, but the date is correctly recorded as 11 November 1757 in Tony Jacques' *Dictionary*, 400.
17 Ratan Singh Bhangu, *Sri Guru Panth Parkash*, 2 Vols., translated by Kulwant Singh (Chandigarh: Institute of Sikh Studies, 2006).

18 Gyani Gyan Singh, *Sri Guru Panth Parkash di Prasravna*, (Amritsar: Gyani Kirpal Singh, 1977); Gyani Gyan Singh, *Twarikh Guru Khalsa*, 2 Vols., 3rd ed, (Amritsar: Bhai Chatter Singh–Jeevan Singh, 2016).
19 A humorous tale about Deep Singh and Banda Bahadur (Sakhi 46), possibly in jest about Deep Singh being afflicted by toothache and Banda Bahadur effecting a miraculous cure; Deep Singh passes muster above all else with the tenth Guru (Sakhi 79) to be awarded the title 'Shaheed' ("Sakhi Shaheedon Singhon ki", I: 470-477); Nawab Kapur Singh founds five deras (dwelling places) in Amritsar (1734) the first of which is headed by Deep Singh with the title 'Shaheed' (Sakhi 90 – "Kapur Singh Nawabi Bhai", II: 84-93). This is definitive testimony coming from Bhangu who had access to authentic history of the period from his illustrious grandfathers: Mehtab Singh Mirankot (paternal) and Sham Singh Karorsinghia (maternal), both contemporaries of Deep Singh. See Bhangu, *Panth Prakash*, Vol. 2 Sakhi 97 for Mehtab Singh and Sukha Singh, Sakhi 110 for Mehtab Singh, and Sakhi 160 for Shyam Singh. Several writers accept the view that Deep Singh's title was awarded before his martyrdom and record his name as Deep Singh Shaheed with the founding of the Budha and Taruna Dal in 1734. See Gopal Singh, *A History of the Sikh People 1469-1988* (New Delhi: Allied Publishers, 1979), f.n. 366-367. Deep Singh finds mention yet again when Ala Singh of Patiala solicits the assistance of the Khalsa against Maler Pathans at Barnala and, after the military victory, Deep Singh leads the thanksgiving prayer (Sakhi 168) "Aur Sakhi Malwae ki turi", II: 770-784.
20 Sukhdyal Singh, *Punjab da Itihas* (Patiala: Panjabi University, 2012), viii.
21 Khushwant Singh, *History*, I: f.n. 27, 113
22 According to them, Dall Singh, the eldest, had no children of his own; these descendants are the progeny of his four brothers.
23 These continue to enjoy a rich oral tradition in the Punjab, usually rendered by dhadhis; this highly stylized genre was founded in the 17th century by the sixth pontificate, Guru Hargobind, and never fails to rouse and inspire.
24 English poetry relies on qualitative meter—stressed (accented)

syllables coming at regular intervals, interspersed with unstressed ones. Punjabi poetry uses a quantitative meter, instead, based on syllabic weight or length—Laghu (short vowel) and Guru (long vowel).

25 John Keegan, *The Face of Battle* (London: Pimlico, 1976), 78.
26 The author personally verified this information with the Tirth Purohit, Kirpa Ram Prabhakar at Haridwar. Although the original custodian has passed away, the genealogy records continue to be held in his name, the office now being managed by his great-nephews.
27 Gyani Gyan Singh (1890) records it variously as 'Deep Singh' or 'Baba Deep Singh Shaheed', 'Shaheed Deep Singh'. Writing at the turn of the 20th century, Gyani Thakur Singh is the first writer to use the honorific, 'Baba,' consistently and thereafter it seems to have stuck.
28 Harjinder Singh Dilgeer, *Sikh Twarikh* (Amritsar: Sikh University Press, 2008), II: 536
29 Indu Banga, "Historical Context of Baba Deep Singh" in compendium of papers presented at *Baba Deep Singh: Jeevan te Yogdaan* National Seminar (Amritsar: Guru Nanak Dev University, 2009), 7.
30 Khushwant Singh, *History*, I: 140 fn 21.
31 Gurdeep Singh Kanwal, *Jeevan Baba Deep Singh ji Shaheed* (Amritsar Jaspal Printing Press), 5.

1. Birth and Belonging

1 Cited in Raijasbir Singh, *Jeevan Baba Deep Singh Shaheed* (Amritsar: Chattar Singh Jeevan Singh, 2003), 150.
2 Kanwal, *Deep Singh*, 15.
3 As recorded in the Shiromani Gurdwara Parbandhak Committee (SGPC) annual calendar.
4 For a summary, see Raijasbir Singh, *Deep Singh*, 337: Gyani Thakur Singh was the first historian to document the birth year as 1739 *Vikram Samvat* (1682 CE) in his *Gurdware Darshan* (1924), 573; this was adopted subsequently by Sohan Singh Ghukewalia (refer his "Baba Deep Singh Shaheed" cited in Raijasbir Singh, *Deep Singh*, 146; and Buta Singh, "Prasang Baba Deep Singh" in *ibid*, 317.

5   Harpal Singh Pannu, "Shaheed Baba Deep Singh ji" in compendium of papers presented at *Baba Deep Singh: Jeevan te Yogdaan* National Seminar (Amritsar: Guru Nanak Dev University, 2009), 68-74.
6   Michael Axworthy, *The Sword of Persia: Nader Shah, from Tribal Warrior to Conquering Tyrant* (New York: I.B. Tauris, 2006).
7   Sumant Dhamija, *Jassa Singh Ahluwalia 1718-1783* (Delhi: Social Science Press, 2011), 3-4; Raijasbir Singh, *Deep Singh*, 22.
8   Teja Singh and Ganda Singh, *Short History of the Sikhs* (Bombay: Orient Longman, 1950), 14; also cited in Bhagat Singh, *A History of the Sikh Misals* (Patiala: Punjabi University, 1993), 6.
9   Catherine Ella Blanshard and Cynthia Talbot, *India before Europe* (New York: Cambridge University Press, 2006), 269: Persian-wheels were widely used in the regions of Lahore, Dipalpur, and Sirhind because of sufficient and easily procurable ground-water supplies: see Pashaura Singh, "Reconsidering the Sacrifice of Guru Arjan" edited by *Gibb Schreffler, Journal of Panjab Studies*, Vol. 18, 2011, 57, http://www.global.ucsb.edu/punjab/sites/secure.lsit.ucsb.edu.gisp.d7_sp/files/sitefiles/journals/volume18/11_InResponse.pdf
10 Abu'l Fazal, *Ain-i-Akbari*, Vol. 2, translated by Colonel Henry Sullivan Jarrett (Calcutta: The Asiatic Society of Bengal, 1891), 316.
11 Irfan Habib, *Economic History of Medieval India 1200-1500* (Pearson Education, 2011), 53.
12 Sarah FD Ansari, *Sufi Saints and State Power: The Pirs of Sind, 1843-1947* (New York: Cambridge University Press, 1992), 27.
13 These rivers further sub-divide the region into somewhat distinctive geo-cultural units. The area southeast of the Sutlej is the Malwa, where the erstwhile cis-Sutlej states flourished; the plains north of this, between the Beas and Sutlej is the Jalandhar or Bist Doab (coined from the first syllables of the two rivers); to its north lies the Majha, the interfluvial tract between the rivers Beas and Ravi (or 'Bari Doab', a term coined by Akbar from the first syllables in Persian of the two rivers), also referred to by historians as the 'Sikh tract' because of its having been centre-stage in the Sikh struggle and eventual sovereignty in the 17-18th centuries; the Rechna Doab, between the Ravi and Chenab, and Jech Doab, between Jhelum and Chenab, are also sometimes considered to be part of Majha.

14 Gyani Gyan Singh records Baba Deep Singh as a Sandhu from Dakoha (near Jalandhar) in *Guru Panth Prakash Part II* (1867) but corrects it to 'Pahuwind' in *Twarikh Guru Khalsa*, Vol. 2, 261.
15 Kahn Singh Nabha, *Guru Shabad Ratnakar Mahan Kosh* (Patiala: Languages Department of Punjab, 1930), 58, http://old.sgpc.net/CDN/Mahankosh.pdf, accessed on 20 April 2020.
16 Raijasbir Singh, *Deep Singh*, 7, 337.
17 Harjinder Singh Dilgeer, *Sikh Twarikh*, Vol. II (Amritsar: Sikh University Press, 2008), 479.
18 Although Pahuwind has a population predominantly of Sandhu jat zamindars, Baba Deep Singh is listed among its 'Khaira Jat Zamindars' who reside mostly in its Western part and number approximately 35 families as against 150 Sandhu families; they hold a fourth of the 1587 village acreage. Sometime in the early 1800s, many Khaira families re-settled on a land grant (jagir) awarded, probably, by Maharaja Ranjit Singh near Patti, a village that later came to be known as 'Shaheed'. Kahn Singh Nabha records Baba Deep Singh's gotra as Khaira although several writers before and after him document it as Sandhu including Gyani Gyan Singh, *Sri Guru Panth Prakash*, 5: 2546; Gyani Thakur Singh, *Sri Gurdware Darshan* (Amritsar: Jeevan Singh Chatter Singh, 2012), 379, and Sohan Singh Ghukewalia, *Baba Deep Singh Shaheed* (Amritsar: Jeevan Singh Chatter Singh), 4.
19 After cremation of the mortal remains, the ashes would be immersed in the Ganges at Haridwar under the auspices of the Tirth Purohit (family priest). It was his traditional responsibility to maintain a record of family deaths and visits, and these records go back several centuries. However, this tradition subsequently underwent a change; most Sikhs now prefer to immerse the ashes in River Sutlej at Patal Puri, a gurdwara in Rupnagar district where the sixth preceptor (Guru Hargobind) was cremated and the ashes of the seventh and eighth preceptors immersed, marking a change in tradition.
20 See Mohinder Murthy in Raijasbir Singh, *Deep Singh*, 252; Simarjit Singh, "Baba Deep Singh nal sanmadit itihasik sthan" in compendium of papers presented at *Baba Deep Singh Jeevan te Yogdaan* National

Seminar (Amritsar: Guru Nanak Dev University, 2009), 119-120; he cites "Malwa Sikh Itihas" by Bhai Visakha Singh and Hoshiar Singh Dulhe from their book *Jattan di gotaan da itihasik verva*.

21 Harjinder Singh Dilgeer, *Guru de Sher*, (Amritsar: Jeevan Singh Chattar Singh, 2011), 406; also cited in Raijasbir Singh, *Deep Singh*, 131; Mehnga Singh Kalsi, *Sirlath Shaheed Baba Deep Singh* (Chandigarh: Unistar Books, 2015), 107; Kalsi records Deep Singh as being one of four brothers (Bhag Singh is the additional one and the youngest).

22 Kalsi, *Baba Deep Singh*, 38.

23 The author personally verified this information in the genealogy register at Haridwar, recorded in 1785 by Dasondha Singh (highlighted in the family tree in Table 1). Ardaman Singh Jhubal, "Baba Deep Singh and Dam Dami Taksal" in compendium of papers presented at *Baba Deep Singh: Jeevan te Yogdaan* National Seminar (Amritsar: Guru Nanak Dev University, 2009), 161-170. 162: Jhubal says that Deep Singh returned to Pahuwind in 1702, married, and rejoined the Guru only in 1706 but this is nowhere corroborated.

24 Kanwal notes Deep Singh's chacha (father's younger brother) also being baptized together with the family, although the name Naudh Singh, differs from the genealogy record; see Kanwal, *Baba Deep Singh*, 19; Tirlok Singh notes that the group included Deepa's extended family, father's younger brother and his family; see his *Deep Singh*, 31.

25 According to Buta Singh, the family converted in the time of Guru Teg Bahadur; see his "Prasang Baba Deep Singh Shaheed" in Raijasbur Singh, *Deep Singh*, 325. According to Gupta, eventually all Majha jats had converted to a man: refer Gupta, *History of the Sikhs*, II: 200.

26 Gupta, *History of the Sikhs*, IV: 15-16.

27 Dhamija, *Jassa Singh Ahluwalia*, 12-13.

28 Pashaura Singh, "Revisiting the Evolution of the Sikh Community" (Journal of Punjab Studies, Vol. 17: 2010), 57-58.

29 WH McLeod, *The A to Z of Sikhism* (Maryland: Scarecrow Press, 2009), 20-21.

30 Michael Barnes, *Interreligious learning: dialogue, spirituality, and the*

Christian imagination (Cambridge: Cambridge University Press, 2012), 245-246.

31 دو عالم منور ز انوار او
همه تشنۀ فیضِ دیدار او

Do aalam munnavar ze anvaare oo. Hamaa tishnaay-e-faiz-edeedaar-e-oo.
ਉਸ ਦੇ ਨੂਰ ਨਾਲ ਦੋਵੇਂ ਜਹਾਨ ਰੋਸ਼ਨ ਹਨ, ਉਸ ਦੇ ਦਰਸ਼ਨਾਂ ਦੀ ਮਿਹਰ ਦੇ ਸਾਰੇ ਪਿਆਸੇ ਹਨ ॥85॥
Both the worlds are illuminated with his spiritual (noor) light. All are anxiously wishful of his bliss and kindness.
—Gyani Mahan Singh, *Tasnifat at-i*-Goya (Amritsar: Khalsa Tract Society, 1963), 108.

32 Bhagat Singh, *Sikh Misals*, 10
33 Indubhusan Banerjee cited in Bhagat Singh, *Sikh Misals*, 10.
34 Gupta, *History*, II: 252-253.
35 Angus Maddison, *Development Centre Studies: The World Economy Historical Statistics* (Paris: OECD Publishing, 2003), 259–261.
36 Will Durant, *The Story of Civilisation*, Vol. 1 (New York: Simon and Schuster, 1935), 475.
37 Sukhdayal Singh, *Punjab da Itihas* (Patiala: Panjabi University, 2012), 263.
38 Bhai Jetha was a devoted Sikh who successively attended upon Guru Arjan and Guru Hargobind, and was one of five Sikhs who accompanied Guru Arjan on his last journey to Lahore where he was martyred in 1606; his four companions included Bidhi Chand. Bhai Jetha attended on Guru Hargobind during his detention in the Gwalior Fort and later, took part in the Guru's battles against imperial troops. He fell fighting at Mehraj on 16 December 1634.
39 Initially given to banditry, Bidhi Chand turned a new leaf when he came in contact with Guru Arjan. He later served as one of Guru Hargobind's military commanders and distinguished himself several times in battle. His best-known exploit was the recovery of two highly prized horses, Dilbagh and Gulbagh, from Mughal stables in the Lahore Fort, employing remarkable guile and resourcefulness along with exceptional daring.

40 Raijasbir Singh, *Deep Singh*, 24.
41 *Ibid*, p. 24.
42 Although Guru Nanak is believed to have built the first gurdwara sometime in 1521-22 in Kartarpur, its details are not known, and in any case, the concept was generalized much later. Until the time of Guru Arjan Dev, the place of Sikh religious activities was known as *Dharamsala*, simply a 'place of faith'. It is only after the Guru Granth Sahib began to be replicated en masse that the modern concept of the gurdwara came to be formalized. Until then, for very long, the Sikh place of congregational worship displayed weapons in lieu of scriptures. It is unlikely if any kind of central place for Sikh congregational worship did exist in Pahuwind during Deepa's infancy, particularly since subaltern communities then were an oppressed lot, with limited freedom of worship. The few that did exist were very often the target of Mughal fury whenever the regime chose to vent their wrath in response to insurrections. Nonetheless, there must have been several families akin to that of Bhagtu's that practiced the Sikh faith, even if they were cautious enough not to profess it openly. It is equally probable that religious teachers (granthis) schooled in Sikh scriptures could be found in most villages for imparting rudimentary education to children as an onerous obligation, if not for a small consideration payable in kind.
43 KS Chawla, *Jivan Baba Deep Singh ji Shaheed* (Amritsar: Khalsa Brothers), 14-15.
44 Khushwant Singh, "Who are the Sikhs," Interview by BBC, 1997, https://www.youtube.com/watch?v=GykzdOXmzG0, accessed on 8 November 2018.
45 'Water stirred with steel' refers to the Sikh baptism ceremony wherein a double-edged steel dagger is used to stir sugar candies (patasa) in water to the recitation of scriptures.

2. At the Feet of the Master

1 'I came into the world charged with a duty to uphold the Right in every place,
   And to destroy sin and evil.

> The only reason I took birth was to see that righteousness may flourish,
> that the Good may live, and tyrants be extirpated.'
> —Guru Gobind Singh, *Bachitter Natak*, Chapter 6, *Dasm Granth*.

2. HR Gupta, *History of the Sikhs*, II: 253-254.
3. Ghukewalia, "Prasang Baba Deep Singh" in Raijasbir Singh, *Deep Singh*, 151; *The Hola Mohalla Festival*, SikhChic.com, available at http://sikhchic.com/article-detail.php?id=119&cat=5
4. Trilok Singh, *Amar Shaheed Baba Deep Singh* (Amritsar: Chattar Singh Jeevan Singh, 2015), 30; it is still not uncommon for Hindu and Sikh pilgrims to walk an entire pilgrimage out of devotion.
5. Ghukewalia records it as '10-15 days': refer "Prasang Baba Deep Singh" in Raijasbir Singh, *Deep Singh*, 153; according to Chawla, the period stretched to three months-and-a-half: refer his *Deep Singh*, 16; but this is unlikely.
6. Raijasbir Singh, *Deep Singh*, 22.
7. Mehnga Singh Kalsi, *Sirlath Shaheed Baba Deep Singh* (Chandigarh: Unistar Books, 2015), 39-40.
8. Gyani Thakar Singh cited in Balkar Singh, "Sikh smriti vich Baba Deep Singh di than" in compendium of papers presented at *Baba Deep Singh: Jeevan te Yogdaan* National Seminar (Amritsar: Guru Nanak Dev University, 2009), 52.
9. Buta Singh, "Prasang Baba Deep Singh Shaheed" in Raijasbir Singh, *Deep Singh*, 323; Ghukewalia, "Prasang Bab Deep Singh" in Raijasbir Singh, *Deep Singh*, 153-154.
10. Buta Singh, "Prasang Baba Deep Singh Shaheed," in Raijasbir Singh, *Deep Singh*, 324.
11. Chawla, *Deep Singh*, 18.
12. *Ibid.*, p. 19.
13. ਸ਼ਕਿਾਰ ਵੇਲੇ ਨਾਲ ਲਜਿਾਂਦੇ । ਹਰ ਪ੍ਰਕਾਰ ਦੀ ਸੇਵਾ ਵਿਚ ਲੱਗੇ ਰਹਿੰਦੇ ।
    Shikar vele nal lijande. Har prakar di sewa vich lage rahnde
    He'd hunt with them and perform multifarious service.
    —Gyani Thakar Singh cited in Balkar Singh, "Sikh smriti," 52; also, Jhabal, "Deep Singh," 162; and Chawla, *Deep Singh*, 19; Aulakh, *Illustrated Stories*, 10-11.

14 Kulwant Singh Choudhary, *Gurdwara Sri Paonta Sahib* (Paonta Sahib: Prabandhak Committee Gurdwara Sri Paonta Sahib, 2015), 10; Interestingly, there is also a contemporary account of a soldier of 17th Battalion, the Sikh Regiment, killing a tiger with fixed bayonet in 1954 near Shivpuri in the jungles of Madhya Pradesh. The slightly bent bayonet along with the stuffed tiger skin and press clippings still adorn the officers' mess of the battalion thereafter aptly christened '17 Sikh The Tiger': 'Shatrujeet', Facebook, https://www.facebook.com/shatrujeet009/posts/17-sikh-the-tiger-battalionthe-year-was-1954-17-sikh-was-located-at-agra-and-com/786048108235393/

15 Most writers suggest a stay of 'several years': Ghukewalia, "Prasang Baba Deep Singh Shaheed," in Raijasbir Singh, *Deep Singh*, 155; Buta Singh, "Prasang Baba Deep Singh Shaheed," in Raijasbir Singh, *Deep Singh*, 325; according to Chawla, his parents came and stayed a month-and-half at Anandpur and then requested the Guru for Deep Singh's return: refer his *Deep Singh*, 20-21.

16 If indeed that was the purpose of his return, his marriage should have eventually taken place at any subsequent opportunity, but never did.

17 Jogeshwar Singh, "Sikh Concept of Dharam Yudh and Baba Deep Singh" in compendium of papers presented at *Baba Deep Singh: Jeevan te Yogdaan* National Seminar (Amritsar: Guru Nanak Dev University, 2009), 138; his claim of Deep Singh's marriage and raising a family is not substantiated in Deep Singh's genealogy record.

18 Aulakh, *Illustrated Stories*, 12.

19 Chawla, *Deep Singh*, 21.

20 Gyani Thakur Singh cited in Raijasbir Singh, *Deep Singh*, 135; also, Chawla, *Deep Singh*, 22-23, 33.

21 Sukhdyal Singh, *Punjab da Itihas*, (Patiala: Panjabi University, 2012), 219, 220-224, 239. Accordingly, this work accepts the Battle of Chamkaur on 7 December 1705 and the Battle of Muktsar on 14-15 January 1706. The date of evacuation of Anandpur is corroborated by Dilgeer, *Sikh Twarikh*, I: 288-289; and Karamjit Malhotra, *The Eighteenth Century in Sikh History* (New Delhi: OUP, 2016), 24. Dilgeer records the evacuation and subsequent move to Chamkaur and Machhiwara differently; see his *Sikh Twarikh*, 1: 288-294.

22 Sukhdyal Singh, *Itihas*, 223-224.
23 Gurdwara Lohgarh Sahib, *Sankhep Itihas (Brief History)*, 8; also, Das Visakha Singh et al, *Itihas*, 1: 277-278, 374-375.
24 During the extended siege of the Anandpur citadel in 1704, these 40 devotees had opted to leave but the Guru insisted that they affix their thumb impressions on the bedawa (disclaimer) as proof that they had disavowed their Guru.
25 See Sukhdyal Singh, *Itihas*, 219-225, for a detailed account of the Guru's journey after evacuating Anandpur until the Battle of Muktsar.
26 Sukhdayal Singh, *Itihas*, 233.
27 Sukhbir Singh Kapoor and Mohinder Kaur Kapoor, *Dasm Granth: An Introductory Study* (New Delhi: Hemkunt, 2009), 20; 'Ranjha' is the male protagonist in *Heer Ranjha*, one of several popular tragic romances of the Punjab.

3. Dam Dama Sahib: Guru Ki Kanshi

1 'Kanshi' is another name for 'Varanasi', the holiest shrine for Hindus and Jains. Guru Gobind Singh envisioned Dam Dama Sahib as a similar central spiritual hub for Sikhism.
2 KS Bajwa, "Takhat Sri Dam Dama Sahib: Establishment and Role in Sikh History", *Sikh Formations Religion, Culture, Theory* 10, Issue 3, 2014, p. 3, https://religiondocbox.com/Hinduism/69730310Takhat-sri-dam-dama-sahib-establishment-and-role-in-sikh-history. html
3 Sarup Singh Koshish, *Guru Diyan Sakhiyan*, Sakhi 89 (Patiala: Panjabi University, 1986), 159; Ganda Singh, *Sri Guru Shobha* (Patiala: Panjab University, 1967), 57 cited in Sukhdyal Singh, *Itihas*, 233.
4 The author obtained this information from the descendants of Bhai Dall Singh at Dam Dama Sahib, Talwandi Sabo.
5 Sukhdyal Singh, *Itihas*, 234; also see Gyani Balwant Singh Kotha Guru, *Sri Dam Dama Guru ki Kanshi* (Bhatinda: Gyani Kaur Singh, 2017), 7, 18-19.
6 Bajwa, "Dam Dama Sahib", 4.
7 *Ibid*, p. 4.
8 *Ibid*, fn 50, 13.
9 Cited in *Gurbilas Patshai Dasvin* in Kotha Guru, *Dam Dama Sahib*, 8.

10 Christopher Shackle, Gurharpal Singh and Arvind-Pal Mandair (Eds.), *Sikh Religion, Culture and Ethnicity* (London: Routledge, 2013), 11–12, 17–19; Bhai Banno was charged by Guru Arjan to proceed to Lahore to have the Adi Granth bound; he chose of his own accord to prepare a copy en route with some alterations, including a hymn by Mira Bai, later installed at his home in Khara Mangat. This version is also referred to as 'Bhai Banno vali Pothi'.

11 Dilgeer, *Guru de Sher*, 316; Gurinder Singh Mann, *The Making of Sikh Scripture* (New York: Oxford University Press, 2001), 16, 21; Mann states that the Guru had used 'another manuscript' to prepare the Adi Granth when denied the Kartarpuri Pothi.

12 Mann, *Sikh Scripture*, 63, 83; Bajwa, "Dam Dama Sahib", 6, fn 25.

13 Aulakh suggests that the Guru dictated from 'other sources'; refer his *Illustrated Stories*, 14.

14 Ghukewalia in Raijasbir Singh, *Deep Singh*, 159.

15 Kotha Guru, *Dam Dama Sahib*, 25.

16 Aulakh, *Illustrated Stories*, 15.

17 Kotha Guru, *Dam Dama Sahib*, 33.

18 Sukhdyal Singh, *Itihas*, 238-239.

19 Bajwa, "Dam Dama Sahib", 5.

20 Kotha Guru, *Dam Dama Sahib*, 30-32; Raja Jai Singh was but 11 years, two months, when he succeeded his father, Raja Vishan (Bishan) Singh, who passed away on 1 January 1700 at Kohat while in the service of the Mughals. After Aurangzeb's death, in the battle for succession that erupted on 8 Jun 1708 among his sons, Raja Jai Singh aligned with Azam Shah, who lost; Guru Gobind Singh had supported Bahadur Shah, who was victorious and succeeded to the throne. Raja Ajit Singh headed the Jodhpur state at the time and there was no 'Raja Bishen Singh' among the Jodhpur royals.

21 Kotha Guru, *Dam Dama Sahib*, 34-35. This narrative needs more research.

22 *Ibid*, 35; he cites Kahn Singh Nabha, *Mahankosh*, 381, 503.

23 *Ibid*., p. 26.

24 The author obtained this information from the descendants of Bhai Dall Singh at Talwandi Sabo.

25 ਟੋਡੀ ਮਹਲਾ ੫
॥ ਸਤਿਗੁਰ ਆਇਓ ਸਰਣਿ ਤੁਹਾਰੀ ॥
ਮਿਲੈ ਸੂਖੁ ਨਾਮੁ ਹਰਿ ਸੋਭਾ ਚਿੰਤਾ ਲਾਹਿ ਹਮਾਰੀ ॥੧॥ ਰਹਾਉ ॥
—Guru Arjan Dev, *SGGS*, 713
Toḍī mėhlā 5.
Saṯgur ā∘i∘o saraṇ ṯuhārī.
Milai sūkẖ nām har sobẖā cẖinṯā lāhi hamārī. ॥1॥ rahā∘o.
Todee, Fifth Mehl:
O True Guru, I have come to Your Sanctuary.
Grant me the peace and glory of the Lord's Name, and remove my anxiety. ॥1॥ Pause ॥
—This information was shared by Baba Banta Singh, Kathavachak (exegete), during Deep Singh's birth anniversary celebrations on 27 January 2022 at Pahuwind.

26 Kotha Guru, *Dam Dama Sahib*, 34-35; Bajwa, "Dam Dama Sahib", 8-9.

27 Simarjit Singh, "Baba Deep Singh ji nal sambandit itihasik sthan," 121.

28 Bajwa, "Dam Dama Sahib", 11-12.

29 ਕਹਯੋ ਸੁ ਆਨੰਦ ਨਗਰ ਸਮਾਣਾ,
ਇਹ ਦਮਦਮਾ ਆਦਿਕ ਪ੍ਯਾ ਪਰਾਨਾ ।
Kahyo Su Anand Nagar Samana
Yeh Damdama aadik Prya Parana.
In *Damdama*, all joy is rife;
Dearer to me than my own life
—Bawa Sumer Singh cited in Bajwa, "Dam Dama Sahib," 11.

30 Sukhdyal Singh, *Itihas*, 238.
31 Bajwa, "Dam Dama Sahib", 10.
32 *Ibid.*, p. 12.
33 Nabha and Bhangu cited in Raijasbir Singh, *Deep Singh,* 52; Mahtab Singh Mirankot is a much-revered Sikh hero and martyr who, along with his companion, Sukha Singh of Mari Kamboh, in a daring feat, killed Massa Rangar in August 1740 for desecrating Harmandir Sahib. Sham Singh Kororia was a member of the Kororsinghia misl that rose to prominence in the mid-18th century; read more at http://www.sikh-history.com/sikhhist/warriors/mahtab.html.

34 Gupta, *History of the Sikhs*, II: 137.
35 Gopal Singh, *A History of the Sikh People 1469-1988* (New Delhi: Allied Publishers, 1979), 268; Balkar Singh, "Sikh Smriti vich Baba Deep Singh ji di than", in compendium of papers presented at *Baba Deep Singh: Jeevan te Yogdaan* National Seminar (Amritsar: Guru Nanak Dev University, 2009), 52; Pannu, "Shaheed Baba Deep Singh ji," 71.
36 "Jatha Shaheedan," http://www.jathashaheedan.com/history.php, accessed on 16 August 2020.
37 Kanwal, *Baba Deep Singh*, 38-39; https://sikhexpo.com/blogs/news/baba-deep-singh-ji-story, accessed on 16 November 2020.
38 Guru Gobind Singh, *Shabad Hazare*, 6, https://www.searchgurbani.com/dasam-granth/shabad/10070/line/1, accessed on 8 December 2019.
39 Gopal Singh, *History*, fn 263.
40 ਹੱਕ ਰਾ ਗੰਜੂਰ ਗੁਰੂ ਗੋਬਿੰਦ ਸਿੰਘ
ਜੁਮਲਾ ਫੈਜ਼ਿ ਨੂਰ ਗੁਰੂ ਗੋਬਿੰਦ ਸਿੰਘ ॥ ੧੦੬ ॥
ਹੱਕ ਹੱਕ ਆਗਾਹ ਗੁਰੂ ਗੋਬਿੰਦ ਸਿੰਘ
ਸ਼ਾਹਿ ਸ਼ਹਨਸ਼ਾਹ ਗੁਰੂ ਗੋਬਿੰਦ ਸਿੰਘ ॥ ੧੦੭ ॥
ਬਰ ਦੋ ਆਲਮ ਸ਼ਾਹ ਗੁਰੂ ਗੋਬਿੰਦ ਸਿੰਘ
ਖ਼ਸਮ ਰਾ ਜਾਂ-ਕਾਹ ਗੁਰੂ ਗੋਬਿੰਦ ਸਿੰਘ ॥ ੧੦੮ ॥
ਫ਼ਾਇਜ਼ੁਲ ਅਨਵਾਰ ਗੁਰੂ ਗੋਬਿੰਦ ਸਿੰਘ
ਕਾਸ਼ਫ਼ੁਲ ਅਸਰਾਰ ਗੁਰੂ ਗੋਬਿੰਦ ਸਿੰਘ ॥ ੧੦੯ ॥
Haka rā gaaṅazūra gurū gobiaṅada siaṅagha
Jumalā faaizi nūra gurū gobiaṅada siaṅagha |106|
Haxka haxka aāgāha gurū gobiaṅada siaṅagha
Shāhi shahanashāha gurū gobiaṅada siaṅagha |107|
Bara do aālama shāha gurū goubiaṅada siaṅagha
Khhasama rā jāṅ-kāha gurū gobiaṅada siaṅagha |108|
Faāeizula anavāra gurū gobiaṅada siaṅagha
Kāshafaula asarāra gurū gobiaṅada siaṅatha |109|
Guru Gobind Singh is the repository of truth
Guru Gobind Singh is the grace of brilliance. |106|
Guru Gobind Singh was the truth for the connoisseurs of truth,
Guru Gobind Singh was the king of kings. |107|
Guru Gobind Singh was the king of both worlds,

And, Guru Gobind Singh was the conqueror of enemy-lives. |108|
Guru Gobind Singh is the bestower of divine radiance.
Guru Gobind Singh is the Revealer of divine mysteries. |109|
—In Bhai Nand Lal, *Ganjnama*, lines 106-109,
https://www.searchgurbani.com/bhai-nand-lal/ganjnama

41 Kotha Guru, *Dam Dama Sahib*, 71; Gurinder Singh Mann, *The Granth of Guru Gobind Singh* (New Delhi: Oxford University Press, 2015), 34-35; Deep Singh compiled and calligraphed a copy of the Dasm Granth in 1747 but this is not available; only a gutka (small prayer book) is now at Dam Dama Sahib with all 'Dasm Granth bani' except the Shastranammala. According to oral tradition, this birh and a recension of the Adi Granth were personal manuscripts of Deep Singh that he carried with him on the move as safari birhs (portable versions).
42 Kotha Guru, *Dam Dama Sahib*, 55.
43 Mann, *The Granth*, 2.
44 *Ibid.*, 26.
45 *Ibid.*, 32; This version is with a family in Delhi,
46 Loehlin cited in Mann, *The Granth*, 205
47 Bajwa, "Dam Dama Sahib", 8.
48 Kotha Guru, *Dam Dama Sahib*, 57.
49 *Ibid*, 57-58.
50 This information was shared with the author by the current generation of Bhai Dall's family.
51 Gopal Singh, *History*, 322 and fn.

4. Founding a Seminary

1 Daura Sakhi cited in Kotha Guru, *Dam Dama Sahib*, 69.
2 Cited in *ibid*, 69-70.
3 *Ibid*, 69.
4 Bajwa, "Dam Dama Sahib", 12; Kotha Guru, *Dam Dama Sahib*, 69.
5 Gyani Gyan Singh cited in Bhagat Singh, *Misals*, 242.
6 Bajwa, "Dam Dama Sahib", 12-13.
7 Sukhdyal Singh, *Itihas*, 239-247.
8 *Ibid*, 243-247.
9 Gupta, *History of the Sikhs*, I: 319-320.

10 Sukhdyal Singh, *Itihas*, 248-249.
11 James Browne, "History of the Sikhs", in *Early European Accounts of the Sikhs*, edited by Ganda Singh, Indian Studies, Past and Present (Calcutta: Indian Studies, Past and Present, 1962), fn 25, 28.
12 Gopal Singh, *History*, 320-322; Ganda Singh, *Life of Banda Singh Bahadur*, 4th ed. (Punjabi University: Patiala, 2016), 17; Aulakh, *Illustrated Stories*, 18.
13 Dilgeer, *Sikh Twarikh*, II: 346; according to Dilgeer, the Guru met Banda briefly at Dehra Dun in February 1695 while on a visit to the area, Banda was then a wandering ascetic. Gupta is of the view that Banda belonged to Sirmaur, was an avid huntsman, and that the Guru had occasion to meet him several times while hunting in the area of Paonta; see Gupta, *History*, II: 3; However, no prior contact between the two has been historically established; see Gopal Singh, *History*, fn. 320.
14 Ganda Singh, *Singh Bahadur*, 160-161.
15 Gokul Chand Narang cited in *Banda Singh Bahadur and Sikh Sovereignty*, edited by Harbans Kaur Sagoo (New Delhi: Deep and Deep, 2001), 94.
16 James Browne, "History of the Sikhs" in *Early European Accounts* by Ganda Singh (ed), 9-42, fn 13, 24.
17 The assassins are named Jamshed Khan and Wasil Beg. The Guru killed Jamshed Khan with his sword while the other assassin was struck down by Sikhs when he tried to flee.
18 Ghukewalia cited in Raijasbir Singh, *Deep Singh*, 161.
19 Khushwant Singh, *History*, I: 101.
20 Ganda Singh, *Banda Singh*, 35-36.
21 Pannu, "Shaheed Baba Deep Singh ji," 71.
22 Khushwant Singh, *History*, I: 101, fn 8; for force levels, see Gupta, *History*, II: 2, 11-12.
23 According to *Akhbarat-e-Darbar-e-Mualla* dated 13 May 1710, the battle began in the morning and lasted until afternoon: see Gupta, *History*, II: 13.
24 DS Saggu, *Battle Tactics and War Manoeuvres of the Sikhs* (Chennai: Notion Press, 2018), 51-57; Ganda Singh, *Banda Singh*, 41-48.
25 Ratan Singh Bhangu, *Sri Guru Panth Parkash*, Vol. 1, Sakhi 40,

Couplet 11, translated by Kulwant Singh (Chandigarh: Institute of Sikh Studies, 2006).
26 Cited in Khushwant Singh, *History*, I: 102.
27 Kamwar Khan cited in Bhagat Singh, *Sikh Misals*, 21.
28 Pannu, "Shaheed Baba Deep Singh ji," 71.
29 Ghukewalia in Raijasbir Singh, *Deep Singh*, 161.
30 Some authors attribute Wazir Khan's death variously to Banda and his commanders, Fateh Singh and Baj Singh; see Saggu, *Battle Tactics*, 55; Gupta, *History*, II: 2, 12-13; Pannu, "Shaheed Baba Deep Singh ji," 71.
31 Gupta, *History*, II: 13.
32 These are the commanders named at the Fateh Burj, Chapper Chiri memorial; Gopal Singh names Baj Singh, Fateh Singh, Karam Singh, Dharam Singh, Sham Singh, and Ali Singh; the last two are known to have joined after abandoning the service of the Nawab of Sirhind; see Gopal Singh, *History*, 340.
33 Aulakh, *Illustrated Stories*, 42.
34 Introductory notes on Gyani Gyan Singh in Raijasbir Singh, *Deep Singh*, 77; Chawla, *Baba Deep Singh*, 61.
35 ਦਿੱਤਾ ਪੰਥ ਰਲ ਬੰਦੇ ਖਿਤਾਬ ਉਸ ਨੂੰ ਬੜੇ ਮਾਨ ਦੇ ਨਾਲ ਵਡਿਆਇਕੇ ਜੀ ।
    ਹੋਇਓ ਜਿੰਦਾ ਸ਼ਹੀਦ ਤੂੰ ਦੀਪ ਸਿੰਘਾ ਇਹ ਆਖਿਆ ਪੰਥ ਸੁਨਾਇਕੇ ਜੀ ।
    Ditta panth rall Bande khitab us nu bade maan nal vadiayike ji
    Hoiyo jinda Shaheed tun Deep Singh ih akhiya panth sunaike ji
    Banda and the *Panth* together conferred this honour hence:
    A living martyr thou shalt be forever now from thence.
    —Ghukewalia cited in Raijasbir Singh, *Deep Singh*, 161.
36 Ghukewalia cited in Raijasbir Singh, *Deep Singh*, 161; Kirpal Singh Badunger, "Shaheed Baba Deep Singh ji: Brahm Gyani" in compendium of papers presented at *Baba Deep Singh: Jeevan te Yogdaan* National Seminar (Amritsar: Guru Nanak Dev University, 2009), 43; Seetal cited in Raijasbir Singh, *Deep Singh*, 54; Das Visakaha Singh et al., *Itihas*, II: 2, 80; Aulakh, *Illustrated Stories*, 19; according to Aulakh, Deep Singh was conferred the title 'Self-respecting Brave Warrior'.
37 Kahn Singh Nabha, *Guru Shabad Ratnakar Mahan Kosh*, (Patiala: Languages Department of Punjab, 1930), 2092, http://old.sgpc.net/CDN/Mahankosh.pdf, accessed on 20 April 2020.

38 ਖਾਲਸਾ ਸੋਇ ਲੜੇ ਹੋਇ ਆਗੈ ॥ (੪੪)
   Khālsā sōi laṛē hōi āgai | (44)
   Khalsa is the one who volunteers to contend in the first rank. (44)
   —Bhai Nand Lal ji, *Tankhahnama*, 106.
39 Bhangu, Episode 79, *Sakhi Shaheedon Singhon ki*, I: 470-477; also Raijasbir Singh, *Deep Singh*, 55-57.
40 Simarjit Singh, "Deep Singh," 122.
41 Conveyed by Pinder Pal Singh, famous Sikh evangelist, in a homily during Deep Singh's birth anniversary celebrations on 26 January 2020 at Pahuwind, Deep Singh's native village; also see Chawla, *Deep Singh*, 63.
42 Chawla, *Deep Singh*, 62-63.
43 Dilgeer, *Sikh Twarikh*, 1: 289.
44 Santokh Singh, *Anandpur di Kahani* (Amritsar: Printwell, 2021), 39-40.
45 With the robust *neem*-based (*Azadirachta indica*) dental hygiene prevalent at the time, such ailments would be improbable in someone in his late 20s. Possibly, the verse relates to somebody else or is, simply, rhyming balderdash.
46 Ghulam Hussein Khan cited in Ganda Singh, *Banda*, 151.
47 Saggu, *Battle Tactics*, 71.
48 Elliot cited in Ganda Singh, *Banda*, 156.
49 Ganda Singh, *Banda*, 157.
50 Saggu, *Battle Tactics*, 72-73.
51 For 'Guru yarvaan' (11th Guru), see Ghukewalia, "Baba Deep Singh Shaheed" in Raijasbir Singh, *Deep Singh*, 162.
52 JS Grewal, "McLeod and Sikh Studies," *Journal of Punjab Studies*, 17 (2010), 1-2, 124.
53 Cited in Ganda Singh, *Early Accounts*, 52.
54 'The order of the Sat-guru [Guru Gobind Singh] was contravened by me, and this is the punishment for it;' cited from the *Mahima Prakash* in Ganda Singh, *Banda*, 151.
55 Paramjit Singh Sidhu, "Baba Deep Singh: Shaheedi Sarup Sancharatmkta" in compendium of papers presented at. *Baba Deep Singh: Jeevan te Yogdaan* National Seminar (Amritsar: Guru Nanak Dev University, 2009), 93; Bhagat Singh, "Martyrdom of Baba

Deep Singh" in *Sikh Struggle and the Misl Period*, eds. Kirpal Singh & Kharak Singh, Vol. 2 (Amritsar: Golden Offset Press, 2013), 111. Gupta along with some historians are of the view that the schism was driven by Mata Sundari who, under pressure from the Mughal government, ordered Banda to retract from his crusade or face excommunication from the Khalsa: see Gupta, *History*, II: 25. This is improbable given that it finds no mention in Banda's own confession at the time of his death.

56 Bhangu, *Panth Parkash*, 230-236; cited in Raijasbir Singh, *Deep Singh*, 11.
57 Dilgeer, *Sikh Twarikh*, II: 456; he mentions the date as 18 October 1723.
58 Gopal Singh, *History*, 359-360: this clash took place after Banda's lifetime, on Diwali 1720. It is likely there was tension all along which precipitated two clashes, one during Banda's lifetime and another afterwards.
59 Dilgeer, *Twarikh*, II: 455-456: according to Dilgeer, there was only one incident, in 1723, precipitated by one Amar Singh, who believed that Banda Bahadur was the 11th Sikh Guru, and that, Amar Singh, was to succeed Banda to the Guruship.
60 Bhagat Singh, *Sikh Misals*, 30: according to Bhagat Singh, Banda had the support of the Khalsa right till the end; even Binod Singh's desertion at Gurdas Nangal stemmed from differences over strategy and tactics; Chawla (*Deep Singh*, 66-67) feels the fault lines appeared much earlier, soon after Chapper Chiri. On reaching Harimandir Sahib, after their sojourn at Anandpur, Banda chose to sit on a chair within the holy sanctum; this was strongly opposed by Deep Singh and many others. Deep Singh castigated him and physically removed him from within the shrine.
61 Balwant Singh Dhillon, *Banda Singh Bahadur* (Amritsar: Singh Brothers, 2016), 67-69.
62 Teja Singh and Ganda Singh, *Short History of the Sikhs* (Bombay: Orient Longman, 1950), 107-108, cited in Bhagat Singh, *Sikh Misals*, 32; Malhotra, *Sikh History*, 19; Rabindra Nath Tagore pays tribute to Banda in his eulogy titled 'Bandi Vir'.
63 Devinder Singh, "Sikh Sangarsh te Baba Deep Singh" in compendium

of papers presented at. *Baba Deep Singh: Jeevan te Yogdaan* National Seminar, 35-41, (Amritsar: Guru Nanak Dev University, 2009), 35.
64 Surinder Kohli, *The Sikh and Sikhism* (New Delhi: Atlantic Publishers & Distributors, 1993), 59.
65 Gopal Singh, *History*, 364.
66 Bhagat Singh, *Sikh Misals*, 436.

5. A Cruel Yoke

1 Bhagat Singh, *Sikh Misals*, 54.
2 *Ibid.*, p. 242
3 Introductory notes on Gyani Gyan Singh in Raijasbir Singh, *Baba Deep Singh*, 77: according to Gyani Gyan Singh, this tallying of the two manuscripts happened over six months in 1760 (*ibid*. 128); this is corroborated by Visakha Singh in his *Itihas* (2: 80) but Deep Singh was martyred in 1757. Besides, it would have been more logical to tally the canon much earlier, before replication.
4 Introductory notes on Gyani Gyan Singh in Raijasbir Singh, *Deep Singh*, 77; also, Bhagat Singh, *Sikh Misals*, 241; the original canon is believed lost in the Greater Holocaust (Vada Ghallughara).
5 Oral tradition suggests that it is currently preserved in a library at Berkeley University, Saudi Arabia, but this is unverified.
6 Kotha Guru, *Dam Dama Sahib*, fn 1, 71; Visakha Singh, *Itihas*, II: 80.
7 Ratan Singh Bhangu, *Sri Guru Panth Parkash*, Vol. 2, Sakhi 136, Couplet 111, translated by Kulwant Singh (Chandigarh: Institute of Sikh Studies, 2006); this suggests there were two manuscripts at Kup: the Dam Dami Bir and another one calligraphed at Amritsar. Also see Raijasbir Singh, *Deep Singh*, 77: according to Gyani Gyan Singh, these were taken to Kabul (*Ibid*. 87), but are now untraced.
8 Gyani Thakur Singh, *Sri Gurdware Darshan*, 576 cited in Raijasbir Singh, *Deep Singh*, 134; Kotha Guru records Deep Singh's compiling of the *Dasm Granth* at Dam Dama Sahib (page 74), and his retaining a personal copy, *Ibid*, 71.
9 Sukhdyal Singh, *Itihas*, 3-4.
10 Kotha Guru, *Dam Dama Sahib*, 74.
11 Mann, *Sikh Scripture*, 38.
12 *Ibid*, 124

13 Visakha Singh, *Itihas*, 1: 397.
14 Kanaihya Lal's *Tareekh-E-Lahore* cited in Bhagat Singh, *Sikh Misals*, 33.
15 Kotha Guru, *Dam Dama Sahib*, 75-76.
16 Badunger, "Shaheed Baba Deep Singh ji: Brahm Gyani," 43; also, Gyani Gyan Singh, "Mukhiye Singhan di Ginti" in *Twarikh Guru Khalsa Pt 2* (Amritsar: Chattar Singh-Jeevan Singh, 2015), 114.
17 Bajwa, "Dam Dama Sahib," 14; Bajwa also cites Karam Singh Historian and Kirpal Singh, *Life of Maharaja Ala Singh of Patiala and his times* (Amritsar: Sikh History Research Department, Khalsa College, 1954), 48-50; Bhangu cited in Raijasbir Singh, *Deep Singh*, 67.
18 Sukhdayal Singh, "Baba Deep Singh ji Shaheed: Jeevan, Sama ate Prapetian," 65.
19 Gupta, *History*, II: 158; Gupta cites Karam Singh to state that this was the first time Ala Singh was baptized and became a 'regular Sikh of Guru Gobind Singh'. Elsewhere, citing Bhangu, Gupta notes that Ala Singh was baptized initially by Nawab Kapur Singh after the same battle; apparently, Kapur Singh was part of this force that came to Ala Singh's assistance. It is likely that Deep Singh baptized Ala Singh in the presence of Kapur Singh. Gupta cites Karam Singh to note a second baptism of Ala Singh by Deep Singh in September 1757 after the Battle of Dharsul (IV: 149). There is no provision for a second or any subsequent baptism in the Sikh code of practice; possibly, this was a token ceremony to honour Deep Singh. Gupta notes a third instance of baptism of Ala Singh by Jassa Singh Ahluwalia in March 1761, apparently, as a stratagem on the part of Ala Singh to pacify the *Dal Khalsa* whom he had displeased by submitting before Abdali after the Third Battle of Panipat (14 January 1761). In effect, Ala Singh never kept any of the outward symbols of the Sikh *maryada* (code) except for a beard which too he trimmed (Gupta, *History*, IV: 28); possibly, for this reason, he is also referred to as Ala *jat* in some accounts: see Qazi Nur Mohammad cited in Saggu, *Battle Tactics*, 202.
20 Bhagat Singh, *Sikh Misals*, 38-39.
21 Dilgeer, *Twarikh*, II: 477.

22 Bhangu, *Sakhi* 90, *Chaupai* 47, 82 (the translation is mine); also Harbans Singh, *The Heritage of the Sikhs* (Calcutta: Asia Publishing House, 1964), 53. And Sikhiwiki, Nawab Kapur Singh, https://www.sikhiwiki.org/index.php/Nawab_Kapur_Singh

23 ਪੰਜ ਭੁਜਗੀਅਨ ਚਰਨੀ ਛੁਹਾਇ ਧਰੋ ਸੀਸ ਮੋਹ ਪਵਤ੍ਰਿ ਕਰਾਇ ।
ਪੰਜ ਭੁਜਗੀਅਨ ਚਰਨ ਬਲ ਪਾਈ . ਸਿੰਘ ਸਸੇ ਹੋਇ ਪ੍ਰਬਤ ਭਏ ਰਾਈ ।੪੭।
Panj bhujagian charni chhuhai. Dharo sees moh pavitre karai.
Panj bhujangian charan payi. Singh saso hoi prbat bhaye rai |47|
He touched the royal robe with the feet of five Singhs,
To make it appropriate to place on his head.
Made holy by touching the feet of five Singhs
Make rabbits to lions and dust to hills instead |47|
—Bhangu, *Panth Prakash*, Vol 2, *Sakhi* 90, *Chaupai* 47, page 82; the translation is mine; Harbans Singh, *The Heritage of the Sikhs* (Calcutta: Asia Publishing House, 1964), 53. https://www.sikhiwiki.org/index.php/Nawab_Kapur_Singh
Also, Gyani Gyan Singh, "Taruna Dal te Budda Dal do naam hone" in *Twarikh Guru Khalsa Pt 2*, 114; and Gyani Gyan Singh, "Panth de Panj jathe hone" in *Twarikh Guru Khalsa Pt 2* ,115.

24 Bhangu, *Panth Parkash*, Vol. 2, Sakhi 90 (translation is mine).
25 Bhangu, *Panth Parkash*, Vol. 2, 50.
26 HS Singha, *Sikh Studies, Book 6* (Delhi: Hemkunt Press, 2005), 37.
27 Gopal Singh, *History*, 367.
28 Gyani Gyan Singh, *Twarikh Guru Khalsa*, Vol 2 (Amritsar: Bhai Chatter Singh – Jeevan Singh, 2016), 115; Bhagat Singh, *Misals*, 242.
29 Gopal Singh, *History*, fn 367; Dilgeer *Sikh Twarikh*, II: 150.
30 Giani Gyan Singh, *Twarikh Guru Khalsa* Vol. 1 (Amritsar: Bhai Chatter Singh—Jeevan Singh, 2016), 116: this happened in 1735, also see Harbans Singh, *The Heritage of the Sikhs* (Calcutta: Asia Publishing House, 1964), 55; Gopal Singh, *History*, 368.
31 Pannu, "Shaheed Baba Deep Singh ji," 72; cavalry was the mainstay of the Khalsa army; also, NK Sinha, *Rise of Sikh Power* (Calcutta: A Mukherjee and Co, 1973), 115-116 cited in Raijasbir Singh, *Deep Singh*, 21.
32 Gopal Singh, *History*, 373-375.
33 Malhotra, *Sikh History*, 38.

34 Gyani Trilok Singh, *Amar Shaheed Baba Deep Singh* (Amritsar: Chattar Singh Jeevan Singh, 2015), 61; Bhagat Singh, "Martyrdom of Baba Deep Singh" in *Sikh Struggle and the Misl Period*, eds. Kirpal Singh & Kharak Singh, Vol. 2 (Amritsar: Golden Offset Press, 2013), 111.
35 Gopal Singh, *History*, 378-380; Dhamija, *Jassa Singh Ahluwalia*, 128-130; BS Nijjar, "Chhota Ghallughara," *The Encyclopedia of Sikhism*, Vol. 1 (Patiala: Punjabi University, 1995), 460–461.

6. The Misl Period

1 Dhamija, *Ahluwalia*, 125; according to Dilgeer (*Twarikh*, II: 492), there were 30 jathas of 100 each; possibly, he meant a 1000 each. One of these was headed by Deep Singh.
2 Gupta, *History*, II: 93.
3 Bhagat Singh, *Sikh Misals*, 385.
4 *Ibid.*, 433, and fn 39 from W. Irvine.
5 George Forster, *A Journey from Bengal to England* Vol. 1 (London: Faulder, 1798), 221.
6 Bhagat Singh, *Sikh Misals*, 433 and fn 38 from Lepel Griffin.
7 Felix Gilbert, "Machiavelli: The Renaissance of the Art of War," in *Makers of Modern Strategy*, ed. Peter Paret (Princeton: Princeton University Press, 1986), 26.
8 BN Goswamy and JS Grewal, *The Mughal and Sikh Rulers and the Vaishnavas of Pindori: A Historical Interpretation of 52 Persian Documents* (Shimla: Indian Institute of Advanced Study, 1969), documents XVIII, XIX, XXIV and XXV 205-11, 227-33.
9 Gyani Gyan Singh, "Singhan ne Paincha nu sodhna" in *Twarikh Guru Khalsa Pt 2*, 140.
10 Bhagat Singh, *Sikh Misals*, 36.
11 Raijasbir Singh, *Deep Singh*, 13; Gopal Singh, *History*, 388; Khushwant Singh, *History*, I: 129-132.
12 Gupta, *History*, II: 106.
13 Gyani Gyan Singh, "Singhan nal vigar te Kot Budhe da janggi" in *Twarikh Guru Khalsa Pt 2*, 151. The author has visited the site of the battle and verified the memorials on ground.
14 Bhagat Singh, *Sikh Misals*, 46; Dilgeer, *Twarikh*, II: 194.
15 Bhagat Singh, *Sikh Misals*, 49

16 *Ibid.*, 40.
17 Khushwant Singh, *Ranjit Singh* (New Delhi: Penguin Books, 2008), 9–14; see Figure 2 for areas under misls in 1780.
18 GC Walker, *Gazetteer of the Lahore District 1893-1894* (Lahore: Panjab Government, 1894), 24.
19 See Bhagat Singh, *Sikh Misals*, 40.
20 Cited in Saggu, *Battle Tactics*, 241.
21 Aulakh, *Illustrated Stories*, 22.
22 Mehnga Singh Kalsi, *Sirlath Shaheed Baba Deep Singh* (Chandigarh: Unistar Books, 2015), 71-73; Bhagat Singh, *Sikh Misals*, 242; Dhamija, *Ahluwalia*, 191; Gopal Singh, *History*, 395.
23 Raijasbir Singh, *Deep Singh*, 77; Miskin, *Tahmas Nama*, 74.
24 Madanjit Kaur, "Natha Singh Shaheed," in *Sikh Struggle and the Misl Period*, eds. Kirpal Singh & Kharak Singh Vol. 2 (Amritsar: Golden Offset Press, 2013), 308-312.
25 Chawla, *Deep Singh*, 98-99.
26 Kotha Guru, *Dam Dama Sahib*, 71, 100; he cites Gyani Gyan Singh (*Gurdham Sangreh*, 260) to record a grant of Rs 50,000 from the *Khalsa Panth* for the construction of the main shrine (*Takth Sahib*), *burj* (tower), water-well, etc: see *ibid.*, fn 1, 59; also see Bajwa, "Dam Dama Sahib," 13. Gyani Gyan Singh lauds Deep Singh for the transformation: *jangal mein mangal* ('forest into paradise'): see stanza 7-8 of *Bisram* 28 in *Panth Prakash Vol II*; George Forster cited in Bhagat Singh (*Sikh Misals*, 34) records that the Sikhs, falling upon his rear, relieved Nadir Shah of much of his booty.
27 Told to the author by the current in-charge of the *Mastuana Foundation* at Dam Dama Sahib.
28 Visakha Singh et al., *Itihas*, II: 82.
29 James Brown cited in Raijasbir Singh, *Deep Singh*, 22; this was an entitlement but in actual fact the misls claimed much less, depending on the harvest.
30 Kotha Guru, *Dam Dama Sahib*, 99-100.
31 Visakha Singh, *Itihas*, II: 82; Gyani Gyan Singh, *Twarikh*, II: 228. The author visited Teona Pujarian, named after head priests of the 'Sidhu' gotra who served at Dam Dama Sahib. An impressive samadh (memorial) stands proudly to the memory of Ran Singh (fifth

head priest—Jathedar—at Dam Dama Sahib) and Jeet Singh. The author also met some prominent members of the family and beheld a well-preserved handwritten recension of Guru Granth Sahib as well as a Hukamnama; while the former is the handiwork of their ancestor, the latter *was* personally transcribed by the tenth Guru and presented to their ancestors. The family also holds handwritten recensions of the Dasm Granth from that period. Their ancestors settled in the village in 1770 after they were granted ownerships rights though they were unable to corroborate this narrative. The handover of the area by the Nawab happened very likely between 1662-1770 because, according to Gyani Gyan Singh, Karam Singh was at the helm at the time, who assumed misl leadership only in early 1762.

32 Kotha Guru, *Dam Dama Sahib*, fn 1, 72.
33 *Ibid.*, p. 96-97
34 *Ibid.*, p. 124-132

7. The Sant-Sipahi

1 Tirlok Singh, *Deep Singh*, 5-11; Aulakh, *Illustrated Stories*, 16-17. The author was unable to verify the narrative on ground. There is no village by the name Peeran Garhi; there are many sites in the vicinity of Talwandi Sabo dedicated to pirs (Muslim saint or holy man); one such site may have been co-located with a garhi (fortalice) which were mostly mud-structures that could not stand the test of time, although some remnants have survived.

2 Jarnail Singh Sabran, *Parupkari Surma*, Youtube: https://www.youtube.com/watch?v=Bpb0GCRHeqU&feature=youtu.be. The author verified the narrative on ground. Today, Pakka Kalan is a large village with a population of over 7000. The notoriety of the Nawab as the abductor of women has survived. Built over an area of some 20-25 acres, with four large gates, his fort has all but disappeared with few vestiges although residents of the area are still referred to as 'kille walas' ('from the fort').

3 Gyani Gyan Singh, *Twarikh Guru Khalsa II*: 229; on request from a Brahmin, the misl took up arms against the Nawab of Jalalabad Lohari in 1825 *Samvat* to right an injustice (1768 CE).

4. Guru Gobind Singh delights in deifying weaponry in his *Shatra Naam Mala*:

ਸ਼ਸਤ੍ਰ ਅਸਤ੍ਰ ਤੁਮਹੀ ਸਿਪਰ ਤੁਮਹੀ ਕਵਚ ਨਿਖੰਗ ॥
ਕਵਚਾਂਤਕ ਤੁਮਹੀ ਬਨੇ ਤੁਮ ਬਯਾਪਕ ਸਰਬੰਗ ॥੨॥

Shastra astra tumhi sipar tumhi kavach nikhang
Kavchatank tumhi bane tum byapak sarbang

'Thou art the arms and weapons, the quiver, and the armour; Thou art the destroyer of the armour and also All Pervading.'
—Sri Shastra Naam Mala, *Dasm Granth*

5. Maurice Keen, *Chivalry* (New Haven: Yale University Press, 2005), 138.

6. ਜਹਾਂ ਜਹਾਂ ਖਾਲਸਾ ਜੀ ਸਾਹਿਬ, ਤਹਾਂ ਤਹਾਂ ਰੱਛਿਆ ਰਿਆਇਤ ।
Jahan jahan Khalsa ji sahib, Tahan tahan racchya riayit
Wherever the Khalsa doth go, may there be protection by His Grace.

7. ਖਾਲਸਾ ਮੇਰੋ ਇਸ਼ਟ ਸੁਹਰਿਦ —*Sarbloh Granth*
Khâlsâ mero isht suhird
'The Pure and my very own ideal'

8. ਜਬ ਆਵ ਕੀ ਅਉਧ ਨਿਦਾਨ ਬਨੈ ਅਤਿ ਹੀ ਰਨ ਮੈ ਤਬ ਜੂਝ ਮਰੋ ॥੨੩੧॥
Jaba Aava Kee Aaudha Nidaan Bani Ati Hee Ran Mai Taba Joojha Maro |231|
'I urge thee O Lord, when the last moment of my life doth come, May I die fighting in the thick of battle.'
—Guru Gobind Singh, *Aukat Bilas, Dasm Granth.* https://www.searchgurbani.com/public/ dasam-granth/page/198

9. PD Bonarjee, *A Handbook of the Fighting Races of India* (Calcutta: Thacker, Spink & Co, 1899), 191.

10. Louis E Fenech, "Martyrdom and the Sikh Tradition" *The Journal of the American Oriental Society*, Vol. 117, No. 4 (Oct.—Dec., 1997), 623-642.

11. Fenech, "Martyrdom", 623-642.

12. Forster, *A Journey*, 333.

13. Cited in Gopal Singh, *History*, 420-421.

14. Qazi Nur Mohammed cited in JS Grewal, (ed.)., *Sikh History from Persian Sources*, 208-209; also, Saggu, *Battle Tactics*, 238-239.

15. Peter Paret, "Introduction," in *Makers of Modern Strategy*, ed. Peter Paret (Princeton: Princeton University Press, 1986), 3.

16 Bhagat Singh, *Sikh Misals*, 436.
17 Ratan Singh Bhangu, *Sri Guru Panth Parkash*, Vol. 2, Sakhi 116, Couplet 41, translated by Kulwant Singh (Chandigarh: Institute of Sikh Studies, 2006).
18 BH Liddell Hart. "The Indirect Approach," in *War*, ed. Lawrence Freedman (New York: OUP, 1994), 232.
19 Most of these strategic terms have been drawn from Robert Greene, *The 33 Strategies of War* (New Delhi: Viva Books, 2006).
20 Winston Churchill quote: https://www.goodreads.com/quotes/37665-battles-are-won-by-slaughter-and-maneuver-thegreater-the
21 Cited in Bhagat Singh, *Sikh Misls*, 438.
22 Cited in Bhangu, *Panth Parkash*, Vol. 2, Sakhi 116, Couplet 37, with reference to the Lesser Holocaust; also, Balwant Singh Dhillon "18th Century Sikh Way of Battle and Tactics" in compendium *Baba Deep Singh: Jeevan te Yogdan* National Seminar (Amritsar: Guru Nanak Dev University, 2009), 173.
23 Cited in Bhangu, *Panth Parkash*, Vol. 2, Sakhi 136, Couplet 146, with reference to the Greater Holocaust.
24 JS Grewal and Irfan Habib, eds., *Sikh History from Persian Sources* (New Delhi: Indian History Congress, 2001), 195-97, 200.
25 Grewal, *Persian Sources*, 199.
26 *Ibid.*, 195
27 Qazi Nur Muhammad, *Jang Nama* (1765), ed. Ganda Singh (Amritsar: Sikh History Research Department, 1939), 50-51.
28 Gopal Singh, *Sikh History*, 440.
29 Francklin cited in Ganda Singh, *Early European Accounts*, 75-76.
30 James Browne, *History of the Origin and Progress of the Sicks* Vol. 2 (London: The East India Company Logegraphic Press, 1788), 25-26 cited in Bhagat Singh, *Sikh Misals*, 43.
31 Attributed to Zakariya Khan, Governor of Lahore, as told to Nadir Shah, Emperor of Persia, in 1739., cited in Bhangu, *Panth Prakash*, Vol. 2, Episode 96.
32 Qazi Nur Muhanmmed, *Jangnama: an eye-witness account of Ahmed Shah Durrani's seventh invasion in 1764* cited in Raj Pal Singh, *The Sikhs: their journey of Five Hundred Years* (Delhi: Bhavna Books, 2003), 120-121; also, Saggu, *Battle Tactics*, 227-239.

33 Ghulam All Khan, *Imacl-ut-Sa'adat*, (Cawnpore, 1864), 71.
34 Colonel ALH Polier, *Swiss Officer in the Mughal Court at Delhi, 1776* cited in Ganda Singh (ed.), *Early Accounts*, 64.
35 Francklin cited in Ganda Singh, *Early Accounts*, 73.
36 Jadunath Sarkar, *Fall of the Mughal Empire*. Vol. 3 (1772-1788) (Calcutta: SN Sarkar, 1938), 148.
37 Syad Muhammad Latif, *History of the Punjab from the Remotest Antiquity to the Present* (Calcutta: The Calcutta Central Press, 1891), 291.
38 Attributed to Zakariya Khan, cited in KS Kang, "Sikh Strategy and Tactics: 18th Century" in compendium of papers presented at. *Baba Deep Singh: Jeevan te Yogdaan* National Seminar (Amritsar: Guru Nanak Dev University, 2009), 17.
39 Cited in Gupta, *History*, II: 114; also, Gopal Singh, *History*, 425.
40 Indubhushan Banerjee cited in Bhagat Singh, *Sikh Misals*, 422.
41 Dhamija, *Ahluwalia*, 11; Bonarjee, *A Handbook*, 85; even McLeod stressed *Jat* cultural patterns and martial traditions in understanding the growth of militancy and the Sikh militant response: see McLeod, *A to Z*, 12-13.
42 Banerjee, *Evolution*, II: 44.
43 Bhagat Singh, *Sikh Misals*, 9; also Banerjee, *Evolution*, II: 124.
44 Ibbetson, *Panjab Castes* (Lahore: Government Printing, 1916), 97, 100.
45 Bonarjee, *Handbook*, 79, 85-86; Ibbetson, *Panjab Castes*, 102, 118-119; RW Falcon, *Handbook on Sikhs: for the use of Regimental Officers* (Allahabad: Pioneer Press, 1896), 64-65.
46 Ibbetson, *Panjab Castes*, 102.
47 Dhamija, *Ahluwalia*, 11; Bhagat Singh, *Sikh Misals*, 43.
48 Gopal Singh, *History*, fn. 214.

8. Review

1 Banga, "Historical Context of Baba Deep Singh," 3.
2 GS Nayyar, "Socio-Political Milieu of Baba Deep Singh" in compendium of papers presented at. *Baba Deep Singh: Jeevan te Yogdaan* National Seminar (Amritsar: Guru Nanak Dev University, 2009), 75.

3   Malcolm Barber, *The New Knighthood: a History of the Order of the Temple (Canto ed.)* (Cambridge, UK: Cambridge University Press, 1995), xxi–xxii.
4   *Baba Deep Singh ji Shaheed ki Katha*, "Utraradh Bisram 50," stanza 12.
5   *Ibid.*, stanza 9
6   His 'landless' status has led many to believe that Deep Singh was a *mazhabi* Sikh. This is contrary to his genealogical record that classifies him as a *jat zamindar* (landowner).
7   Cunningham, *History*, 107-108; also see Gyani Gyan Singh, *Twarikh Guru Khalsa*, "Satvin Misal Shaheedan di," III: 226-230; territorial conquest and occupation of landholdings began when Karam Singh assumed misl leadership.
8   Bhai Nand Lal, *Tankhanamah*, 106-128.
9   Lord Moran, *The Anatomy of Courage.* (Boston: Houghton Mifflin Company, 1967), 159-160.

9. Right to Go to War

1   Refer the calendar for that year. Available at: https:// www.drikpanchang.com/calendars/indian/indiancalendar.html?year=1757. Also see Pal Singh Purewal *Jantri* (Mohali: Punjab School Education Board, 1994), 309.
2   Jacques, *Dictionary*, 400.
3   Gupta, *History*, II: 128-132.
4   Miskin, *Tahmas Nama*, 46.
5   Gopal Singh, *History*, 394.
6   Khushwant Singh, *History of the Sikhs*, I: 138.
7   Gupta, *History*, II: 128 – 132; Saggu, *Battle Tactics*, 100; Gopal Singh, *History*, 394.
8   Trilok Singh, *Amar Shaheed Baba Deep Singh* (Amritsar: Chattar Singh Jeevan Singh, 2015), 65-70; Mehnga Singh Kalsi, *Sirlath Shaheed Baba Deep Singh* (Chandigarh: Unistar Books, 2015), 84-85; according to Kalsi, the raid took place at night; Aulakh, *Illustrated Stories*, 26-27: Aulakh notes that the raids took place in the evening, when the tired enemy had just settled down to rest for the night.
9   Bhagat Singh, "Martyrdom of Baba Deep Singh" in *Sikh Struggle and*

the Misl Period, eds. Kirpal Singh & Kharak Singh Vol. 2 (Amritsar: Golden Offset Press, 2013), 111.

10 Pyara Singh Padam, *Sankhep Sikh Itihas* (Amritsar: Singh Brothers, 2014), 126.

11 The *dhoti* or *chaadra* is a rectangular piece of unstitched cloth usually around 4.5 metres long, worn as a traditional men's garment all through the Indian subcontinent. The *Kacchera* is a specially designed undergarment akin to boxer shorts in appearance with a tie-knot (drawstring). It is one of the five Sikh articles of faith called the Five Ks (ਪੰਜ ਕ੍ਕਾਰ) ordained by Guru Gobind Singh at the *Baisakhi Amrit Sanskar* in March 1699; symbolizes 'sexual restraint'.

12 Khushwant Singh, *History*, I: 139.

13 Gupta, *History*, II: 132.

14 Raijasbir Singh, *Deep Singh*, 264; a 'kabit' (Hindi 'kavita') is a poem in any meter.

15 Gupta, *History*, II: 134; Gopal Singh, *History*, 394; Raijasbir Singh (*Deep Singh*, 7) states that Amritsar was plundered in May 1757; also see Saggu, *Battle Tactics*, 300; according to Bhagat Singh (*Sikh Misals*, 243), this happened in October 1757 but May is more likely as part of the general action against Sikhs in the wake of Durrani's invasion and retreat. Dharam Singh cites 1 May 1757 as the date of demolition under the command of Sarbuland Khan: see his "Baba Deep Singh Shaheed da Kav-Bimb" in compendium of papers presented at. *Baba Deep Singh: Jeevan te Yogdaan* National Seminar (Amritsar: Guru Nanak Dev University, 2009), 111, 115.

16 See Jhubal, "Baba Deep Singh and Dam Dami Taksal," 166; Aulakh, *Illustrated Stories*, 30; also, Gyani Gyan Singh, "Amritsar di betabii" in *Twarikh Guru Khalsa Pt 2*, 174.

17 Pannu, "Shaheed Baba Deep Singh ji," 73.

18 Gupta, *History*, II: 158: Ala Singh was baptized by Deep Singh earlier in 1731 in gratitude for military assistance against Rai Kalha and his allies. Gupta, *History*, IV: 121, 149. Ala Singh was the first from the *Phulkian* states to be baptized, initially by Nawab Kapur Singh (Gupta, *History*, IV: 147). He would be baptized a third time by Jassa Singh Ahluwalia in March 1761, apparently, as a stratagem to pacify the *Dal Khalsa* displeased with him for submitting before

Abdali after the Third Battle of Panipat (14 January 1761); all this when actually he never kept any of the outward symbols of a Sikh, only a trimmed beard: see Gupta, *History*, IV: 28.

10. Taking up the Gauntlet

1 Gyani Gyan Singh, *Twarikh*, II: 227.
2 This information was conveyed to the author by the descendants of Bhai Dall Singh at Talwandi Sabo.
3 The author toured these villages; there is only a faint memory among a few elders of this history along with a sense of pride in their forbears for having fought for honor.
4 This name is not found in the genealogy record of Deep Singh's immediate family (Table 1); possibly, a distant relative.
5 Gyani Gyan Singh, *Panth Prakash Vol II*, "Utraradh Bisram 50," stanza 14; also, Raijasbir Singh, *Deep Singh*, 128.
6 Raijasbir Singh, *Deep Singh*, 142; a *dohra* is a self-contained rhyming couplet, in this case each line has 4 + 4 feet.
7 Much of this information was conveyed to the author while interacting with the clergy during his visit to the Lakhi Jungle gurdwara.
8 The author toured these villages; very few retain the memory of this participation.
9 Gyani Gyan Singh puts the additional strength at 1000: see Raijasbir Singh, *Deep Singh*, 74.
10 Gyani Gyan Singh, *Panth Prakash II, Baba Deep Singh ji Shaheed di katha*, "Utraradh Bisram 50," stanza 18.
11 ਚੁ ਕਾਰ ਅਜ਼ ਹਮਹ ਹੀਲਤੇ ਦਰ ਗੁਜ਼ਸ਼ਤ ॥ ਹਲਾਲ ਅਸਤ ਬੁਰਦਨ ਬ ਸ਼ਮਸੀਰ ਦਸਤ ॥੨੨॥
—Guru Gobind Singh, *Zafarnamah*
Chu kar az hameh heel-te dar guzasht, Halal ast burdan b-shamshir dast (22)
When all stratagems fail in the fight for justice, it is legitimate to unsheathe the sword.
12 ਜਬ ਆਵ ਕੀ ਅਉਧ ਨਿਦਾਨ ਬਨੈ ਅਤਿ ਹੀ ਰਨ ਮੈ ਤਬ ਜੂਝ ਮਰੋਂ
—Guru Gobind Singh, *Chandi Charitra*
Jab av ki audh nidaan bane ut heeran mein tab joojh maron
When the last moment of my life doth come, may I die fighting in the thick of battle.

13 In Raijasbir Singh, *Deep Singh*, 303; a 'vaar' is a heroic ode or ballad that generally narrates the story of Punjabi folk heroes.
14 In Raijasbir Singh, *Deep Singh*, 184.
15 Clifford Hopewell, *James Bowie Texas Fighting Man, A Biography* (Austin, TX: Eakin Press, 1994), 126; Stephen L Hardin, *Texian Iliad*. (Austin, TX: University of Texas Press, 1994), 124.
16 Visakha Singh, *Itihas*, I: 377.
17 Cited in Raijasbir Singh, *Deep Singh*, 254.
18 Naudh Singh was *Sandhu* by caste and, according to popular lore, Deep Singh's cousin, their mothers being real sisters. Initially, he was part of Gujar Singh Bhangi's jatha but joined the Shaheed misl on the reorganization of the Dal Khalsa into twelve misls in 1748. He is supposed to have been baptized by Deep Singh. His descendants live in village Chicha near Amritsar. However, Gyani Gyan Singh records his surname (mistakenly) as 'Gill' (see "Utraradh Bisram 50," stanza 48).
19 Sohan Singh Seetal, "Shaheedi Baba Deep Singh ji" in Raijasbir Singh, *Deep Singh*, 233.

11. The Face Off

1 Based on Tahmas Khan Miskin, *Tahmas Nama*. Abridged and translated by P. Setu Madhav Rao. (Bombay: Popular Prakashan, 1967), 61-62; Raijasbir Singh, *Deep Singh*, 50-51; Gupta, *History*, II: 135-136.
2 Miskin, *Tahmas Nama*, vii.
3 *Ibid.*, p. 153
4 Raijasbir Singh, *Deep Singh*, 108.
5 According to Miskin (*Tahmas Nama*, 52), Prince Taimur had an army of approx ten-fifteen thousand under his command with a train of artillery.
6 Gyani Gyan Singh, "Amritsar di Betabi" in *Shamsher Khalsa, Part 2*, Episode-116, 75.
7 Raijasbir Singh, *Deep Singh*, 185; the author confirmed this from village elders at *Gohalwar* as received information from their forefathers. They even accompanied the author to the site of a fortalice that existed at the time; the elders had seen its remnants

though now there is no trace, the area being under intensive cultivation.
8   Gyani Gyan Singh, *Shamsher Khalsa Part 2*, "Dharam Yudh"; also, *Raj Khalsa Part 1*, "Satvin Misal Shaheedan di".
9   Khushwant Singh, *History*, I: 139-140: Khushwant Singh describes Deep Singh's army as comprising some 5000 peasants armed with hatchets, swords, and spears; Patwant Singh, *The Sikhs*, (London: Harper & Collins: 1999), 88, refers to their strength as a mere 'handful':
10 As told to the author by Nihang Kashmir Singh of Taruna Dal in village Chabba.
11 Gyani Gyan Singh, *Panth Prakash II*, "Utraradh Bisram 50," stanza 28.
12 Baron De Jomini, "Strategy and Grand Tactics" in *War*, ed. Lawrence Freedman (New York: OUP, 1994), 214.
13 Carl Von Clausewitz, "Key Concepts" in *War*, ed. Lawrence Freedman (New York: OUP, 1994), 208.
14 GC Walker, *Gazetteer of the Lahore District 1893-1894* (Lahore: Panjab Government, 1894), 2.
15 *Ibid.*, p. 144
16 *Ibid.*, p. 15-17
17 When the first census was held in as late as 1881, the rural population in the area stood at almost 80% (compared to the urban), and the average population per village at 684. Muslims accounted for maximum houses followed by Sikhs and Hindus. This was despite the marked increase in the population of Sikhs in the Sikh *Raj*: see *Gazetteer of the Amritsar District 1883-4* (Calcutta: Punjab Government, 1884), 15, Table VII.

12. The Battle

1   Khushwant Singh, *History*, I: fn 27, 113.
2   Aulakh, *Illustrated Stories*, 32-34
3   ਦੀਨ ਮਜ਼ਬ ਦਾ ਮੱਚਿਆ ਜੰਗ ਆ ਕੇ ਹੋਵੇ ਨਿਕਲ ਮੈਦਾਨ ਕੁਰਬਾਨ ਅੱਗੇ ।
    ਪਿਛਾਂਹ ਹੱਟੇ ਸੋ ਮਰੇਗਾ ਹੋ ਕਾਫਰ, ਸਾਰੇ ਹੱਲਾ ਕਰ ਵਧੇ ਜਵਾਨ ਅੱਗੇ ।
    *Deen mazab da machiya jang aake hove nikal maidan kurban agge
    pichhan hatte so marega ho kafir, saare hulla kar vadho jawan agge*

This battle is over race and creed—
take courage and do glorious deed.
Whoever turns his back to flee
shall die and this I pledge to thee!

—Kartar Singh Kalaswalia, *Jauhar Khalsa* cited in Raijasbir Singh, *Deep Singh*, 187.

4 Sohan Singh Seetal in "Shaheedi Baba Deep Singh ji" cited in Raijasbir Singh, *Deep Singh*, 234.

5 ਥੋੜੇ ਸਘਿ ਤੇ ਬਹੁਤੇ ਮੁਸਲਮਾਨ ਹੈਸਨ....। –
Thoreh Singh te bahute musalman haisan....
Fewer Singhs there were and more Muslims.

—Kartar Singh Kalasvalia, "Jauhar Khalsa" cited in Raijasbir Singh, *Deep Singh*, 186.

6 Cited in Raijasbir Singh, *Deep Singh*, 187.

7 In Raijasbir Singh, *Deep Singh*, 187.

8 "Utraradh Bisram 50," *Panth Prakash* II, stanza 36.

9 ਪਰੇ ਬਨ ਖੇਤਾਂ ਵਚਿ ਲੜ ਰਹੇ ਤੇਗਾਂ ਚਲਦਆਿਂ ਖੂਬ ਲਸ਼ਿਕਾਰ ਪੈ ਰਹੇ ।
Pare ban khetanvich larh rahe tegan chaldian khub lishkar paye rahe 186
The Sikhs now fought in small groups (*pare*) as their swords caught the glint of the sun all across the wide expanse of the battlefield.

—Kartar Singh Kalasvalia, *Jauhar Khalsa*, cited in Raijasbir Singh, *Deep Singh*, 186.

10 'Tahli' is the Indian Rosewood, a tree native to the Indian subcontinent. The shrine Tahla Sahib that marks the place of Deep Singh's injury takes its name from a thicket of Tahli trees in the area at the time of battle which may also have provided good camouflage and concealment to the enemy.

11 Kanwal, *Deep Singh*, 70.

12 Gyani Gyan Singh, "Utraradh Bisram 50," *Sri Guru Panth Prakash, Vol II*, stanza 37.

13 *Ibid.*, stanza 38.

14 Raijasbir Singh, *Deep Singh*, p. 188; also, Gyani Gyan Singh, "Utraradh Bisram 50," stanza 40.

15 *Ibid.*, stanza 40-41.

16 *Ibid.*, stanza 42-43.

17 "Indian Units of Measurement" Wikipedia, accessed 20 January

2020. See under Akbar Weights and Measure. The conversion rate for the *ser* was @ .637.7 grams; the *katcha ser*, prevalent at the time, was multiplicative 2.5 inverse of the *pukka ser*: 1 *pukka ser* = 2.5 *katcha ser*; 30 *katcha ser* would be 12 *pukka ser* = 7.68 kilograms. https:// en.wikipedia.org/wiki/Indian_units_of_measurement

18   Naudh Singh was not 'Gill' but a 'Sandhu' from village Chicha near Amritsar.
19   Cited in Raijasbir Singh, *Deep Singh*, 137.
20   Pannu, "Shaheed Baba Deep Singh ji," 74.
21   ਬੈਂਤ ॥ ਰਾਮਸਰ ਦੇ ਨੇੜੇ ਖਲੋ ਕਰਕੇ, ਬਾਬਾ ਦੀਪ ਸਿੰਘ ਜ਼ੋਰ ਲਗਾ ਦਿੱਤਾ ।
ਵਾਂਗਰ ਗੋਲੇ ਜਾਂ ਗੇਂਦ ਦੇ ਸੀਸ ਤਾਈਂ, ਹੱਥੋਂ ਜ਼ੋਰ ਘੁਮਾ ਚਲਾ ਦਿੱਤਾ ।
ਡਿੱਗਾ ਵਿਚ ਪਰਕਰਮਾ ਦੇ ਜਾ ਕਰਕੇ, ਬ੍ਰਹਮ ਸ਼ਕਤੀ ਨੇ ਐਸਾ ਉਡਾ ਦਿੱਤਾ ।
ਜਦੋਂ ਸੀਸ ਪਰਕਰਮਾ ਦੇ ਵਿਚ ਡਿਗਯਾ, ਤਦੋਂ ਸਿੰਘ ਨੇ ਫਰਜ਼ ਨਿਭਾ ਦਿੱਤਾ ।
Baint. Ramsar de nede khalo karke, Baba Deep Singh zor laga ditta Vangar gole jan gaind de sees tayin, hathon zor ghuma chala ditta
Dhigga vich parkarma de ja karke, brahm shakti ne aisa uda ditta
Jadon sees parkarma de vich digya, tadon singh ne pharaz Nabhaditta
Beside Ramsar as Deep Singh stood, robustly did he throw;
His severed head, he flung it far and spinning it did go.
   It landed in *Parkarma*; he'd used his spiritual power,
   With this he fully accomplished then his pledge in that true hour.
—Trilok Siingh Dirvesh, *Prasang Baba Deep Singh ji Shaheed* cited in Raijasbir Singh, *Deep Singh*, 296; a 'baint' in Arabic and Persian poetry has two lines though the number of syllables per line can vary. In this verse, each line has two parts, with perfect end-rhymes.
22   Gyani Gyan Singh, "Satvin Misal Shaheedan di" in *Twarikh Guru Khalsa Pt 3*; also, *Raj Khalsa* (Part 1), 36; this is at variance with his *Sri Guru Panth Prakash II*, "Uttraradh Bisram 50," stanza 54-57 in which he records that Deep Singh was decapitated near Chabba while duelling with Aman Khan, and fought on till Ramsar where he died. Gyani Gyan Singh, however, erroneously records the year of battle as 1824 Samvat (1767 CE) instead of 1814 Samvat (1757 CE) in the concluding stanza of Utraradh Bisram 50.
23   ਸ਼ਹੀਦ ਸਾਬਰ-ਅਲੀ ਖਾਨ ਬਢ ।
ਪਾਂਚ ਹਜ਼ਾਰੀ ਜੁੱਝਯੋ ਤਹਿ ਖੜ ।
ਦੂਦ ਜੁਧ ਕਰਿ ਸੁੱਧ ਉਦਾਰਾ ।
ਹੀਰਾ ਸਿੰਘ ਨੇ ਤਿਸ ਕੋ ਮਾਰਾ ॥੨੨॥

> *Sayyed Sabar-Ali Khan Khan badd*
> *Panch hazari jujhyo tahkhad*
> *Dud jud ker sudh udara*
> *Hira singh ne tis ko mara |77|*
> Sayed Sabar-Ali was a commander great
> In-charge five thousand men in state
> He took to single combat fight,
> Was killed by Hira Singh outright.
> —Gyani Gyan Singh, "Utraradh Bisram 50," stanza 77;
> also, Ghukewalia cited in Raijasbir Singh,
> *Deep Singh*, 191-192.

24 Gyani Gyan Singh, "Utraradh Bisram 50", stanza 60 (Mahat Singh), stanza 75 (Ram Singh).

13. Battle Review

1 Dharam Singh states that Deep Singh fought two duels and killed both his adversaries, Sarbuland Khan and Yakub Khan; see his "Baba Deep Singh Shaheed da Kav-Bimb," 115.
2 Raijasbir Singh, *Deep Singh*, 133-138; there is no historical evidence of a battle fought in the area during Nadir Shah's invasion, nor the desecration of Harimandir Sahib. Gyani Thakur Singh also leaves many questions unanswered: why would Deep Singh leave Dam Dama Sahib with only one companion when he was the head of a misl? That too with Sukha Singh Ramgarhia who was never part of the Shaheed misl? Why should the Lahore army mobilize and be waiting in strength for barely thirty Sikhs?
3 Bhagat Singh, *Sikh Misals*, 41-42; Gupta, *History*, IV: 123-124.
4 "The Third Battle of Panipat" Wikipedia. Available at: https://en.wikipedia.org/wiki/Third_Battle_of_Panipat; his name appears in history even in 1767: see Miskin, *Tahmas Nama*, 116.
5 Gupta, *History*, II: 164
6 Jacques, *Dictionary*, 400.
7 Kanwal, *Baba Deep Singh*, 65.
8 Gupta, *History*, II: 164.
9 Gyani Gyan Singh, "Utraradh Bisram 50," Stanza 60 (Mahit Singh), Stanza 61 (Ram Singh).

10 Badunger, "Shaheed Baba Deep Singh ji: Brahm Gyani," 45-46; he has added Deep Singh at the top and suffixed 'Shaheed' to all the names. The memorial includes neither Deep Singh's name (although his leadership is acknowledged), nor the suffix.
11 The date should read 30 *Kartik*, 1814 *Samvat*, or 11 Nov 1757 CE.
12 In his "Utraradh Bisram 50," *Panth Prakash*, "Satvin Misal Shaheedan di" (Raj Khalsa Part 1), and "Dharam Yudh" (Shamsher Khalsa Part 2), Gyani Gyan Singh records Deep Singh's death and cremation at Ramsar.
13 Davinderpal Singh, *The Golden Temple and the City of Amritsar* (Amritsar: Sikh Book Company, 2018), 35.
14 Soon after the formal handing over of the keys of Harimandir Sahib to Sikhs by the British administration on 20 Jan 1922, the Gurdwara Act followed in 1925 (*ibid.*, 53,55), allowing Sikhs to execute an elaborate plan for the modernization of the premises. At the time, there were some eighty-four bungas around the temple of various shapes and sizes (*ibid.*, 42), mostly overlooking the narrow parikrama that circumambulated the sarovar (lake). Since these were all private residences, often the activities of the lodgers were woefully anything but spiritual, and the gurdwara administration had long faced excoriating criticism for their inability to act. The Parikrama Scheme empowered the SGPC to acquire these bungas 1950 onwards. By 1972, all but the Ramgarhia and Shaheed Bunga had been demolished (*ibid.*, 43).
15 Several of these cenotaph-shrines are, in fact, large gurdwaras whereas some are marked only by a small room with a nishaan sahib (Sikh flag) although fund collection is ongoing for further construction. Many include a symbolic samadh.
16 The piece of land measuring some 1.75 acres still stands in the name of the Central Waqf Council, the national Muslim body that oversees Muslim religious and charitable property in India.
17 Kotha Guru, *Dam Dama Sahib*, 66.
18 ਦਹਿਨੇ ਹਾਥ ਤੇਗ ਖ਼ਰ ਧਾਰਾ
    ਵਜ਼ਨ ਜਾਹਿ ਥਾਂ ਸੇਰ ਅਠਾਰਾਂ
    dahine hath teg khar dhara
    vajan jah tha ser atharan

A broadsword held in his right hand:
it weighed a full eighteen *ser* grand.
　　　　　—Gyani Gyan Singh, "Utraradh Bisram 50", stanza 58.
ਲੈ ਕੇ ਹੱਥ ਵਿਚ ਖੰਡਾ ਠਾਰਾਂ ਸੇਰ ਦਾ,
ਰਣ ਕੁਦਿਆਂ ਜਾਂ ਬੁੱਢਾ ਜਥੇਦਾਰ
Lai ke hath vich khanda tharan ser da,
Ran kudiyan jan buddha jathedar
With broadsword 18 *ser* to wield,
　The hoary Jathedar takes the field
　　　　　—Kewal Singh Nirdosh in Raijasbir Singh, *Deep Singh*, 273.
ਅਠਾਰਾਂ ਸੇਰੀ ਵਜ਼ਨ ਖੰਡਾ ਬਾਬੇ ਨੇ ਫੜਿਆ
atharan seri vazan khanda babe ne phadia
　Baba [Deep Singh] held a *khanda* of 18 *seri*
　　　　　—Kanwal, *Deep Singh*, 69.

19　ਬਾਰਾਂ ਸੇਰ ਪੁੱਕਾ ਖੰਡਾ ਹੱਥ ਹੈਸੀ ਸੂਰਮੇ ਦੇ
　　Baraan ser pukka khanda hath haisi soormey de
　　The daring warrior wielded a 12 *ser pukka* broadsword.
　　　　　—Trilok Singh Dervesh in Raijasbir Singh, *Deep Singh*, 287.
20　"Indian Units of Measurement." See under Akbar Weights and Measures; the conversion rate was revised to .870 grams in 1833, and to .933 grams in 1956, when India switched to the metric system. https://en.wikipedia.org/wiki/Indian_units_of_measurement
21　Simarjit Singh, "Baba Deep Singh nal sanbandit itihasik sthan," 125.
22　"*Akal Takth* Weapons' Display." Filmed 12 February 2008 at *Akal Takth*, Amritsar. Video Part 1—7.16 mins; Part 2—7.10 mins. Par 1: https:// www.youtube.com/watch?v=tRrDR9lJhSk#action=share; time 3.44 min; Part 2: https://www.youtube.com/watch?v=nArLYH-IJ9g
23　On enquiring of a functionary during the weapon display at the *Akal Takth*, the author was informed that Deep Singh's broadsword weighed 2.5 kilograms.
24　The great Rajput warrior, Maharana Pratap of Mewar (late 16th century) is similarly portrayed by oral traditions to have carried two swords weighing 25 kilos each in addition to an 80-kilos spear, while his entire armour tipped the scales at 72 kilos. Historians, however, continue to question these figures.

25 Balwinder Singh & Jaura Singh, "Baba Deep Singh ji Shaheed de Shaster" in compendium of papers presented at. *Baba Deep Singh: Jeevan te Yogdaan* National Seminar (Amritsar: Guru Nanak Dev University, 2009), 130.
26 Gyani Gyan Singh cites the weight of the mace as 30 ser, or 7.7 kilograms: see "Utraradh Bisram 50," Stanza 46.
27 Bhagat Singh, *Sikh Misals*, 435: 'A Sikh soldier carried on his person an iron load of about 20 kgs.' Gupta, *History*, IV: 375: this comprised generally two swords, spears, lances, pikes, sabres, two-edged daggers, bow-and-arrow, muskets, matchlocks, battle-axes, shield, and coat-of-mail.
28 Balwinder Singh and Jaura Singh, "Baba Deep Singh Shaheed de Shaster," 130-131; the author also confirmed this with the clergy at *Bunga Mastuana* at Dam Dama Sahib.
29 Rao, *Tahmas Namah*, 61-62.
30 Gupta, *History*, IV: 123; Fauja Singh, *The City of Amritsar: An Introduction*, edited Fauja Singh (Patiala: Punjabi University, 2000), 82-83. Accessed 10 Dec 2019: https://www.allaboutsikhs.com/harmandir-sahib/installation-of-holy-granth-at-harimandir. According to Fauja Singh, only Gurbaksh Singh was among the five men martyred.
31 Patwant Singh, *The Sikhs*, 88.
32 Cited in R Palmer, "Frederick the Great, Guibert, Bulow: From Dynastic to National War," in *Makers of Modern Strategy*, ed. Peter Paret (Princeton: Princeton University Press, 1986), 97.

Table 2: Circumstances of Deep Singh Martyrdom

33 Napoleon, "Maximes," in *War*, ed. Lawrence Freedman (New York: OUP, 1994), 216.
34 Gyani Gyan Singh, "Uttraradh Bisram 50", *Panth Prakash II*, stanzas 30-33, 45-47, 58-72. Gyani Gyan Singh, "Satvin Misal Shaheedan," in *Raj Khalsa Part 1*, 36.
35 Gyani Thakar Singh, *Sri Gurdware Darshan* in Raijasbir Singh, *Deep Singh*, 137.
36 Raijasbir Singh, *Deep Singh*, 143.
37 *Ibid.*, 171

38 *Ibid.*, 187-190
39 *Ibid.*, 210-211
40 *Ibid.*, 240-244
41 *Ibid.*, 257-258
42 *Ibid.*, 273
43 *Ibid.*, 290, 295, 296
44 *Ibid.*, 309
45 *Ibid.*, 333-334
46 Kanwal, *Deep Singh*, 70-71.

Table 3: Summary of Prominent Duels

47 Gyani Gyan Singh, "Uttraradh Bisram 50" in *Panth Prakash* II, stanzas 33-35, 47-52, 75-95.
48 Kalaswalia in Raijasbir Singh, *Jauhar Khalsa*, 187, 191-192.
49 In Raijasbir Singh, *Deep Singh*, 235, 237-238.
50 The author obtained this information by interacting with the clergy in Naudh Singh's native village, Chicha, near Amritsar.

Table 4: Places of Martyrdom

51 Gyani Gyan Singh, "Uttraradh Bisram 50", stanzas 75-95.
52 In Raijasbir Singh, *Deep Singh*, 187, 190-192.
53 *Ibid.*, 235, 237-238.
54 Kanwal, *Deep Singh*, 71-72.

Table 5: Cenotaphs: Documented versus On-Ground

55 Karam Singh, *Amritsar*, 64; Baba Praga was a Chhibber from village Karyala. He was a notable figure in Sikh history and participated in many battles. His loyalty and spiritual devotion to different Gurus, particularly Guru Arjan Dev, finds mention in *Suraj Prakash*.

14. Tryst with Harimandir Sahib

1 'Kos' is an Indian unit of measurement now archaic; one kos was equal to two miles, or 3.2 kilometer.
2 'Katcha ser' was the unit of weight at the time; 18 *ser* would be about 4.6 kg; refer section on Deep Singh's broadsword above.
3 Gyani Gyan Singh, *Twarikh Sri Amritsar* (Amritsar: Kendriya Singh

Sabha, 1923), 54. Karam Singh suggests that Deep Singh laid the foundations that year (1764): see Karam Singh, *Twarikh Amritsar* (Amritsar, Chattar Singh Jeevan Singh: 2020), 49; in the event, it begs the question why a pre-decided site of the Bunga should coincide with his place of martyrdom. Gyani Gyan Singh incorrectly records the year of Deep Singh's martyrdom as 1824 *Bikrami* (1767 CE) in his *Panth Prakash* Vol II, "Baba Deep Singh Shaheed ki katha" (Sakhi 50).

4 Gyani Gyan Singh, *Amritsar*, 49-56.
5 This information was shared by Davinderpal Singh who has authored a book on the city.
6 Son of Jassa Singh *Ramgarhia* who succeeded his father and fought alongside Maharaja Ranjit Singh in the Battle of Kasur (1807 CE); died 1816 CE.
7 It is built within the *laldori* where ownership was by possession alone with no registered titles. No definitive information is available about its exact date of construction. Quite likely, the shrine began as a modest cenotaph and was enlarged incrementally over the years, particularly after 1764 CE. The entire area later became the dominion of Jassa Singh Ramgarhia, known as *Katra Ramgarhia*, established sometime in the mid-1750's and was the biggest settlement in Amritsar: see Karam Singh, *Amritsar*, 16.
8 The excavation began after a gurmatta was passed to the effect by the Dal Khalsa during Vaisakhi on 30 March 1747: see Gupta, *History*, II: 81.
9 Malhotra, *Sikh History*, 41; Bhagat Singh, *Sikh Misals*, 119.
10 Prithipal Singh Kapur, "Jassa Singh Ramgarhia" in *Sikh Struggle and the Misl Period*, eds. Kirpal Singh & Kharak Singh Vol 2 (Amritsar: Golden Offset Press, 2013), 283-384
11 Karam Singh, *Amritsar*, 16.
12 Simarjit Singh, "Baba Deep Singh," 125.
13 Gopal Singh, *History*, fn 394-395; Piara Singh Padam, *Sankhep Sikh Itihas* (Amritsar: Singh Brothers, 2014), 95.
14 This view was projected by many of the participating academics at the *Baba Deep Singh: Jeevan te Yogdaan* National Seminar at Guru Nanak Dev University in January 2009 held to commemorate

Deep Singh's the Semiquincentennial (250th) anniversary of his martyrdom. The author was also present.
15 Kahn Singh Nabha, *Guru Shabad Ratnakar Mahan Kosh* (Patiala: Languages Department of Punjab, 1930), 2092. Accessed 20 April 2020. http://old.sgpc.net/CDN/Mahankosh.pdf
16 Miskin, *Tahmas Nama*, 61-62
17 *Ibid.*, IX.
18 Bhagat Singh, *Sikh Misals*, 244, fns 7-8.
19 Raijasbir Singh, *Deep Singh*, 339.
20 Trilok Singh Dervesh cited in Raijasbir Singh, *Deep Singh*, 296.
21 This view was expressed by the Sikh Historical Research Board, located within the premises of the Golden Temple.

Epilogue

1 Gyani Gyan Singh, "Satvin misl shaheedan di" in *Twarikh Guru Khalsa Pt 2*, 226-230; also, in Gyani Gyan Singh *Raj Khalsa*, "Satvin Misal Shaheedan di".
2 The author found no memorial at Churasta Attari, possibly, it has disappeared over time; there is also no separate memorial for Basant Singh at Tharra Sahib, although a Basant Singh is included among the other martyrs. It is possible that since the two battles were so close in time, the memorials have been combined.
3 Khushwant Singh, *History*, I: 140.
4 Gupta, *History*, II: 137-140; Gupta also cites Bhaktmal, II: 347; also Miskin, *Tahmas Nama*, 63.
5 Bhagat Singh, *Sikh Misals*, 41-42; Gupta, *History*, IV: 123-124.
6 Gupta, *History*, II: 173-174.
7 Madanjit Kaur, "Natha Singh Shaheed" in *Sikh Struggle and the Misl Period*, eds. Kirpal Singh & Kharak Singh Vol 2 (Amritsar: Golden Offset Press, 2013), 308-312.
8 Gupta, *History*, II: 183: supposedly kept in the main Dharamshala at Kabul (see fn on same page), but this remains unverified.
9 Colonel Polier in Ganda Singh, *European Accounts*, 59 fn. 22.
10 Surinder Singh Johar, *The Heritage of Amritsar* (New Delhi: Sundeep Prakashan, 1978), 69; Saggu, *Battle Tactics*, 301-302. Abdali is also known to have suffered from a painful carbuncle on his nose for a large part of his adult life.

11 Cited in Gupta, *History*, II: 188
12 Gupta, *History*, IV: 30-31.
13 *Ibid.*, IV: 31.
14 *Ibid.*, IV: 31-33.
15 Gyani Gyan Singh, "Satvin Misal Shaheedan di" in *Twarikh Guru Khalsa, Part 2*, 228; also, Gyani Gyan Singh, *Raj Khalsa 1*: 37. According to Lepel Griffin cited in Bhagat Singh, Sudh Singh was martyred in 1762 fighting the Mohammedan Governor of Jalandhar; see Bhagat Singh, *Misals*, 246.
16 Gyani Gyan Singh, "Satvin Misal Shaheedan di" in *Twarikh Guru Khalsa, Part 2*, 228; also in Rajasbir Singh, *Deep Singh*, 129; Saggu (*Battle Tactics*, 165) mentions the battle along with names of the principal Sikhs but records the date as 1 December 1764; so does Malhotra, *Sikh History*, 46; and Bhagat Singh, "Afghan Invasions of Punjab including Battle of Panipat" in *Sikh Struggle and the Misl Period*, eds. Kirpal Singh & Kharak Singh Vol 2 (Amritsar: Golden Offset Press, 2013), 127; Gupta, *History*, II: 216. Gurbaksh Singh's place of birth was *Leel* near Khem Karan, now across the IB in Pakistan: see Bhagat Singh, *Misals*, 242 and Bhangu's Sakhi 156 (Vol: II); Gupta records it incorrectly as *Gaggobhua* near Taran Taran: Gupta, *History*, II: 209. There is another gurdwara in village Bhalwanke-Darajke, about a mile from Pahuwind, which commemorates his night-halt. By another account, Bhai Gurbaksh Singh was the great nephew of Bhai Mati Das Chhibber who was martyred along with Guru Teg Bahadur in 1675 at Delhi.
17 Qazi Nur Mohammad, *Jang Namah*, ed. Ganda Singh (Amritsar: Khalsa College, 1939), 35.
18 Introductory note to Gyani Gyan Singh in Raijasbir Singh, *Deep Singh*, 129.
19 Davinderpal Singh, *The Golden Temple & the City of Amritsar* (Amritsar: The Sikh Book Company, 2018), 133. The *Shaheed Bunga* had been built earlier in 1764: see Gyani Gyani Singh, *Twarikh Sri Amritsar*, 54. It was now rebuilt along with the sanctum.
20 Baron Von Hugel cited in BL Grover and Alka Mehta, *A New Look at Modern Indian History* (New Delhi: S Chand, 2018), 144.
21 India Today: https://www.indiatoday.in/india/story/

maharajaranjit-singh-voted-greatest-leader-of-all-times-1652824-2020-03-05
22 Gopal Singh, *History*, 328.
23 Kirpal Singh, "Introduction" in *Sikh Struggle and the Misl Period*, eds. Kirpal Singh & Kharak Singh Vol. 2 (Amritsar: Golden Offset Press, 2013), xvi-xvii.
24 Gupta, *History*, III: 166-170.
25 For this estimate of Sikh casualties, see Gupta, *History*, II: 256
26 Lepel Griffin, *Ranjit Singh* (Oxford: Clarendon Press, 1892), 71.
27 He died on 23 March 1823 while delivering the *coup de grace* in the Battle of Nowshera (Afghanistan).
28 Banga, "Deep Singh," 5-6.

Appendix A: Deep Singh in Verse

1 Kanwal, *Deep Singh*, 12.
2 Indian poetry tends to include the name of the poet generally towards the end of the poem, a tradition ignored in these translations.
3 Kanwal, *Deep Singh*, 14.
4 *Ibid.*, 11.
5 *Ibid.*, 19-20.
6 Bhangu, *Pracheen Panth Prakash* Sakhi 79 Vol 1. Most versions are without the last couplet (20), cited by Raijasbir Singh, *Deep Singh*, 57, taken from an SGPC publication (1984) of the work; the reference here is to Deep Singh whose bunga is located on the south side of *Harimandir Sahib*, Amritsar.
7 Kanwal, *Deep Singh*, 38-39.
8 Ratan Singh Bhangu, *Sri Guru Panth Parkash*, Vol. 1, Sakhi 46, Couplets 1-2, translated by Kulwant Singh (Chandigarh: Institute of Sikh Studies, 2006).
9 In Raijasbir Singh, *Deep Singh*, 54; 'diwan' is Hindi for 'a seated gathering', usually formal and with an important personage in chair, in this case, Banda Singh Bahadur; 'jawan' means 'youth'. In fact, Deep Singh belonged to Pahuwind and not Chakoyi as mentioned herein.
10 Ghukewalia, "Deep Singh," in Raijasbir Singh, *Deep Singh*, 161-162.
11 Kanwal, *Deep Singh*, 63-64.

12 In Raijasbir Singh, *Deep Singh*, 183.
13 *Ibid.*, 271; a 'pauri' is a poem with a poetic meter generally employed for heroic ballads; in this case, each line is of six feet with perfect end-rhyme.
14 *Ibid.*, 232-233; a 'korda' is a poem generally with 13 syllables per line; this one has rhyming couplets.
15 *Ibid.*, 168.
16 *Ibid.*, 188.
17 Gyani Gyan Singh, "Utraradh Bisram 50", *Panth Prakash*, stanzas 33-35.
18 In Raijasbir Singh, *Deep Singh*, 307-309
19 *Ibid.*, 187.
20 Gyani Gyan Singh, "Utraradh Bisram 50", stanza 45.
21 *Ibid.*, stanza 46.
22 *Ibid.*, stanza 47.
23 *Ibid.*, stanzas 48-53.
24 *Ibid.*, stanzas 54-58
25 In Raijasbir Singh, *Deep Singh*, 241; also, Gyani Gyani Singh, "Utraradh Bisram 50", stanzas 54-59.
26 *Ibid.*, 242
27 *Ibid.*, 188
28 *Ibid.*, 189
29 *Ibid.*, 143
30 *Ibid.*, 171-172; 'phirna chhand' is a poetic measure that is varied within a larger piece to provide contrast and relief.
31 Gyani Gyan Singh, "Utraradh Bisram 50", stanzas 78-89.
32 Seetal cited in Raijasbir Singh, *Deep Singh*, 238; Gyani Gyan Singh also records both duels in his "Utararadh Bisram 50": with Zabardast Khan (Stanzas 78-89), Rustam Khan (Stanza 90-91).
33 Gyani Gyan Singh, "Utararadh Bisram 50", stanzas 90-91.
34 *Ibid.*, Stanza 77.
35 *Ibid.*, Stanza 92.
36 Kanwal, *Deep Singh*, 71-72

Appendix B: Competing Claims of Birth and Belonging

1 Das Visakha Singh et al., *Malwa Sikh Itihas* vol 1 (Amritsar: Chattar Singh, Jiwan Singh, 1998), 375.

2   Gyani Balwant Singh Kotha Guru, *Sri Dam Dama Guru ki Kanshi*. (Bhatinda: Gyani Kaur Singh, 2017), 70.
3   Verified by the author on interacting with the head granthi (priest) at the Gurm Gurdwara.
4   Das Visakha Singh et al, *Itihas* 1: 277-278, 374-375.
5   Niranjan Singh Sathi cited in Mehnga Singh Kalsi. *Sirlath Shaheed Baba Deep Singh* (Chandigarh: Unistar Books, 2015), 35.
6   The author interacted with village elders at Gurm who expressed ignorance of any genealogy records for their claim; nor were they aware of any kinship ties between Deep Singh and Baba Naudh Singh.
7   Kotha Guru, *Dam Dama Sahib*, 72.
8   Das Visakha Singh et al., *Itihas*, 1: 278; II: 109.

Appendix C: Origin and Evolution of Sikhism

1   Gurdwara Sacha Sauda stands in Farooqabad (Pakistan) in commemoration of the event.
2   Andre Wink, *Al-Hind: The Making of the Indo-Islamic World* (Boston: Brill Academic, 2002), 51, 204-205.
3   KS Lal, *Growth of Muslim Population in Medieval India (1000-1800)* (Delhi: Research Publications in Social Sciences, 1973), 211-217.
4   Will Durant, *The Story of Civilization: Our Oriental Heritage Vol. 1* (New York: Simon & Schuster, 1976), 458-472.
5   *Babur-Nama: Memoirs of Zehir-Ded-Din Muhammed Baber: Emperor of Hindustan* Vol 1 (1826). Translated by John Leyden and William Erskene (London: OUP, 2011), 140.
6   ਆਪੈ ਦੋਸੁ ਨ ਦੇਈ ਕਰਤਾ ਜਮੁ ਕਰਿ ਮੁਗਲੁ ਚੜਾਇਆ ॥
    ਏਤੀ ਮਾਰ ਪਈ ਕਰਲਾਣੇ ਤੈਂ ਕੀ ਦਰਦੁ ਨ ਆਇਆ ॥੧॥
    ਕਰਤਾ ਤੂੰ ਸਭਨਾ ਕਾ ਸੋਈ ॥
    ਜੇ ਸਕਤਾ ਸਕਤੇ ਕਉ ਮਾਰੇ ਤਾ ਮਨਿ ਰੋਸੁ ਨ ਹੋਈ ॥੧॥ ਰਹਾਉ ॥
    ਸਕਤਾ ਸੀਹੁ ਮਾਰੇ ਪੈ ਵਗੈ ਖਸਮੈ ਸਾ ਪੁਰਸਾਈ ॥
    ਰਤਨ ਵਿਗਾੜਿ ਵਿਗੋਏ ਕੁਤੀ ਮੁਇਆ ਸਾਰ ਨ ਕਾਈ
        —Guru Nanak Dev, Sri Guru Granth Sahib, 360 (lines 12-14)
    Āpai ḍos na ḍeºī kartā jam kar mugal chaṛāºiºā.
    Ėtī mār paºī karlāṇe taiṅ kī ḍaraḍ na āºiºā. ॥1॥
    Kartā tūṅ sabhnā kā soºī.

Je saktā sakte ka∘o māre tā man ros na ho∘ī. ||1|| *rahā∘o.*
Saktā sīhu māre pai vagai khasmai sā pursā∘ī.
Ratan vigāṛ vigo∘e kutīṅ mu∘i∘ā sār na kā∘ī.

'The Creator Himself does not take the blame but sent the Mughal as the messenger of death.
There was so much slaughter that people screamed. Did You not feel any compassion, Lord? ||1||
If a powerful tiger attacks and kills a flock of sheep, its master must answer for it.
This priceless country is laid waste and defiled by dogs, and none attends to the dead.'

7 Pashaura Singh. "Revisiting the Evolution of the Sikh Community." *Journal of Punjab Studies* Vol. 17, (2010), 57.
8 HS Gill, *Baba Nanak* (New Delhi: Harman Publishing, 2003), 6.
9 *Ibid.*, 4.
10 Nikky-guninder Kaur Singh, *The feminine principle in the Sikh Vision of the Transcendent* (Cambridge: Cambridge University Press, 1993), 172.
11 ਅਵੱਲ ਅਲਹ ਨੂਰ ਉਪਾਯਾ ਕੁਦਰਤ ਦੇ ਸਬ ਬੰਦੇ
    ਏਕ ਨੂਰ ਸੇ ਸਬ ਜਗੁ ਉਪਜਯਿਾ ਕੌਣ ਭਲੇ ਕੋ ਮੰਦੇ
    Aval alah nūr upā∘i∘ā kudrat ke sabh bande.
    Ėk nūr te sabh jag upji∘ā ka∘un bhale ko mande. ||1||

'First, God created the Light; then, by His Creative Power, fashioned all mortal beings.
When from One Light the entire universe has emerged, how can one be good and another bad?' ||1||
        —Bhagat Kabir, Sri Guru Granth Sahib, 1349, line 19

12 Gopal Singh, *History*, 7.
13 ਘਾਲਿ ਖਾਇ ਕਿਛੁ ਹਥਹੁ ਦੇਇ ॥
    ਨਾਨਕ ਰਾਹੁ ਪਛਾਣਹਿ ਸੇਇ ॥੧॥
    Ghaal khaae kishh haththahu dhaee ||
    naanak raahu pashhaanehi saee ||1||

'One who works for what he eats, and gives away some to the needy.
O Nanak, he has found the Path.'
        —Guru Nanak, Sri Guru Granth Sahib, 1245, line 19

14 ਧੌਲੁ ਧਰਮੁ ਦਇਆ ਕਾ ਪੂਤੁ ॥
   Dhoul dharam da⸱iā kā pūt.
   'All religion is born of compassion.'
   —Sri Guru Granth Sahib, 3, line 13

15 ਸਚਹੁ ਓਰੈ ਸਭੁ ਕੋ ਉਪਰਿ ਸਚੁ ਆਚਾਰੁ ॥੫॥
   sachahu ourai sabh ko oupar sach aachaar ॥5॥
   'Truth is higher than everything, but higher still is truthful living.' ॥5॥
   —Guru Nanak, Sri Guru Granth Sahib, 62, line 12

16 ਕਬੀਰ ਹਜ ਕਾਬੇ ਹਉ ਜਾਇ ਥਾ ਆਗੈ ਮਿਲਿਆ ਖੁਦਾਇ ॥
   ਸਾਂਈ ਮੁਝ ਸਿਉ ਲਰਿ ਪਰਿਆ ਤੁਝੈ ਕਿਨਿਹੁ ਫੁਰਮਾਈ ਗਾਇ ॥੧੯੭॥
   Kabīr haj kābe ha⸱o jā⸱e thā āgai mili⸱ā khudā⸱e.
   Sāñ⸱ī mujh si⸱o lar pari⸱ā ṯujhai kinih furmā⸱ī gā⸱e. ॥197॥
   Kabeer, I was going on a pilgrimage to Mecca, and God met me on the way
   He scolded me and asked, 'Who told you that I am only there?'
   —Kabir, Sri Guru Granth Sahib, 1375.

17 ਵਡਾ ਸਾਹਿਬੁ ਊਚਾ ਥਾਉ ॥
   ਊਚੇ ਉਪਰਿ ਊਚਾ ਨਾਉ ॥
   ਏਵਡੁ ਊਚਾ ਹੋਵੈ ਕੋਇ ॥
   ਤਿਸੁ ਊਚੇ ਕਉ ਜਾਣੈ ਸੋਇ ॥
   vadaa saahib oochaa thaa-o.
   oochay upar oochaa naa-o.
   ayvad oochaa hovai ko-ay.
   tis oochay ka-o jaanai so-ay.
   jayvad aap jaanai aap aap.
   Great is the Master, high is His Heavenly Home.
   Highest of the High, above all is His Name.
   Only one as Great and as High as God
   can know His Lofty and Exalted State.
   Only He Himself can know Himself.
   —Guru Nanak, The *Japji*, Stanza 24
   Guru Nanak, Sri Guru Granth Sahib, 5 (lines 9-10)

18 ਭੰਡਿ ਜੰਮੀਐ ਭੰਡਿ ਨਿੰਮੀਐ ਭੰਡਿ ਮੰਗਣੁ ਵੀਆਹੁ ॥
   ਭੰਡਹੁ ਹੋਵੈ ਦੋਸਤੀ ਭੰਡਹੁ ਚਲੈ ਰਾਹੁ ॥
   ਭੰਡੁ ਮੁਆ ਭੰਡੁ ਭਾਲੀਐ ਭੰਡਿ ਹੋਵੈ ਬੰਧਾਨੁ ॥
   ਸੋ ਕਿਉ ਮੰਦਾ ਆਖੀਐ ਜਿਤੁ ਜੰਮਹਿ ਰਾਜਾਨ ॥

Bhand jammī▫ai bhand nimmī▫ai bhand mangaṇ vī▫āhu.
Bhandahu hovai ḏostī bhandahu chalai rāhu
Bhand mu▫ā bhand bhālī▫ai bhand hovai bandhān.
So ki▫o mandā ākhī▫ai jiṯ jameh rājān.
'From woman, man is born; within her, conceived; to woman he is engaged and wed.
Woman becomes his friend; through her, future generations come. When his woman dies, he seeks another; to woman, he is bound. So why call her bad who gives birth to kings?'
— Sri Guru Granth Sahib, 473, lines 8-9.

19 WH McLeod, *The Sikhs: History, Religion, and Society* (New York: Columbia University Press, 1989), 31.

20 ਮਰਣੁ ਮੁਣਸਾ ਸੂਰਿਆ ਹਕੁ ਹੈ ਜੋ ਹੋਇ ਮਰਨਿ ਪਰਵਾਣੋ ॥
Maraṇ muṇsā sūri▫ā hak hai jo ho▫e maran parvāṇo.
'The death of brave heroes is blessed, if it is approved by God.'
— Guru Nanak Dev, Sri Guru Granth Sahib, 579, line 19.

21 Mohammed Iqbal. *Zarb-e-Kaleem-013 Shukar-o-Shikayat (Thankscum-Complaint)*. Accessed 20 January 2020. http://iqbalurdu.blogspot.com/2011/04/zarb-e-kaleem-013-shukar-o-shikayat.html

22 Mohammad Iqbal, *Bang-e-Dra-143 Nanak*. Accessed 2 April 2020. http://iqbalurdu.blogspot.com/2011/04/bang-e-dra-143-nanak.html

23 Wilfred Smith, *On Understanding Islam* (The Hague: Mouton, 1981), 179.

24 Gurinder Singh Mann, *The Making of Sikh Scripture* (New York: Oxford University Press, 2001), 6.

25 *Ibid.*, 10.

26 *Ibid.*, 13.

27 Jaswinder Dhillon, *Studies in Sikh Philosophy and Culture* (Amritsar: Guru Nanak Dev University, 2004), 19. According to Gyani Gyan Singh, Guru Amar Das purchased the land from landholders in 1572 CE: refer Gyani Gyan Singh, *Twarikh Sri Amritsar* (Amritsar: Kendra Singh Sabha, 1977), 4.

28 ਨਾ ਤੂ ਆਵਹਿ ਵਸਿ ਬਹੁਤੁ ਘਿਣਾਵਣੇ ॥
ਨਾ ਤੂ ਆਵਹਿ ਵਸਿ ਬੇਦ ਪੜਾਵਣੇ ॥
ਨਾ ਤੂ ਆਵਹਿ ਵਸਿ ਤੀਰਥਿ ਨਾਈਐ ॥
ਨਾ ਤੂ ਆਵਹਿ ਵਸਿ ਧਰਤੀ ਧਾਈਐ ॥

ਨਾ ਤੂ ਆਵਹਿ ਵਸਿ ਕਿਤੈ ਸਿਆਣਪੈ ॥
ਨਾ ਤੂ ਆਵਹਿ ਵਸਿ ਬਹੁਤਾ ਦਾਨੁ ਦੇ ॥
ਸਭੁ ਕੋ ਤੇਰੈ ਵਸਿ ਅਗਮ ਅਗੋਚਰਾ ॥

—Guru Arjan Dev, Sri Guru Granth Sahib,
Line 9-11, 962.

Nā tū āvahi vas bahut ghiṇāvaṇe.
Nā tū āvahi vas bed paṛāvaṇe.
Nā tū āvahi vas tirath nā॰ī॰ai.
Nā tū āvahi vas dhartī dhā॰ī॰ai.
Nā tū āvahi vas kitai si॰āṇpai.
Nā tū āvahi vas bahutā dān de.
Sabh ko terai vas agam agocharā.

None may fathom or know You,
O Supreme Being through contempt.
Nor by studying the Vedas;
Nor by bathing at the holy places;
Nor through mendicancy and wandering all over the world;
Nor through tricks of the mind;
Nor by huge donations to charity.
All are under Your power,
O inaccessible, unfathomable Lord!

29 ਪੇਖਨ ਸੁਨਨ ਸੁਨਾਵਨੋ ਮਨ ਮਹਿ ਦ੍ਰਿੜੀਐ ਸਾਚੁ ॥
Pekhan sunan sunāvano man mèh ḍariṛ॰ī॰ai sāch.
See, hear, speak and implant the True Lord within your mind.

—Guru Arjan Dev,
Sri Guru Granth Sahib, 706.

30 Pashaura Singh, "Revisiting Evolution," 57-58.
31 Khushwant Singh, *History of the Sikhs*, I: 54–56, 294–295.
32 Harbans Singh, *The Heritage of the Sikhs* (Calcutta: Asia Publishing House, 1964), 10.
33 An old text that provides some details of the process is the *Gurbilas Chhevin Patshahi*, written in 1718; also see Fauja Singh, *The City of Amritsar*, accessed 10 December 2019. https://www.allaboutsikhs.com/harmandir-sahib/installation-of-holy-granth-at-harimandir
34 Mann, *Sikh Scripture*, 21; now in the custody of Karamjit Singh Sodhi of Kartarpur, also see *ibid.*, 15.

35 ਸੂਹੀ ਮਹਲਾ ੫ ॥
Sūhī mēhlā 5.
ਸੰਤਾ ਕੇ ਕਾਰਜਿ ਆਪਿ ਖਲੋਇਆ ਹਰਿ ਕੰਮੁ ਕਰਾਵਣਿ ਆਇਆ ਰਾਮ ॥
ਧਰਤਿ ਸੁਹਾਵੀ ਤਾਲੁ ਸੁਹਾਵਾ ਵਿਚਿ ਅੰਮ੍ਰਿਤ ਜਲੁ ਛਾਇਆ ਰਾਮ ॥
ਅੰਮ੍ਰਿਤ ਜਲੁ ਛਾਇਆ ਪੂਰਨ ਸਾਜੁ ਕਰਾਇਆ ਸਗਲ ਮਨੋਰਥ ਪੂਰੇ ॥
ਜੈ ਜੈ ਕਾਰੁ ਭਇਆ ਜਗ ਅੰਤਰਿ ਲਾਥੇ ਸਗਲ ਵਿਸੂਰੇ ॥
Santā ke kāraj āp khalo˳i˳ā har kamm karāvaṇ ā˳i˳ā rām.
Dharat suhāvī ṭāl suhāvā vich amrit jal chhā˳i˳ā rām.
Amrit jal chhā˳i˳ā pūran sāj karā˳i˳ā sagal manorath pūre.
Jai jai kār bha˳i˳ā jag anṭar lāthe sagal visūre.

The Lord Himself has stood by to resolve the affairs of Saints, and complete their tasks.

The land and pool are beautiful, within it is contained the Ambrosial Water.

The Ambrosial Water is full up and my job is complete, all my desires fulfilled.

Felicitations are pouring in from all over the world, and my sorrows are dissipated.

—Guru Arjan Dev,
Sri Guru Granth Sahib, line 15, 783.

36 Mann, *Sikh Scripture*, 4-5.

37 Ahmed Sirhindi *Maktubat-i-Imam Rabbani* Vol. 1 Letter No. 163, Lahore 1964 cited in Bhagat Singh, *History of the Sikh Misals* (Patiala: Punjabi University, 1993), 8.

38 J. Gordon Melton, *Faiths Across Time: 5,000 Years of Religious History* (Santa Barbara: ABC-CLIO, 2014), III: 1163.

39 *The Jahangirnama: Memoirs of Jahangir, Emperor of India,* Translated, edited, and annotated by Wheeler M. Thackston, (New York: Oxford University Press, 1999), 59.

40 GC Walker, *Gazetteer of the Lahore District 1893-1894* (Lahore: Panjab Government, 1894), 31.

41 Pashaura Singh, "Reconsidering the Sacrifice of Guru Arjan," *Journal of Panjab Studies.* Edited by *Gibb Schreffler Vol. 18,* (2011), 305: http://www.global.ucsb.edu/punjab/sites/secure.lsit.ucsb.edu.gisp.d7_sp/files/sitefiles/journals/volume18/11_InResponse.pdf

42 Pashaura Singh, "Revisiting Evolution," 66.

43 ਸੂਰਬੀਰ ਬਚਨ ਕੇ ਬਲੀ ॥
   Sūrbīr bachan ke balī.
   'The true man of courage is a man of his word.'
   —Sri Guru Granth Sahib, 392, line 16.

44 Syad Mohammad Latif, *History of the Panjab* (Calcutta: Central Press, 1891), 259-260.

45 Sushil Pandit, "Truth About Kashmir: Story of Kashmir and Kashmiri Hindus," talk at IIT Madras 6 October 2016. Video (watch 2.07.40 to 2.09.25 recorder timing). https://www.youtube.com/watch?v=FhiXbwPKN9Y; also, JS Grewal, *The Sikhs of the Punjab* (New Delhi: Cambridge University Press, 2014), 72.

46 ਭੈ ਕਾਹੂ ਕਉ ਦੇਤ ਨਹਿ ਨਹਿ ਭੈ ਮਾਨਤ ਆਨ ॥
   ਕਹੁ ਨਾਨਕ ਸੁਨਿ ਰੇ ਮਨਾ ਗਿਆਨੀ ਤਾਹਿ ਬਖਾਨਿ ॥ ੧੬ ॥
   Bhai kāhū kaᵒo det neh neh bhai mānat ān.
   Kaho Nānak sun re manā giᵒānī tāhi bakhān.
   —Sri Guru Granth Sahib, 1427, line 7
   One who does not frighten anyone, and who is not afraid of anyone else,
   Says Nanak, listen, mind: call him spiritually wise. ॥16॥

47 Will Durant, *The Story of Civilization: Our Oriental Heritage Vol. 1* (New York: Simon & Schuster, 1976), 458-472; also see Felix Gilbert, "Machiavelli: The Renaissance of the Art of War," in *Makers of Modern Strategy*, ed. Peter Paret (Princeton: Princeton University Press, 1986), 26; the author contends that even early Christianity cast a pacifying and enervating influence.

48 JD Cunningham, *A History of the Sikhs* (Delhi: Asia Educational Services, 1994 [1849]), 38.

49 ਹਥਿਆਰ ਪੰਜੇ ਬਨ ਕੇ ਦਰਸ਼ਨ ਆਵਣਾ ।
   'hathiar panje bann ke darsan avana'.
   'Appear before the Guru with five weapons on your person'
   —In Ganda Singh, ed., *Hukamname* (Patiala: Punjabi University, 1967), 179, 194; Pashaura Singh, "Revisiting," 61-62: this must be understood in its militaristic context.

50 John Malcolm, *Sketch of the Sikhs* (London: John Murray, 1812), 190.

51 Cunningham, *The Sikhs*, 82.

52 Cited in Gopal Singh, *History*, 328-329.

53 Chhanda Chatterjee. "Rabindranath Tagore's Use of Guru Gobind Singh as a Nationalist Icon" in *Tagore and Nationalism*, ed. KL Tuteja and Kaustav Chakraborty (Shimla: Indian Institute of Advanced Studies, 2017), 257-266.
54 Rabindranath Tagore (1888). *Guru Gobind Singh*. Translated by Anurag Singh: https://profanuraagsingh.wordpress.com/2015/06/29/gurugobind-singh-a-poem-by-tagore/
55 Christopher Shackle, Gurharpal Singh and Arvind-Pal Mandair, eds., *Sikh Religion, Culture and Ethnicity*. (London: Routledge, 2013), 11–12, 17–19.
56 Banga, "Deep Singh," 7.
57 *Encyclopaedia Britannica*, s.v. 'Sikhism'. Accessed 10 April 2020 https://www.britannica.com/topic/Sikhism
58 Gopal Singh, *History*, 421.
59 ਸਤਿਗੁਰ ਨਾਨਕ ਪ੍ਰਗਟਿਆ ਮਿਟੀ ਧੁੰਧੁ ਜਗਿ ਚਾਨਣੁ ਹੋਆ।
ਜਿਉ ਕਰਿ ਸੂਰਜੁ ਨਿਕਲਿਆ ਤਾਰੇ ਛਪਿ ਅੰਧੇਰੁ ਪਲੋਆ।
Satiguru Naanaku Pragatiaa Mitee Dhundhu Jagi Chaananu Hoaa |
Jiu Kari Sooraju Nikaliaa Taaray Chhipay Andhyru Paloaa |
—Bhai Gurdas. *Vaaran. Vaar 1, Pauri 27*, 1-2

Select Bibliography

"Akal Takth Weapons' Display", filmed 12 February 2008 at Akal Takth, Amritsar. Video Part 1—7.16 mins; Part 2—7.10 mins, Part 1: https://www.youtube.com/watch?v=tRrDR9lJhSk#action=share; time 3.44 min, Part 2: https://www.youtube.com/watch?v=nArLYH-IJ9g

Ali, Babu Rajab. *Babu Rajab Ali di Chonvin Kavita*. Patiala: Punjabi University, 1986.

Ansari, Sarah FD. *Sufi Saints and State Power: the Pirs of Sind, 1843-1947*. New York: Cambridge University Press, 1992.

Asher, Catherine Ella and Cynthia Talbot. *India before Europe*. New York: Cambridge University Press, 2006.

Aulakh, Ajit Singh. *Illustrated Stories of Baba Deep Singh ji Shaheed, Baba Banda Singh ji Bahadur, Bhai Mani Singh ji Shaheed*. Amritsar: Chattar Singh Jeevan Singh, 2010.

Axworthy, Michael. *The Sword of Persia: Nader Shah, from Tribal Warrior to Conquering Tyrant*. IB Tauris, 2006.

Babur-Nama Memoirs of Zehir-Ed-Din Muhammed baber: Emperor of Hindustan, Vol. 1, translated by John Leyden and William Erskene. London: Oxford University Press, 2011.

Badunger, Kirpal Singh. "Shaheed Baba Deep Singh ji: Brahm Gyani" in compendium of papers presented at *Baba Deep Singh: Jeevan te Yogdaan* National Seminar. Amritsar: Guru Nanak Dev University, 29-30 January 2009, p. 42-47.

Bajwa, KS. "Takhat Sri Dam Dama Sahib: Establishment and Role in Sikh History", *Sikh Formations: Religion, Culture, Theory 10*, Issue 3, 2014. https://religiondocbox.com/Hinduism/69730310-Takhat-sridam-dama-sahib-establishment-and-role-in-sikh-history.html

Banerjee, Indubhusan. *Evolution of the Khalsa: the Reformation*, Vol. 2. Calcutta: A Mukherjee & Co, 1947.

Banga, Indu. "Historical Context of Baba Deep Singh" in compendium of papers presented at *Baba Deep Singh: Jeevan te Yogdaan* National Seminar. Amritsar: Guru Nanak Dev University, 29-30 January 2009, p. 3-7.

Barber, Malcolm. *The new knighthood: a history of the Order of the Temple, Canto ed.* Cambridge, UK: Cambridge University Press, 1995.

Barnes, Michael SJ. *Interreligious learning: dialogue, spirituality, and the Christian imagination.* Cambridge: Cambridge University Press, 2012.

"Battle of Amritsar (1757)", Wikipedia, https://en.wikipedia.org/wiki/Battle_of_Amritsar (1757)

"Bhai Mani Singh," Sikhiwiki, accessed on 22 April 2020, https://www.sikhiwiki.org/index.php/Bhai_Mani_Singh_Shaheed.

Bhangu, Ratan Singh. *Sri Gur Panth Parkash*, Vol. 1 and 2, translated by Kulwant Singh, Institute of Sikh Studies, Chandigarh, 2006.

Bonarjee, PD. *A Handbook of the Fighting Races of India.* Calcutta: Thacker, Spink & Co, 1899.

Browne, James. "History of the Origin and Progress of the Sicks" in *Early European Accounts of the Sikhs*, edited by Ganda Singh. Calcutta: Indian Studies, Past and Present, 1962, p. 9-42.

"Rudolph Bultmann", Wikipedia, accessed on 22 April 2020, https://en.wikipedia.org/wiki/Rudolf_Bultmann

Chatrik, Dhani Ram. *Chatrik Ratnavali.* Patiala: Punjabi University, 1975.

Chatterjee, Chhanda. "Rabindranath Tagore's Use of Guru Gobind Singh as a Nationalist Icon" in *Tagore and Nationalism,* edited by K.L. Tuteja and Kaustav Chakraborty, Indian Institute of Advanced Studies, Shimla, 2017, p. 257-266.

Chawla, Kartar Singh. *Jivan Baba Deep Singh ji Shaheed.* Amritsar, Khalsa Brothers.

Choudhary, Kulwant Singh. *Gurdwara Sri Paonta Sahib.* Paonta Sahib: Prabandhak Committee Gurdwara Sri Paonta Sahib, 2015.

Churchill, Winston. *Quotes, Goodreads,* https://www.goodreads.com/quotes/37665-battles-are-won-by-slaughter-and-maneuver-thegreater-the

Clausewitz, Carl Von. "Key Concepts" in *War,* ed. Lawrence Freedman. New York: Oxford University Press, 1994, p. 206-211.

Clifford, Hopewell. *James Bowie Texas Fighting Man: A Biography.* TX: Eakin Press, Austin, 1994.

Cunningham, JD. *A History of the* Sikhs. Delhi: Asia Educational Services, 1994.

Dalrymple, William. *Return of a King: The Battle for Afghanistan, 1839-42.* New York, Random House, 2013.

Dervesh, Trilok Singh. *Prasang Baba Deep Singh ji Shaheed*, Meher Singh Surinder Singh, Amritsar, n.d.

Dhamija, Sumant. *Jassa Singh Ahluwalia (1718-1783)*. Delhi: Social Science Press, 2011.

Dhillon, Balwant Singh. "18vi sadi di Sikh yudh kala atte janggi vivhar" in compendium of papers presented at *Baba Deep Singh: Jeevan te Yogdaan* National Seminar. Amritsar: Guru Nanak Dev University, 29-30 January 2009, p. 171-177.

Dhillon, Jaswinder. *Studies in Sikh Philosophy and Culture*. Amritsar: Guru Nanak Dev University, 2004.

Dilbar, Daya Singh. "Vaar Baba Deep Singh ji Shaheed" in *Dilbar Vaaran*, Meher Singh Surinder Singh, Amritsar, 1972.

Dilgeer, Harjinder Singh. *Guru de Sher*. Amritsar: Jeevan Singh Chattar Singh, 2011.

Dilgeer, Harjinder Singh. *Sikh Twarikh*, 5 vols. Amritsar, Sikh University Press, 2008.

Durant, Will. *The Story of Civilization: Our Oriental Heritage*, Vol. 1. New York, Simon & Schuster, 1976.

Encyclopaedia Britannica, s.v. "Sikhism", accessed on 10 April 2020, https:// www.britannica.com/topic/Sikhism

Falcon, Captain RW. *Handbook on Sikhs: for the use of Regimental Officers*. Allahabad: Pioneer Press, 1896.

Fazal, Abu'l. *Ain-i-Akbari*, Vol. 2, translated by Colonel Henry Sullivan Jarrett, The Asiatic Society of Bengal, Calcutta, 1891.

Fenech, Louis E. "Martyrdom and the Sikh Tradition", *The Journal of the American Oriental Society*, Vol. 117, No. 4, October-December, 1997, p. 623-642.

Forster, George. *A Journey from Bengal to England through the Northern part of India, Kashmir, Afghanistan, and Persia, and into Russia, by the Caspian Sea*, 2 Vols. London: Faulder, 1798.

Gazetteer of the Amritsar District 1883-4. Calcutta: Punjab Government, 1884.

Ghukewalia, Sohan Singh. *Baba Deep Singh Shaheed*, Jeevan Singh Chatter Singh, Amritsar, n.d.

Gilbert, Felix. "Machiavelli: The Renaissance of the Art of War" in *Makers of Modern Strategy*, ed. Peter Paret. Princeton: Princeton University Press, 1986, p. 11-31.

Gill, HS. *Baba Nanak*. New Delhi: Harman Publishing, 2003.

Goswamy, BN and JS Grewal. *The Mughal and Sikh Rulers and the Vaishnavas of Pindori: A Historical Interpretation of 52 Persian Documents*. Shimla: Indian Institute of Advanced Study, 1969.

Greene, Robert. *The 33 Strategies of War*. New Delhi: Viva Books, 2006.

Grewal, JS. *The Sikhs of the Punjab*. New Delhi: Cambridge University Press, 2014.

Grewal, JS and Irfan Habib. eds. *Sikh History from Persian* Sources. New Delhi: Indian History Congress, 2001.

Grewal, JS. "WH McLeod and Sikh Studies" in *Journal of Punjab Studies*, 17, 2010, 1-2, p. 115–142.

Griffin, Lepel. *Ranjit Singh*. Oxford: Clarendon Press, 1892.

Grover, BL and Alka Mehta. *A New Look at Modern Indian History*. New Delhi: S. Chand, 2018.

Gupta, HR. *History of the Sikhs*, 5 Vols., 3rd ed. New Delhi: Munshiram Manoharlal Publishers, 2007.

Gurdas, Bhai. *Vaaran*, Vaar 1, Pauri 27, p. 1-2.

Gurdwara Lohgarh Sahib Patshain, 10 *Sankhep Itihas*, n.d.

Guru Nanak Dev University, *Baba Deep Singh: Jeevan te Yogdaan*, compendium of papers presented at National Seminar, Amritsar, 29-30 January 2009.

Habib, Irfan. *Economic History of Medieval India, 1200-1500*, Vol. 8, Part 1. Delhi: Pearson Education, 2011.

Hardin, Stephen L. *Texian Iliad*, TX: University of Texas Press, Austin, 1994.

Hopewell, Clifford. *James Bowie Texas Fighting Man: A Biography*, TX: Eakin Press, Austin, 1994.

Howard, Michael. "The Dimensions of Strategy" in *War*, ed. Lawrence Freedman, New York: Oxford University Press, 1994, p. 197-202.

Ibbetson, Denzil Charles. *Panjab Castes*, Lahore: Government Printing, Punjab, 1916.

"Indian Units of Measurement," Wikipedia, https://en.wikipedia.org/wiki/Indian_units_of_measurement

Iqbal, Mohammed. *Zarb-e-Kaleem-013 Shukar-o-Shikayat*, accessed on 20 January 2020, http://iqbalurdu.blogspot.com/2011/04/zarb-ekaleem-013-shukar-o-shikayat.html

Iqbal, Mohammad. *Bang-e-Dra-143 Nanak*, accessed on 2 April 2020, http://iqbalurdu.blogspot.com/2011/04/bang-e-dra-143-nanak.html

India Today, 5 March 2020, https://www.indiatoday.in/india/story/maharaja-ranjit-singh-voted-greatest-leader-of-alltimes-1652824-2020-03-05

Jacques, Tony. *Dictionary of Battles and Sieges*. Westport: Greenwood, 2007.

"Jatha Shaheedan," http://www.jathashaheedan.com/history.php

Jhubal, Ardaman Singh. "Baba Deep Singh and Dam Dami Taksal" in compendium of papers presented at *Baba Deep Singh: Jeevan te Yogdaan* National Seminar. Amritsar: Guru Nanak Dev University, 29-30 January 2009, p. 161-170.

Johar, Surinder Singh. *The Heritage of Amritsar*. New Delhi: Sundeep Prakashan, 1978.

Jomini, Baron De. "Strategy and Grand Tactics" in *War*, ed. Lawrence Freedman. New York: Oxford University Press, 1994, p. 112-213.

Journal of Indian History, Vol. XXVI, Part 1, April 1948, Serial No. 76.

Kalaswalia, Kartar Singh. *Jauhar Khalsa*, Bhai Jwahir Singh Kirpal Singh, Amritsar, n.d.

Kalsi, Mehnga Singh. *Sirlath Shaheed Baba Deep Singh*. Chandigarh: Unistar Books, 2015.

Kang, KS. "Sikh Strategy and Tactics: 18th Century" in compendium of papers presented at *Baba Deep Singh: Jeevan te Yogdaan* National Seminar. Amritsar: Guru Nanak Dev University, 2009, p. 8-24.

Kanwal, Gurdeep Singh. *Jeevan Baba Deep Singh ji Shaheed*. Amritsar: Jaspal Printing Press, n.d.

Kapoor, Sukhbir Singh and Mohinder Kaur Kapoor. *Dasm Granth An Introductory Study*. New Delhi: Hemkunt, 2009.

Kapur, Prithipal Singh. "Jassa Singh Ramgarhia" in *Sikh Struggle and the Misl Period*, eds. Kirpal Singh & Kharak Singh, Vol. 2. Amritsar: Golden Offset Press, 2013, p. 280-288.

Kaur, Kanwalpreet. "Weapons of the 18th Century" in compendium of papers presented at *Baba Deep Singh: Jeevan te Yogdaan* National Seminar. Amritsar: Guru Nanak Dev University, 29-30 January 2009, p. 83-88.

Kaur, Madanjit. "Natha Singh Shaheed" in *Sikh Struggle and the Misl Period*, eds. Kirpal Singh & Kharak Singh, Vol. 2. Amritsar: Golden Offset Press, 2013, p. 308-312.

Keegan, John. *The Face of Battle*. London: Pimlico, 1976.

Keen, Maurice Hugh. *Chivalry*. New Haven: Yale University Press, 2005.

Khan, Ghulam All. *Imacl-ut-Sa'adat*, Cawnpore, n.p, 1864.

Kohli, Surinder. *The Sikh and Sikhism*. New Delhi: Atlantic Publishers & Distributors, 1993.

Koshish, Sarup Singh. *Guru Diyan Sakhiyan*, Sakhi 89. Patiala: Panjabi University, 1986.

Kotha Guru, Gyani Balwant Singh. *Sri Dam Dama Guru ki Kanshi*. Bhatinda: Gyani Kaur Singh, 2017.

Lal, KS. *Growth of Muslim Population in Medieval India (1000-1800)*. Delhi: Research Publications in Social Sciences, 1973.

Latif, Syad Muhammad. *History of the Punjab from the Remotest Antiquity to the Present*. Calcutta: The Calcutta Central Press, 1891.

Liddell Hart, BH. "The Indirect Approach" in *War*, ed. Lawrence Freedman. New York: Oxford University Press, 1994, p. 231-232.

Maddison, Angus. *Development Centre Studies: The World Economy Historical Statistics*. Paris: OECD Publishing, 2003.

Mahan Singh Gyani. *Tasnifat at-i-Goya*. Amritsar: Khalsa Tract Society, 1963.

Malcolm, John. *Sketch of the Sikhs*. London: John Murray, 1812.

Malhotra, Karamjit K. *The Eighteenth Century in Sikh History*. New Delhi: Oxford University Press, 2016.

Mann, Gurinder Singh. *The Granth of Guru Gobind Singh*. New Delhi: Oxford University Press, 2015.

Mann, Gurinder Singh. *The Making of Sikh Scripture*. New York: Oxford University Press, 2001.

McLeod, WH. *The A to Z of Sikhism*. Maryland: Scarecrow Press, 2009.

McLeod, WH. *The Sikhs: History, Religion, and Society*. New York: Columbia University Press, 1989.

McLeod, WH. "The Sikh Struggle in the Eighteenth Century and its

Relevance for Today" *History of Religions*, Vol. 31, No. 4. 1992, p. 344-362, available at www.jstor.org/stable/1062799

Melton, J. Gordon. *Faiths Across Time: 5000 Years of Religious History*. 4 Vols., ABC-CLIO, Santa Barbara, 2013.

Miskin, Tahmas Khan. *Tahmas Nama*, abridged and translated by P. Setu Madhav Rao, Popular Prakashan, Bombay, 1967.

"Misl", Wikipedia, https://wikivisually.com/wiki/Misl

Moran, Lord. *The Anatomy of Courage*. Boston: Houghton Mifflin Company, 1967.

Muhammad, Qazi Nur. *Jang Namah (1764-1765)*, Ed. Ganda Singh. Amritsar: Sikh History Research Department, 1939.

Murti, Mohinder. *Teg de Dhani*. Amritsar: Singh Brothers, 1949.

Nabha, Kahn Singh. *Guru Shabad Ratnakar Mahan Kosh*. Patiala: Languages Department of Punjab, 1930, accessed on 20 April 2020, http://old.sgpc.net/CDN/Mahankosh.pdf

Nabha, Kahn Singh. *Mahankosh Encyclopedia of Sikh Literature*, English translation by Punjabi University, Patiala, 2006.

Nahar, Nirmal Singh. "Shaheed Baba Deep Singh," in *Shaheedi Qurbanian*. Amritsar: Meher Singh Surinder Singh, 1984.

Nand Lal, Bhai. *Tankhanamah*, accessed on 20 April 2020, https://www.searchgurbani.com/bhai-nand-lal/tankahnama

Nand Lal, Bhai. *Ganjnama*, accessed on 17 April 2020, https://www.searchgurbani.com/bhai-nand-lal/ganjnama

Napoleon. "Maximes" in *War*, ed. Lawrence Freedman. New York: Oxford University Press, 1994, p. 114-216.

"Nawab Kapur Singh," Sikhwiki, accessed on 10 October 2018, https://www.sikhiwiki.org/index.php/Nawab_Kapur_Singh

Nayyar, GS. "Socio-Political Milieu of Baba Deep Singh" in compendium of papers presented at *Baba Deep Singh: Jeevan te Yogdaan* National Seminar. Amritsar: Guru Nanak Dev University, 29-30 January 2009, p. 75-81.

Nijjar, BS. "Chhota Ghallughara", *The Encyclopedia of Sikhism*, Vol. 1. Patiala: Punjabi University, 1995.

Nirdosh, Kewal Singh. "Vaar Baba Deep Singh" in *Dhadi Prasang*, Chandigarh, 2000.

Pandit, Sushil. "Truth About Kashmir: Story of Kashmir and Kashmiri

Hindus," Talk at IIT Madras, 6 October 2016, Video, 2.13.50 hrs., https://www.youtube.com/watch?v=FhiXbwPKN9Y

Padam, Piara Singh. *Sankhep Sikh Itihas*. Amritsar: Singh Brothers, 2014.

Palmer, R. "Frederick the Great, Guibert, Bulow: From Dynastic to National War" in *Makers of Modern Strategy*, ed. Peter Paret. Princeton: Princeton University Press, 1986, p. 91-119.

Pannu, Harpal Singh "Shaheed Baba Deep Singh ji" in compendium of papers presented at *Baba Deep Singh: Jeevan te Yogdaan* National Seminar. Amritsar: Guru Nanak Dev University, 29-30 January 2009, p. 68-74.

Paret, Peter. "Introduction", in *Makers of Modern Strategy*, ed. Peter Paret. Princeton: Princeton University Press, 1986, p. 3-8.

Polier, Colonel A.L.H. Swiss Officer in the Mughal Court at Delhi, 1776.

"Punjab Doabs", Wikipedia, https://upload.wikimedia.org/wikipedia/commons/c/c3/PunjabDoabs.png

Purewal, Pal Singh. *Jantri*. Mohali: Punjab School Education Board, 1994.

Saggu, DS. *Battle Tactics and War Manoeuvres of the* Sikhs. Chennai: Notion Press, 2018.

Sagoo, Harbans Kaur. *Banda Singh Bahadur and Sikh Sovereignty*, Ed. Harbans Kaur Sagoo. New Delhi: Deep and Deep, 2001.

Saraf, Babu Firozedin. *Saraf Rachnavali*. Patiala: Punjabi University, 1973.

Sarkar, Jadunath. *Fall of the Mughal Empire 1772-1788*, Vol. 3. Calcutta: SN Sarkar, 1938.

17 Sikh "The Tiger", accessed on 11 April 2020, https://www.facebook.com/shatrujeet009/posts/17-sikh-the-tiger-battalionthe-year-was-1954-17-sikh-was-located-at-agra-and-com/786048108235393/

Seetal, Sohan Singh Seetal. "Shaheed Baba Deep Singh" in *Merian Dhadi Vaaran*, Part 2, Youtube video, 57.14 minutes, https://www.youtube.com/watch?v=I_B-ftAuSYY

Shackle, Christopher. Gurharpal Singh and Arvind-Pal Mandair, eds. *Sikh Religion, Culture and Ethnicity*. London: Routledge, 2013.

Shiromani Gurdwara Parbandhak Committee (SGPC), annual calendar.

Shaheed, Charan Singh. *Rachnavali*. Patiala: Punjabi University, 1975.

"Shatrujeet", Facebook, https://www.facebook.com/shatrujeet009/posts/17-sikh-the-tiger-battalionthe-year-was-1954-17-sikh-waslocated-at-agra-and-com/786048108235393/

"SikhExpo", accessed on 16 November 2020, https://sikhexpo.com/blogs/news/baba-deep-singh-ji-story

Sidhu, Paramjit Singh. "Baba Deep Singh: Shaheedi Sarup Sancharatmkta" in compendium of papers presented at *Baba Deep Singh: Jeevan te Yogdaan* National Seminar. Amritsar: Guru Nanak Dev University, 29-30 January 2009, p. 89-110.

Singh, Balkar. "Sikh smriti vich Baba Deep Singh di than" in compendium of papers presented at *Baba Deep Singh: Jeevan te Yogdaan* National Seminar. Amritsar: Guru Nanak Dev University, 29-30 January 2009, p. 48-57.

Singh, Balwinder and Jaura Singh. "Baba Deep Singh Shaheed de Shaster" in compendium of papers presented at *Baba Deep Singh: Jeevan te Yogdaan* National Seminar. Amritsar: Guru Nanak Dev University, 29-30 January 2009, p. 127-131.

Singh, Bhagat. *A History of the Sikh Misals*. Patiala: Punjabi University, 1993.

Singh, Bhagat. "Martyrdom of Baba Deep Singh" in *Sikh Struggle and the Misl Period*, eds. Kirpal Singh & Kharak Singh, Vol. 2. Amritsar: Golden Offset Press, 2013, p. 110-112.

Singh, Bhagat. "Afghan Invasions of Punjab including the Battle of Panipat" in *Sikh Struggle and the Misl Period*, eds. Kirpal Singh & Kharak Singh, Vol. 2. Amritsar: Golden Offset Press, 2013, p. 117-136.

Singh, Buta. *Prasang Baba Deep Singh Shaheed*, Harbhajan Singh Harcharan Singh, Amritsar, n.d.

Singh, Das Visakha and Sant Sipahi Janet Pura. *Malwa Sikh Itihas*, 3 vols. Amritsar: Chattar Singh, Jiwan Singh, 1998.

Singh, Davinderpal. *The Golden Temple & the City of Amritsar*. Amritsar: The Sikh Book Company, 2018.

Singh, Devinder Singh. "Sikh Sangarsh te Baba Deep Singh" in compendium of papers presented at *Baba Deep Singh: Jeevan te Yogdaan* National Seminar. Amritsar: Guru Nanak Dev University, 29-30 January 2009, p. 35-41.

Singh, Dharam. "Baba Deep Singh Shaheed da Kav-Bimb" in compendium of papers presented at *Baba Deep Singh: Jeevan te Yogdaan* National Seminar. Amritsar: Guru Nanak Dev University, 29-30 January 2009, p. 111-118.

Singh, Fauja. *The City of Amritsar: An Introduction*, Ed. Fauja Singh,

Punjabi University, Patiala, 2000, accessed on 10 December 2019, https://www.allaboutsikhs.com/harmandir-sahib/installation-ofholy-granth-at-harimandir

Singh, Ganda. *Early European Accounts of the Sikhs and History of Origin and Progress of the Sikhs*, Ed. Ganda Singh. Delhi: Today and Tomorrow's Printers and Publishers, 1974.

Singh, Ganda. *Life of Banda Singh Bahadur*, 4th ed. Patiala: Punjabi University, 2016.

Singh, Ganda. *Hukamname*, Ed. Ganda Singh. Patiala: Punjabi University, 1967.

Singh, Ganda. *Sri Guru Shobha*. Patiala: Panjabi University, 1967.

Singh, Gopal. *A History of the Sikh People 1469-1988*. New Delhi: Allied Publishers, 1979.

Singh, Guru Gobind. *Aukat Bilas,* accessed on 11 November 2019, https://www.searchgurbani.com/public/dasam-granth/page/198

Singh, Guru Gobind. *Bachitter Natak, Dasm Granth,* accessed on 10 September 2019, https://www.searchgurbani.com/public/dasamgranth/page/117

Singh, Guru Gobind. *Shabad Hazare, Dasm Grath,* accessed on 8 December 2019, https://www.searchgurbani.com/dasam-granth/shabad/10070/line/1

Singh, Guru Gobind. *Shatranamala, Dasm Granth,* accessed on 20 September 2019, https://www.searchgurbani.com/public/dasamgranth/page/1327

Singh, Guru Gobind. *Zafarnamah, Dasm Granth,* accessed on 22 September 2019, https://www.searchgurbani.com/public/dasam-granth/page/2748

Singh, Gyani Gyan. *Sri Guru Panth Parkash di Prasravna*, Gyani Kirpal Singh, Amritsar, 1977, or Bhai Baljinder Singh, https://archive.org/details/PanthParkash1/mode/2up

Singh, Gyani Gyan. *Twarikh Guru Khalsa*, 2 Vols., 3rd ed. Amritsar: Bhai Chatter Singh Jeevan Singh, 2016.

Singh, Gyani Gyan. *Twarikh Sri Amritsar*. Amritsar: Kendriya Singh Sabha, 1923.

Singh, Gyani Mahan. *Tasnifat at-i-Goya*. Amritsar: Khalsa Tract Society, 1963.

Singh, Gyani Trilok. *Amar Shaheed Baba Deep Singh*. Amritsar: Chattar Singh Jeevan Singh, 2015.

Singh, Harbans. *The Heritage of the Sikhs*. Calcutta: Asia Publishing House, 1964.

Singh, Jarnail Sabran. *Parupkari Surma*, Youtube, https://www.youtube.com/watch?v=Bpb0GCRHeqU&feature=youtu.be

Singh, Jogeshwar. "Sikh Concept of Dharam Yudh and Baba Deep Singh" in compendium of papers presented at *Baba Deep Singh: Jeevan te Yogdaan* National Seminar. Amritsar: Guru Nanak Dev University, 2009, p. 132-140.

Singh, Kamalroop and Gurinder Singh Mann. *The Granth of Guru Gobind Singh*. New Delhi: Oxford University Press, 2015.

Singh, Karam. *Twarikh Amritsar*. Amritsar: Chattar Singh Jeevan Singh, 2020.

Singh, Khushwant. *A History of the Sikhs*, Vol. 1. New Delhi: Oxford University Press, 1999.

Singh, Khushwant. "Who are the Sikhs," Interview by BBC in 1997, accessed on 8 November 2018, https://www.youtube.com/watch?v=GykzdOXmzG0

Singh, Khushwant. *Ranjit Singh*. New Delhi: Penguin Books, 2008.

Singh, Kirpal. "Introduction" in *Sikh Struggle and the Misl Period*, eds. Kirpal Singh & Kharak Singh, Vol. 2. Amritsar: Golden Offset Press, 2013, p. xvi-xxvi.

Singh, Kirpal. *Life of Maharaja Ala Singh of Patiala and his times*. Amritsar: Sikh History Research Department, Khalsa College, 1954.

Singh, Nikky-guninder Kaur. *The Feminine Principle in the Sikh Vision of the Transcendent*. Cambridge: Cambridge University Press, 1993.

Singh, Pashaura. "Reconsidering the Sacrifice of Guru Arjan," Ed. *Gibb Schreffler, Journal of Panjab Studies*, Vol. 18, 2011, p. 305, http://www.global.ucsb.edu/punjab/sites/secure.lsit.ucsb.edu.gisp.d7_sp/files/sitefiles/journals/volume18/11_InResponse.pdf

Singh, Pashaura. "Revisiting the Evolution of the Sikh Community," *Journal of Punjab Studies*, Vol. 17, 2010.

Singh, Patwant. *The Sikhs*. London: Harper & Collins, 1999.

Singh, Raj Pal. *The Sikhs: their journey of Five Hundred Years*. Delhi: Bhavna Books, 2003.

Singh, Raijasbir. *Jeevan Baba Deep Singh Shaheed*. Amritsar: Chattar Singh Jeevan Singh, 2003.

Singh, Santokh. *Anandpuri di* Kahani. Amritsar: Printwell, 2021.

Singh, Simarjit. "Baba Deep Singh nal sanbandit itihasik sthan" in compendium of papers presented at *Baba Deep Singh: Jeevan te Yogdaan* National Seminar. Amritsar: Guru Nanak Dev University, 29-30 January 2009, p. 119-126.

Singh, SP. *Inner Dynamics of Guru Granth Sahib.* Amritsar: Guru Nanak Dev University, 2004.

Singh, Sukhdyal. *Punjab da Itihas.* Patiala: Panjabi University, 2012.

Singh, Sukhdyal. "Baba Deep Singh ji Shaheed: Jeevan, Sama ate Prapetian" in compendium of papers presented at *Baba Deep Singh: Jeevan te Yogdaan* National Seminar. Amritsar: Guru Nanak Dev University, 29-30 January 2009, p. 58-67.

Singh, Teja and Ganda Singh. *Short History of the Sikhs.* Bombay: Orient Longman, 1950.

Singh, Gyani Thakur. *Sri Gurdware Darshan.* Amritsar: Jeevan Singh Chatter Singh, 2012.

Singha, HS. *Sikh Studies*, Book 6. Delhi: Hemkunt Press, 2005.

Sinha, NK. *Rise of Sikh Power.* Calcutta: A. Mukherjee and Co, 1973.

Sirhindi, Ahmed. *Maktubat-i-Imam Rabbani*, Vol. 1, Letter No 163, Lahore, 1964.

Smith, Wilfred. *On Understanding Islam.* The Hague: Mouton, 1981.

Steinbach, Henry. *The Punjab—being a brief account of the Country of the Sikhs*. London: Smith, Elder and Co, 1845.

Tagore, Rabindranath. *Guru Gobind Singh*, translated by Anurag Singh, https://profanuraagsingh.wordpress.com/2015/06/29/gurugobind-singh-a-poem-by-tagore/

The Hola Mohalla Festival, SikhChic.com, available at http://sikhchic.com/article-detail.php?id=119&cat=5

The Jahangirnama: Memoirs of Jahangir, Emperor of India, translated, edited, and annotated by Wheeler M. Thackston. New York: Oxford University Press, 1999.

"The Third Battle of Panipat," Wikipedia, available at https://en.wikipedia.org/wiki/Third_Battle_of_Panipat

Walker, GC. *Gazetteer of the Lahore District 1893-1894.* Lahore: Panjab Government, 1894.

Wink, Andre. *Al-Hind: The Making of the Indo-Islamic World.* Boston: Brill Academic, 2002.

Index

A

Adina Beg, 87, 89, 90, 208
Ahmed Shah Durrani, 85, 101, 171, 199, 210, 211
  daring raid by Sikhs, 125–128
  fourth invasion, 123–125
Ajit Singh, 27, 293
Akal Bunga (Akal Takht), 11, 68, 74, 87, 198, 285
Akbar, 6, 179, 273, 294
Akhand Path, 38
Ala Singh, 73, 76, 83, 114, 128, 211, 317, 326
  Aid by Deep Singh, 73, 128
Amritsar, 6, 7, 11, 15, 27, 45, 61, 68–69, 75–79, 81, 82, 85, 87, 123, 127, 129, 142, 145–148, 155, 163–165, 168, 171, 175, 176, 178, 181, 198, 207–215, 220, 273
Anandpur, 20–22, 24–26, 24–27, 30, 35, 36, 39, 40, 43, 44, 53, 60–61, 68, 75, 113, 115, 210, 220, 264–265, 277–278
  evacuation by Guru Gobind Singh, 26–29
Attar Singh, Mastuana, 92
Aurangzeb, 10, 12, 31, 51, 216, 278
  death, 51

B

Babur, 268, 269, 273
Balwant Singh
  fights with Rustam Khan, 258–261
  fights with Zabardast Khan, 253–258
Banda Bahadur, 52–54, 60, 65, 72, 96, 111, 114, 115, 265
  capture, 62, 66
  Deep Singh joins, 55–56
  execution, 56, 62, 63, 65, 71
  factionalism, Tatt and Bandei Khalsa, 64–66, 229–230
  fall, 62–63
  first Sikh sovereign state, 52, 53, 55, 56
  meets Guru Gobind Singh, 54–55, 56
  military campaigns, 52–54, 56–58
  national hero, 65-66
  panthic investiture of Deep Singh, 59–61
  search of cause for his fall, 63–65
  Sirhind battle, 56–59
Bandei Khalsa, 64
bargirs, 84
Battle of Chamkaur, 27, 43
Battle of Gohalwar-Amritsar, 6, 7, 11, 15, 27, 45, 68, 75, 76, 77, 79, 82, 85, 87, 123, 127, 129, 133, 137, 141, 142, 145, 147, 148, 163, 164, 175, 181, 194, 207, 208, 210, 215, 220, 273
  Balwant Singh *versus* Zabardast Khan and Rustam Khan, 166–167
  caring for the dead and wounded, 168–169
  Chabba-Chatiwind, 155–158
  cunning plan, 161
  Deep Singh *versus* Aman Khan, 162–164
  Deep Singh *versus* Yakub Khan, 161–162
  Deep Singh's khanda, 178–180
  deployment and tactics, 144–145
  determined Sikh advance, 161
  Dyal Singh *versus* Amir Jan Khan, 158–159
  eye-witness account, 105, 138, 140, 177, 208
  face of, 160–161
  force levels, 143–144
  Lahore Army, 143–144
  Naudh Singh *versus* Mir Jan Khan, 162
  phases, 145–146
  prequel, xx
  Ram Singh and Mahat Singh, 168
  Ramsar and beyond, 164–165
  Sikh attack and breakthrough, 151–155
  Sikh retaliation, 207–209

Index

strategy and tactics, 102
summary of duels, 188–190
summary of epitaphs, (Table 5) 191-195
terrain, 146–147
war aims, 144
Battle of Muktsar, 29
Battle of Sirhind, 56-59
Bhagat Singh, Shaheed, xxiv, 13, 217
Bhagel Singh Karorsinghia, 13, 215
Bhagtu, 3–5, 17, 18–22, 30, 264
Bhai Dall Singh (1706 CE), xxii, 33, 44, 229, 309, 310, 329
Bhai Gurdas, 274
Bhai Mani Sngh, 23, 25, 26, 35, 36–38, 42, 43–45, 61, 64, 69, 71, 77, 113, 114, 202, 265
Bhai Nand Lal, 24, 42, 119, 312, 316, 327, vii
Bhangani, 14, 40, 56
Bhangu, Ratan Singh, 40, 58, 151, 226
Budha Dal, 74–75, 75, 82, 211
Bunga, 198, 205, 207, 212, 216, 262, 285, 295, 339

C

Chabba, 136, 140, 144–147, 155, 156, 163–167, 170–180, 184–191, 197–198, 204, 205, 219, 220, 239, 248, 249, 263
Chapper-Chiri, 57
Charat Singh Sukerchakia, 115
Chattivind, 262
Chhota Ghallughara (Lesser Holocaust), 77, 80

D

Dal Khalsa, 66, 75, 82, 83, 125, 128, 188, 208, 210, 286, 319, 329, 340
Dam Dama Sahib, 27, 33, 34, 36, 37, 39, 40, 42, 44, 45, 49, 50, 51, 66–71, 67, 68, 69, 71–72, 75, 91–92, 94, 114, 171, 174, 178, 180, 207, 264–266, 265, 281
   Deep Singh, first Jathedar, 44
   development, 91-93
   Guru Gobind Singh arrives, 33
   Guru Ki Kashi, 39
Dam Dami Bir, 37, 68
Darbara Singh, 72
Dasm Granth, 18, 41–44, 69, 70, 98, 279, 280
   editing, 41–44

Deep Singh
   in aid of Ala Singh, 73
   baptism, 16, 17, 29, 40, 48, 50, 98, 264, 279
   birth, 3–7, 5, 6, 15, 18, 264, 266
   birth and belonging, conflicting claims of, 8, 9, 15
   blessings of a saint, 223–224
   brief return to Pahuwind, 25–26, 50, 224
   celebration of anniversaries, xv-xvi
   Chhota Ghallughara (Lesser Holocaust), 77, 80
   conflicting claims of birth and belonging, xxiv, 3
   courage and resolve, 133–135, 230–231
   duel with Aman Khan, 170
   duel with Shah Jamal, 184, 249
   duel with Yakub Khan, 170, 185, 205
   early years, 10
   editing Dasm Granth, 41
   elimination of informers, 84–85
   family tree, 8
   final battle, xx, 123-206
   first Jathedar, 40, 44, 49, 281
   iconic appeal, xv–xviii, 119
   investing Kapur Singh with Nawab title, 73
   jatha, 75
   Jeonda Shaheed, 40, 43, 226–227
   joins Banda Bahadur, 52, 55–56
   Khanda, 178–180
   panthic investiture, 59–61
   preparing granth, role in, 37
   returns to Dam Dama Sahib, 66
   scholastic achievement, 68–70
   Shaheed misl, xxiv, 61, 81, 90, 91, 116, 127, 131, 180, 198, 199, 206, 209, 211, 212, 217
   shaheed title, xxiv, 40-43, 227
   shaheedavalan dera, 41, 74, 82
   summary of duels, 188–190
   summoned by Guru Gobind Singh at Dam Dama Sahib, 25
   true Khalsa warrior-saint, 118
   tutelage under Guru Gobind Singh, 113, 265
   united with Banda Bahadur, 55–56
Deras, 74, 82
Dewan Lakhpat Rai, 76

Dhirmal, 35
Dina, 29, 31, 32, 68, 172, 265

E

elimination of informers, 84–85

F

Face of Battle, xxii, 160–161
Farrukh Siyar, 66
Fateh Singh, 27, 49, 50, 59

G

Ghallughara, 68, 81, 173, 209
   Chhota (Lesser Holocaust), 80
   Wada (Greater Holocaust), 68, 81, 105, 173, 209
Gohalwar, 123, 124, 127, 139, 142–145, 147, 151, 152, 155, 156, 169, 173, 186, 187, 188, 219
Goindval Pothi, 273–274
Gurbaksh Singh, 50, 61, 72, 75, 76, 92, 127, 179, 181, 207, 208, 211, 212
Gurdwara Act, 336
Gurdwara Bachaona Sahib, 176, 182
Gurdwara Janamsthan, 7
Gurdwara Lakeer Sahib, 133
Gurdwara Lalkar Sahib, 127, 153
Gurdwara Rakabganj, 215
Gurdwara Rann Niti Sahib, 151
Gurdwara Shaheedganj, 198, 199
Gurdwara Sisgang, 215
Gurm, 8, 29, 264–266
Guru Amar Das, 39, 273
Guru Angad Dev, 39, 273
Guru Arjan, 4, 9, 10, 11, 35, 39, 111, 133, 272, 274, 276
Guru Gobind Singh, 12, 20, 22, 26, 27, 32, 34, 35, 37, 41, 42, 50, 51, 54, 56, 60, 61, 66, 98, 106, 111, 117, 151, 214, 265, 278–281
   adi granth, 35–40
   Banda Bahadur, 52–54
   Dam Dama Sahib, 33–35
   Dasm Granth, editing, 41–44
   Death, 54
   Dina, 31
   evacuation of Anandpur, 26–29
   meeting the emperor, 51–52
   national hero, 54–55
Guru Har Rai, 132
Guru Hargobind, 11–13, 19, 34, 39, 52, 111, 132, 198, 277, 279

Guru Nanak, 19, 34, 38, 52, 132, 201, 219, 268, 273, 275, 279, 282, 283
Guru Ram Das, 39
Guru Teg Bahadur, 12, 34, 38, 56, 91, 215, 216, 275, 278, 281
Guru-ke-bagh, 147, 167, 168, 174, 188, 190, 195
Gyani Gyan Singh, xxi, xxii, 6–7, 7, 36, 50, 72, 86, 116, 130, 131, 136, 141, 143, 150, 151, 155, 156, 157, 159, 160, 165, 166, 168, 170, 171, 173, 175, 177, 178, 196, 197, 198, 200, 202, 205, 207, 220, 235, 240, 241, 242, 244, 255
Gyani Thakur Singh, 163

H

Haji Attai Khan, 139, 141, 143, 144, 145, 152, 155, 164, 165, 172
Harimandir Sahib, 14, 37, 45, 64, 69, 75, 133, 138, 142, 144–147, 163, 170, 175, 176, 179, 196, 198, 200, 210–216

I

Indus Valley Civilization, 268
Iqbal, 271

J

Jahan Khan, 126, 127, 138–140, 140–146, 141, 142, 143, 152–158, 153, 154, 155, 156, 158, 161, 165, 171, 172, 174, 199, 208, 234
Jaspat Rai, 78
Jassa Singh Ahluwalia, 72, 78, 80, 82, 86, 89, 90, 102, 115, 124, 199, 208, 211, 301
Jassa Singh Ramgarhia, 74, 83, 199, 215, 216
Jats, 10, 37, 75, 111–112, 112, 274
Jehangir, 277
Jeonda Shaheed, 40–41
Jeoni, 4–5, 17, 20
Jujhar Singh, 27, 28

K

Kahn Singh Nabha, 7, 59, 201, 295, 315, 340
Kapur Singh, 13, 72–74, 73, 74, 80, 82, 86, 114, 115, 151, 319
Kapura Brar, 29
Karam Singh, 72, 74, 92, 180, 211–212
Kartarpur pothi, 35
Kaura Mal, 85
Kesho Ram, 24

Khalsa, 19
  building the tradition, 70–72
  helm, 72
  Khalsa ji, 83
  helm, 72
Khanda (broadsword), 178-180

L

Lahore, 5, 7 10, 34–35, 68, 70, 71, 76, 77, 79, 81, 85, 87, 89, 90, 105, 107, 123, 124, 126, 138–147, 151–155, 165, 169, 171, 172, 178, 207–209
Lakhi Jungle, 34
Lakhpat Rai, 76, 79

M

Maha Singh, 30–31
Maharana Pratap, 158
Mai Bhago of Jhabbal, 13
Manji Sahib, 91, 174, 190, 192, 195, 262, 263
Martyrdom, role in nationhood, 214–218
Massa Rangar, 69
Mata Gujri, 27
Mata Sundari, 25, 42, 64, 69
Mehtab Singh, 69, 194
Miskin, Tahmas Khan, 105, 140–143, 209
Misls 82–93, 104, 111, 124, 128, 198, 199, 211
  founding of, 91–93
Muktas, 31
Muktsar battle, 29–32
Muslim conquest, 268

N

Naudh Singh, 131, 135, 136, 151, 152, 161, 162, 172, 179, 202
  fights with Mir Jan Khan, 242–244
Nawab Kapur Singh, 74
  of Singhpura, 13
Nawab of Malerkotla, 56–57, 73
Nawab Zabat Khan, 92
Niccolò Machiavelli, 84

O

Origin and Evolution of Sikhism, 267–283
Ottoman empire, 5

P

Pahuwind, xvi, xvii, xxiii, 5–15, 20, 25, 26, 30, 50, 67, 117, 224–225, 264–266, 326

Panda Vahi, xxi, xxiii, 6–10, 111, 123, 292
Parikrama Scheme, 176
Pero, 6
Phulkian misl, 83
Punjab—geo-cultural units, 6-7, 268

R

Rabindra Nath Tagore, 281
Rai Shamir, 29
Raijasbir Singh, xxii, 7, 151, 219
Raja Jai Singh Mirza, 38
Raja of Jaipur, 38, 278, 308
Raja of Jodhpur, 38, 308
Rajputs, in aid of, 90–91
Rakabgang, 215
Rakhi, 87
Ram Rauni, 81, 127, 199
Ranjit Singh, 74, 83, 86, 92, 111, 115, 199, 203, 212, 217, 282
Ranjit Singh, Maharaja, 74, 83, 86, 92, 111, 199, 203, 212–217, 282
Ratan Singh Bhangu, 6, 40

S

Sacha Sauda, 267–268, 270
Sahib Devan, 25, 45
Saleem Shah, 34
Sant-Sipahi, 16, 50, 61, 94–114, 117, 119, 271, 280, 294, 323
  Jat, 111–112
  spiritual warrior, 98–102
  strategy and tactics, 102–107
  unlikely encomium, 107–110
Sarai Amanat Khan, 142, 147
Shah Alam II, 110, 215
Shaheed Bunga, 198, 205, 206, 212, 262, 285
Shaheedan Jatha, 73–76
Shaheeds, 74, 82, 90, 92, 99, 115, 211
Shazadpurias, 92
Shiromani Gurdwara Parbandhak Committee (SGPC), 51, 70, 176
Sialkot, 89, 90, 92, 212
  under Sikh sway, 89–90
Sikh casualties, 146, 178, 191, 217
Sikh Empire, 66, 213–214
Sikhism, 9, 34, 38–39, 100, 111, 132, 267–268, 283
  conciliatory vision, 269–279
  creed formalizing, 273–274
  defense of all faiths, 278

formalizing the creed, 273
founding of the Khalsa, 19, 53, 113, 133, 212, 278-280
martyrdom and militarization, 276–277
modern legacy, 282–283
Muslim Conquest, 268–269
origin, 13, 111, 200, 267–268
praise by enemy, 110
rising fortunes, 210–212
strategy and tactics, 54, 102-107
Sirhind battle, 56–59
Sobha Singh, 199
Solkhian, 60
spiritual warrior, 98–102
Strategy and tactics, 102–107
Sukha Singh, 13, 26, 69, 76, 78, 80, 86, 163, 171, 184, 202
Sukhdyal Singh, 27, 52

T

Tahla Sahib, 156, 163, 177, 191, 198, 204, 205, 220
Takhte Taus, 215
Talwandi Sabo (Takht Sri Dam Dama Sahib), xxii, 25, 26, 33–36, 40, 44, 66, 67, 76, 90, 92, 96, 117, 128, 132, 219, 281, 295
Tara Singh of Vaan, 13, 71

Tarn Taran, 7– 10, 14, 15, 132, 133, 135, 136, 140, 142, 144, 147, 151, 171, 178, 181, 193, 194, 276
Taru Singh of Poohla, 13
Taruna Dal, 74–76, 76, 211, 220, 285, 287
Tat-Bandeyi Khalsa controversy, 115
Tatt Khalsa, 66
Teona Pujarian, 92
Tharra Sahib, 192, 195, 208
The Sikh Regiment, xvii, 217, 306
Tirth Purohit, 7

U

Udham Singh, Shaheed, 217
Unequal contest, 85–86
Unlikely encomium, 107–110

V

Village Varpal, 159, 175, 195

W

Wada Ghallughara, 81, 209
Wazir Khan, 52, 56–59, 95-96, 114

Y

Yahya Khan, 78–80, 79

Z

Zafarnamah, 31, 32, 70, 100
Zakariya Khan, 70–71, 77, 78
Zorawar Singh, 27, 293